THE USSR IN THIRD WORLD CONFLICTS

THE USSR IN THIRD WORLD CONFLICTS

Soviet arms and diplomacy in local wars 1945–1980

BRUCE D. PORTER

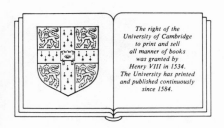

The right of the
University of Cambridge
to print and sell
all manner of books
was granted by
Henry VIII in 1534.
The University has printed
and published continuously
since 1584.

CAMBRIDGE UNIVERSITY PRESS

Cambridge
London   New York   New Rochelle
Melbourne   Sydney

Published by the Press Syndicate of the University of Cambridge
The Pitt Building, Trumpington Street, Cambridge CB2 1RP
32 East 57th Street, New York, NY 10022, USA
296 Beaconsfield Parade, Middle Park, Melbourne 3206, Australia

First published 1984

Printed in the United States of America

Library of Congress Cataloging in Publication Data
Porter, Bruce D.
The USSR in Third World conflicts.
Revision of author's thesis (Ph.D.) – Harvard Univer-
sity, 1979.
1. Soviet Union – Military policy. 2. Soviet Union –
Military relations – Developing countries. 3. Developing
countries – Military relations – Soviet Union. 4. Military
history, Modern – 20th century. 5. World politics –
1945 – . I. Title. II. Title: USSR in Third
World conflicts.
UA770.P666   1984   355'.0335'47   83–26265
ISBN 0 521 26308 5

CONTENTS

PREFACE

The USSR in Third World Conflicts was written principally under the auspices of the Center for International Affairs (CFIA) at Harvard University during the academic year of 1979–80. I was serving at the time as a postdoctoral fellow in the newly formed program in national security studies at CFIA. As with most books, however, the genealogy of this work is rather more complicated than that. It originally was a doctoral dissertation, written in partial fulfillment of the requirements for a Ph.D. in political science at Harvard University. The dissertation was completed in the autumn of 1979, a few months after my fellowship at CFIA had actually begun. When I left CFIA roughly one year later, the work of transforming the dissertation into a book had been largely completed, but some additional research and a thoroughgoing revision were still called for. This final reworking took place at an unconscionably slow pace from 1981 to 1983, while I was employed full-time as a research analyst of Soviet foreign policy at Radio Free Europe/Radio Liberty, Inc., in Munich, West Germany.

The long gestation period of this book (alas, typical of doctoral dissertations that see print) necessitates numerous acknowledgments. I am particularly indebted to three persons: Professors Adam Ulam and Samuel P. Huntington of Harvard University, and Keith Bush, Director of Research at Radio Liberty. Adam Ulam originally encouraged me to write a dissertation on the topic of Soviet involvement in Third World conflicts on the basis of a paper I presented in a graduate seminar he taught; he later became the principal adviser of the dissertation and provided constant intellectual inspiration and needed moral support. Samuel Huntington was the second reader of the dissertation; his incisive analysis and commentary on the work as it unfolded were major factors in shaping it. He also made possible the one-year postdoctoral fellowship at CFIA that enabled me to turn an unwieldy dissertation into something resembling a book. Since the time I left CFIA, Dr. Huntington has tenaciously encouraged me to finish the book, and without his encouragement this work probably would never have been finished. I owe him much. Keith Bush of Radio Liberty also encouraged me to devote spare hours to a second revision and arranged for needed secretarial assistance.

A number of professional colleagues read individual chapters of the work at various stages of its development and provided useful criticism: Kenneth Adelman, Don Carlisle, Jorge Dominguez, Lawrence Ekpebu, Thane Gustafson, Paul Henze, Patrick Moore, Laurie Mylroie, David Powell, William Quandt, Gary Samore, Steve Sestanovich, John J. Stremlau, and Manfred W. Wenner. I am very appreciative of the assistance they rendered, but I am, of course, wholly responsible for the factual accuracy and conclusions of the book.

The Danforth Foundation provided financial assistance that enabled me to work full-time on a doctoral dissertation during my last year as a graduate student at Harvard. The Smith-Richardson Foundation provided the grant to CFIA that made possible the one-year postdoctoral fellowship mentioned earlier. Radio Free Europe/Radio Liberty, Inc., provided funds for secretarial assistance in the final preparation of the manuscript. Without the support of these institutions, the book could never have been completed.

Finally, I wish to thank my wife, Susan, and my children, David, Christopher, and Lisa, for their encouragement and support. They bore the burden of having a preoccupied scholar in the house, and they managed to keep my feet on the ground whenever my head was in the clouds. My thanks to them comes last, but it is far from least.

1
INTRODUCTION

The principal foundations which all states have are good laws and powerful armies. Since there can be no good laws where there are not strong armies, I shall set aside any discussion of laws and proceed to speak of armies.

Niccolo Macchiavelli, *The Prince*

As the 1970s progressed, the problem of Soviet military involvement in Third World conflicts came to assume an increasingly prominent place on the U.S. foreign policy agenda. The USSR attempted – by means of diplomacy, military advisers, arms shipments, and occasionally troops – to influence the course of at least eight localized conflicts during the decade. The list of those conflicts reads like a roll call of the decade's most dangerous international crises and hot spots: the Indo-Pakistani war, the Yom Kippur war, the war in Vietnam, the Angolan civil war, the Ogaden war, the intra-Communist clash in Indochina (Vietnam's invasion of Cambodia and China's incursion into Vietnam), South Yemen's brief clash with Yemen, and the civil war in Afghanistan. The USSR had been involved militarily in local conflicts before, of course, but the magnitude, scope, and apparent success of its efforts in the 1970s were perhaps without precedent.

In the 1950s and 1960s the Soviet Union's involvement in local conflicts, though often receiving considerable publicity, generally took place on a modest scale with respect to the actual volume of military equipment delivered to Third World clients at war. The main exceptions to this pattern were the massive Soviet arms shipments to the regimes in Pyongyang and Hanoi during the Korean war and the war in Vietnam. Although Moscow, prior to 1969, had transferred massive quantities of arms to Egypt, Syria, Indonesia, and India, and lesser amounts to some 20 additional countries, those shipments usually had preceded or followed the period of actual hostilities. The Kremlin had displayed its penchant for caution by refraining from large-scale arms shipments to regimes immediately engaged in conflict – particularly non-Communist regimes – and by minimizing any direct participation by Soviet personnel in combat or combat support. Commencing with the war of attrition in the Middle East (1969–70), the Soviet Union's historical policy of restraint in this regard changed markedly. In that conflict, over 10,000 Soviet military advisers engaged in a wide range of combat-support operations: Soviet troops

1

manned SAM installations; Soviet pilots flew combat missions; and Moscow transferred thousands of tons of weaponry to the Arabs. It was the USSR's first massive military effort on behalf of a non-Communist client at war since its effort to back the Kuomintang in China in the 1920s. Events in the following decade proved that the Soviet role in the war of attrition was not an anomaly. The 1970s witnessed three massive Soviet airlifts and sealifts of arms to client regimes at war, the deployment in combat of over 40,000 Soviet-armed Cuban troops in Africa, and the outright invasion and occupation of a Third World country by the USSR – all phenomena unheard of during the Cold War.

Inevitably, concern that the Soviets were running rampant in the Third World served to erode public support for détente in the United States, solidify support for increased military spending, and hasten the development of the Sino-American rapprochement. During the October war, and again during the Angolan crisis, U.S. Secretary of State Henry Kissinger warned that Moscow's actions imperiled the entire Soviet-American relationship and undermined prospects for a stable international order. Shortly after the Ogaden war, Dmitri K. Simes observed that "the new pattern of Soviet imperial gunboat diplomacy threatens to modify the rules of the international game." By 1979, Robert Legvold could state that turmoil in the Third World had overwhelmed all other considerations in the superpower rivalry, "save the growth and increased projection of Soviet military power whose menace it serves to accentuate." President Carter's state-of-the-union address in January 1980, shortly following the invasion of Afghanistan, identified "the steady growth and increased projection of Soviet military power beyond its own borders" as one of three principal challenges facing the United States. That challenge is certain to remain a critical one throughout the 1980s and beyond.[1]

This book is intended as a study of the USSR's military and diplomatic involvement in Third World conflicts from 1945 to 1980. The study was motivated to a considerable extent by an awareness of the growing importance to U.S. foreign policy of understanding Soviet policy toward the Third World and particularly toward Third World conflicts. This book does not, however, treat Soviet involvement in Third World conflicts principally as a problem in U.S. foreign policy.[2] Rather, the intent is to understand Soviet foreign policy in its own right.

This study is designed primarily to illuminate certain of the *tactical* and *operational aspects* of the USSR's policy in local conflicts. In this respect

---

[1] Quotations are from Henry Kissinger, *Department of State Bulletin (DOSB)* LXIX(October 29, 1973):528, and *DOSB* LXXII(February 23, 1976); Dmitri K. Simes, "Detente, Russian Style," *Foreign Policy* No. 32(Fall 1978):54; Robert Legvold, "The Super Rivals: Conflict in the Third World," *Foreign Affairs* 57(Spring 1979):755; Jimmy Carter, "The State of the Union," *Presidential Documents* 16(January 28, 1980):195.

[2] I have written elsewhere on the subject of appropriate U.S. policy toward Soviet involvement in local conflicts. See Bruce D. Porter, "Washington, Moscow, and Third World Conflict in the 1980s," in Samuel P. Huntington, ed., *The Strategic Imperative: New Policies for American Security* (Cambridge, Mass.: Ballinger, 1982), 253–300.

it departs from the main trend among studies of Soviet policy toward the Third World. The tendency has been for scholars and analysts either to focus on certain general features of Soviet ideology and thinking that pertain to the Third World or to evaluate the USSR's strategic aims and interests in specific regions of the world. Such aspects of the problem are by no means overlooked in this study, but the intention is to focus on a somewhat different, relatively neglected, echelon of policy: the tactical methods and operational approaches of the USSR in local conflicts generally. The terms *tactical* and *operational* refer here not only to the military details of the Soviet Union's involvement in conflicts but also to the entire range of implemental steps, both diplomatic and military, that the USSR has employed in attempting to influence specific conflicts.[3]

I have chosen the case-study approach to accomplish this end. By comparative analysis of five cases of Soviet military involvement in local conflicts, I have attempted to better understand in what specific ways the Soviet Union has sought to achieve its aims in local conflicts, what characteristic patterns can be traced in Soviet operations, and what practical lessons the USSR has learned over time in the implementation of policy in local conflicts. Each case treats the USSR's involvement in a given conflict as a single overall operation in which many facets of policy must be coordinated and on which many factors bear. For example, each case study treats the Soviet-American relationship as one factor bearing on the conflict at hand; however, the emphasis is not on how the conflict influenced relations between Washington and Moscow but on how specific Soviet-American interactions during the conflict contributed to shaping its course and outcome.

The main difficulty in undertaking such a study has been in obtaining accurate and pertinent information on Soviet diplomatic activities and arms shipments during the conflicts in question. The nature of the subject is such that few totally reliable sources exist, and even some normally credible sources must be treated with caution. I have been forced to take a fairly eclectic approach to obtaining information, relying on whatever sources have provided information that has seemed reliable, whether local newspapers, journalistic reports, memoirs, speeches, interviews, or information from Western intelligence sources that has managed to make its way into public sources. Soviet sources have been used whenever possible, but they have been, frankly, not very illuminating, save in a few instances. I have tried to use great caution in evaluating all sources, but occasionally have made personal judgments as to whether or not credibility could be attributed to certain sources that could not be independently confirmed.

---

[3] After this book was written, a study was published that covers at least some of the same ground, and that does treat certain operational aspects of Soviet involvement in Third World Conflicts. I highly recommend this study by Stephen T. Hosmer and Thomas W. Wolfe, *Soviet Policy and Practice toward Third World Conflicts* (Lexington-Lexington Books, 1983).

Wherever this has been the case, I have tried to make appropriate qualifications in the text.

The study is organized as follows. This chapter is intended as an introduction to the work as a whole. Chapter 2 is a historical survey of the USSR's involvement in Third World conflicts, tracing the evolution of Soviet policy through four distinct stages in the postwar period. Some attention is also given to the period from 1917 until World War II, as background for what follows. This survey is meant principally to provide an overall framework for the case studies that follow. Chapter 3 reviews postwar Soviet advances in the military capabilities necessary for projecting conventional power abroad. It reviews trends in five areas: arms exports, naval power, transport capabilities, the establishment of military support facilities abroad, and the employment of Soviet, East European, and Cuban military advisers and troops in local conflicts. Chapter 3 also discusses the implications of Moscow's achievement of nuclear parity for its behavior in local conflicts.

Chapter 4 is a brief introduction to the case studies, explaining why the five specific conflicts were selected for study and setting forth the parameters of comparison used in analyzing the cases. Chapters 5 through 9 constitute the heart of the work: case studies of Soviet involvement in the Yemeni civil war (1962–8), the Nigerian civil war (1969–70), the Yom Kippur war (1973), the Angolan civil war (1975–6), and the Ogaden war (1977–8). The case studies are organized identically, using the categories established in Chapter 4: the local dispute; the diplomatic relationship between the USSR and its client; Soviet weapons shipments and other military assistance; the roles of Soviet and East European advisers (and, where appropriate, Cuban troops); Soviet-American interactions; the China factor; the outcome of the conflict from the perspective of Soviet interests. Chapter 10, the conclusion of the work, summarizes the findings of the case studies using a comparative approach; it is organized according to the same outline used for the case studies. The concluding chapter also draws somewhat on the historical information in Chapter 2 concerning conflicts other than the five case studies. This is done in order to clarify just what is characteristic and what is exceptional about Soviet policy in the five conflicts selected for study.

2
THE USSR IN LOCAL CONFLICTS: A HISTORICAL OVERVIEW

> In short, the Communists everywhere support every revolutionary
> movement against the existing social and political order of things.
> Karl Marx and Friedrich Engels, *The Communist Manifesto*

Between 1945 and 1980, well over 100 separate wars took place around
the globe, the vast majority of them in or between developing countries.[1]
The Soviet Union was involved as a major arms supplier and diplomatic
actor in some 20 of these conflicts. Although these figures suggest that
the USSR steered clear of local wars far more often than not, involvement in 20 conflicts nevertheless represents an extraordinarily high level
of foreign commitment for a country that prior to World War II only
rarely had acted as a major supplier of arms, or even as a principal
diplomatic actor, in conflicts outside Europe. Furthermore, under the tsars,
and during the first two decades of Soviet rule, Russia had generally
avoided any kind of involvement in conflicts not on or near its borders,
whereas most of the conflicts in which it became involved after 1945 took
place in regions of Asia, Africa, and the Middle East that were not contiguous to the Soviet Union.

At least three factors contributed to the USSR's enhanced diplomatic
and military roles in local conflicts after 1945. First, and most obvious,
was the vast expansion of Soviet military power that took place as a
result of the war with Nazi Germany. Huge stocks of surplus armaments,
large and well-trained military forces, and (within four years after the
war) possession of nuclear weapons all made it simply much more feasible for the USSR to play a larger role in world affairs after 1945 than
was previously possible. Second, the rapid decolonization of Asia, Africa,
and the Middle East that followed World War II left a power vacuum
in what came to be known as "the Third World." The retreat from empire
by the European colonial powers gave rise to a whole host of new nations,
impoverished and militarily weak, thereby opening up numerous opportunities for the USSR to seek influence in regions once beyond its
reach and making possible the establishment of supplier-client relation-

---

[1] Istvan Kende, "Local Wars in Asia, Africa and Latin America, 1945–1969," Stockholm International Peace Research Institute (SIPRI), in *Armaments and Disarmaments in the Nuclear Age: A Handbook* (Atlantic Highlands, N.J.: Humanities Press,
1976), 174–5.

Table 2.1. *The USSR in local conflicts, 1945–80*

Stage 1 (1945–53)	Chinese civil war (1945–9)
	Korean war (1950–3)
Stage 2 (1953–64)	Suez war (1956)
	Indonesian conflicts (1958–65)
	Congo crisis and civil war (1960–4)
	Laotian civil war (1960–1)
	Algeria vs. Morocco (1963)
	Yemeni civil war (arms shipments via Egypt) (1962–4)
Stage 3 (1965–72)	Yemeni civil war (direct Soviet involvement) (1965–9)
	War in Vietnam (through Paris peace accords) (1965–72)
	Nigerian civil war (1967–70)
	Six-day war (1967)
	War of attrition (1969–70)
	Indo-Pakistani war (1971)
Stage 4 (1973–80)	Yom Kippur war (1973)
	War in Vietnam (through fall of Saigon) (1973–5)
	Angolan civil war (1975–6)
	Ogaden war (1977–8)
	Vietnam vs. Cambodia (1978–9)
	China vs. Vietnam (1979)
	South Yemen vs. Yemen (1979)
	Afghan civil war (1978–)

ships with regimes that had not even existed before the war. Third, the building of nuclear arsenals by the United States and the Soviet Union, together with the development of a permanent U.S. commitment to the defense of Western Europe, soon led to a complete East-West standoff, a stalemate on the European continent. Soviet ambitions had to be channeled elsewhere, and the Third World, if only because of its instability, must have appeared to present a more appealing venue for the pursuit of those ambitions than Europe itself.

The Soviet Union's involvement in Third World conflicts from 1945 to 1980 evolved through roughly four stages, as depicted by Table 2.1. Each successive stage represented a broadening of either the physical magnitude or the geographical scope of Soviet efforts to provide military assistance to Third World regimes at war. This chapter will review each of the four stages in turn in order to provide historical background for the case studies in later chapters. First, however, a look at the USSR's behavior in local conflicts and its role as an arms supplier prior to World War II may be in order. During the interwar years the USSR was a militarily weak power, with very limited capabilities for exporting arms or projecting military force abroad; its involvement in foreign conflicts was of necessity fairly minimal and largely defensive in nature. Also, the few conflicts in which it did become involved were not centered in the Third World, because today's large numbers of developing independent nation-states did not even come into being until after World War II. This was nevertheless an important formative period for Soviet conduct that must have had considerable influence on the course of Soviet foreign policy after 1945.

The formative period: revolution and retreat (1917–41)

The Bolshevik revolution was conceived in armed uprisings and propagated by military force. The Red Army undertook an astonishing number of tasks in the first few years of Soviet rule: It defeated three separate White armies; it invaded and occupied Ukraine, Belorussia, Azerbaijan, Armenia, and Georgia; it assisted the Soviet leaders in gaining control over the Moslem borderlands and the Far East; it helped establish satellite regimes in Outer Mongolia, Tannu-Tuva (Urankhai), and northern Iran; and it unsuccessfully attempted to invade Poland and establish a Red government in Warsaw. By November 1922, five years after the revolution, Soviet power extended over most of the territory of the former Russian Empire, a remarkable achievement by any measure. Although numerous factors contributed to the Bolshevik victory – propaganda, superior organization, astute political and diplomatic maneuvering, the incompetence and disunity of the Whites – the establishment of Soviet rule depended more on raw military force than on anything else. Without the Red Army the revolution would have failed – this lesson made a deep impression on the Soviet leaders, and it played a major role in shaping their attitude toward the uses and utility of military power.

Subversion and support for foreign revolutions also played central roles in Soviet policy during the early years. Although the Communist uprisings that took place in Europe shortly following the Russian revolution were too small and too short-lived to be considered "local conflicts" for purposes of this study, Moscow's support for them was indicative of the revolutionary commitment and internationalist ambitions of the new Soviet leadership. Bolshevik efforts to foment revolution abroad were confined mostly to propaganda and rhetoric, support and encouragement for foreign Communist parties, and the dispatching of agents such as Karl Radek, Eugen Levin, and M. N. Roy into Europe and Asia with the specific mission of exploiting revolutionary opportunities. But some military efforts were also made. Arms transfers, if they can be called that, began in the first few months after the revolution, when small arms and ammunition were smuggled into Finland in support of an abortive Communist uprising. A more direct attempt at military support for revolution occurred after the Hungarian Soviet Republic headed by Bela Kun was established in March 1919. The commander in chief of the Red Army in Moscow ordered some of his troops to travel toward eastern Galicia and Bukovina in order to establish direct contact with Kun, but before the plan could be carried out, the troops were transferred to the Urals front in order to meet a White offensive. Between 1919 and 1924, the Kremlin supported a number of other Communist and workers' uprisings: the Spartacist uprising in Berlin early in 1919, the declaration of a Bavarian Soviet Republic in Munich in March 1919, the *Märzaktion* in northern Germany a year later, German uprisings in the fall of 1923, an attempted revolution by the Bulgarian Communist party in September 1923, and a one-day coup in Estonia in December 1924. Moscow was unable to offer significant military assistance to any of these movements, and they all failed quickly.

The failure of these Communist uprisings in Europe was a factor in turning the Bolshevik leaders eastward in pursuit of their revolutionary aspirations. Shortly prior to the October revolution, Lenin had published *Imperialism: The Highest Stage of Capitalism*, in which he had significantly further developed Marx's theory of the evolution of capitalism. Lenin asserted that the process whereby huge monopolies came to dominate the capitalist economic system eventually forced the Western industrial powers to undertake imperialist conquests of foreign colonies in order to find outlets for investment and profit. Imperialism would temporarily forestall the inevitable collapse of the capitalist mode of production. Indeed, without its colonies to exploit, capitalism would long since have perished. In the summer of 1920, following the failure of the Spartacist uprising, the Bavarian Soviet Republic, and the *Märzaktion*, Lenin returned to some of the concepts he had developed in *Imperialism*. Recognizing the futility of overthrowing capitalism by a frontal assault, the Soviet leader conceived a strategy of weakening the imperialist powers by striking at them from the rear – by encouraging national revolutionary movements in their colonial empires.

Lenin articulated this strategy in his draft theses on the national and colonial questions prepared for the Second Comintern Congress, and in his speech to that congress, which met in July of 1920. According to Lenin, the Soviets had to pursue a policy that would achieve the closest possible alliance between Soviet Russia and "all the national and colonial liberation movements."[2] This union was the key to the eventual overthrow of capitalism:

> At this Congress we see taking place a union between revolutionary proletarians of the capitalist, advanced countries, and countries where there is no or hardly any proletariat, i.e., the oppressed masses of colonial, Eastern countries...World imperialism shall fall when the revolutionary onslaught of the exploited and oppressed workers in each country...merges with

[2] Vladimir I. Lenin, *Polnoe sobranie sochinenii*, 4th ed., vol. 31 (Moscow, 1950), 124.

the revolutionary onslaught of hundreds of millions of people who have hitherto stood beyond the pale of history.[3]

Lenin freely admitted that "it is beyond doubt that any national movement can only be a bourgeois-democratic movement," but he insisted that Communists support such movements so long as they were "genuinely revolutionary." He made clear that this alliance with bourgeois liberation movements in colonial and underdeveloped countries would be a temporary expedient, and he stressed that the genuine proletarian parties in those countries, however small they might be, must not actually merge with the bourgeois nationalist movements, but must only work with them for a time, even as they prepared to undermine these movements in the long run.[4] Lenin's viewpoint prevailed over strong opposition at the congress. For the next several years the Soviet regime and the Comintern pursued a policy of lending support to national revolutionary movements and encouraging local Communists – where such existed – to cooperate with them in a "united-front" strategy.

One consequence of the new emphasis on cooperating with local nationalists was a shift in Soviet policy toward Turkey. Moscow began to explore the possibility of rapprochement with the nationalist movement of Mustapha Kemal Pasha, recognizing that the tiny, newly formed Communist party of Turkey had no prospect of winning popular support. Kemal was then fighting the Greek army, which was attempting to occupy Anatolia under the terms of the Treaty of Sèvres, and the Soviet leadership evidently believed that victory by Kemal would undermine the influence of Great Britain and other Western powers in the Near East, thereby serving Soviet security interests, as well as contributing in a roundabout manner to the revolutionary struggle in Europe.[5] Following difficult negotiations, a treaty of friendship was signed on March 16, 1921, between the Soviet government and Kemal's nationalist regime in Ankara. In the course of the following 15 months, the Kremlin turned over to Kemal's nationalist army enough military supplies to equip perhaps three divisions. It also extended a substantial amount of financial credit for military purchases. Although it was not decisive, the Soviet aid contributed to Kemal's eventual victory over the Greek army in the autumn of 1922. This can be considered the first historical case of Soviet military assistance to a foreign regime at war.

A second early example of Soviet diplomatic and military involvement in a local conflict took place from 1923 to 1927, when Moscow provided assistance to the Kuomintang, the Canton-based National

---

[3] *Ibid.*, 207–8.
[4] *Ibid.*, 216–17.
[5] An excellent treatment of this subject is Harish Kapur, *Soviet Russia and Asia, 1917–1927: A Study of Soviet Policy towards Turkey, Iran and Afghanistan* (Geneva: Michael Joseph, 1966).

Revolutionary party of Dr. Sun Yat-sen, in its struggle to unite a divided China under its leadership. This was the first major test of Lenin's united-front strategy, and it ended in disaster. The entire episode was one of the most complex undertakings in Soviet diplomatic history: In addition to maintaining diplomatic relations with the truncated government of the "Chinese Republic" in Peking, Moscow established relations with the Kuomintang and with a number of the warlords who controlled various regions of China; it also exerted considerable control over the small Chinese Communist party, which after 1922 entered into a united front with the Kuomintang. The Kuomintang-Communist front, which was engineered largely through the efforts of Soviet diplomat Adolf Joffe, gave the Kremlin a channel through which it was able to influence Kuomintang policies for a number of years.

In January 1923, Sun and Joffe signed an agreement effectively establishing a political and military alliance. The following August, a Nationalist general, Chiang Kai-shek, visited Moscow to discuss Soviet assistance to the Kuomintang. During his visit, Mikhail Borodin, a Comintern agent who became the chief of Soviet efforts inside China until 1927, left for China with a delegation that included several military advisers, all veterans of the civil war and graduates of the Red Army military academy. These Soviet advisers helped establish, staff, and finance the Whampoa military academy, a training school for officers near Canton. In May 1925, another large body of Soviet advisers arrived in Canton with the mission of training officers of the National Revolutionary Army (NRA) in the field. The Soviet Union shipped some military equipment to the NRA via Vladivostok, including over 23,000 small arms and large amounts of ammunition; Soviet sources estimated the value of the weapons sent by December 1925 at $2 million. As the civil war in China intensified, some Soviet advisers – and apparently some troops – participated in actual combat alongside units of the NRA. During the first months of Chiang's highly successful northern expedition, the USSR provided some long-range radio equipment, and Soviet planes occasionally undertook tactical bombing, reconnaissance, and supply missions in support of the Nationalist army. The number of Soviet advisers working in China may have reached over 1,000.[6]

Stalin's professed intention of having the Chinese Communists squeeze the Kuomintang like a lemon before throwing it away was, ironically, fulfilled in reverse. Dissension between the Communists and the Nationalists in the united front grew steadily, leading to a number of tense situations and incidents, to a split in the Kuomintang, and eventually, in April 1927, to a brutal massacre of Communists in

[6] Joseph E. Thach, Jr., "Soviet Military Assistance to Nationalist China 1923–41," Parts I and II, *Military Review* (August 1977):72–82, and *Military Review* (September 1977):49–56.

Shanghai by their Nationalist allies. The Shanghai massacre led to a complete break in Soviet-Nationalist relations and meant the virtual collapse of the whole Soviet effort in China. Although it ended in failure, the Kremlin's effort to assist the Nationalists undoubtedly was a seminal event in the development of Soviet approaches toward local conflicts and the political uses of foreign military assistance. The experience taught the Kremlin leadership the risks inherent in linking the foreign policy fortunes of the Soviet Union too closely to the fate of local Communist parties; also, the Shanghai massacre dramatized the importance of correctly assessing the local balance of forces and the local political situation by intelligence gathering and research. Finally, the failure in China probably contributed to the marked wariness and caution with which the Soviet Union was to treat involvement in local conflicts for at least the following 40 years.

The Shanghai massacre meant the end, for the time being at least, of the strategy of forming united fronts with nationalist movements, as articulated by Lenin seven years earlier. After 1927, the national bourgeoisie fell out of favor as a tool for promoting revolution in the colonial world. Serious efforts to foment revolution abroad virtually ceased during the 1930s, as the USSR began to turn inward and concentrate on the building of "socialism in one country." Direct threats to the USSR's own national security, in the meantime, came to outweigh and subsume all other foreign policy considerations. The Japanese occupation of Manchuria in September 1931 and Hitler's accession to power in Germany in January 1933 confronted Soviet Russia with the prospect of facing hostile expansionist powers on two fronts. In order to cope with the threat of a two-front war, the outlines of which became increasingly plain as the decade progressed, the Comintern began to concentrate on building an *international* united front against the potential enemies of the Soviet Union. Soviet involvement in local conflicts during the 1930s should be viewed as one aspect of an overall policy intended to prevent or delay the vastly larger conflagration that threatened, rather than as the pursuit of revolutionary gains, as had been the case perhaps in the previous decade.

From 1931 to 1943 the USSR provided substantial military assistance to two provincial rulers of Sinkiang, Chin Shu-jen (1931–3) and General Sheng Shih-ts'ai (1933–43), then embroiled in small conflicts with other warlords:

> The Soviets were first asked for direct military assistance against other Chinese warlords in 1934, and they forthwith provided two brigades of NKVD troops and combat air support to General Sheng. Again in 1937 Sheng turned to the Soviets for aid, and again troops and air cover were sent...arms and uniforms were also provided for a Sinkiang army of 10,000 men, a Soviet military aircraft assembly factory was built at Urumchi...and sev-

eral hundred Soviet flyers trained at a clandestine aviation training school at Kuldzha in 1938–39.[7]

By offering aid to the Sinkiang warlords, the USSR was able to establish a significant military presence in an area that would be of considerable strategic importance should a war with Tokyo break out.

Moscow had resumed relations with the Kuomintang, then in power in Peking, in 1932. As the Sino-Japanese conflict began to escalate into a full-scale war in the summer of 1937, Nationalist China and the Soviet Union, in August, concluded a mutual nonaggression pact. The terms of the treaty apparently called for Russia to provide arms and military supplies in exchange for raw materials. Massive arms shipments were trucked via Sinkiang to Lanchow in northwestern China; the exact numbers of weapons sent are uncertain, but included were hundreds of combat planes, thousands of machine guns, and numerous artillery pieces and trucks. According to some estimates, the Soviet Union equipped between 10 and 20 Chinese divisions at that time. An entire squadron of Soviet bombers and fighters and their pilots, allegedly volunteers, entered combat on behalf of the Nationalists in December 1937. Many of the aircraft sent to the Nationalists were built in the Urumchi factory in Sinkiang.

Between 1935 and 1939, numerous border incidents threatened to trigger a Soviet-Japanese war. Two large battles took place – at Lake Khasan in the summer of 1938 and in the Khalkin-gol region from May to September of 1939 – involving as many as 50,000 troops and hundreds of aircraft. In each case the military contest was indecisive, and the status quo ante was restored, but these battles underscored the risks of a full-scale war between Moscow and Tokyo. In this context, Soviet assistance to the Nationalists became an integral part of the USSR's own defense policy, somewhat akin to U.S. Lend-Lease assistance to Great Britain.

A similar fundamental concern with national security was a central factor in Stalin's decision to intervene in the Spanish civil war, 1936–9. Adam Ulam has written that "nothing was further from the Soviet government's intentions than a satellite Spain,"[8] for the USSR was at that time trying to win the trust and cooperation of Britain and France in order to forge an anti-Fascist coalition. The Spanish Communists were ordered to pursue a strictly proper united front with Spain's Republicans, and Moscow did its utmost to keep its own involvement discreet. For this reason, no Soviet soldiers were sent to join the 40,000-man International Brigade recruited by the Comintern from around the world. But more than 2,000 Red Army advisers and weapons specialists went to Spain, and the Soviet government mounted a major

[7] Raymond L. Garthoff, *Soviet Military Policy: An Historical Analysis* (New York: Praeger, 1966), 16.
[8] Adam Ulam, *Expansion and Coexistence: Soviet Foreign Policy 1917-1973*, 2nd ed. (New York: Praeger, 1974), 245; see also pp. 243–4.

effort to transport military equipment to the Loyalists. A credit of $85 million was extended to the Republican government, and Soviet, Spanish, and other merchant vessels transported massive amounts of equipment to Spain. Franco's forces sank or captured several Soviet ships during the war, with some loss of life. A German military attaché who attempted to trace the Soviet shipments made the following estimate of their total:

> ...164 vessels loaded with 242 aircraft, 703 guns, 27 antiaircraft guns, 731 tanks, 1,386 trucks, 69,200 tons of other war material, 29,125 tons of ammunition, as well as 28,049 tons of petrol, 100 rifle-machine guns, 500 howitzers, 187 tractors, 325 tons of medical stores, 27,278 tons of crude oil, 5,650 tons of lubricants, 450 tons of clothing – and 920 officers and men.[9]

Two Western historians, Hugh Thomas and Louis Fischer, believe that the attaché underestimated the real totals.[10] The figures illustrate that Moscow was capable of massive intervention in a distant conflict prior to World War II – albeit only by means of sealift, a relatively slow and inflexible instrument.

Gradually Stalin's commitment to preventing a Fascist victory in Spain waned; the complexity of maintaining the distant supply line was almost beyond Soviet capabilities anyway. Once the Soviet Union became convinced that London, Paris, and Washington were not interested in an alliance with the USSR against Nazi Germany, Stalin began to explore the possibility of an accommodation with Germany. This eventually led to the Molotov-Ribbentrop nonaggression pact of August 1939. Europe stepped to the brink of conflagration.

Thus, from the October revolution until World War II, the Soviet Union was a major arms supplier in three conflicts – the Kuomintang-Nationalist struggle, the Sino-Japanese war, and the Spanish civil war – and it made a number of smaller attempts to influence local disputes or support local revolutionaries by military means. All of these conflicts occurred in nearby regions of traditional Russian interest, and this pattern was to persist for a number of years after World War II. Only in the mid-1950s did the USSR begin serious efforts to advance its influence in areas of the Third World beyond the traditional perimeter of Russian interest, and only then did arms exports become a major tool of Soviet foreign policy. Nevertheless, in the interwar years the Kremlin learned valuable practical lessons about the nature of local conflicts, the limits and possibilities of military assistance, and the logistical challenges of transporting arms and rendering military aid from a distance.

[9] Louis Fischer, *Russia's Road from War to Peace: Soviet Foreign Relations 1917–1941* (New York: Harper & Row, 1969), 280.
[10] *Ibid.*, pp. 280–2; Hugh Thomas, *The Spanish Civil War* (New York: Harper & Brothers, 1961), 635–6. Thomas (pp. 640–3) gives a register of the Soviet arms shipments reported by the German attaché.

Stage 1: the two-camps period (1945–53)

Stage 1 of postwar Soviet involvement in Third World conflicts corresponded with the last eight years of Stalin's rule. The only significant examples of Soviet involvement in local conflicts during that period were on behalf of Communist regimes contiguous to the USSR. Even routine Soviet weapons transfers went almost exclusively to Communist regimes and movements in Europe and Asia. The aging and dogmatic Josef Stalin, it seems, failed to grasp the potential importance of the emerging nations of the Third World. At the nineteenth congress of the Communist party of the Soviet Union (CPSU) in October 1952, both Stalin and Georgii Malenkov, his closest deputy, articulated the viewpoint that the world was divided basically into only two camps – imperialist and socialist. The newly independent nations were mere pawns of the former colonial powers, their bourgeois leaders the chief enemies of the national liberation movements and unworthy candidates for Soviet support.[11] This viewpoint sharply narrowed the potential scope of Soviet foreign policy efforts and largely accounts for the halfheartedness of Moscow's attempts to court non-Communist regimes during that period.

There was one notable exception to the general Soviet policy between 1945 and 1953 of transferring arms only to Communist clients: In 1947, Moscow evidently encouraged Czechoslovakia to supply the Israeli Haganah with equipment, thousands of small arms, ammunition, and a number of Messerschmitt fighter planes. The Soviet leadership evidently believed that support for Israel would serve to weaken the British position in the Middle East; only later, under Khrushchev, did the Kremlin come to view the rising force of Arab nationalism as a superior lever for advancing its influence in that region.

The first major instance of Soviet involvement in a post–World War II conflict occurred in China. After an uneasy truce during the war with Japan, the civil war between the Nationalists and the Communists had resumed on a larger scale than ever before. Predictably, the USSR offered military aid to Mao Tse-tung's forces, while the United States provided large quantities of arms and much ill-heeded advice to Chiang Kai-shek, but both powers were quite unprepared for the rapid and total victory of the Kungch'antang (the Chinese Communist party) on the mainland by late 1949. Soviet involvement in the Chinese civil war was cautious and clandestine and probably was not a deciding factor in the war. The Soviet army turned over large stores of captured Japanese arms to the Communists as it withdrew from Manchuria, and it allowed them to assume a powerful strategic position in that territory. Moscow nevertheless continued to recognize the Nationalist government for several months after its eventual defeat had become obvious and in other ways indicated a reluctance to offer full support

---

[11]*Pravda*, October 6 and 9, 1952.

to Mao.[12] The reasons behind Stalin's extreme caution at this juncture are somewhat obscure. Possibly he incorrectly assessed the relative political and military strengths of the contending parties in China; also, he may have been concerned that too open a show of support for the Red forces would trigger firmer U.S. support of Chiang Kai-shek.

The victory of the Chinese Communists and the USSR's successful consolidation of its hegemony in Eastern Europe were no doubt encouraging to Stalin and his colleagues. Together with the first Soviet nuclear explosion in August 1949, these events tempered their perceptions of Soviet weakness vis-à-vis the United States and encouraged a more activist foreign policy in support of revolutionary movements abroad. A spate of Communist uprisings in various parts of Asia accompanied the Chinese Communists' victorious sweep downward from Manchuria. The Indochinese struggle had already begun, and in 1947 and 1948 uprisings were attempted in Indonesia, the Philippines, Malaya, and parts of India. The boost of confidence that Mao's victory gave to the world Communist movement was likely a contributing factor in Stalin's decision to back North Korea's invasion of the Republic of Korea in late June of 1950. Secretary of State Acheson's public demarcation of a U.S. defense perimeter that excluded Korea almost certainly was another contributing factor, for it is unlikely the Kremlin would have allowed Pyongyang to attack South Korea if it had calculated in advance on a massive U.S. military response.

Much more than the Chinese civil war had been, the Korean war was an indirect struggle between the Soviet Union and the United States. The divided status of Korea was itself a product of U.S.-Soviet jockeying for influence in Asia immediately after the defeat of Japan, and the Korean war rapidly saw the domestic issue of who would rule Korea submerged by the strategic rivalry of the superpowers. Washington supported Syngman Rhee's regime with aircraft, naval vessels, hundreds of tanks, and more than 210,000 U.S. troops. The USSR provided tanks, aircraft, and advisers to Kim Il Sung's army, and in November Peking entered the war with tens of thousands of its own troops after repeated warnings that an American crossing of the 38th parallel would not go unresisted. Three years and over a million casualties later, a final armistice ended the war, leaving Korea with a more or less status quo ante bellum political structure. The international order, however, did not return to ante bellum status. The war in Korea marked the real beginning of an intensive cold war between the USSR and the United States; any quick or simple reconciliation became inconceivable. American defense spending more than tripled

---

[12] Shortly after World War II, Stalin is reported to have told a group of visiting Chinese Communists that "the development of the uprising in China had no prospect, and that the Chinese comrades should seek a *modus vivendi* with Chiang Kaichek." Vladimir Dedijer, *Tito* (New York: Simon & Schuster, 1953), 322. After the fall of Peking, when the Nationalists moved their capital to Canton, the Soviet ambassador was one of the few foreign representatives to move with them.

during the course of the Korean war and did not come down much afterward, while U.S. military forces increased from 1.46 million to 3.64 million at the height of the war. Soviet armed forces were also increased substantially during the war, possibly by as much as 3 million men. The conflict in Korea greatly accelerated the solidification of NATO (founded in April 1949 under the impetus of the Berlin blockade) and thus portended the future relationship between the United States and the Soviet Union as one of protracted stalemate in Europe and of vicarious local wars fought for marginal geographical gains and incremental political advantages.

By 1953, after eight years of groping and experimenting on the part of the World War II victors, a new balance of power had emerged in the world. The Soviet Union and the United States both possessed nuclear weapons and large, standing military forces. The Soviet economy had been restored to its prewar production levels and in many sectors was surpassing them. The United States had demonstrated its determination to pursue a policy of "containment" vis-à-vis Communist expansion in any part of the globe, and the USSR had shown both the inclination and the capacity to pose local challenges to U.S. preeminence in areas adjacent to its territory, particularly in areas controlled by local Communist regimes.

Stage 2: the turn to the Third World (1954–64)

The death of Stalin and the subsequent destalinization of Soviet Russia led to significant changes in the foreign policy of the USSR. Among the many shifts in policy was a new outlook and approach toward the developing nations. The new Soviet leaders recognized that the process of decolonization offered plentiful opportunities for political gains, and they undertook several initiatives designed to win the favor of previously maligned "national bourgeois" leaders in the Middle East and South Asia. The Soviet Union, in effect, discovered the Third World. This shift in Soviet thinking and foreign policy, which became increasingly evident over the period from 1953 to 1956, amounted to a restoration of Lenin's vision of forging a united front between the nationalist aspirations of the developing world and the revolutionary, anti-Western objectives of the Soviet regime.

Moscow's post-Stalinist courtship of the Third World began innocently enough: In July 1953 the Soviet representative to the United Nations Economic and Social Council announced that the USSR would contribute 4 million rubles to the UN program of technical assistance to underdeveloped nations. This reversed a long history of opposition of the program and signaled the beginning of a major effort to court the Third World. Malenkov spoke favorably of India and Burma in a speech to the Supreme Soviet in August 1953; a five-year trade agreement with India was signed in September 1953; in 1954, Afghanistan became the first Third World nation to receive credits from Russia since World War II; in February 1955, the first major Soviet economic aid project in one of the less developed nations was announced, the Bhilai steel mill in India, costing over $100 million; in June 1955, Prime Minister Nehru of India made a landmark visit to the Soviet Union, followed a few months later by a highly publicized tour of India, Burma, and Afghanistan by Khrushchev and Bulganin. None of these overtures led to major superpower competition, none seemed particularly threatening to American or European interests, and none of them prepared the Western powers for the surprising announcement on September 17, 1955, that Gamal Abdel Nasser's nationalist regime in Egypt had signed a $250-million arms agreement with Czechoslovakia: "Under the terms of the agreement Cairo was to obtain Soviet MiG-15 and -17 jet fighters, Ilyushin-28 jet bombers, medium and heavy tanks, artillery, submarines, torpedo boats, two destroyers, and ammunition."[13] Although Czechoslovakia was the supplier of record for the military aid, Nasser revealed several months later that the agreement had actually been negotiated with the USSR.

The announcement of that agreement caused deep concern in Western capitals. The problem was not simply that the weapons deal might precipitate a new arms race in the Middle East and greatly heighten tensions there, as both Harold Macmillan and John Foster Dulles warned; far more than just the regional balance of power was at stake: The Soviet Union, in reaching over the confining walls of the Baghdad Pact, had discovered in arms sales a potent instrument for manipulating regional tensions to its own advantage. The September announcement electrified militant Arab nationalists throughout the Middle East and revealed to the Third World an alternative to military dependence on the West.

Khrushchev codified the Soviet Union's new approach toward national liberation movements in the Third World at the twentieth congress of the CPSU in 1956. He spoke of "the emergence in the world arena of a group of peace-loving European and Asian states which have proclaimed nonparticipation in blocs as a principle of their foreign policy." The nonaligned states, together with the socialist nations, formed "a vast peace zone." Khrushchev explained in detail the significance of decolonization for Soviet foreign policy:

> The present disintegration of the imperialist colonial system is a postwar development of world-historical significance...
> The new period in world history, predicted by Lenin, when

---

[13] Oles M. Smolansky, *The Soviet Union and the Arab East under Khrushchev* (Lewisburg, Bucknell University Press, 1974), 30–1. The agreement was a barter arrangement (Egyptian cotton and rice in exchange for the arms), so the figure of $250 million is only a Western estimate of the value of the weapons. See U.S. Congress, Subcommittee on Foreign Economic Policy of the Joint Economic Committee, *New Directions in the Soviet Economy*, 89th Congress, 2d sess. (Washington: U.S. Government Printing Office, 1966), 965.

the peoples of the East would play an active part in deciding the destinies of the entire world and become a new and mighty factor in international relations, has arrived...

Today they need not go begging to their former oppressors for modern equipment. They can get it in the socialist countries, free from any political or military obligations.

The very fact that the Soviet Union and other countries of the socialist camp exist, that they are ready to help the underdeveloped nations with their industrial development on terms of equality and mutual benefit, is a major stumbling block to colonial policy.[14]

Similar commitments to support for national liberation movements can be found in the keynote addresses at every congress of the CPSU since 1956 and in vast quantities of Soviet media commentary and scholarly writing.

For nearly two decades following the arms deal with Egypt, the Middle East was the focal point of Soviet efforts to work with the national liberation movements in the Third World. Syria and Yemen became the next Arab nations to receive Soviet arms. Early in 1956, Syria concluded an agreement with Prague, and arms deliveries began in March (via Egypt, because Syrian facilities were inadequate for receiving the weapons). A similar agreement was reached with Yemen, and deliveries began in October 1956. Czechoslovak and Soviet military advisers traveled to Egypt, Syria, and Yemen to assist in weapons maintenance and pilot training.

Moscow's debut as an arms supplier in the Middle East opened a new era in Soviet foreign policy; arms exports from the Soviet Union and its East European allies multiplied dramatically after 1955. According to the Stockholm International Peace Research Institute:

The pattern, and the values, of Soviet arms supplies to the third world countries clearly show the change in policy after 1955...Until 1955, arms suppliers to the third world were small, and were exclusively directed to socialist countries – particularly North Korea. The big increase in the flow of weapons to non-aligned countries began after 1955.[15]

In addition to a continuing flow of arms into Egypt, Syria, and Yemen, Soviet weapons were delivered for the first time to Afghanistan in 1956, Iraq and Indonesia in 1958, and Guinea in 1959. Between 1960 and 1964, 11 additional nations became recipients of Soviet military

[14] *Pravda*, February 15, 1956.
[15] SIPRI, *The Arms Trade with the Third World* (New York: Humanities Press, 1971), 188–9; see also p. 190.

aid.[16] Although estimates vary, the total amount of Soviet weapons exports to nonaligned countries from 1954 to 1964 exceeded $2.7 billion.[17] The sudden turn to the Third World is further illustrated by the fact that nearly 80 percent of all Soviet arms exports during stage 2 went to non-Communist nations, compared with a negligible amount before 1955.

Under Khrushchev, the USSR began to exert its influence in regional conflicts beyond the traditional bounds of Russian military activity. In sharp contrast with the Stalinist era, most such efforts were on behalf of non-Communist clients. The military scale of Soviet involvement in Third World conflicts was quite modest, however, particularly if account is taken of the quantity of Soviet weapons actually employed in combat. For example, Soviet arms shipments to the Arabs contributed to the tension preceding the Suez war in October-November 1956, but those arms were not used in the war. The tanks and heavy equipment that the Imam Ahmed in Yemen received from the USSR likewise sat idle during the Yemen-Aden border clashes of 1957–9. The USSR's military involvement in the Congo crisis was confined largely to providing 15 transport planes, 5 of which flew under UN aegis, and to shipments of small arms. Moscow rushed 300 tanks and a few MiG fighters to Algeria during its brief border war with Morocco in 1963, but the conflict was terminated too quickly for the weapons to play a major role.

Under Khrushchev, the USSR's largest military assistance program to a Third World country involved in conflict was in Indonesia, where from 1958 to 1965 more than $1 billion worth of arms were sent to back Sukarno in three successive conflicts: the Sumatran rebellion (1958–60), the crusade against Dutch possession of West Irian (1961–2), and the "Crush Malaysia" campaign (1963–5). The Soviet investment was massive, but the vast majority of the weapons were never used in combat. The Sumatran rebellion, the most serious of the three conflicts, was put down largely with weapons Sukarno already had, and Indonesian military actions in the other two conflicts amounted to no more than a few commando raids. The Kremlin probably was willing to make such large commitments of military assistance in the early 1960s precisely because they were symbolic commitments, and the chance of confrontation with the Western powers was fairly small.

In 1960–1, the Soviet Union undertook two small interventions in quick succession in the Congo and in Laos. The scale of Soviet military involvement was modest in each instance, but the diplomatic significance of the events was considerable. The Congo intervention began

---

[16] The new recipients were Laos, India, Morocco, Algeria, Sudan, Ghana, Mali, Cambodia, Somalia, Tanzania (via Zanzibar), and Zaire. This does not include a modest gift to Nepal. SIPRI, *The Arms Trade Registers* (Cambridge: M.I.T. Press, 1975).

[17] *SIPRI Yearbook of Armaments and Disarmaments* (Cambridge: M.I.T. Press, 1976), 220. CIA estimates are somewhat higher than SIPRI estimates.

in the summer of 1960, when Moscow offered support to the government of Patrice Lumumba in Leopoldville in its effort to suppress a secessionist rebellion in Katanga. The USSR's involvement began under the umbrella of UN efforts to aid Lumumba, but it became unilateral after the Congolese prime minister became disaffected with the assistance being rendered by UN authorities. Soviet involvement in the crisis was boisterous and highly publicized, though the actual assistance provided amounted largely to trucks, small arms, and provision of transport planes. At the height of the crisis, Lumumba was ousted in a coup, and his successors promptly expelled the Soviets from the Congo. Despite that setback, the crisis gave Moscow an opportunity to flex its muscle for the first time ever in a sub-Saharan conflict, providing a lesson to African nationalists they would not soon forget.

Soviet involvement in the Laotian civil war in 1960–1 was also on a very modest scale – military assistance to the united front of Souvanna Phouma and the Pathet Lao amounted to no more than a few million dollars in small arms – but it was probably the most politically successful military assistance effort made under Khrushchev. A Soviet airlift (including some planes flown in from the Congo) enabled the united front to rout the U.S.-supported forces of General Phoumi Nosavan and to win control of four-fifths of the country by May 1961, only a few months after the first Soviet air sorties began. The political outcome was highly favorable from Moscow's point of view. The United States suspended aid to Phoumi, forcing him to acquiesce in a coalition government. The Geneva Accords of July 1962 then guaranteed the neutrality of Laos.

The USSR undertook considerably larger arms shipments to a Third World state at war the following year, when the Imam Ahmed was overthrown by a military coup in Yemen. By means of accelerated arms shipments to Egypt, Moscow in effect underwrote Nasser's intervention in the ensuing civil war between the new Republican government and the Royalist tribesmen who rallied to the Imam. So long as Khrushchev was in power, however, the Soviet involvement remained indirect, and all Soviet military assistance to the Republicans passed through Cairo.

The Cuban missile crisis, the Berlin crisis, and the numerous smaller wars and crises that fueled U.S.-Soviet tensions during Khrushchev's tenure in power left the impression that the world had passed through an extraordinarily dangerous period. Khrushchev's own flamboyant, threatening style confirmed this impression, and the West (as well as the East) was in some measure relieved when he was deposed by a more somber-looking collective of apparatchiks. In retrospect, however, Soviet military activities in the Third World under Khrushchev were on a far smaller scale and of much more limited scope than they would later become. The USSR simply did not possess the military means – including a favorable balance in strategic nuclear weapons

– necessary for projecting its power abroad in a major way. The Soviet leadership evidently recognized the necessity of rectifying this short-coming if Moscow was to acquire influence in the world commensurate with that enjoyed by Washington. Thomas Wolfe noted that the Soviet drive to gain "global politico-military maneuverability" began in the early 1960s:

> Only gradually toward the end of the Khrushchev decade did it also come to be recognized that there was a need for more mobile and versatile forces, either for asserting a Soviet presence in distant areas of political contention or for possible use in local conflict situations in which it might not be expedient to invoke the threat of immediate nuclear holocaust.[18]

This effort did not begin to produce significant results until the latter part of the decade. In the meantime, the deployment of Soviet inter-continental nuclear missiles had also speeded up noticeably, particularly after the Cuban missile crisis. By the time Khrushchev was ousted from power, the USSR possessed nearly three times as many ICBMs as it had in 1962 (200 compared with 75).

Stage 3: nascent globalism (1965–72)

The accession of Brezhnev and Kosygin to power in October 1964 seems to have marked the beginning of a third stage of Soviet military involvement in Third World conflicts. At the twenty-third congress of the CPSU in March 1966, Brezhnev made an unusually strong and lengthy statement affirming the Soviet Union's commitment to support movements engaged in "wars of national liberation." The thoroughgoing *Realpolitik* of the new leaders manifested itself in their willingness to provide material assistance even to military governments and conservative regimes in the Third World, as long as doing so would advance Soviet interests. From 1965 to 1972, the USSR exported roughly $6.5 billion worth of arms to developing countries; seven additional countries became recipients of Soviet arms for the first time.[19] The new Soviet leaders showed themselves to be somewhat bolder than Khrushchev in their use of military force and assistance to gain political advantage in the Third World, and the military scale of Soviet involvement in local conflicts during stage 3 was markedly larger, on the average, than during stage 2.

During the period from 1965 to 1972, the Soviet Union refined and expanded its military assistance programs, improved its sealift and

[18] Thomas W. Wolfe, "The Projection of Soviet Power," *Military Review* (February 1969):64–5.

[19] The new recipients were Pakistan, Iran, South Yemen, Ethiopia, Nigeria, Cyprus, and Uganda. Small gifts were also made to Mauritania and the People's Republic of the Congo. SIPRI, *The Arms Trade Registers*.

airlift capabilities, and made progress in the quality and quantity of its assault forces, both airborne and amphibious. The Soviet fleet grew in size, and the geographical scope of its routine operations was extended. Although the USSR's power projection capabilities still lagged considerably behind those of the United States, these advances helped pave the way for greater Soviet assertiveness in distant conflicts. Because many of the new forces were of marginal utility for defending the homeland, clearly it would seem that they were assembled with the intention of enhancing the Kremlin's ability to influence events in more distant parts of the world. The Soviet Union also made great progress in redressing the nuclear imbalance with the United States during this time, expanding its ICBM force from 270 delivery vehicles in 1965 to over 1,500 by 1972; the number of Soviet submarine-launched ballistic missiles also increased, from 120 to 560. The USSR's achievement of effective nuclear parity undoubtedly increased the self-confidence of the Soviet leadership, while enhancing the USSR's international image as a superpower equal to the United States. It also somewhat reduced the risks for the Soviet Union in becoming involved in local conflicts, because the United States was not likely to threaten massive retaliation in such instances without overwhelming nuclear superiority.

Following Soviet Premier Alexei Kosygin's visit to Hanoi in February 1965, Soviet military aid to North Vietnam increased massively. Both Moscow and Peking had been supplying some arms to North Vietnam for several years prior to 1965, but only after the United States under President Lyndon B. Johnson began to greatly increase its own ground forces in Vietnam did Soviet aid to North Vietnam increase dramatically. The U.S. entry into the war on a massive scale not only transformed Indochina into a primary axis of the superpower rivalry but also intensified Sino-Soviet competition for influence with Hanoi. Failure to arm North Vietnam unreservedly might have made the USSR vulnerable to Chinese charges of not supporting national liberation movements and might have damaged Soviet prestige with Communist parties around the world. Indeed, competition with Peking may have been a greater factor drawing the Soviet Union into the conflict as an arms supplier than was competition with Washington, but the war provided an excellent opportunity to tie down U.S. forces in Vietnam and force Washington to expend enormous sums of fiscal, political, and moral capital in defending a country of secondary strategic significance.

From 1965 until the signing of the Paris peace agreements in 1972, the USSR delivered over $3 billion worth of weaponry to North Vietnam in its largest and ultimately one of its most successful attempts to influence the outcome of a local conflict. Hanoi also received arms from China, but by far the greater bulk of its military equipment came from the Soviet Union. American intelligence reports indicated that through at least 1971 North Vietnam never suffered from shortages of arms, ammunition, transport vehicles, or other military equipment, U.S. bombing raids notwithstanding.[20] Without the military assistance received from the Soviet Union, it is doubtful that North Vietnam and its guerrilla allies in the south could have prevailed in the war.

Despite the magnitude of the USSR's commitment to North Vietnam from 1965 to 1972, the Soviet leadership did not hesitate to provide a number of Arab nations with large quantities of arms during the same period, nor did it refrain from making other efforts at military involvement in the Third World. This fact alone illustrates the USSR's progress in establishing itself as a power capable of exerting its influence, by military or other means, in diverse regions of the globe.

Egypt accumulated Soviet weaponry for over a decade following the Suez war, only to see the bulk of it destroyed on the ground during the six-day war of June 1967. The extreme brevity of that conflict made it impossible for the Soviet Union to stage an airlift of weaponry to the Arabs; although an effort was made to resupply Egypt's losses, none of the supplies reached their destination before the cease-fire. The Kremlin was reduced to making threatening, but ineffectual, noises in the background. Egypt's humiliation was a catastrophe for the USSR, one of such proportions that it had the effect of undermining Soviet influence in Cairo, once Moscow proved unable, as the Arabs' principal ally, to reverse the defeat and recover the lost territories after six years of effort. In the short term, however, the defeat provided the catalyst for a vastly increased Soviet presence in the Middle East. Alvin Z. Rubinstein observed that "defeat transformed the Soviet-Egyptian relationship. The massive flow of Soviet aid after the June War restored Egypt's military capabilities and intensified interactions between the two countries on all levels."[21] The huge quantities of arms and advisers that were poured into Egypt after the conflict were many times larger than any previous extension of Soviet power beyond the Eurasian land mass; the arms alone amounted to more than $4.5 billion from 1967 to 1973.

When Nasser withdrew his troops from Yemen following the June war, the USSR immediately stepped in as the first-line arms supplier and mainstay of the Republican regime in Sana, engineering hasty airlifts and sealifts of MiGs and tanks that just sufficed to rescue the capital city from a 70-day Royalist siege. The obscurity of the conflict belies its significance, for the Yemeni civil war was the first clear-cut historical case of Soviet power rescuing a non-Communist regime from otherwise certain military defeat. The war also provided the first confirmed instance in the postwar period of Soviet fighter pilots engaging

[20] National Security Council memorandum No. 1, reproduced in *Congressional Record*, May 10, 1972.
[21] Alvin Z. Rubinstein, *Red Star on the Nile: The Soviet-Egyptian Influence Relationship Since the June War* (Princeton University Press, 1977), xi.

in combat in the Third World. The Yemeni civil war is treated as a case study in Chapter 5.

Brezhnev and Kosygin revealed the pragmatic bent of their politics at the time of the Nigerian civil war (1967–70), when Moscow backed the campaign of the federal military government (FMG) against secessionist Biafra. The war produced several departures from past Soviet practice – the Soviet Union rendered aid to a conservative military government that was also a British Commonwealth member and a recipient of massive British military assistance in a war against an avowedly progressive, nationalist regime that professed to be exercising self-determination. Nigeria had received arms from 20 countries before the war, including Czechoslovakia, but not the USSR. Only Britain and the Soviet Union, however, were willing to supply arms once the civil war began. Soviet arms shipments commenced in August 1967 and continued at intervals throughout the war; they included heavy artillery, MiG-17 fighters, and Il-28 bombers, in addition to small arms and transport vehicles. It was the Soviet Union's first large military supply operation in sub-Saharan Africa, and though Lagos certainly would have won the war without Soviet arms, the Kremlin's willingness to aid the FMG won it considerable favor in black Africa, strengthened Soviet ties with previously aloof Nigeria, and prodded Lagos toward the nonaligned foreign policy it has pursued ever since. The Soviet role in the Nigerian civil war is examined closely in Chapter 6.

The Soviet invasion of Czechoslovakia in August 1968 briefly soured the USSR's relations with the West and with some Third World countries. Prior to that invasion, the prevailing opinion in the West was that the new Soviet leadership had advanced beyond the use of brute force in Eastern Europe; that invasion caused a reassessment of Soviet intentions and objectives and a slowing of an already slow movement toward an East-West détente. Czechoslovakia is not in the Third World, and hence that invasion is outside the scope of this work, but militarily it portended some of the same tactics that would later be used by Moscow in Afghanistan: the element of surprise, the use of airborne troops to seize and hold key points, the manufacture of an "invitation" to intervene, and the promulgation (in the case of Afghanistan, an elaboration) after the fact of a doctrine justifying the intervention as an act necessitated by Socialist solidarity. The so-called Brezhnev doctrine that asserted the irreversibility of Communist revolutions and the limited sovereignty of Socialist states had been formulated principally to justify the invasion of Czechoslovakia, but its potential implications for the Third World would later become apparent in the 1970s, when several Communist and revolutionary leftist regimes came to power in Asia and Africa. The age-old diplomatic dictates of credibility and prestige seemed to require that the USSR commit its military power to defending these new regimes, if they were threatened.

The war of attrition (1969–70) witnessed a level of direct participation in combat by Soviet soldiers that had been unparalleled in any earlier post–World War II conflict: Soviet pilots flew combat missions, Soviet advisers participated at all levels of tactical and logistical planning, and Soviet crews manned SAM installations and fired SAMs at Israeli jets. Despite such extraordinary efforts, Israel managed throughout the conflict to continue making effective air strikes against Egypt, thereby embarrassing Moscow perhaps as much as or more than the Arabs. The war ground to a halt in midsummer of 1970 in what amounted to a tactical defeat for Egypt, amid signs that even Nasser was coming to recognize the limitations of Soviet power and assistance in achieving concrete gains against Israel. Anwar Sadat's succession to the Egyptian presidency after Nasser's death in September soon led to further signs of a slow Egyptian drift away from Moscow.

The growing strain in Soviet-Egyptian relations was obscured temporarily by the signing in August 1971 of an Egyptian-Soviet treaty of friendship and cooperation and by a massive influx of Soviet advisers into Egypt. By 1972 there were some 20,000 Soviet advisers working in Egypt, and the USSR enjoyed privileged access to five Egyptian ports and eight airfields, six of which were under its exclusive control. This impressive infrastructure did not last long. In July 1972, Sadat stunned the world by announcing nationalization of the Soviet-built military facilities in Egypt and by ordering Soviet military advisers to leave Egypt (some civilian advisers remained). Although Moscow made a brief comeback in its relations with Cairo during 1973, the expulsion order of July 1972 portended the eventual complete collapse of the Soviet position in Egypt that took place in the years following the October 1973 war.

The final conflict in which the Soviet Union was involved during this third phase was the Indo-Pakistani war of 1971. Former U.S. Secretary of State Henry Kissinger has portrayed this conflict as "the naked recourse to force by a partner of the Soviet Union backed by Soviet arms and buttressed by Soviet assurances."[22] This characterization is perhaps somewhat too harsh. During the first several months of 1971, as the political crisis in East Pakistan was worsening and the probability of an Indo-Pakistani conflict was increasing, the Soviet Union seems to have acted with a measure of caution, perhaps hoping that in the event of a flare-up it could play the role of mediator, much as it had done at the time of the short-lived Indo-Pakistani war of 1966. The Soviet news media denounced Pakistani repression of the Bengalis in East Pakistan, but at the same time they called for a peaceful resolution of the problem.

On August 9, the Soviet Union and India signed a treaty of friendship and cooperation. Although preparations for the conclusion of such a treaty had been under way prior to the outbreak of the crisis in East Pakistan, the practical effect of the treaty, coming when it did, was to accelerate the drift toward conflict. India then believed that it had

[22] Henry Kissinger, *White House Years* (Boston: Little, Brown, 1979), 913.

obtained a needed measure of assurance against the possibility of either Chinese or U.S. intervention. Some Soviet arms had been entering India throughout the year, and their volume increased sharply in November with the start of an airlift from the USSR and the arrival of Soviet freighters carrying some 5,000 tons of military hardware. Whether or not the Soviet leadership wanted to encourage an Indian invasion of East Pakistan, its failure to exercise restraint in the provision of arms at this time plainly contributed to that end. India invaded East Pakistan in force around December 4, engulfing the subcontinent in a 14-day war. No new Soviet arms are known to have arrived in India during the period of full-scale hostilities, but Moscow openly backed India in its public pronouncements and through vigorous diplomacy, both in the UN and vis-à-vis the United States. The outcome of the conflict must be seen as a diplomatic success for the Soviet Union. The war dismembered Pakistan, an ally of both the United States and the People's Republic of China (PRC), and it greatly strengthened Soviet ties with India.

It seems clear that from 1965 to 1972 there were significant increases in the scale and scope of Soviet military and diplomatic involvement in Third World conflicts. The USSR undertook massive programs of military assistance to both North Vietnam and Egypt, escalated the level of its involvement in Yemen, and by means of weapons shipments and skillful diplomacy won notable political gains in Nigeria and South Asia. Soviet weaponry, advisers, and even some troops were used by the Kremlin more extensively than ever before to further its influence in the Third World. Nevertheless, the wholesale destruction of Soviet weaponry in the June war, Israel's tactical victory in the war of attrition in 1970, and Sadat's expulsion of Soviet advisers in 1972 hardly boded well for the USSR's future in the Middle East. Nor did Moscow then have much to show for its large commitment in Indochina. Paradoxically, the very regions in which the Soviet Union had devoted its greatest energies were those that, until 1972 at least, had yielded the least in terms of solid achievements. This may have been in part because the Middle East and Indochina were also the areas in which the United States was then making its greatest efforts to support pro-Western regimes and to counteract Soviet influence.

Stage 4: the achievement of global power (1973–80)

At the beginning of the 1970s, both the Soviet Union and the United States deliberately sought to effect a measure of rapprochement in their relations. Although this was not the first period of détente in postwar history, it was the most enthusiastically publicized and most conscientiously pursued, with agreements being reached on a number of outstanding East-West issues. A quadripartite agreement on Berlin was signed; a U.S.-Soviet summit meeting in Moscow concluded a historic agreement on strategic arms limitation, as well as several other accords on trade and cooperation; Brezhnev paid a return visit to the United States; a peace treaty was signed in Paris that brought hostilities in Vietnam to a temporary end.

It was a heady time, but the achievements were short-lived. The United States had pursued a policy of détente at least partly on the assumption that it would restrain Soviet military activity abroad and narrow the range of acceptable international behavior. Instead, the 1970s were years of unprecedented Soviet military involvement in Third World conflicts, beginning with the Yom Kippur war and ending with the invasion of Afghanistan. The result was growing U.S. disillusionment with the term *détente* and the policy it then represented.

The Yom Kippur war marked the beginning of this disillusionment. It can be seen as the opening of a fourth phase of Soviet involvement in Third World conflicts. Although prior to October 1973 the USSR had been a principal actor in a number of Arab-Israeli conflicts, as discussed earlier, never had it been so intensely and directly involved during actual hostilities. Indeed, it was "the first time that the Soviet Union had ever engaged in a massive continuous resupply of a non-Communist client during the actual course of full hostilities."[23] Nearly 1,000 flights of transport planes and some 30 Soviet cargo vessels delivered upward of 100,000 tons of arms to the Arabs in the course of the conflict. This arms supply operation was considerably larger than any previous Soviet effort of a comparable nature in the Third World; also without historical parallel was the wide range of activities undertaken by military personnel from the USSR. Soviet advisers drove tanks from Latakia to Damascus, operated radar equipment, repaired weapons damaged in combat, and manned air defenses at Syrian ports; Soviet advisers are reported to have accompanied Syrian ground units everywhere except at the front, with at least one adviser assigned to every Syrian command post from the battalion level up; seven Soviet airborne divisions were placed on alert during the greater part of the war, and the Soviet fleet in the Mediterranean was increased to around 90 ships, including a number of amphibious assault vessels. The USSR had never done anything quite like it before. Furthermore, following the cease-fire, a Cuban armored brigade was deployed on the Syrian front; although it never engaged in combat, this deployment can be seen in retrospect as a portent of things to come in other Third World conflicts.

The pattern of Soviet diplomacy in the October war was not unlike that in previous Middle East conflicts – the Kremlin acted with caution, it sought to exert a measure of restraint over the Arabs, it made a last-minute threat to intervene directly – but these similarities do not hide the fact that in this war there were significant advances in the scale and scope of Soviet military involvement in a local conflict. More

[23] Jon D. Glassman, *Arms for the Arabs* (Baltimore: Johns Hopkins University Press, 1975), 131.

important still, the events of this war confirmed the newfound status of the USSR as a global power, this by virtue of the fact that Moscow conducted the resupply operation in the face of the virtual certainty that it would trigger vigorous countermeasures from the United States, with the attendant risks of confrontation, and the fact that the hostilities were terminated largely as a result of face-to-face U.S.-Soviet negotiations held in Moscow. The Yom Kippur war is the subject of the case study found in Chapter 7.

Although Moscow managed against considerable odds to salvage from the Yom Kippur war a military stalemate and a moral victory for the Arabs, it suffered almost total collapse of its influence in Egypt shortly thereafter. Having achieved his minimal goals in the October war, Sadat became convinced that Egypt could not afford another war and that the Sinai could more easily be won back by diplomatic means. Renewed U.S. interest in a Middle East settlement, and the pressure placed on Washington as a result of the cartelization of the world petroleum market, made such a diplomatic alternative feasible and left Sadat with little use for the Soviets; also, by the end of the war he had come to regard them with deep distrust. Throughout 1974 and 1975 the Soviet Union's ties with Egypt eroded, whereas U.S.-Egyptian relations improved. In the spring of 1976, Sadat abruptly cancelled the 1971 treaty of friendship and cooperation with the USSR and terminated Soviet access to Egyptian naval facilities, essentially bringing to an end 20 years of extensive cooperation between Cairo and Moscow.

Although the middle of the decade found the USSR being pushed out of its former prominent role in the Middle East, Soviet prospects appeared considerably brighter in Indochina, where the position of the Thieu regime in Saigon was steadily becoming weaker. During the early months of 1974, and continuing into the summer of that year, Viet Cong and North Vietnamese units undertook a cautious offensive in the south, consisting principally of selected attacks against particularly vulnerable targets. The surprising success of this offensive, combined with the lack of any meaningful deterrent response from the United States, encouraged Hanoi to broaden its offensive. One and one-half years after the October war and less than two and one-half years after the signing of the Paris peace agreements, Saigon fell. Regular divisions of the North Vietnamese army, equipped with Soviet weapons, entered Saigon on April 30, 1975, to achieve for Hanoi its long-sought goal of political control of the south.

The fall of Saigon must be regarded as a watershed event in postwar history. Washington's defeat in Indochina shattered American and world perceptions of U.S. invincibility and demonstrated that a military alliance with the United States was not an absolute guarantee of security for a Third World country. While the United States fell into a troubled period of neoisolationism and self-effacement in its foreign policy, the Soviet leadership received a needed boost in confidence; the principal lessons of that war for the Kremlin were not about the limitations of military power but about its manifest political utility. The fall of South Vietnam, in fact, marked the beginning of a highly successful strategic offensive by the USSR in the Third World. Between April 1975 and January 1979, there occurred no less than seven successful armed seizures of power or territory by pro-Soviet Communist or radical leftist parties in the Third World. Pro-Soviet revolutionary regimes came to power as the result of violent conflicts or coups in South Vietnam, Laos, Angola, Ethiopia, Afghanistan, South Yemen, and Cambodia. Soviet arms played a role in the majority of these instances.

This series of military victories by Soviet allies in the Third World coincided with, and was at least partly the result of, a shift in the thinking of the Soviet leadership regarding national liberation movements. By the late 1960s, the leadership in the Kremlin had already begun to recognize that the national bourgeoisie in the Third World was not proving to be a reliable ally in advancing Soviet interests abroad. In 1968, for example, Professor R. Ulyanovsky wrote the following in *Pravda*:

> In the period of struggle against colonial regimes the national bourgeoisie was often at the head of the struggle. In the present stage of the national-liberation struggle *the national bourgeoisie already has demonstrated its inability to continue to play that role*. This does not mean of course that it has everywhere ceased to participate in the anti-imperialist struggle...
>
> The historical tendency in the national-liberation movement is toward the gradual and ever-growing role of the working class...In a number of countries this position has gained ground, and a block of left-wing forces is forming, with the working class playing an active role.[24]

Numerous similar pronouncements can be found in Soviet sources during the late 1960s and 1970s.[25] This seems to have reflected not merely a new ideological nuance but an actual shift in Soviet strategy toward lesser support for nationalist bourgeois leaders and greater reliance of Marxist parties and other left-wing revolutionary groups in the Third World.

Donald Zagoria has suggested that this shift in the USSR's approach to the Third World had its origins in the numerous setbacks suffered in backing regimes led by national bourgeoisie:

[24] *Pravda*, January 3, 1968.
[25] See, for example, A. Iskenderov, "The National Liberation Movement in Our Time," in *The Third World, Problems and Prospects: Current Stages of the National Liberation Struggle* (Moscow: Progress Publishers, 1970), 11–43; A. Kiva, "Strany sotsialisticheskoi orientatsii: nekotorye osobennosti politicheskogo razvitiya," *Mezhdunarodnaya zhizn'* (September 1973):38–47.

> Having realized the error of the excessive cooperation with un-
> reliable "bourgeois nationalist" leaders in the 1950s and 1960s,
> the Soviets have come up with a new strategy for the 1970s and
> 1980s. They continue, in some cases, such as Iraq, Syria, and
> Algeria, for example, to support non-communist "socialists" of
> one kind or another. But now that more orthodox Marxist-Len-
> inist groups have proliferated in many parts of Asia and Africa,
> the new element in the Soviet strategy is to help communist
> parties gain state power.[26]

The Soviet experience in Egypt may have been the most important
single factor behind this reassessment in strategy, but the experience
of failure in the Sudan, Ghana, Indonesia, Algeria, and the Congo no
doubt also played a role.

This development in Soviet policy should be seen largely as a tactical shift. It did not mean that in the future Moscow would concentrate its efforts solely on radical, ideologically motivated movements
and regimes. There was recognition that, in the words of one Soviet
commentator, "the struggle against imperialism is being waged by
different social forces, by radical, moderate, and even conservative
regimes."[27] The USSR's approach to the Third World in the latter half
of the 1970s continued to be broadly opportunistic, though never for-
getting that the ideological fervor and disciplined organization of radical clients made them the most effective allies.

There was significant expansion in the Soviet Union's military assistance programs in the Third World after 1972. The regimes targeted
for assistance were by no means all Marxist-Leninist. According to one
official U.S. estimate, Soviet arms exports to developing countries
reached a value of roughly $16.5 billion from 1973 through 1977. A
different U.S. agency estimated Soviet arms exports in the period from
1974 to 1978 at some $14.8 billion. According to this second study,
the Soviet Union exported more fighter planes, bombers, tanks, anti-
aircraft pieces, and artillery pieces that did the United States in that
time, and total Soviet deliveries of weapons worldwide were about 10
percent above U.S. deliveries. The USSR, however, provided substantially fewer services, such as maintenance and training, to its clients
that did the United States. The Stockholm Institute for Peace Research, in a study first released in 1982, also concluded that the Soviet
Union had surpassed the United States as the world's largest exporter
of arms.[28] Arms shipments were, of course, only one element making

---

[26] Donald Zagoria, "Into the Breach: New Soviet Alliances in the Third World," *Foreign Affairs* 57(Spring 1979):738. See also Francis Fukuyama, "A New Soviet Strategy" *Lommentary* 24 (October 1979): 52 ff.

[27] Kiva, "Strany sotsialisticheskoi orientatsii," 38.

[28] U.S. Arms Control and Disarmament Agency, *World Military Expenditures and Arms
Transfers 1968–1977*, p. 155; Central Intelligence Agency, "Arms Flows to LDCs –
U.S.-Soviet Comparisons, 1974–77" (Washington, D.C., 1978); *Frankfurter Rund-
schau*, March 8, 1982. See also U.S. Department of State, "Conventional Arms
Transfers in the Third World, 1972–81," Special Report No. 102.

possible the USSR's military activism in the Third World in the late 1970s. A growth in power projection capabilities was another; this will be examined in detail in the following chapter.

The fall of South Vietnam in 1975 and the painful reassessment of national purposes that it elicited in the United States helped create the international climate that made possible the subsequent Soviet-Cuban intervention in the civil war in Angola. The import of the Angolan civil war in 1975–6 went far beyond the relatively modest strategic significance of this West African country. It was the first (and thus far only) historical case of truly massive Soviet military involvement in a sub-Saharan conflict; furthermore, Angola lay completely outside the traditional perimeter of Soviet or Russian interests. It also marked the first large-scale deployment of Cuban troops on behalf of a Soviet client state.

The Angolan civil war was waged between three competing national liberation movements; the Soviet Union supported the most urban and best organized of the three, the Marxist MPLA, with which it had a long history of ties. Arms shipments from the USSR to the MPLA had begun as early as August 1974, but not until November 1975, when Portuguese rule in Angola formally came to an end, did Soviet arms shipments increase to massive scale. By the end of the conflict, Moscow had shipped over $300 million worth of arms to the MPLA, including several hundred tanks and armored personnel carriers. Of greater consequence than the arms shipments, however, was the deployment in Angola of the Cuban expeditionary force, which in only a few months was expanded into a force of nearly 20,000 troops by February 1976. The Cuban effort began tentatively and somewhat haphazardly, but it proved surprisingly effective, probably because of close coordination with Moscow and because of Soviet arms shipments, logistical and transport assistance, and financing. The result of the Soviet-Cuban intervention in this war was complete triumph of the MPLA in all parts of the country except the rural south. The conflict also proved to be an embarrassing diplomatic fiasco for the United States, whose own program of covert support to a rival movement fighting the MPLA was cut short by congressional fiat. The USSR's involvement in the Angolan civil war is analyzed in detail in Chapter 8.

Prior to the civil war in Angola, the USSR's principal shortcoming in undertaking to influence the outcomes of Third World conflicts was the Kremlin's reluctance to employ Soviet troops in foreign combat. Advisers simply cannot substitute for trained soldiers, and most Third World armies are not able to use modern weapons to good advantage. The introduction of Cuban troops into Angola and the attendant triumph of the MPLA showed the Soviet leadership a new way in which Soviet power could be exerted in distant conflicts – provided, of course, that Castro went along. It was a lesson that the leadership of the Kremlin put to good use only two years later in the Ogaden war.

The war between Ethiopia and Somalia over the Ogaden in 1977– 8 was, in terms of actual fighting, even larger than the conflict in Angola, and its strategic significance was greater. When the war began, as the result of the Somali offensive in the summer of 1977, the Soviet Union was attempting to maintain close ties with both Somalia, a long-time ally, and the radical leftist regime of Lieutenant Colonel Mengistu Haile-Mariam. It even appears that for a short time during the conflict, Soviet arms were being shipped to both combatants. Following the expulsion of Soviet advisers from Somalia in November 1977, the Soviet Union began a massive airlift of arms to Ethiopia, with the eventual value of the arms delivered running to roughly $1 billion. As in Angola, Cuban troops, many flown in on Soviet planes, played the decisive role in the war. Moscow and Havana coordinated their efforts so carefully that in some cases arriving Cuban troops were outfitted immediately with Soviet equipment and dispatched directly to the front. The number of Cuban soldiers was somewhat less than in Angola, but the volume of arms deliveries was nearly three times as great, and Soviet advisers were more directly involved in the Ethiopian campaign than they had been in Angola. At least two high-ranking Soviet officers flew into Ethiopia to oversee parts of the operation, giving the Kremlin an unusual degree of direct control over the direction of the fighting.

The United States made no serious effort to resist or deter the Soviet-Cuban intervention, and it proceeded with few international impediments. It was, in fact, the first time in postwar history that a large Soviet military operation had taken place outside Eastern Europe without any other major power becoming involved militarily. The loss of Somalia as an ally meant the loss of the largest Soviet military base outside the Warsaw Pact, but the overall consequences of the war were highly positive for the Soviet Union. Ethiopia has 10 times the population of Somalia, vastly greater natural resources, and greater influence in Africa. Although the USSR's involvement in the war temporarily strained its relations with the Arab League, which supported Somalia, the conflict had the effect of transforming Ethiopia into a loyal ally of the Soviet Union. This gave Moscow a new channel of influence in the Red Sea region and thus partly compensated for the loss of its close relationship with Cairo a few years earlier.

During an 18-month period following Ethiopia's victory in the Ogaden, the Soviet Union became involved on a relatively modest scale in three conflicts in the developing world: Vietnam's military takeover of Cambodia, the short Sino-Vietnamese conflict that followed, and South Yemen's attack on Yemen (Sana) in the fall of 1978. The first two of these conflicts may be seen as part of the aftermath of the U.S. withdrawal from Vietnam, a withdrawal that led to intensified rivalry between Moscow and Peking in Southeast Asia. The conflict between the two Yemens may have arisen at least partly from a desire on the part of the Soviet leadership to reenter the Middle East, even if only by demonstrating its influence over the course of events on the periphery of the region.

The November 3, 1978, signing of a treaty of alliance between the Soviet Union and Vietnam, by giving Hanoi a needed measure of reassurance, undoubtedly encouraged Vietnam to launch a full-scale military operation against the pro-Chinese regime of Pol Pot in a conflict that the U.S. national security adviser, Zbigniew Brzezinski, called "the first case of a proxy war between the Soviet Union and China."[29] It is not clear if the USSR actually shipped arms to Vietnam during the course of this fighting – Vietnam, after all, was already well equipped with both Soviet and captured U.S. weapons – but Soviet diplomatic support for Hanoi was a paramount factor in the conflict. The recognition of the PRC by the United States in December 1978 also may have contributed to Vietnam's decision to invade Cambodia. American recognition almost certainly influenced Peking's decision to respond to Hanoi's capture of Phnom Penh by mounting a punitive incursion into Vietnam, beginning on February 17, 1979. In this instance the USSR is known to have undertaken an airlift of arms to Vietnam, starting only five days after China opened hostilities; Moscow also demonstrated its support for Hanoi by means of naval deployments and verbal warnings directed at China.

It is difficult to estimate just how much influence the Kremlin had on the decision of the People's Democratic Republic of Yemen to attack Yemen in February 1979. Nearly 1,000 Soviet advisers are reported to have been stationed in South Yemen at the time of the attack, along with some 500 or more Cuban advisers. Being heavily dependent on Soviet economic and military assistance, it is difficult to imagine that the regime in Aden would have launched the attack without at least consulting Moscow. In any event, the U.S. State Department protested the role played by Soviet advisers in the conflict. The war ended fairly quickly, partly as a result of Saudi mediation and partly as a consequence of a strong show of U.S. support for the threatened regime in Sana.

In April 1978, a violent coup in Afghanistan overthrew the military regime of President Mohammad Daoud, replacing it with a pro-Soviet regime headed by Nur Mohammad Taraki, leader of the People's party or Khalq party. This set the stage for growing Soviet military involvement in Afghanistan. Taraki's regime met with widespread opposition among Moslem tribes in the countryside, and that plunged Afghanistan into a bitter civil war. In June 1978, large numbers of Soviet military advisers began entering the country in order to assist Taraki in quelling the insurgency. The Soviet presence increased steadily, and scores of Soviet advisers were reported to have been assassinated during the first year of the civil war. In September 1979, following a summer of

[29] CBS television interview, January 8, 1978. Reported in *Facts on File*, January 13, 1978.

mounting opposition and conflict in the country, Taraki was killed in a palace shoot-out and replaced by Hafizullah Amin, who had been Taraki's prime minister. Amin, though ostensibly pro-Soviet, was too independent-minded for Moscow's liking; furthermore, his repressive approach toward governing the country was a rallying point for the opposition. The situation deteriorated further, with the Afghan army itself disintegrating and unable to defend the regime effectively against the widespread insurgency that threatened it.

On December 24 the Soviet Union commenced a large airlift of Soviet troops into Afghanistan, followed a few days later by motorized rifle divisions crossing the Soviet-Afghan border. The immediate aims of the Soviet invasion, evidently, were not only to defend the Communist revolution in Afghanistan but also to install a more effective and more pliable government. Amin was killed, reportedly by a vanguard of the Soviet invasion force. Babrak Karmal, Afghan ambassador to Czechoslovakia and a leader of the Parcham faction of the Afghan Communist movement, was brought to Kabul from Prague to head a new government. Soviet troops then began the difficult task of subduing Mujahideen resistance in Afghanistan, a resistance whose ranks were swelled greatly by a nationalist reaction to the Soviet invasion itself.

The invasion of Afghanistan marked the first time that the USSR had ever intervened directly in a Third World country with large numbers of its own military forces. The number of soldiers involved eventually exceeded by a factor of 4 or 5 the numbers of Cuban troops deployed in Angola or Ethiopia. At one level, the invasion can be seen as the crowning event of a decade during which the USSR's military involvement in the Third World, and particularly in Third World conflicts, expanded massively. It seems improbable that the Soviet leadership would have dared to undertake such a radical and risk-laden step had the experience of the preceding decade not convinced them of the reality of a new world political and military balance. Signs of the Soviet leadership's growing confidence could be seen in various pronouncements hailing "the mighty progress" of the national liberation movements, speaking of an increasingly favorable "correlation of forces," and claiming that a "fundamental restructuring of international relations" was taking place.

On another level, however, the Soviet experience in Afghanistan proved to be a textbook demonstration of the potential pitfalls of superpower intervention in a Third World country. At the time of this writing, over five years after the first Soviet advisers entered Afghanistan and nearly four years after the invasion, the Soviet Union still had not been able to establish control of the Afghan countryside nor strengthen the Karmal regime to such an extent that it could stand on its own. Despite all the military advances made by the Soviet Union in the 1970s, despite greatly enhanced Soviet capabilities for power projection, and despite the experience gained in numerous successful

interventions by proxy, the USSR found it extremely difficult to subdue a tribal rebellion in an impoverished country situated right on its
frontier. The invasion also had the effects of worsening Soviet relations
with the Moslem countries, giving considerable impetus to higher defense spending in the United States, and hastening the momentum of
the Sino-American rapprochement. It is quite possible that Moscow
will yet manage to turn the situation in Afghanistan around and reap
what historians in retrospect will regard as a strategic success from
occupation of that country, but the price that it will have to pay to
do this almost certainly will be vastly higher than the Soviet leadership could have estimated in 1979.

3
SOVIET POWER PROJECTION: ADVANCES IN POSTWAR MILITARY CAPABILITIES

> As Peter grew older his nursery began to look more and more like an arsenal.
>
> Vasili Klyuchevsky, *Peter the Great*

It is not possible for a country to conduct global diplomacy without the military capabilities necessary to project its power for considerable distances beyond its borders. Ray Cline has observed that "unlike economic power, or for that matter strategic-nuclear power, the capability of non-nuclear military forces wanes quite rapidly with distance. Armed forces which could be formidable on home ground, such as those of Switzerland, may have very little capability even a short distance beyond national borders."[1] After World War II, the Soviet Union had by far the largest standing army in Europe, but this force, though formidable, did not give Moscow much influence over the outcomes of political and military events in the vast majority of the world that was not contiguous or near to the USSR's borders. The Soviet Union was a superpower, but its limited military reach meant that, unlike the United States, it was not a global power.

The Kremlin had managed as early as the Spanish civil war (1936–8) to muster sufficient sealift capabilities to furnish the Loyalist forces with massive quantities of arms, but this had proved a slow and clumsy operation, ultimately futile. Until the late 1960s and early 1970s, Moscow was sorely deficient in those kinds of military forces suitable for rapid and versatile projection of power abroad. This deficiency naturally limited the scope and magnitude of the USSR's involvement in Third World conflicts. By the 1970s, however, nearly two decades of massive investment in mobile forces began to yield results, enabling the Soviet Union to begin acting as a truly global power in world affairs. The USSR's growing military reach made it technically feasible to undertake massive involvements in the October war, the Angolan civil war, the Ogaden war, and the civil war in Afghanistan.

The Soviet achievement should not be underestimated, for the challenge of maintaining an enduring capability to project power at will is immense. It requires large stocks of surplus weapons for shipment to client states,

---

[1] Ray S. Cline, *World Power Assessment 1977: A Calculus of Strategic Drift* (Boulder: Westview, 1977), 125.

a versatile blue-water navy that can function effectively in distant oceans, substantial sealift and airlift capacity, foreign-based support facilities from which to support or stage distant operations, and thousands of well-trained troops and technical advisers who can be sent abroad on short notice if necessary. This chapter will review postwar Soviet advances in all of these areas. It will also review briefly the USSR's acquisition of a large and secure second-strike nuclear capability, which has provided Moscow with the margin of safety necessary for taking the risks entailed in greater involvement in local conflicts.

Weapons shipments

World War II resulted in technological and structural transformation of the Soviet armaments industry. During the war years, nearly half of the Soviet national GNP was devoted to defense spending, as the USSR manufactured over 100,000 major combat aircraft, tanks, and armored vehicles and several million small arms. Despite the devastation caused by the Nazi invasion, the end of the war found the USSR in possession of the world's second largest armaments industry, a massive complex of factories and laboratories that provided the foundation for future Soviet military might. This industry, together with huge supplies of surplus war material, made it possible for Moscow to become a major exporter of weapons for the first time in Russian history. Whereas in the interwar period (1930–9) the USSR had supplied less than 6 percent of total world exports of combat aircraft and tanks, and only a fraction of 1 percent of the exports of other types of weapons, in the first two decades of the postwar period the USSR took substantial shares of the world market in almost all categories: by one estimate, 37 percent in tanks, 29 percent in submarines, 27 percent in patrol vessels, 4 percent in warships, 14 percent in transport aircraft, 6 percent in trainer aircraft, 28 percent in helicopters, and 28 percent in combat aircraft.[2]

Although a substantial fraction of the Soviet Union's arms exports from 1945–80 went to its Warsaw Pact allies, exports to Third World nations increasingly came to dominate Soviet arms sales over this period, beginning in the mid-1950s. From 1973–77, for example, the USSR exported an estimated 23.4 billion dollars of armaments, only 7.8 billion of which, or one-third, went to the Warsaw Pact. The U.S. State Department has estimated that from 1955, when Soviet arms shipments to the Third World

---

[2] Robert E. Harkavy, *The Arms Trade and International Systems* (Cambridge: Ballinger, 1975), 60–76. Harkavy's estimate extends only to 1968, but from 1969 to 1980, the USSR continued to maintain a large share of the international market, averaging roughly a third of world weapons exports over this period. More precise figures are easily calculated from the tables in the annual publication, *World Military Expenditures and Arms Transfers*, published by the U.S. Arms Control and Disarmament Agency. SIPRI has made estimates of the Soviet share of arms exports to the Third World. See SIPRI, *The Arms Trade Registers*, 152–4; SIPRI, *The Arms Trade with the Third World*, 11; and *SIPRI Yearbook*, 1977, 306–7. SIPRI data tends, if anything, to underestimate Soviet arms exports.

began in earnest, until 1981, the USSR exported some $70 billion of arms and military assistance to the Third World – a remarkable sum for a country that could hardly meet its own requirements prior to World War II. Dollar estimates of Soviet weapons exports, however, are notoriously inaccurate. A better picture of Soviet arms sales to the Third World can be had by analyzing the *number* of individual weapons systems of various types that the USSR has exported abroad. (Numbers of specific types of weapons, rather than dollar amounts, is also the method generally employed in the case studies that follow.) The State Department in 1982 published the following estimates of the numbers of Soviet weapons of various types delivered to the Third World from 1972 to 1981; also shown is the percentage of total world exports represented by each category:

Tanks/self-propelled guns	13,200	(41.5%)
Light armor	14,225	(37.6%)
Artillery (over 100 mm)	16,400	(30.1%)
Large surface warships	46	(17.8%)
Small surface warships	189	(18.7%)
Guided missile patrol boats	97	(64.6%)
Submarines	17	(23.6%)
Supersonic combat aircraft	3,705	(55.8%)
Subsonic combat aircraft	570	(27.6%)
Helicopters	1,345	(24.5%)
Other military aircraft	510	(8.8%)
Surface-to-air missiles	23,250	(65.0%)

These figures, better than dollar amounts, give some idea of the magnitude of Soviet investment and involvement in the Third World during the 1970s. Particularly noteworthy are the massive Soviet deliveries of tanks, supersonic aircraft, and surface-to-air missiles, in all of which categories the USSR holds nearly half or more of the world market.[3]

The geographical distribution of Soviet arms exports has been heavily skewed toward the Middle East and North African regions of the world. Between 1956 and 1979, roughly 53 percent of all Soviet arms deliveries

---

[3] Figures on Soviet deliveries to the Warsaw Pact and the Third World from 1973 to 1979 are from U.S. Arms Control and Disarmament Agency, *World Military Expenditures and Arms Transfers 1968–1977*, 155. The $70 billion figure is from U.S. Department of State, *Conventional Arms Transfers in the Third World, 1972–1981* (August, 1982), 12–13; this publication also provides an annual breakdown of the numbers. On the problems associated with dollar values, see Edward T. Fei, "Understanding Arms Transfers and Military Expenditures: Data Problems," in Stephanie Neumann and Robert Harkavy, eds., *Arms Transfers in the Modern World* (New York: Praeger, 1977), 37–46; see also Edward Laurence and Ronald Sherwin, "Understanding Arms Transfers through Data Analysis," in Uri Ra'anan, et al., eds., *Arms Transfers to the Third World: The Military Buildup in Less Industrial Countries* (Boulder: Westview, 1978), 87–106.

to the Third World were to the Middle East, and another 20 percent were to North Africa. The heavy Soviet investment in these two adjoining regions identifies them as the main focal point of Soviet interests in the Third World.[4]

Overall responsibility for the Soviet military assistance program rests with the State Committee for Foreign Economic Relations (*Gosudarstvennii Komitet SSSR po Vneshnim Ekonomicheskim Svyazam*), a member organ of the Council of Ministers. The specific subdivision charged with administering the program is the Chief Engineering Directorate, which acts as the negotiator and supplier in arms agreements. This directorate coordinates with the Ministry of Defense on the types and quantities of weapons to be provided and with the External Relations Directorate of the General Staff on necessary technical assistance. It also coordinates with the Ministry of Foreign Trade and the Ministry of the Maritime Fleet to arrange for the shipment of military equipment. The role of the Politburo of the CPSU Central Committee in this process is probably similar to its role in actual weapons procurement: It resolves controversies and problems that arise; it intervenes whenever the particular political concerns of its members are at stake; it exercises close control over particularly large or sensitive arms deals.[5] Top-ranking Politburo members are often present at the signing of large arms deals.

The term *military assistance* is somewhat of a misnomer, inasmuch as the USSR rarely makes outright grants of military equipment to a recipient.[6] The normal practice is to sell the equipment at low or even below-cost prices, with generous repayment arrangements and concessionary interest rates. The contracts vary, but Moscow normally extends credit at 2, 2.5, or 3 percent interest, sometimes higher. Repayment is usually stretched over 12 years or longer.[7] A client nation is occasionally allowed

---

[4] Central Intelligence Agency (National Foreign Assessment Center), *Communist Aid Activities in Non-Communist Less Developed Countries, 1979 and 1954–79* (Washington, D.C., October 1980), 14. Percentages calculated from Table A-2. See also Leo Tansky, "Soviet Foreign Aid: Scope, Direction, and Trends," Joint Economic Committee of Congress, *Soviet Economic Prospects for the Seventies* (Washington: U.S. Government Printing Office, 1973), 773.

[5] U.S. Arms Control and Disarmament Agency, *The International Transfer of Conventional Arms*, a report to the Congress, 93rd Congress, 2d sess., 1974, p. 37; Arthur J. Alexander, *Decision-Making in Soviet Weapons Procurement*, Adelphi Papers Nos. 147–8 (London: International Institute for Strategic Studies, 1978), 8–11.

[6] Exceptions would be the three Mi-8 transport helicopters given to Peru in May 1973 and various aircraft given to national rulers for their private use. Afghanistan, during the course of the postwar period, received a number of outright grants and the most favorable purchase terms of any nation (a 25-year grace period on a 50-year loan).

[7] Franklyn D. Holzman, *International Trade under Communism* (New York: Basic Books, 1976), 180–1; W. Joshua and S. P. Gilbert, *Arms for the Third World: Soviet Military Aid Diplomacy* (Baltimore: Johns Hopkins University Press, 1969), 104.

ιo repay its loan with its own "soft" currency, and sometimes barter arrangements are worked out. Robert E. Harkavy has identified seven customary modes of transferring arms between nations.[8] Of these, the Soviet Union has employed five – sales, licensing, final assembly of finished parts by the recipient nation, loans, and retransfers via an intermediary nation – but straight export sales dominate heavily. Examples of the less common transfer modes include licensing for manufacture of MiG-21 fighters in India, the first phase of which (1966–7) included the assembly of finished parts in India, the loan of 15 Il-14 transport planes to the Congo (Zaire) in 1960, and the transferring of weapons via Egypt to Nigeria, Sudan, Guinea, and Ghana. Retransferring can be carried out legally only if permission is received, because Soviet arms contracts include restrictive clauses forbidding transfers without approval, much like those found in Western arms sales agreements.

The actual economic burden to the Soviet Union of its military assistance to developing nations is probably quite low, despite the below-cost sale prices and the concessionary interest rates. This is because substantial portions of the weapons transferred to Third World countries are relatively obsolete and of diminishing practical utility for the Soviet armed forces. By selling surplus arms, the USSR acquires real resources and saves itself the costs of storage and maintenance. The capital costs for research, machinery, and construction (but not labor and materials) would also have to be discounted in calculating the real costs to the Soviet Union of its arms export program, because those capital costs are necessitated by the nation's own defense needs.[9]

The construction of a blue-water navy

One of the most significant developments in the USSR's ability to intervene in local wars has been the massive naval construction program it began in the mid-1950s. As a land power bordered by some 10 nations and in close proximity to the various armed forces in Europe, China, and Japan, the USSR in the first four decades of its existence devoted most of its naval investments to coastal defense.[10] It has never had to be as concerned about defending sea-lanes as has the United States, which is more dependent on overseas sources for raw materials and which must keep open the sea-lanes to its European allies. But after World War II, the creation of a large modern navy able to deploy substantial forces in distant

---

[8] Harkavy, *The Arms Trade*, 144. The seven modes are export sales or grants, licensing, final assembly of finished parts, loans, retransfers, co-development and production, and the sale of single weapons intended as manufacturing prototypes.

[9] The question is treated in greater detail in Bruce D. Porter, *Soviet Military Intervention: Russian Arms and Diplomacy in Third World Conflicts, 1958–1978*, Appendix C, 481–3. Doctoral dissertation, Harvard University, 1979.

[10] "The Soviet Union operates more small combat craft...than the remainder of the world's navies combined." *Understanding Soviet Naval Developments* (Washington, D.C.: Office of the Chief of Naval Operations, 1975), 25.

oceans became a necessity if the Soviet Union was to develop a global reach approaching that of the United States. The fact that the Soviet leaders indeed implemented rapid construction of the first blue-water navy in Russian history is one evidence of their determination to extend the geographical reach of Soviet power.

The postwar buildup of Soviet naval forces can be dated roughly from the year 1956, when Admiral Sergei Gorshkov became commander in chief of the navy. Gorshkov presided over the transformation of the Soviet navy into a modern, versatile, and sizable fleet. His vision of the navy's mission seems to have significantly shaped the entire construction program of the fleet and the parallel evolution of Soviet naval strategy. Gorshkov envisioned the creation of a "balanced navy," which he defined as a navy "capable of conducting combat operations under differing circumstances" and "able to support state interests at sea in peacetime."[11] In the 1970s he particularly emphasized the role of the navy in countering Western aggression against Third World nations and acting as "a deterrent to military adventurists." He also described the navy as an ambassador of the Socialist nations, displaying Soviet achievements and friendship around the world and "strengthening the international influence of the Soviet Union."[12]

Much of the expansion of the Soviet navy can be attributed to the new strategic missions assigned the fleets of both superpowers. The most significant development under Gorshkov was the expansion of the Soviet ballistic submarine force, involving the construction of numerous attack submarines and surface ships intended for antisubmarine warfare. But many of the new Soviet surface ships – which the USSR invariably claims are for antisubmarine warfare – are powerful open-ocean combatants that could be used for establishing an offshore presence near a regional conflict or for displaying Soviet military power in foreign ports.

The *Petya*-class escort introduced in 1961 and the *Kynda*-class missile cruiser deployed in 1964 were the first modern surface warships wholly designed and produced after Gorshkov became commander in chief of the navy. The lead time necessary for the design and construction of the *Kynda* suggests that the decision to build a modern surface fleet probably was made no later than the time of the Suez crisis. From 1961 to 1979 the USSR built three classes of escort ships, five classes of destroyer/ASW vessels, four classes of new cruisers, two types of small carriers, and at least two types of amphibious landing vessels. The total number of new large warships deployed was over 200. It amounted to the creation of an entire surface fleet in two decades

---

[11] Sergei Gorshkov, "Guarding the Conquests of the Great October Revolution," *Morskoi Sbornik* (October 1967).

[12] Sergei Gorshkov, "Navies as Peacetime Instruments of the Aggressive Policy of Imperialist States," *Morskoi Sbornik* (December 1972):17. This was one installment of a lengthy series of articles by Gorshkov entitled "Navies in War and Peace."

– an event somewhat reminiscent of Imperial Germany's naval buildup prior to World War I.

Of particular significance was the unveiling in 1967 of the *Moskva* helicopter carrier, Russia's first air-capable warship. It was followed two years later by a sister ship, the *Leningrad*. The Soviets claimed that the *Leningrad* and the *Moskva* were for antisubmarine warfare, but Western analysts consider them capable of supporting amphibious assaults.[13] The United States has seven helicopter carriers, all intended for use in support of landing operations. In 1975 the USSR added the first real attack carrier to its fleet, the 38,000-ton *Kiev*. A second carrier, the *Minsk*, was completed the next year, and two more, the *Kharkov* and the *Novorossisk*, were scheduled for commissioning in 1980 and 1983. Employing a small number of V/STOL fighter aircraft and devoting much of its deck space to other weapons systems, the *Kiev* cannot be compared with any of the American aircraft carriers, but it was a significant addition to the Soviet fleet.

As of 1979 the USSR did not have any heavy attack carriers, whereas the American fleet had 13. These attack carriers are the principal reason that Washington has enjoyed superior global naval capacities over Moscow, and most Western analysts had long considered it unlikely that the Soviet Union would ever build heavy carriers, because of their great expense and increasing vulnerability.[14] But in August 1979, U.S. intelligence and naval experts revealed that a large-deck, nuclear-powered attack carrier was under construction in the Murmansk area. In December, Admiral Gorshkov confirmed the report to American diplomats. The construction of the carrier, apparently in the 75,000-ton class, seems to be a development of great consequence for the future of the Soviet Union's capacity to project power abroad.[15]

In 1961, Soviet warships carried out small-scale exercises in the Norwegian Sea for the first time, and the following year ships from the Black Sea fleet traveled via the Atlantic to join the Arctic fleet, also for the first time. In 1963, Soviet ships in the northeast Atlantic engaged in maneuvers that included circumnavigation of the British Isles; thereafter, such exercises became routine. In 1964, Russian warships were first deployed for a sustained period in the Mediterranean, relying on anchorage resupply for support. Thirty-nine Soviet combat ships made the transit between the Black Sea and Mediterranean Sea that year, far more than in any previous postwar year. By 1970 the

---

[13] Jonathan T. Howe, "Soviet Beachhead in the Third World," *U.S. Naval Institute Proceedings* 94(October 1968):60–7; Thomas W. Wolfe, "The Projection of Soviet Power," *Military Review* (February 1969):68–9.

[14] Robert Waring Herrick, *Soviet Naval Strategy: Fifty Years of Theory and Practice* (Annapolis: U.S. Naval Institute, 1968), 153–5; *Understanding Soviet Naval Developments*, 25.

[15] *New York Times*, August 21, 1979, and December 17, 1979.

number of annual transits reached 125.[16] The Mediterranean exercises continued each year from 1964 to 1967, when, after the June war, the number of ships increased, and the average length of individual deployment nearly doubled. In 1967, for the first time, a naval presence was maintained in the winter, marking the beginning of a permanent Soviet naval presence in the Mediterranean.[17] Also in 1967, Soviet research vessels began surveying the Indian Ocean, and the following year a squadron of three surface warships, a nuclear submarine, and a tanker visited 10 Indian Ocean ports from March to July. After 1971 the USSR began maintaining a small but virtually permanent task force of from 10 to 20 ships in the Indian Ocean.

In 1970 the Soviet navy conducted worldwide maneuvers known as "Okean." Contingents from all the Soviet fleets engaged in large-scale exercises in the Baltic Sea, the Arctic Ocean, the Black Sea, the Mediterranean, the North Atlantic, and the Pacific as far south as the South China Sea. More than 200 ships participated, coordinated from Moscow on a real-time basis, in a display of naval power and of command and coordination capabilities that was impressive for a power that only a decade earlier had had little experience on the open seas. Five years later, Okean 75 took place; it involved around 220 ships, deployed even farther afield than in 1970 (some ships operated in the Caribbean, off the west coast of Africa, and in the Indian Ocean). J. William Middendorf II, U.S. secretary of the navy, asserted at the time that this exercise demonstrated the capability of the Soviet navy to operate effectively in all oceans of the world. Some idea of the growing impact and magnitude of the Soviet naval effort can be gained from Table 3.1, which shows the numbers of ship-days logged by Soviet warships in the Atlantic, Mediterranean, and Indian Ocean beginning in 1964. In the mid-1960s the expanding Soviet navy began an extensive program of port visits to Third World nations. Prior to 1964 the Russian combat fleet had visited only three developing countries: Egypt in 1956, Syria in 1957, and Indonesia in 1959 and 1962. From 1964 to 1972, Soviet warships visited at least 38 additional Third World nations, many of which received multiple visits at more than one port. The total number of visits was well over 300.[18]

The USSR has also devoted resources to enhancing its capability for distant amphibious assault missions. In the summer of 1964, ref-

---

[16] Robert G. Weinland, "Soviet Transits of the Turkish Straits, 1945–70," in Michael MccGwire, ed., *Soviet Naval Developments: Capability and Context* (New York: Praeger, 1973), 325–43.

[17] William H. J. Manthorpe, Jr., "The Soviet Navy in 1975," *U.S. Naval Institute Proceedings* 102(May 1976):206–7.

[18] Data derived from a tabulation of Soviet port visits, 1953–72, in Michael MccGwire et al., eds., *Soviet Naval Policy: Objectives and Constraints* (New York: Praeger, 1975), 389–418. See also Anne M. Kelly, "Port Visits and the 'International Mission' of the Soviet Navy," in Michael MccGwire and John McDonnell, eds., *Soviet Naval Influence: Domestic and Foreign Dimensions* (New York: Praeger, 1977), 510–29.

Table 3.1. *Ship-days logged by Soviet warships*

	Mediterranean	Indian	Atlantic
1964	1,500		1,000 +
1965	2,800		1,200 +
1966	4,400		2,500 +
1967	8,100		3,750
1968	11,000	1,800	5,000 +
1969	15,000	3,700	7,500
1970	16,500	3,600	12,000
1971	19,000	3,800	15,000 +
1972	18,000	8,800	16,000 +
1973	20,600	8,600	14,800
1974	20,200	10,500	13,000
1975	20,000	7,200	12,000
1976	18,600	7,300	12,000

Sources: Robert G. Weinland, "Soviet Naval Operations: 10 Years of Change," in MccGwire et al., eds., *Soviet Naval Policy* (New York: Praeger, 1975), 375–86; Albert E. Graham, "Soviet Strategy and Policy in the Indian Ocean," and Paul J. Murphy, "Trends in Soviet Naval Force Structure," in Paul J. Murphy, ed., *Naval Power in Soviet Policy* (Washington, D.C.: U.S. Air Force, 1978), 130–1, 278. These sources are not precisely compatible; all figures are rounded to the nearest 100 and should be considered estimates.

erences to the existence of "naval infantry" or marine units in the armed forces first appeared in the Soviet press. Russian marine units had seen limited action in World War II, and similar units had existed periodically in Russian history since 1704, but their reactivation in 1964 was seen by many Western analysts as evidence that the Kremlin desired a small amphibious strike force for possible interventionary use. In September 1964 the Soviet naval infantry (apparently a branch of the navy) participated in joint Warsaw Pact maneuvers in Bulgaria; they have played a limited role in various maneuvers since then. The numbers of naval infantry grew from 3,000–5,000 in 1965 to 8,000 in October 1969 to 15,000 or more by mid-1972.[19] Their numbers were reported to be increasing as of 1980, though this remained a modest force indeed alongside the much larger U.S. Marine Corps force of 188,000 troops.

In 1966 the 4,000-ton *Alligator* class of tank landing ships was added to the Soviet fleet. An *Alligator* can carry 375 troops and 28 tanks. By 1976, 20 *Alligator*-class vessels had been built, 14 of which were still in operation in 1980. Beginning in 1975, the fleet also acquired 13

[19] Information on the Soviet marines is from John F. Meehan III, "The Soviet 'Marine Corps'," *Military Review* LII(October 1972):84–94; Charles W. Stockwell, "The Soviet Naval Infantry," in MccGwire, ed., *Soviet Naval Developments*, 172–5; Charles G. Pritchard, "Soviet Amphibious Force Projection," in MccGwire and McDonnell, eds., *Soviet Naval Influence*, 246–77.

Ropucha-class landing ships of Polish construction. Roughly the same size as the *Alligator*-class vessels, but engineered with roll-on/roll-off capability and with a higher troop-to-vehicle ratio, the *Ropuchas* were a significant addition to the USSR's overall potential for distant assault operations. The upward trend in amphibious assault capability continued in 1978, when the 13,000-ton *Ivan Rogov* was launched, the first of a new class of amphibious craft of highly modern design. The *Ivan Rogov*, nearly three times the size of the *Alligator*-class ships, is heavily armed and capable of carrying a battalion of infantry and up to 40 tanks. It will provide the Soviet armed forces with long-range, long-endurance assault capability surpassing that offered by previous Soviet ships.[20] Much larger numbers of small landing craft, including the world's largest flotilla of high-speed naval hovercraft, would permit larger-scale operations, but at a much shorter range.

There have been numerous historical instances of the USSR deploying warships so as to influence – politically and militarily – the courses of conflicts in the Third World. Although the Soviet fleet has not engaged in actual combat in any of these conflicts, it has proved its value as a diplomatic instrument and passive deterrent force. During the six-day war, the Soviet Mediterranean fleet shadowed the U.S. Sixth Fleet, and after the war a Soviet naval presence in Port Said helped to deter Israeli strikes against Egypt. In the fall of 1970, a group of Soviet combat vessels was deployed in the eastern Mediterranean, presumably to deter any U.S. intervention in the Jordanian crisis, and two months later Soviet gunboats were dispatched to Conakry, Guinea, after it was invaded from the sea by a small Portuguese force. Countervailing naval forces were deployed in the Indian Ocean from December 1971 to January 1972, evidently to discourage any U.S. intervention in the Indo-Pakistani war. The next year, during the October war, massive Soviet naval forces in the Mediterranean were deployed in a formation clearly intended to influence U.S. actions; *Alligator* tank landing ships were used to transport Moroccan troops to Syria. During the Angolan civil war, a small Soviet task force established itself offshore from Angola. A Soviet squadron of some seven major warships and a number of submarines was sent into the South China Sea during the 1979 border war between China and Vietnam. These are only some of the more prominent of the numerous examples that could be given.[21]

The 1980s are likely to be a decade of increasing involvement by the Soviet navy in the affairs and conflicts of the Third World. Perhaps the plainest indication of this was the intensive shipbuilding program

[20] *Strategic Survey* (1979):45; *Defense Daily*, March 21, 1980, 118; *Jane's Fighting Ships 1979–80* (New York: Franklin Watts, 1979), 548–50; *Jane's Fighting Ships 1983–84* (London: Jane's Publishing, 1983), 542–4.
[21] See James M. McConnell and Bradford Dismukes, eds., *Soviet Naval Diplomacy* (London: Pergamon, 1978).

that was under way in the Soviet Union at the beginning of the decade. As of 1980 the USSR was constructing four new classes of nuclear-powered cruisers, including a number of 32,000-ton battle cruisers with heavy guns for shore bombardment. Although such guns would be of little value against a modern missile-equipped fleet, they could have tremendous impact on a local conflict, even if only passively deployed. Also under construction was the new *Berezina* class of heavily armed, 40,000-ton logistics craft intended to replenish and sustain Soviet warships on the high seas. However, the most telling indicator of Moscow's naval ambitions was perhaps the large capital investment being made in expansion and refurbishing of shipyards.[22] This suggested that Soviet naval construction in the 1980s would accelerate markedly and that the USSR was seeking to attain parity in the one category of military power in which it had remained decidedly inferior to the United States in the past.

Advances in transport capabilities

Another area in which Soviet power projection capabilities have been improved significantly is that of airlift and sealift (i.e., transport vehicles for military equipment and troops). The USSR can rely on land transportation to meet most of its own defense needs, but airlift and sealift capability is necessary if arms and equipment are to be transferred to a Third World client during a local conflict. Airlift is essential for rapid and flexible response in a crisis, but only sealift can handle the tonnage involved in massive or protracted weapons shipments.

Voennaya Transportnaya Aviatsia (military transport aviation) is the branch of the Soviet air force responsible for transporting supplies, weapons, and personnel within the Soviet Union and to foreign regions. VTA relies primarily on three types of aircraft for long-range transport: the Antonov-12, the Antonov-22, and the Ilyushin-76 (Table 3.2). The An-22 and the Il-76 are much better suited for transferring large weapons to a distant client quickly, and they are the principal aircraft Moscow has relied on in making arms shipments to the Middle East and Africa. VTA's aggregate lift capacity in millions of ton-miles grew from 11.4 in 1965 to 19.4 in 1970 to 26.4 in 1977. Its lift capacity increased more than one-third between 1970 and 1977, despite a reduction in the total number of planes because of retirements of An-12s. If additional air transport were critically needed, *Aeroflot*, the Soviet civilian airline, could increase cargo capacities by about 25 percent and triple the number of passengers. *Aeroflot* personnel played a key role in the invasion of Czechoslovakia in 1968, during which

[22] *New York Times*, December 10 and 17, 1979.

Table 3.2. *VTA's principal long-range transport planes*

Plane	Year deployed	Number in VTA service 1979	Power-plant	Maximum cargo (kg)	Range with maximum load (km)	Troops[a] Pax	Troops[a] Para
An-12	1956	650	Turboprop	20,000	3,600	100	65
An-22	1965	40	Turboprop	80,000	5,000	200	150
Il-76	1971	100	Jet	40,000	5,000	150	120

[a]Pax, passengers (infantry): Para, paratroops
Source: Peter Borgart, "The Soviet Transport Air Force," *International Defense Review* (June 1979):945–50.

two entire Soviet divisions were ferried to a single airfield in less than 18 hours.[23]

Despite the impressive gains of VTA during the 1970s, the USSR has continued to expand its airlift capability. In 1979 it was learned that the USSR was undertaking the manufacture of a new transport plane, the An-400, with a larger capacity than the American C–5. Its estimated cargo capacity will be on the order of 120,000 kilograms, 1.5 times greater than that of the An-22.[24]

In addition to making possible rapid, large-scale weapons shipments to distant regions of the globe, the Soviet air transport force gives the USSR a credible instrument for intervention with airborne troops. VTA's fleet of roughly 600 An-12 tactical lift planes alone could airlift one airborne division with full combat equipment and supplies for three days to a distance of 2,000 kilometers. The An-22s and Il-76s could also be used to ferry paratroops, and to even greater distances. The troop component of this airborne threat will be examined in a later section.

Sealift is primarily the responsibility of the Soviet merchant marine, rather than the navy. The USSR's maritime fleet grew from 590 ships with a combined capacity of 3.3 million deadweight tons in 1959 to an inventory of some 1,600 vessels carrying roughly 16 million deadweight tons in 1975.[25] Western experts disagree whether this growth was undertaken primarily for economic reasons – to earn hard currency and improve the balance of payments – or for political and military reasons, such as replenishing warships, displaying the Red flag and Soviet technology around the world, threatening Western shipping interests, pursuing military research and reconnaissance, and providing military transport.[26] In either case, the military potential of this merchant fleet is real, and certainly this was taken into account in designing it. Controlled by the navy, the merchant marine in 1976 included some 1,650 modern, highly automated ships, nearly 500 of which were ideal for long-range military transport. The entire merchant marine is coordinated from Moscow by an automatic control system, with computer centers at major ports on the Black Sea and Baltic Sea and in the Far East. "It is believed that most officers of

[23] Robert P. Berman, *Soviet Air Power in Transition* (Washington: The Brookings Institution, 1978), 36; John M. Collins and Anthony H. Cordesman, *Imbalance of Power: Shifting U.S.-Soviet Military Strengths* (San Rafael: Presidio Press, 1978), 193–5; Alfred L. Monks, "Air Forces," in David R. Jones, ed., *Soviet Armed Forces Review Annual 1977* (Gulf Breeze, Fla.: Academic International, 1977), 53.

[24] Peter Borgart, "The Soviet Transport Air Force," *International Defense Review* (June 1979):948–50.

[25] Richard T. Ackley, "The Merchant Fleet," in MccGwire and McDonnell, eds., *Soviet Naval Influence*, 298; *Understanding Soviet Naval Developments*, 39.

[26] A proponent of the economic viewpoint is Robert E. Athay, *The Economics of Soviet Merchant Shipping* (Chapel Hill, N.C.: University of North Carolina Press, 1971). An opposite viewpoint is found in Verner R. Carlson, "The Soviet Maritime Threat," *U.S. Naval Institute Proceedings* 93(May 1967):41–8.

the merchant fleet are naval reservists who regularly provide the Soviet
Navy with information [on foreign ports and ships]."[27] During the
Vietnam war, millions of tons of equipment were moved by Soviet
freighters from Black Sea ports around the Cape of Good Hope to
Haiphong, and merchant ships carried the bulk of Soviet supplies to
the Arabs in 1973, to Angola in 1975–6, and to Ethiopia in 1977–8. In
the late 1970s the Soviets began adding roll-on/roll-off vessels to the
maritime fleet, a concept borrowed from American designs for military
transport ships. Although only a fraction of the total merchant fleet
would be used for military transport at any given time, the fleet's large
size makes it a fairly simple matter for the USSR to provide weapons
to any nation that has a port. In this respect, the Kremlin has increased its flexibility of action greatly since the time of Stalin.

The establishment of foreign facilities for military support

Projection of military power is facilitated considerably by access to
military bases and support facilities abroad.[28] This is another area in
which the USSR has made significant progress since the 1950s, though
not without considerable difficulty and numerous setbacks. In 1973,
a naval attaché from a Western country was reported to have asked
a high-ranking Soviet officer what his greatest difficulty was as a
result of the USSR's shift to forward naval deployment. Without hes-
itation, the officer replied "Bases."[29] Formally, the USSR denies that
it maintains bases abroad, because that is viewed as an imperialist
practice, and in fact it does not maintain anywhere near the number
of large military complexes that the United States has. Principally,
it has sought to gain access to already-existing support facilities around
the world.

The simplest and least politically sensitive types of facilities maintained by the USSR are naval anchorages or deep-sea mooring buoys
located in international waters. After moving into the Mediterranean
and the Indian Ocean, the Soviet navy established an extensive system
of such anchorages in each area. Soviet ships are regularly refueled
and replenished while lying at such anchorages. Table 3.3 lists the
known locations of such facilities. Of greater political significance
and practical usefulness are the air and port facilities in Third World
countries to which the Soviet armed forces have special access, sometimes on a virtually permanent lease basis. A common pattern has

[27] Donald C. Daniel, "Merchant Marine," in Jones, ed., *Soviet Armed Forces Review
Annual*, 87.
[28] SIPRI defines a "base" as any facilities used to support armed forces deployed
abroad, including "installations for (a) accommodation, (b) catering, (c) health
services, (d) stockpile of equipment, ammunition, fuel, etc., (e) repairs and maintenance, (f) communications, and (g) transportation." *SIPRI Yearbook*, 1972, 247.
[29] U.S. Congress, Senate Committee on Commerce and National Ocean Policy, *Soviet
Oceans Development*, 94th Congress, October 1976, 146.

Table 3.3. *Soviet anchorages and deep-sea mooring buoys in international waters*[a]

Mediterranean
  West of Alexandria
  Two, east and west of Crete, in the Aegean Sea
  Hammammet Bay, east of Tunis
  Off Spanish Alboran, near Gibraltar
  Near Malta
  Gulf of Sidra, off Libya
  East of Sicily
  West of Lebanon (?)

Indian Ocean
  Near Massawa in the Red Sea[d]
  Near the Maldives
  Near Seychelles Islands[b]
  Near Cargados Carajos Islands[b]
  Off Mauritius[c]
  Southwest of Madagascar[c]
  Near Diego Garcia[c]
  In Mozambique channel[c]
  In Arabian Sea[c]
  Off St. Brandon group
  Chagos Archipelago[b]

[a]The facilities are anchorages except as noted.
[b]Anchorages and buoys.
[c]Buoys only
[d]A floating dry-dock towed from Berbera in 1977.
Sources: F. M. Murphy, "The Soviet Navy in the Mediterranean," *U.S. Naval Institute Proceedings* 93(March 1967):38–44; Albert E. Graham, "Soviet Strategy and Policy in the Indian Ocean," 286–7; *African Contemporary Record, 1977–78;* U.S. Senate, Armed Services Committee, *Disapprove Construction Projects on the Island of Diego Garcia.*

been for the USSR to build facilities for a client nation in exchange for right of access to them. Support facilities in the Third World used by the Soviet Union since 1945 are listed in Table 3.4. The USSR's troubles in establishing permanent facilities are evidenced by the fact that the two largest complexes – in Egypt and Somalia – were closed to Soviet use in 1974 and 1977, respectively.

The most extensive complex of Soviet facilities was in Egypt. Soviet activity there reached a peak after the signing of the Soviet-Egyptian treaty of friendship and cooperation in May 1971. By mid-1972, six airfields were being used by the Soviets, all of which they controlled, and only three of which were shared with the Egyptian air force. The Soviet Mediterranean fleet made extensive use of four Egyptian harbors – Port Said, Alexandria, Mersa Matruh, and Sollum – and sometimes

Table 3.4. *Military support facilities in Third World used by the USSR, 1945–80*[a]

Host country	Place	Function
Algeria	Algiers	Refueling station
	Oran	Refueling station
	Mers El Kebir	Water and battery charging
	Anaba	Airfield
Angola	Luanda	Airfield
Egypt	Alexandria[b]	Port facilities
	Port Said[b]	Port facilities
	Mersa Matruh[b]	Naval base and airfield
	Sollum[b]	Port facilities
	Assuan[b]	Airfield
	Beni Suef[b]	Airfield
	Cairo West[b]	Airfield
	El Mansoura[b]	Airfield
	Inchas[b]	Airfield
	Jiyanklis[b]	Airfield
Ethiopia	Dahlak Islands	Port facilities
Guinea	Conakry[b]	Airfield
Iraq	Umm Qasr	Port facilities
	Basrah	Port facilities
	Al Fau	Port facilities
Somalia	Berbera[b]	Large naval base and missile support facility; airfield
	Mogadishu[b]	Port and dockyard facilities; airfield
	Kisimayu[b]	Port facilities
	Uanle Uen[b]	Airfield
	Hargeisa[b]	Airfield
	Galcaio[b]	Airfield
South Yemen	Socotra Island	Port facilities
	Turba	Port facilities
	Lahej	Airfield
	Mukalla	Airfield; berthing facilities under construction?
	Aden	Port facilities; airfield; air defenses
	Perim Island	Port; airfield under construction?
Syria	Latakia	Port facilities
Vietnam	Cam Ranh Bay	Submarine docking and replenishing; other naval facilities; airfields; communications and intelligence facilities
Yemen	Hodeida[b]	Port facilities

[a]This register includes only facilities to which the USSR has enjoyed special access. It does not include ports or airfields routinely used by the USSR and other nations for commercial purposes, refueling, etc.
[b]Access terminated.

Sources: "Foreign Military Presence, 1971: Armed Forces and Major Bases," *SIPRI Yearbook*, 1972, 259–61; Murphy, ed., *Naval Power in Soviet Policy*, 198, 260–1, 284; Brian Crozier, "The Soviet Presence in Somalia," *Conflict Studies* No. 54(February 1975); *Facts on File*, May 11, 1979; *New York Times*, June 10 and 18 and October 28, 1980; *Frankfurter Allgemeine Zeitung*, October 31, 1980; U.S. Department of Defense, *Soviet Military Power*, 2nd ed. (Washington: U.S. Government Printing Office, 1983).

called at Berenice on the Red Sea. Perhaps never was the tenuousness of superpower influence in the Third World more dramatically illustrated than on July 18, 1972, when Anwar Sadat announced that the Soviet military mission had been terminated and that the military facilities built by the USSR would become the exclusive property of the Egyptian government.

The nationalization of the bases included the airfields and the port facilities being built at Mersa Matruh, but Soviet ships were not prevented from continuing to use the various harbors. But by 1974 Egypt was apparently pressuring Moscow to reduce its use of Egyptian ports, for Soviet activity dropped significantly. In May 1975, Soviet warships were denied entrance to Mersa Matruh and Sollum, and their use of the port at Alexandria was tightly restricted. In March 1976, Sadat ordered the Soviet submarine support operation at Alexandria to withdraw within a month. The USSR's access to the massive complex of facilities it had built was terminated less than four years after the Soviet heyday in Egypt. One result was a noticeable drop in the number of ship-days logged by Soviet ships in the Mediterranean.

The Soviet facilities constructed at Berbera, Somalia, between 1962 and 1976 were perhaps the nearest thing to a full-fledged, Western-type military base that the USSR possessed anywhere in the Third World. The Berbera complex at one time encompassed a good-size deep-water port, barracks housing for over 1,000 personnel, a long-range high-frequency communications center that was apparently a key center of Soviet command and control in the Indian Ocean, a large petroleum storage area, and an airstrip more than 13,000 feet in length. Between late 1973 and 1976 the Soviet Union constructed a sophisticated handling and storage facility for conventional missiles at the Berbera site, the only one of its kind outside the USSR. Like the Soviet complex in Egypt, the facilities at Berbera were clearly intended to serve the USSR's larger strategic purposes, not merely to provide military support to Mogadishu. And like the Egyptian facilities, the Berbera complex and other Soviet facilities in Somalia were nationalized in November 1977, at the time of President Siad's expulsion of Soviet advisers. It is worth noting, however, that the Soviet Union was to some degree able to offset the loss of the facilities in Egypt and Somalia by increasing its already existing presence in Syria and South Yemen after 1974 and by acquiring naval facilities in the Dahlak Islands of Ethiopia.

Soviet advisers and combat troops

Traditionally the USSR has been extremely cautious about employing its armed forces outside its own borders or, since World War II, outside the perimeter of the Warsaw Pact. Although prior to 1979 Soviet advisers, pilots, and commanders had occasionally participated in a limited way in certain local conflicts, the invasion of Afghanistan marked

the first time the Soviet Union had deployed regular tactical formations of ground troops in a Third World country. This restraint may
have originated at least partly from the Red Army's debacle on the
Vistula in 1920 during its revolutionary campaign against Poland.
On that occasion Lenin is reported to have declared that in the future
the USSR should offer only indirect support to revolutionary movements abroad and should never commit its own troops in direct participation.[30] Whether or not his words were reported accurately, that
counsel does conform with subsequent Soviet policy, at least until
1979. It was a policy that sharply limited Soviet influence in local
conflicts. Without trained and effective troops on the ground, weapons
shipments were often of little value to a Third World country at war.
The USSR partially compensated for its evident policy of not deploying regular ground troops abroad by sending technical and military advisers in large numbers to Third World clients. Though not
nearly as effective as combat troops would have been, the advisers
provided the training and expertise necessary for client states to employ Soviet military equipment. According to U.S. intelligence estimates, 6,880 military personnel from the Soviet Union and Eastern
Europe were employed as advisers in the less developed nations in
1974.[31] Nearly 4,000 of them were stationed in the Middle East. The
figure was considerably higher before Sadat expelled several thousand Soviet military advisers from Egypt in July 1972.

The cost of supporting Soviet military advisers can be a considerable drain on a Third World state:

> In the case of Soviet technical advisers, the LDC is required to
> pay the foreign exchange costs of transportation to and from the
> country and many local costs such as housing and medical care.
> These costs are often covered by grants under Western and
> Chinese technical aid. It has been estimated that in the aggre-
> gate, roughly 15 to 20 percent of drawings on Soviet project
> credits have gone to pay the costs of such technical assistance;
> in some of the more backward nations, however, the figure has
> reached 25 to 30 percent.[32]

The high costs of hosting Soviet advisers, as well as the feeling in
many Third World countries that their attitude toward local nationals
is arrogant and condescending, have made them rather unpopular in
most host nations. Even if it were somehow possible for a client state
to dispense with their services, however, Moscow would no doubt
insist on sending a contingent of advisers to every weapons customer,

---

[30] Chiang Kai-shek, *Soviet Russia in China: A Summing-up at Seventy* (New York:
Farrar, Strauss and Cudahy, 1957), 22.
[31] Central Intelligence Agency, *Handbook of Economic Statistics, 1975* (Washington:
CIA, 1975), 69. This compares with an estimated 24,440 economic advisers.
[32] Holzman, *International Trade under Communism*, 183.

for they provide the Kremlin with a valuable political presence and with intelligence reports on local conditions and the uses to which the Soviet arms are being put. Although Soviet advisers are not intended to participate in combat, a number have perished in local conflicts.[33]

The participation of Soviet-armed Cuban troops in Third World conflicts beginning with the Angolan civil war dramatically increased the potential effectiveness of Soviet arms in local conflicts and no doubt made Moscow appear a more promising ally to certain Third World regimes. In addition to playing a major role in training local army units, Cuban soldiers in Angola, Ethiopia, and elsewhere have fulfilled many assignments usually avoided by Soviet advisers: manning artillery, deploying trained units for armored fighting, flying combat planes in airborne support and assault missions, offering front-line logistical and technical assistance, and engaging infantry and guerrillas in direct ground combat. As many as 4,000 Cuban troops may have suffered casualties in Angola and Ethiopia.[34]

Cuba's political ties in Africa can be traced back to the first months after the Cuban revolution. Ernesto "Che" Guevara visited Africa and Asia in 1959, and further important contacts between Havana and several African nations were made in September 1961 at the first conference of nonaligned nations in Belgrade. Cuban advisers visited Algeria as early as 1963, and a small Cuban expeditionary force fought against Moise Tshombe in the Congo (Zaire) in 1964–5. The Congo (Brazzaville) also became the site of an important Cuban training center for guerrillas. Soldiers and officers from the MPLA, the PAIGC, the Eritrean Liberation Front, ZAPU, FRELIMO, Algeria, Zanzibar, and the PLO have received training from the Cubans, either in Havana or in Africa. Cuban leader Fidel Castro enhanced his prestige in the Third World by hosting the tricontinental conference in January 1966 and the sixth nonaligned nations conference in September 1979. By 1978 Cuba had diplomatic relations with 31 of the 49 African countries. At the time of the Angolan conflict, Castro declared that "our people is both a Latin-American and a Latin African people. Millions of Africans were shipped to Cuba as slaves by the colonialists, and a great part of Cuban blood is African blood."[35] Although Africa was the primary setting for Cuban involvement, Cuban troops were also sent to South Yemen, and to Syria following the October war. Table 3.5 shows estimates, taken largely from U.S. State Department sources, of the numbers of Cuban troops and advisers stationed in Third World nations as of 1978. Many of Cuba's soldiers abroad are believed to be

---

[33] Rough estimates of the number of casualties may be found in Avigdor Haselkorn, "Soviet Military Casualties in Third World Conflicts," *Conflict* 2(1980):73–85.

[34] Interview: David Smith, U.S. State Department.

[35] *Granma Weekly Review*, March 28, 1976.

Table 3.5. *Cubans in Africa and the Middle East, 1977–8*

Country	Number and function
Angola	19,000 military; 4,000 civilians
Algeria	35 medical aides
Benin	10–20 security advisers
Cape Verde	10–15 medical aides
Congo	300 military; 100–150 technicians
Equatorial Guinea	300–400, about half military
Ethiopia	16,000–17,000, mostly military
Guinea	300–500, mostly military
Guinea-Bissau	100–200, two-thirds military
Libya	100–125 military advisers
Madagascar	30 military advisers
Mozambique	800, half military
Soa Tome and Principe	75–80 medical aides
Sierra Leone	100–125 military advisers
South Yemen	1,000–2,000, mostly military
Tanzania	100–300 civilians
Uganda	A handful of military (?)

Sources: New York Times, November 17, 1977; Jorge I. Dominguez, "Sources of Cuban Foreign Policy," *Harvard International Review* (April/May 1979):6; Interview, David Smith, U.S. State Department.

drawn from Havana's well-trained reserves of 90,000 troops.[36] In addition to their military role, thousands of them have been involved in construction, medical and health service, education, and other forms of development assistance.

Cuba claims to have made the decisions to intervene in Angola and Ethiopia independent of the USSR, but the ideological links between Moscow and Havana, the close party ties, and Cuba's heavy economic dependence on the Soviet Union argue that Castro would neither have wished nor dared to act independently. A Soviet diplomat, Rudolf Shliapnikov, once declared of Cuba's dependence on the USSR, "We have only to say that repairs are being held up at Baku for three weeks and that's that."[37] Certainly the Cubans could never intervene in foreign conflicts without Soviet financing, weapons, and transport, and for this reason many Western observers have come to regard the Cuban troops in Angola and Ethiopia, if not elsewhere, as surrogate or proxy forces for the Soviet Union. Nevertheless, Castro and other Cuban leaders seem to relish playing the role of international revolutionaries, and a number of scholars have argued that Cuba's foreign

[36] The total Cuban regular armed forces number 121,000; army reserves number 90,000, and the People's Militia 200,000. *Defense and Foreign Affairs Handbook, 1976–77* (Washington: Copley & Associates, 1976), 108–9.
[37] Hugh Thomas, *Cuba or the Pursuit of Freedom* (London: Eyre and Spottiswoode, 1971), 1475.

policy ambitions are not so much subordinate to as parallel with those of the Soviet Union.[38] The case studies in Chapters 8 and 9 will provide additional insights into this question. Whatever the nuances of the Soviet-Cuban relationship, it is clear that from 1975 to 1978 Castro provided the Kremlin with the tool it required for translating its practice of weapons shipments into greater influence on the courses of local conflicts in Africa.

The Soviet invasion of Afghanistan, beginning on Christmas Eve 1979, was a fitting culmination to a decade during which Moscow's traditional restraint with respect to the use of its own forces abroad had continually slackened. The large number of troops involved – over 85,000 by mid-January – surpassed by far the number of troops deployed by Cuba in Angola and Ethiopia combined. The geographical location of Afghanistan and the large commitment of manpower required to subdue the rebellion made it wholly unfeasible for Moscow to employ Cubans or other proxies in this instance. In sending its own soldiers into Afghanistan, the Kremlin not only crossed a historic threshold but also acquired political and military experience that could conceivably facilitate future deployments of Soviet troops in Third World conflicts.

The spearhead of the invasion was the Soviet 105th Airborne Guards Division. It was airlifted into Kabul December 24–6 by roughly 250 flights of Il-76 and other transport planes. Airborne units also seized key points along the highways and tunnels lying between the USSR and the cities of Afghanistan in order to provide a secure route for the ground troops that followed. The swiftness and efficiency of the airborne assault surprised and impressed Western analysts considerably. The deployment in Afghanistan suggests that airborne forces are likely to be a key component of any direct intervention by the Soviet armed forces in the future.

A standard Soviet airborne division incorporates two parachute regiments, an artillery regiment, and an armored regiment, the latter equipped with 107 light-armored vehicles known as the *Boevaia Mashina Desantnaia* (BMD). Introduced in 1973, the BMD is a nine-ton, highly mobile, fully amphibious tank with considerable firepower for its size; it mounts three machine guns, a 73-mm main gun, and an antitank missile launcher, and it can carry six men at speeds of up

[38] Jorge Dominguez, "Sources of Cuban Foreign Policy," *Harvard International Review* (April/May 1979):1, 6–7; Zdenek Cervenka and Colin Legum, "Cuba: The New Communist Power in Africa,"*African Contemporary Record 1977–78*, A103–16; Nelson P. Valdes, "Revolutionary Solidarity in Angola," in Cole Blasier and Carmelo Mesa-Lago, eds., *Cuba in the World* (University of Pittsburgh, 1979), 87–117. Said Yusuf Abdi reviews both sides of the issue in "Cuba's Role in Africa: Revolutionary or Reactionary?" *Horn of Africa* 1(October-December 1978):17–24. For an opposing view, see Hugh Thomas, "Cuba's 'Civilizing Mission' – Lessons of the African Adventures," *Encounter* (February 1978):51–5; Brian Crozier, "The Surrogate Forces of the Soviet Union," *Conflict Studies* No. 92(1978):1–3.

to 40 miles per hour. These divisions also carry substantial quantities of antiaircraft guns, artillery, and antitank weapons.

The Red Army was the first army in the world to conduct an airborne drop of combat troops (in Soviet Central Asia in the early 1920s), and the Kremlin's interest in airborne forces has continued unabated since then. Soviet airborne operations were sharply limited in World War II because of the wholesale destruction of the army's air transport aircraft during Germany's Operation Barbarossa, but the airborne forces were reorganized after the war into three corps of 100,000 men and placed under a special directorate in the Ministry of Defense. The airborne troops played a key role in the occupation of Czechoslovakia in 1968. By 1973 they were organized into seven (and later eight) well-equipped divisions of over 8,000 men each. Placed on alert during the October war, these airborne divisions rendered Brezhnev's implied threat to intervene unilaterally in the conflict quite credible; that event, analyzed in Chapter 7, first illustrated the potential of these airborne divisions for intervention in Third World conflicts. The invasion of Afghanistan dramatically demonstrated their actual capability.

Shortly after the initial operations of the airborne forces in Afghanistan, five motorized rifle divisions entered the country – the 5th, 16th, 66th, 357th, and 360th. If fully equipped, these five divisions together would have deployed 1,750 tanks and 2,250 personnel carriers, but intelligence reports indicated that at least some of the divisions were not at full strength. The divisions were centered in Afghan cities and were employed principally to secure airfields, highways, and political centers. Air force units operating MiG-21 and MiG-23 fighters provided support to the overall Soviet operation.[39]

The occupation of Afghanistan demonstrated that in certain situations the Kremlin is willing to deploy ground forces for combat in the Third World. However, Afghanistan is contiguous to the Soviet Union; the logistical challenges and political risks of deploying and sustaining a large ground force in a country not adjacent to the USSR would be vastly greater. As of 1980, in fact, the Soviet Union's military transport capabilities and access to bases abroad would not have enabled it to undertake a foreign military intervention using its own troops and equipment on anywhere near the same scale and at the same distance as the U.S. military involvement in Vietnam. But the USSR has enjoyed superior power projection capabilities over the United States in some parts of Asia and the Middle East, and the Soviet leadership would seem to be abandoning some of its traditional

[39]Information on the Soviet airborne divisions and the invasion of Afghanistan is from the following sources: Kenneth Allard, "A Clear and Present Danger: Soviet Airborne Intervention." Unpublished seminar paper, Harvard University; *Aviation Week & Space Technology*, January 14, 1980; *New York Times*, January 8, 17, and 23, 1980; *Department of Defense Current News Summary and Selected Statements*, December 1979 through April 1980.

caution and restraint with respect to the use of Soviet armed forces outside the Warsaw Pact.

Soviet nuclear capabilities and local conflicts

From 1945 until roughly the mid-1960s, Washington maintained meaningful superiority over Moscow in strategic nuclear weapons. The key to this superiority was the U.S. capability to destroy with a first strike Soviet nuclear delivery vehicles in sufficient number to significantly blunt the effect of any all-out retaliatory strike. Although the Soviet Union, in such an eventuality, would have retained enough residual forces to make a serious counterattack against the United States, it could have retaliated only at the risk of inviting the whole-sale destruction of its cities by a U.S. second strike; any calculation of the ultimate outcome undoubtedly counseled prudence in the Kremlin. The risks and potential costs of escalation of a confrontation to the nuclear level were higher for the USSR during this period than for the United States.

The nuclear superiority of the United States exerted a tacit but pervasive influence on diplomatic and military developments around the world. It counterbalanced the Soviet advantage in conventional ground forces in Europe, and it deterred Moscow from making too overt its challenges to U.S. interests in the Third World. The latter consequence came about because of the risks of escalation implicit in any crisis or local conflict in which both the United States and the USSR were involved. Washington's nuclear advantage was by no means a tractable instrument – it could not prevent the USSR from putting pressure on Berlin, nor could it prevent the Soviets from indirectly and cautiously supporting revolutionary movements around the world. Above all, it was an insufficient factor in the total equation to guarantee diplomatic and political outcomes favorable to the West when certain other factors were missing.[40] But, logically, it must have had a certain dampening effect on Soviet assertiveness and latitude of action in the Third World and elsewhere.

As the 1960s progressed, the political advantages enjoyed by the United States as a result of its nuclear superiority began to erode in consequence of the USSR's buildup of its sea-based nuclear forces,

---

[40] Barry M. Blechman and Stephen S. Kaplan, *Force Without War: U.S. Armed Forces as a Political Instrument* (Washington: The Brookings Institution, 1979), 127–9, argue that the strategic weapons balance did not influence the outcomes of crisis incidents in which both the United States and the Soviet Union were involved. The argument is based principally on a statistical breakdown of the outcomes of incidents that occurred during various eras of the strategic balance; however, the study does not (and perhaps could not) separate out all the other factors that came to bear in each situation, nor is it possible to measure or know how many times the USSR refrained from taking action (i.e., times when no incident occurred) precisely because of its leaders' perceptions of the strategic balance.

the severalfold expansion of its ICBM forces, and the hardening of its missile silos. Robert McNamara, in January 1968, declared that the USSR "had achieved, and most likely will maintain over the fore-seeable future, an actual and credible second strike capability."[41] That same year the Soviet Union deployed for the first time a medium-range ballistic missile (the SS-N-6) aboard a nuclear-powered sub-marine; that was followed by rapid deployment of nuclear-powered submarines with medium-range missiles and, in 1974, long-range missiles. The existence of this fleet made the Soviet second-strike force secure throughout the 1970s. Long before the U.S. Minuteman force became significantly vulnerable to a Soviet first strike, Soviet ICBM and SLBM invulnerability had radically altered the nuclear equation – by greatly reducing the utility of an American first strike, it lowered the threshold of risk for Moscow in local conflicts. In effect, the Soviet achievement of a secure second-strike force gave the USSR a kind of protective umbrella behind which it could exploit its advantage in conventional forces and its ties with revolutionary regimes and par-ties in the Third World.

Soviet theorists were well aware of the consequences of what was happening. One Soviet scholar, V. V. Zhurkin, in a work on U.S. be-havior in local crises and conflicts, asserted that as a result of the Soviet attainment of nuclear parity, "the hopes of the USA for employing nuclear blackmail as a means of obtaining its goals in international crises were exploded."[42] Other Soviet writers identified the year 1970 – when the USSR is said to have achieved nuclear parity – as the beginning of a new phase in international relations, one more favor-able to the achievement of Soviet aims.[43] It seems to be no accident that the USSR's more openly offensive approach toward conflict and revolution in the Third World after 1970 correlated with its achieve-ment of effective nuclear parity. The shift from nuclear imbalance to approximate parity per se was not a sufficient cause for (though it was a necessary condition for) the Soviet Union's more activist role in global affairs during the 1970s. Generally speaking, the will, in-tentions, diplomatic abilities, and strategy of national leadership are more critical factors in shaping the course of world events than are military capabilities alone, either nuclear or conventional. The fol-lowing case studies will illustrate the extent to which this was so in the Soviet Union's efforts to influence the courses of five specific local conflicts.

[41] *Statement Before the Senate Armed Services Committee on the FY 1969–73 Defense Program and the 1969 Defense Budget*, January 22, 1968, 46–7.

[42] V. V. Zhurkin, *SShA i mezhdunarodno-politicheskiye krizisy* (Moscow: Nauka, 1975), 49.

[43] See, for example, G. A. Trofimenko, "Vneshnyaya politika SShA v 70-e gody: dek-laratsii i praktika," *SShA* (December 1976):15; G. A. Trofimenko, "Sovetsko-amer-ikanskie soglasheniya ob ogranichenii strategicheskikh vooruzhenii," *SShA* (September 1972):7; K. M. Georgiev and M. O. Kolosev, "Sovetsko-amerikanskie otnosheniia na novom etape," *SShA* (March 1973):13.

4
THE CASE STUDIES: A FRAMEWORK FOR ANALYSIS

> Investigators, however, who have paid careful attention to more than one country or area...have soon discovered the intellectual power that is inherent in such comparisons.
>
> Karl Deutsch

The preceding three chapters have presented a considerable amount of general material on the USSR's involvement in Third World conflicts, including historical background, Soviet ideological perspectives, and development of military capabilities that made such involvement possible. This establishes the necessary foundation for exploring more closely the USSR's policy and behavior in specific local wars. Five conflicts in which the Soviet Union was involved have been chosen as case studies for this purpose. This chapter will elaborate the criteria of their selection and outline the framework to be used in analyzing them.

The criteria of selection

In singling out conflicts for case study, only the postwar era was considered – most examples of Soviet involvement in local conflicts took place after 1945 anyway, and it is the period most relevant to contemporary Soviet policy and current American concerns. Moscow was involved militarily in at least 20 conflicts in the Third World between 1945 and 1980 (see Table 2.1). These 20 conflicts were narrowed down to five by applying the following criteria:

The contenders were non-Communist. This restriction eliminates the Chinese civil war, the Korean war, the Laotian civil war, the war in Vietnam, Hanoi's invasion of Cambodia, the Sino-Vietnamese border war of 1979, and the civil war in Afghanistan. These wars were considered briefly in Chapter 2, but the case studies will concentrate on Soviet intervention on behalf of non-Communist clients. Western commentators occasionally refer to the government of the MPLA in Angola or to the Ethiopian Dergue as Communist, but it is more correct to identify them as radical leftist, pro-Soviet regimes. The Kremlin does not officially recognize either Angola or Ethiopia as Communist states; when representatives from the MPLA or from the Commission to Organize the Party of the Working People of Ethiopia have attended congresses of the CPSU or other official conferences, they have not been referred to as "fraternal, socialist parties," but as "national-democratic parties" or as "revolutionary vanguard parties." Moscow's policy toward non-Communist combatants differs noticeably from its policies when one or both contenders are Communist and all the complicating factors of party ties, ideology, and the world Communist movement come into play. Furthermore, the latter three conflicts are as yet too recent for historical study, and numerous excellent studies are already available on the earlier wars in China, Korea, Laos, and Vietnam. It seems appropriate to focus on conflicts that have received less scholarly attention.

Soviet arms shipments took place during the course of hostilities, not prior to or after the violent stages of the conflict. This criterion restricts the case studies to those instances in which the USSR chose to become involved actively and militarily in a conflict. Shipping arms to a country at war would seem to represent a higher level of risk – and commitment – than transferring arms in peacetime. Although the USSR supplied arms to Egypt prior to the Suez war in 1956 and supplied massive amounts of arms to the Arab world both before and after the six-day war in June 1967, these conflicts were not selected as case studies, for Soviet arms were not delivered during the period of actual combat (in the latter case, probably because time did not allow it). Likewise, in the Indo-Pakistani war of 1971, no known arms shipments from the USSR to India took place during the war itself (December 4–17), even though Moscow clearly favored the Indian side in the dispute and had provided New Delhi with many weapons shortly prior to the conflict. If the war had been prolonged or had not gone so well for India, it is probable that the USSR would have organized an emergency airlift of arms, but it proved unnecessary.

Soviet arms played a significant role in determining the course of hostilities. This criterion eliminates from the list the USSR's involvement in the Indonesian civil war (the Sumatran rebellion) of 1958–9, the Algerian-Moroccan border war of 1963, and the Indo-Pakistani dispute of September 1965. It is true that some Soviet weapons shipments took place in connection with these conflicts, but it can be argued that Soviet assistance was a marginal factor in all three conflicts, at least in terms of its impact on the course of the fighting. The USSR shipped a number of fighter planes, ships, and jeeps to Indonesia at the time of the Sumatran rebellion, but this equipment saw little use in combat, particularly not in the decisive campaigns of the war. Soviet aid to Algeria in the 1963 border war was modest, and most of the arms arrived after the worst of the hostilities were over. The USSR cut off military supplies to Morocco during the war, but they were resumed (via Czechoslovakia) shortly afterward. Formally, Moscow's position was one of neutrality. In the case of the Indo-Pakistani conflict in 1965, Soviet shipments of arms to India took place during the hostilities (again under prior agreements), but the quantity was small and largely symbolic. Although leaning to India, Moscow was loath to have relations with Pakistan deteriorate. Eventually the Soviets acted as mediators of the dispute, winning a measure of favor from both sides at Tashkent in January 1966.

Wars of attrition and other nonconventional wars are excluded. These are wars in which traditional land battles for control of territory do not take place; rather, the primary goal of one contender is to wear down the will and resources of the other by unconventional tactics: intermittent guerrilla strikes, propaganda, armed raids, manuevers, shelling, bombing, and so forth. They are excluded because it is difficult to define when they begin and end and because the nature of Soviet involvement in such wars logically would differ somewhat from that in more conventional conflicts.

Indonesia's disputes with the Dutch over West Irian and with Malaysia are often listed in historical works as wars, but never were more than a few commando raids undertaken, involving less than 100 troops at a time. The Soviet Union shipped massive volumes of heavy weapons to Indonesia during this time – tanks, ships, planes, and so forth – most of which sat idle and was never used in combat. Likewise, the prolonged Congo crisis of the early 1960s involved little warfare that could be described as conventional. Yemen's campaign against British Aden from 1957 to 1959 and South Yemen's brief war with Yemen in 1979 fall into a similar category: The warfare was limited to sporadic commando raids by guerrillas at least partly equipped with Soviet weapons. Such conflicts cannot readily be compared with more traditional wars.

The war of attrition between Egypt and Israel in 1969–70 witnessed massive Soviet military involvement, possibly the largest postwar extension of Soviet conventional forces beyond the perimeter of the Warsaw Pact up to that time. It was not a full-scale war on the order of the six-day war in June 1967 or the Yom Kippur war in October 1973, but in many respects it was a more clearly defined conventional conflict than were some of the other conflicts selected for study, such as the Yemeni civil war or even the Angolan civil war. Nevertheless, given that only a limited number of cases could be singled out for study, this conflict was reluctantly excluded both because of its less than full-scale nature and in order not to focus the overall study too heavily on the Middle East region.

These four criteria reduce the list of conflicts in Table 2.1 to five: the Yemeni civil war, the Nigerian civil war, the October war, the civil war in Angola, and the Ogaden war. The five cases chosen for study represent every conventional-style land conflict in the Third World between 1945 and 1980 in which the Soviet Union provided significant military assistance to a non-Communist client during the course of full hostilities.

The parameters of comparison

In order to achieve a measure of rigor in the analysis and to facilitate recognition of patterns and trends in Soviet policy, the case studies are organized according to a fixed outline, using seven parameters of comparison. Each chapter opens with a summary of the given conflict and a brief review of related international events. Following this introduction, each chapter is divided into seven sections:

The local dispute. This section reviews in detail the issues and forces causing the local conflict, including its historical background. The purpose is to determine what types of disputes are conducive to Soviet intervention, how local conditions affect and constrain Soviet actions, and whether or not Moscow is able to exploit local issues to its own advantage. Studies of Soviet foreign policy toward the Third World are often criticized for concentrating excessively on the global and strategic implications of Soviet behavior, while ignoring the dynamics of local politics and the regional balance of forces. In order to counter this tendency, the case studies devote a large amount of attention to the nature and underlying causes of the local dispute. This section in each chapter will also review Soviet commentary on the conflict to determine what ideological justifications are employed and how Soviet analysts perceive the conflict's place within "the international class struggle": Which issues are emphasized and which downplayed or ignored? Does the Soviet "line" shift as the conflict progresses? What factors make the conflict a "war of national liberation"?

The diplomatic relationship between the USSR and its client. This section examines, insofar as the public record allows, the genesis of the relationship and of subsequent arms agreements and the unfolding of the bilateral relationship: Did the initiative come from Moscow or from the Third World client? What talks and negotiations preceded the offering of aid, and what was the substance of those talks? Did the USSR's involvement develop from an existing or previous program of military assistance, or was the crisis an opportunity to probe for influence in an area where prior contacts had been limited? Did the relationship develop smoothly, or were there open disagreements and friction? Did Moscow exert any kind of pressure on its client or attempt to manipulate its actions in a certain direction? By what means were contacts maintained and developed during the war? Did the USSR seek to develop ties with local Communist or workers' parties? Finally, who exerted the most influence on whom?

Weapons shipments and other military aids. As far as the data allow, this section attempts to specify the volume and types of weapons and other military equipment delivered to the Soviet client. The "weapons mix" is analyzed for what it reveals about the USSR's intentions and the level of its commitment: Were the weapons clearly intended for defensive purposes, or could they also be used offensively? Were key weapons withheld from the client that might have made a difference in the course or the outcome of the conflict? Did the volume of weaponry shipped exceed or fall short of the client's needs? Were the weapons tailored to suit obvious military requirements, or was the choice of weapons a poor one? How did the Soviet weaponry perform under the given environmental and military conditions? The timing of the weapons shipments may also reveal something about the factors bearing on Soviet policy: Did the USSR begin transferring weapons before or after the positions of key regional and Western powers were known? Did it begin before or after it was evident which side would win? Rapid, intense shipments suggest a strong commitment to a client's battlefield success, particularly if they occur at critical junctures in the fighting. More leisurely shipments suggest a lesser commitment, even hesitancy, which could come from uncertainty about the desirable or probable outcome, about the reliability of the client, or about likely Western responses. Delays in shipments may reveal disagreements between Moscow and the client government. Examined in isolation, the flow of weapons is not a decisive indicator, because it may be influenced by other factors, but together with other evidence it may add to our understanding of Soviet behavior during the conflict.

The role of Soviet and East European advisers. This section considers to what extent, if any, Soviet and East European military and technical advisers, and combat personnel such as pilots, gunnery crews, and line officers, played a role in the conflict. Where applicable, the role of Cuban troops will also be considered in this section: What was the extent of involvement by the advisers or troops? When did they arrive, and did they play a role in actual combat? What was their relationship with the local nationals? How decisive was their role in the conflict?

Soviet-American interactions. This section reviews diplomatic interactions between the USSR and the United States during the conflict in order to assess the influence of U.S. diplomatic and military actions on Soviet policy and the impact of the superpower relationship on local wars. The extent of U.S. involvement on either side of the conflict will be reviewed, as well as the Soviet view of that involvement. The potential of the crisis to have led to superpower confrontation will be evaluated. This section is not intended to review U.S. policy toward the conflict as a whole, but only to assess the impact of American actions on Soviet behavior.

The China factor. The People's Republic of China (PRC) has been a troublesome and disturbing factor in Soviet foreign policy since 1949, increasingly so since the Sino-Soviet split became serious in the late 1950s and early 1960s. The repercussions of that split have affected Soviet policy even in remote parts of the globe. Peking, particularly in the 1960s, charged the Soviet leadership with revisionism – with not pursuing a genuinely Leninist policy of fostering world revolution, supporting national liberation movements, and standing up to imperialism in local conflicts. While engaging in counter polemics against Maoism, the Kremlin leaders felt compelled to pursue a more aggressive policy in the Third World so as to refute the Chinese accusations, win the support of local Communist parties, and cultivate favor with nationalist regimes. This section considers the influence of the PRC on Soviet behavior in the given conflict. China's influence takes three forms: It may be largely rhetorical and diplomatic, such as when Peking accuses the Soviets of errors or insufficient ardor in supporting a local state; it may take the form of active competition to win the favor of the client state; or China may seek to counter Soviet influence by providing arms and other aid to the opposite side. China plays some role in almost all of the case studies under consideration, and by examining the nature of that role and how it has evolved, one can better understand the significance and impact of the Sino-Soviet split on Moscow's involvement in Third World conflicts.

The outcome. The final section evaluates the impact of Soviet diplomacy and arms shipments on the course and outcome of the war. It attempts to determine if the Soviet involvement was militarily decisive and how the outcome might have differed (in broadest outline only) if Moscow had not intervened. The section also weighs the immediate benefits and losses deriving to the Soviet Union from its effort. In cases in which significant short-term gains were realized, subsequent events will be chronicled to see if the gains proved to be more or less permanent, or if they were rapidly lost in the long run. The goal is to assess the utility for Moscow of its involvement in local conflicts and to determine if the Soviet leadership has learned lessons over time that have improved its approach and tactics.

Chapter 10, the conclusion of this work, will summarize the findings of the case studies using the same basic outline presented here. Recurring patterns and significant trends in Soviet policy will be identified and discussed, with reference principally to the case studies, but also to some of the other conflicts reviewed in the first chapter. Chapter 10 offers a general overview of the nature and evolution of Soviet military involvement in local conflicts over the course of some three decades.

5
THE YEMENI CIVIL WAR

> The world should know that we cannot negotiate with an Egyptian
> pistol at our heads and Ilyushins in our sky.
>
> Imam Muhammad al-Badr

The term *quagmire* might appropriately be applied to the Soviet Union's
long years of involvement in the Yemeni civil war. As the conflict dragged
on year after year, with little progress made on either side, Moscow felt
steadily compelled to increase its commitment to the revolutionary regime
in Sana, eventually investing over $500 million of military assistance in
an effort to ensure its survival. Yet, after backing the Yemen Arab Republic
(YAR) for eight years, even rescuing it from total collapse in 1967–8, by
1970 the USSR was left with few tangible returns to show for its investment. The Soviet Union nevertheless continued to court the YAR assid-
uously throughout the 1970s.

The tenacity of the Soviet Union's efforts to win influence in Yemen
evidently derived from its intense interest in the Arabian peninsula and
in the strategic sea-lanes of the Middle East. Impoverished and backward
Yemen has virtually no natural resources of interest to a superpower, and
its military strength is marginal, but its frontier with Saudi Arabia, its
proximity to Ethiopia, and its position on the Strait of Bab el-Mandeb
make its geographical location alone a valuable strategic asset. The USSR's
involvement in the Yemeni civil war was almost certainly but one facet
of a broader effort to win influence in the littoral countries along the Red
Sea and the Gulf of Aden: Saudi Arabia, Egypt, Sudan, Ethiopia, Djibouti,
Somalia, Yemen, and South Yemen. The pattern of Soviet diplomacy in
the region during the 1960s and 1970s strongly suggests that establishing
a controlling presence on the Red Sea waterway was a principal goal of
the USSR; perhaps nowhere else in the Third World have Soviet foreign
policy initiatives been so extensive and persistent.

The Yemeni civil war began September 25, 1962, when a military coup
led by Colonel Abdullah al-Sallal overthrew Muhammad al-Badr, who had
succeeded to the ancient imamate but a week earlier. The imam escaped
from his palace in Sana while it was under bombardment by Russian
tanks purchased by his father a few years earlier. Fleeing northward, he
rallied the mountain tribesmen in the north and east of Yemen to the
royal family's cause; Sallal, meanwhile, organized a Revolutionary Coun-

cil in Sana that proclaimed the establishment of the Yemeni Arab Republic (YAR), with himself as president. The ensuing civil war dragged on nearly eight years and led to varying levels of foreign involvement on the part of Saudi Arabia, Egypt, British Aden, Jordan, Iran, the United States, and the Soviet Union. In terms of manpower and national prestige, Egypt was the most heavily committed of the outside powers, but from the beginning the Soviet Union was the principal underwriter and arms supplier of the new republic.

The civil war made Yemen the fulcrum of a deep-rooted rivalry between the revolutionary and traditional regimes of the Middle East. Egypt, Syria, and Iraq supported the republican cause; Jordan, Morocco, Pakistan, Iran, and Saudi Arabia stood behind the Royalists. Only two days after Sallal's coup, Egyptian military units began arriving by air at Sana and Taiz, the vanguard of a force that eventually numbered more than 70,000 troops and gave Cairo considerable control over the foreign and defense policies of the YAR. In November, Egypt signed a mutual defense treaty with the YAR; Saudi Arabia meanwhile offered shelter and support to the imam. The war widened in December when Egypt undertook the first of numerous bombing missions against Saudi towns near the Yemeni border. The Saudis responded by increasing their material and financial support to the imam, with the result that Riyadh and Cairo found themselves embroiled in a proxy war from which neither could extricate itself for several years. The intransigence and factionalism of the Yemeni combatants tended to pull both their Arab and their Soviet supporters ever deeper into the quagmire as diplomatic efforts to end the conflict failed one after another. This occurred despite the fact that Egypt, Saudi Arabia, and the USSR managed to manipulate the Royalists and the Republicans to a certain extent because of the total Yemeni dependence on them for arms, money, and support.[1]

The war took the form of a protracted stalemate that lasted until the Royalists abandoned the fight because of defections by their tribal supporters and the termination of Saudi assistance. Throughout the conflict the Republicans controlled the cities and towns on the coastal plain of southern and western Yemen, while the imam's tribal forces dominated the mountainous land to the north and east. Neither force could dislodge nor defeat the other. Table 5.1 shows the chronology of the war's major events, illustrating how periods of Republican offensives and Royalist counteroffensives were punctuated by periods of negotiation and outside mediation intended to make possible a mutual Saudi and Egyptian withdrawal. At the outbreak of the war, the Royalist forces outnumbered the Republican forces by 10 to 1, and only the intervention of Egypt saved

---

[1] The war became such a quagmire for Egypt that Nasser took to referring to it as "my Vietnam." A. I. Dawisha, "Intervention in the Yemen: An Analysis of Egyptian Perceptions and Policies," *The Middle East Journal* 29(Winter 1975):55. In an interview with *Look* magazine, the Egyptian leader admitted that the Yemeni intervention had been a miscalculation: "We never thought that it would lead to what it did." Reported in *The Times* (London), March 5, 1968. Moscow's sentiments were no doubt similar.

Table 5.1. *A chronology of the Yemeni civil war, 1962–70, showing stages of Soviet involvement*

Stage 1

Sept. 26, 1962	The Republican coup	Imam al-Badr deposed; republic declared in Sana
Oct. 1962	Egyptian troops arrive in Yemen	
Feb.–Mar. 1963	Ramadan offensive	Republican forces push Royalists deeper into mountains; Marib and Harib fall
Nov. 1962–Aug. 1963ᵃ	*U.S. and UN attempts at mediation.*	*Saudi Arabia and Egypt agree to withdraw; UN mission goes to Yemen; mediation breaks down*
Apr.–Dec. 1963	War resumes	War stalemated; little military action
Jan. 1964	*Cairo summit*	*Serious Saudi-Egyptian effort to negotiate a solution*
Jan.–Mar. 1964	Royalist counteroffensive	Republican transportation disrupted; some territory gained
Apr. 23–29, 1964	Nasser visits Yemen	Egypt decides to increase its assistance to YAR
Jun.–Sept. 1964	Haradh offensive	50,000 Egyptian troops clear mountain country between Sada and Hajja; Royalist headquarters captured; imam flees
Sept. 5–12, 1964	*Alexandria summit conference*	*Negotiations conducted that eventually lead to conclusion of "Erkwit cease-fire" in November*
Dec. 1964–Jul. 1965	Royalist counteroffensive	Very successful; territory regained; culminated in Taif manifesto, a proclamation of coordinated efforts to be made by Saudis and Royalists against the YAR
Aug. 22–24, 1965	*Jeddah agreement*	*A negotiated settlement between Cairo and Riyadh; both sides to sponsor a peace conference and to work for mutual withdrawal*
Nov. 23–Dec. 21, 1965	*Haradh conference*	*Direct negotiations between Royalists and Republicans sponsored by Saudi Arabia and Egypt; the talks are unfruitful and break down*

Table 5.1. *(cont.)*

Stage 2		
Jan.–Sept. 1966	Fighting resumes	A period of partial Egyptian withdrawal; USSR begins some direct arms shipments to YAR
Oct. 1966–May 1967	Hostilities intensify	Egyptian bombing raids resume; regional tension heightens
Jun. 1967	Six-day war between Israel and Arab states	Egypt's military shattered; Nasser no longer able to afford intervention in Yemen
Aug. 29–Sept. 1, 1967	*Khartoum summit conference*	*Khartoum agreement negotiated; Egypt will withdraw its forces, and Saudi Arabia will cease supporting Royalists*
Oct.–Dec. 1967	Egypt withdraws	Royalists advance and surround Sana
Stage 3		
Feb. 1968–Sept. 1969	Republican counteroffensive	Siege of Sana broken (Feb. 1968) with Soviet assistance; all major towns and villages recaptured
Jan. 1969	Saudis cease payments to Royalists	
Jan.–Feb. 1970	Royalist offensive	The last serious Royalist effort; Sada retaken
Jul. 1970	*Saudi Arabia recognizes YAR*	*War ends*

[a]Italic entries mark periods of attempted negotiation or mediation.

the fledgling YAR from a quick defeat. When Nasser finally withdrew from Yemen in November 1967, the Republican government survived against considerably larger forces because of a rapidly organized and determined Soviet effort to supply the besieged capital city with arms and support. Once Egypt had left the country and it became clear that Sana nevertheless could not be taken, tribal support for the Royalist cause began to ebb.

The USSR's involvement in the Yemeni civil war spanned the last two years of Khrushchev's rule and the first six years of the Brezhnev era. The Soviet commitment evolved through three stages. From October 1962 until December 1965, Soviet military aid was channeled solely through Egypt, and the USSR's direct involvement was confined to economic assistance, propaganda, and diplomacy. A second stage opened early in 1966, following the Haradh conference, when the Jeddah agreement between Saudi Arabia and Egypt began to break down. Nasser's commitment to sustain Republican Yemen with his own troops was faltering at this time, leading Moscow to supply small quantities of arms directly to Sana. Czechoslovakia also provided some military assistance. The Egyptian troops were not withdrawn, however, and the bulk of Soviet aid during this period continued to flow through Cairo. The third and most serious stage of Soviet involvement began late in 1967, when Nasser finally was compelled to bring home his 70,000 troops in the Yemen because of Egypt's defeat in the June war with Israel. With the Egyptian expeditionary force removed, the Royalists enjoyed a definite military advantage over the Republicans. The Soviet Union undertook a series of transport airlifts and sealifts of military equipment to Sana and Hodeida. Soviet arms, ammunition, combat aircraft, tanks, and a host of military and technical advisers assisted in breaking a threatening Royalist siege of the Republican capital, ensuring the latter's survival and eventual victory in the war. Soviet arms shipments continued to play a role in the remaining hostilities, which essentially ended in March 1970, when Saudi Arabia helped mediate a reconciliation between the YAR and most of the Royalist tribes. Riyadh recognized the YAR in July of that year.

The local dispute

Yemen in 1962 was one of the most isolated and backward countries in the world, a feudal anachronism ripe for revolution. Despite a population of roughly 4.5 million, no financial or commercial institutions existed; there was not even a national currency. There was not a single sewage system, there were no factories, and electricity was available to only about 3 percent of the population. William Brown wrote that "there was not a single ministry capable of performing a public service function," and Edgar O'Ballance characterized Yemen as "the last genuine medieval country and people left in the world."[2] Yemen was governed by a corrupt oligarchy of Sayyid officials.[3] Justice was arbitrary and cruel, slavery was common, and taxation was oppressive. The fear and hatred engendered by the Imam Ahmed's rule had inspired a long series of conspiracies and assassination attempts against him, none of which had succeeded, though he was seriously injured more than once.

The forces of revolution that engulfed the imamate after Ahmed's death had been building for some time. Since World War II, a long period of decline had taken place in Yemen's agricultural production and handicraft industries, the result of drought, oppressive taxation, and a steady decline in foreign demand for primitive Yemeni goods. During the 1950s, many young people and military personnel were sent abroad to study in Egypt, Western Europe, America, and the Soviet bloc; they returned with new

---

[2] William R. Brown, "The Yemeni Dilemma," *The Middle East Journal* 17(Autumn 1963):355–7; Edgar O'Ballance, *The War in the Yemen* (Hamden: Archon, 1971), 9, 17–42. Brown was deputy principal officer at the U.S. Legation in Taiz, 1960–2; O'Ballance was a correspondent who covered the civil war firsthand.

[3] The Sayyids were members of the Zeidi sect who claimed direct descent from the prophet Mohammed. The Zeidi and Shafii sects were the two prominent Islamic groups in Yemen.

ideas and an acute awareness of Yemen's backwardness. An estimated 50,000 to 75,000 Yemenis joined the labor force of neighboring Aden, where they, too, came under the influence of foreign ideas and saw an affluence not known at home. The military was subject to modernizing influences through the agency of Egyptian and Soviet advisers the imam brought to Sana to assist in training the army. As the military increased in effectiveness, and as its store of modern arms (mostly Soviet) grew, it became a potential source of opposition to the imam and the Sayyid bureaucracy. The potent force of Arab nationalism was also rising in the Middle East, and it was not possible to seal it off from Yemen entirely, given the ready availability of cheap transistor radios in Yemeni towns.

The demise of the imamate was preceded by rebellions of the Hashib, Bakil, and other tribes in 1959 and by bombing incidents in Taiz, Ibb, and Sana during 1960 and 1961. In December 1961, Ahmed published a sensational poem denouncing Nasser's effort to foster socialism in Egypt as contrary to the principles of Islam. Cairo responded by broadcasting a call for revolution in Yemen, an appeal continued thereafter in regular broadcasts by Yemeni nationalists cooperating with Nasser. In August 1962, demonstrations against the imam occurred in several secular schools, and these in turn precipitated the first public protest march ever held in Sana. It ended with soldiers killing several demonstrators. Riots took place again early in September at schools in Sana and Taiz; pictures of the imam were torn down and replaced by portraits of Nasser.

Only one week after the death of Imam Ahmed on September 19, 1962, Cairo's appeal for a revolution in Sana found a response in the form of the coup described earlier. Although local conditions made Yemen ripe for revolution, the coup that toppled the imam's son was at least partly the result of a complex conspiracy masterminded and directed from Egypt. Cairo's elaborate preparations enabled Egyptian troops to arrive by air within 48 hours of the coup; supply ships began arriving as early as October 1. Once the civil war broke out, Yemen divided along the incipient lines of conflict that had existed prior to the revolution. The Republicans were a diverse and divided coalition of urban intellectuals, army officers, and Shafii merchants, united principally by common opposition to the imamate. They generally agreed on the need for a more liberal government and for economic modernization of Yemen, but they shared no single conception of how to pursue these ends, and divisions in their ranks became manifest over time. The Royalists drew their main support from the Zeidi tribes in the north who had traditionally supported the imam and who were again willing to offer their guns in his defense if the price was right. These tribesmen had rallied to Imam Ahmed when his succession to the throne was challenged in 1948, and again during the rebellion of the militia in 1955, events that portended the civil war. The central goal of the Royalist leaders was restoration of the imamate, but the Zeidi sheiks and their tribesmen were at least equally interested in assuring their local autonomy, obtaining gold and weapons, and expelling foreigners such as the Egyptians from their country. They were also motivated to an extent by religious fervor, but the Imam al-Badr found that their loyalty could be assured only at a price. This made the financial support of Saudi Arabia crucial for the Royalist cause.

Four main factors made the dispute a natural candidate for the USSR's attention and involvement: (1) The Republican government was a revolutionary regime dedicated to modernization, a fact that made a Soviet commitment both feasible and ideologically justifiable. (2) The Republicans were desperate for foreign assistance, without which they could not survive. (3) Egypt's prestige was behind the Republican cause, thus offering Moscow an opportunity to strengthen ties with Nasser. (4) The USSR's military and economic assistance to Yemen during the late 1950s had acquainted Soviet officers and diplomats with the country and had forged ties with many of the Yemeni officers who came to power in 1962. This latter fact gave rise to the irony that the Soviet arms shipped to the imam prior to 1962 became the very lever by which the USSR won influence with the antimonarchist forces that overthrew the imam.[4]

Because Yemen had never been a colony or protectorate of a European power, Soviet commentators had some difficulty portraying the civil war as a war of national liberation. The problem was compounded by the fact that Moscow had been a supporter of the imam for several years prior to the 1962 coup. This dilemma was tacitly acknowledged in a *Pravda* commentary of October 3, 1962:

> The people of Yemen have a glorious history of struggle against imperialism and colonialism for the national independence of their homeland. Their just fight for independence has always received friendly backing from the Soviet Union, which established official relations with Yemen as early as 1928. A treaty of friendship and trade was signed at the same time and was renewed in 1955 . . .
>
> However, the absolute feudal regime in Yemen served as an obstacle to the country's progress and kept the people of the nation in darkness and ignorance, stifling all aspirations toward democratic forms of government.

The article also stated that "the birth of the new republic on the Arabian Peninsula is causing alarm among the imperialist powers," and throughout the conflict the Soviet news media portrayed the struggle as one between the progressive Republican regime, backed by the world's progressive forces, and the Royalists, who were allegedly pawns of the capitalist states and multinational oil companies. Aramco, "the boss of things in Saudi Arabia," was said to be behind Riyadh's involvement, and the Soviet news media charged that U.S. and British arms, planes, and pilots were entering Yemen via British

---

[4] Shortly after coming to power, Sallal asserted that Imam Ahmed's arms deal with the USSR in 1956 had laid the groundwork for the revolution. *New York Times*, October 7, 1962.

Aden and Saudi Arabia. Considerable attention was also devoted to the alleged involvement of thousands of Western mercenaries on the Royalist side.[5] In fact, the number of mercenaries involved in the war was quite small, and the involvement of the United States and Britain was marginal, but the ideological imperative of interpreting the conflict as a war of national liberation required that the central role of imperialism be postulated. The People's Republic of China was far more involved in Yemen than any of the Western powers; yet Soviet ideological pronouncements placed the greatest stress on U.S. and West European involvement.

The diplomatic relationship between the USSR and its client

For decades prior to the civil war the Soviet Union had cultivated a relationship with Yemen as part of a broader effort to erode British influence in the Middle East. Diplomatic ties between the Kremlin and the imamate were first opened in 1928 when a 10-year treaty of friendship and cooperation was signed in Sana. It was the first such treaty between Moscow and an Arab country, and it resulted in a modest trade relationship that lasted until late 1938, when the Soviet mission was recalled. World War II intervened before a new mission could be sent. During the 1950s, Moscow sought the favor of the Imam Ahmed, who had come to power in 1948, by supporting Yemen's claim to British Aden. Relations were formally opened on November 1, 1955, the anniversary of the original treaty of friendship.[6] Arms from the USSR and Czechoslovakia began to arrive one year later, and a Soviet technical mission was established in Sana. Between 1956 and 1960, when Soviet-Yemeni relations cooled somewhat, approximately $30 million in arms were shipped to the imam, including over 60 attack and training aircraft, some 30 T-54 tanks, and a number of armored

---

[5] For representative Soviet commentary on the war, see the following: *Pravda*, October 10, 1962; B. Cherkasov, "In the New Yemen," *International Affairs* (June 1963):40–4; *Pravda*, August 7, 1965; *Pravda*, November 16, 1967; *Izvestia*, November 19, 1967; N. Farizov, "Intervention in the Yemen," *International Affairs* (March 1968):122; *Pravda*, December 9, 10, 12, 23, 25, 26, 27, and 29, 1967; *Izvestia*, December 19, 1967; G. Mirskii, "Arabskie Narody Prodolzhayut Borby," *Mirovaya Ekonomika i Mezhdunardoniye Otnoshenia* (March 1967):124; B. Izakov, "Agoniya starogo rezhima v Iemene," *Novoe Vremya* (December 15, 1967):20.

[6] The first move to reestablish formal ties occurred in October 1955, when Daniel Solod, the Soviet ambassador to Egypt, met with the acting Yemeni foreign minister in Cairo. They signed a renewal of the original 1928 agreement. Five months later a trade agreement was signed that may have included secret clauses on arms deliveries.

personnel carriers, antiaircraft guns, and helicopters.[7] Few of these weapons ever saw action in the war against Aden, but they served to strengthen Soviet ties with Yemen, particularly with the military. Relations advanced in numerous ways: The USSR assisted Yemen in building a much-needed port at Hodeida that opened in April 1961; several Soviet and East European technical missions traveled to Yemen; Yemeni students and officers studied in Czechoslovakia and the USSR. In June 1956 and again in January 1958, Crown Prince Muhammad al-Badr visited the Soviet Union and Eastern Europe, seeking assistance of various kinds from the very powers that later would be supplying his enemies.

Moscow's extensive experience in Yemen and its strong ties with the military there made the establishment in 1962 of a military assistance relationship with the YAR relatively easy. The USSR and Egypt (then the United Arab Republic, UAR) recognized the YAR on September 29, 1962, less than three days after Sallal's coup took place. The unusual rapidity of the Soviet recognition suggests the possibility that Cairo had informed Moscow in advance about the plot against the imam; prior consultation with Moscow would have been a logical step, because the survival of the YAR would depend on the USSR's willingness to supply arms to the Egyptian expeditionary force. Within two days of the coup, Sallal informed Nikita Khrushchev by telegram of the establishment of the YAR, stating, "We have forever replaced the monarchy with a Republican regime founded on respect for human dignity and rights, as well as on socialist justice and equality among the sons of men." Khrushchev responded in a telegram to Sallal on October 1, declaring that "foreign interference of any kind in Yemen's internal affairs is intolerable."[8]

On October 18, 1962, the Soviet Union and the YAR renewed a technical assistance agreement originally signed with the Imam Ahmed. Although the agreement was of little direct military significance, it did signal to Sana that the Soviets were willing to follow up their diplomatic recognition with concrete forms of assistance. A Soviet military delegation arrived in Egypt the same month; the impending war in Yemen must have been the first item of discussion, because Egypt's intervention required large volumes of Soviet arms and assistance. During the first week of November, a YAR delegation

---

[7] SIPRI, *The Arms Trade Registers*, 65–6; Joshua and Gibert, *Arms for the Third World*, 12; Eric Macro, *Yemen and the Western World* (London: Hurst, 1968), 118–19. The conflict with Aden became quite hot in 1957 when Yemeni incursions across the frontier triggered a major British operation against Yemen. The heavy Soviet weapons saw almost no use in this conflict, partly because the imam forbade their use (though he had purchased them), recognizing the potential power they gave the military. See O'Ballance, *War in the Yemen*, 55–6. According to Marshall Goldman, *Soviet Foreign Aid* (New York: Praeger, 1967), 152, the planes were eventually scrapped and melted down to make license plates.

[8] *Pravda*, October 2 and 3, 1962.

visited Prague and then spent four days in Moscow (November 9–12). The delegation met with Marshal Rodion Malinovsky, the Minister of Defense, and other defense and foreign affairs officials.[9] Almost certainly this occasion marked the Republican's first personal plea for direct military assistance, something Moscow evidently saw fit to deny for the time being.

Throughout November and December, scores of Soviet advisers arrived in Yemen, and additional technical assistance agreements were signed. In June 1963, when it appeared that U.S. mediation had led to a Saudi-Egyptian agreement on mutual withdrawal, President Sallal embarked on a foreign tour, visiting several Arab capitals and East European countries, including the USSR. His goal was to ensure a supply of armaments and equipment to Sana in the event of an Egyptian withdrawal. He was not successful:

> Nasser insisted that all such material assistance be sent to the UAR for re-distribution, which meant in practice that the bulk was kept back by Egypt for its own use. Only a small proportion got through to the Yemenis, and this amount was regulated according to how the Yemenis responded to current Egyptian wishes.[10]

Fortunately for the Republican regime, the American mediation broke down, and Egypt remained entrenched in Yemen.

Less than a year later, Sallal was again forced to petition Moscow for aid. Following the Cairo summit meeting of January 1964 and the subsequent Royalist offensive (see Table 5.1), it appeared that Nasser's commitment to Sana was failing anew. In March, Sallal again traveled to the USSR, this time for a 15-day visit. He was given red-carpet treatment, meeting at least twice with Khrushchev and being accompanied for much of the trip by Leonid Brezhnev, who at that time was a member of the Politburo and Soviet head of state. One source suggests that Sallal was actually able to negotiate an agreement for direct arms shipments, but that the UAR objected to it.[11] He finally returned home with a renewal of the 1955 friendship treaty and two separate credit agreements, reportedly worth over $70 million, for several civilian construction projects.[12] About a month later, Nasser visited Yemen personally and decided to increase rather than reduce his military commitment there, once again saving the Republicans from certain defeat. In May 1964, Khrushchev visited the UAR

---

[9] *Pravda*, November 10 and 11, 1962.
[10] O'Ballance, *War in the Yemen*, 107.
[11] SIPRI, *The Arms Trade with the Third World*, 567. O'Ballance, *War in the Yemen*, 125, writes nothing of the UAR's objections, but does confirm that the Soviets offered direct shipments of Czech arms to Sallal during this visit. He notes that the agreement meant little in practice, because goods went first to Egypt, and "only a small proportion was allowed to trickle into the Yemen."
[12] *Pravda*, March 22 and 26, 1964; *Izvestia*, March 26, 1964.

for 16 days to attend the opening of the first stage of the Aswan Dam. Sallal joined Khrushchev and Nasser for a Red Sea cruise on Nasser's yacht. The situation in Yemen required extensive discussion, because Egypt was preparing to launch a major offensive against the Royalists. Sallal was apparently his usual overbearing self, for Nasser is reported to have told an exasperated Khrushchev, "I just wanted you to see what I have to put up with."[13] No doubt the visit strengthened the Soviet leader's conviction that Soviet arms were best placed in the control of Egypt, not the YAR.

The Haradh offensive in the summer of 1964 was the largest operation of the war, involving some 50,000 heavily armed Egyptian troops who systematically advanced on the mountain strongholds of the Royalists, capturing their headquarters and forcing the imam to flee. But in 1965 the Royalists launched a highly successful counter-offensive that retook almost all of the territory they had lost. Saudi Arabia cooperated closely with the Royalists, and it appeared that their victory would be assured unless Nasser were willing to commit further resources to Yemen's defense. Instead, he chose the path of negotiation, traveling to Jeddah to meet with King Faisal August 22–24. There they signed the Jeddah agreement, providing for a cease-fire, withdrawal of Egyptian troops, and termination of Saudi support to the Royalists. Both Nasser and Faisal undertook steps to ensure the success of the agreement, including convening a peace conference at Haradh (November 24 to December 24, 1965). The Haradh talks ultimately broke down, but Cairo decided to undertake a partial withdrawal anyway.

Immediately following this trip to Jeddah, Nasser flew to Moscow to confer with the Soviet leaders for five days. It seems likely that these talks centered on possible policy options in Yemen should Egypt withdraw or should the peace conference break down. The Republicans, however, were evidently not willing to depend on Nasser's commitment to their survival, nor did they trust his negotiating skills. Before the Jeddah meeting, but while the Royalist offensive was still in full swing, Hassan al-Amri, the new Republican president, met on August 7, 1965, with the Soviet chargé d'affaires in Sana to discuss the situation. "The Soviet envoy expressed his country's readiness to extend every aid to the Yemeni people."[14] On November 21, just prior to the Haradh peace talks, al-Amri met with the Soviet ambassador again to discuss "technical assistance."[15] It is possible that the Soviet

[13] Malcolm Kerr, *The Arab Cold War: Gamal 'Abd Al-Nasir and His Rivals, 1958–1970*, 3rd ed. (London: Oxford University Press, 1971), 112. This anecdote was related to Kerr by a Soviet journalist who was with Khrushchev's entourage in Cairo in May 1964. Sallal also visited the Soviet Union briefly in June 1964 en route to Peking.

[14] Sana Radio, August 7, 1965.

[15] Sana Radio, November 21, 1965. Hassan al-Amri represented the Republicans at this time, because Sallal was temporarily out of favor with the Egyptians and the Republican leadership. Sallal recovered his position in 1966, only to be deposed by a military coup in October 1967.

Union offered direct arms shipments during these meetings and that Nasser acquiesced during his Moscow visit. If so, this marked the beginning of the second stage of Soviet involvement. According to Royalist sources, Soviet arms began to arrive in Yemen by sea while the Haradh conference was still under way; if these sources can be trusted, this suggests that the USSR either did not expect or did not desire the conference's success.[16]

In May 1966, Alexei Kosygin, Chairman of the Council of Ministers of the USSR, visited Egypt for eight days. Hassan al-Amri was in Cairo at the time, but the Egyptians are said to have prevented him from meeting with Kosygin until an hour before the Soviet premier's departure. Kosygin himself is reported to have insisted on the meeting. The YAR president made the usual request for more arms deliveries, to which Kosygin wryly replied "that he had already sent enough to equip a Yemeni army of five million men."[17] Kosygin offered to equip a Yemeni army of 18,000 men with arms from East Germany, but Nasser firmly vetoed the proposal. Egypt's reservations about direct arms shipments to Sana no doubt reduced the flow of Soviet arms during this second stage below what it otherwise might have been.

The third and final stage of Soviet involvement in the Yemeni conflict began after the June war with Israel, when it became apparent that Nasser could not afford to keep his troops in Yemen much longer. During July and August, numerous high-level exchanges took place between Egypt and the USSR, and although the primary subject of these talks was no doubt Egypt's own security problems, the subject of Yemen must also have come up. At the Khartoum summit conference, August 29 to September 1, 1967, Faisal and Nasser reached an agreement on mutual disengagement from Yemen patterned after the Jeddah agreement of 1965. This time, Nasser began withdrawing his troops immediately, and by early December the Republican army faced the larger Royalist forces alone for the first time. By December 1 the Royalists succeeded in blocking the main roads to Sana, and a 70-day siege of the capital city began.

The Republicans had anticipated just such a development even before the Khartoum conference. Early in August, Abdullah Jizailan, deputy premier of the YAR, had been sent to Moscow, probably in order to persuade the Soviets that direct arms shipments were a necessity. A Soviet military delegation went to Yemen a few weeks later to assess the situation firsthand. It is not clear precisely when an agreement on direct arms shipments was reached, but MiG fighters began to arrive in mid-November. In the meantime, Sallal had been overthrown in a military coup on November 5 and replaced by Hassan al-Amri. The Kremlin hastened to note its approval of the new Yemeni

---

[16] *The Times* (London), January 13, 1966.
[17] Kerr, *The Arab Cold War*, 112–13. If Kosygin really said this, his claim was an obvious exaggeration, because the Soviet army itself did not have 5 million soldiers at the time. The entire population of Yemen was under that figure.

government, and relations proceeded with hardly a pause. A second Yemeni delegation visited Moscow from November 25 to December 2, "at the invitation of the Soviet government." This Yemeni delegation was headed by Foreign Minister Hassan Makki. It was met at the airport by Marshal Andrei Grechko, the new Soviet Minister of Defense, and other officials.[18] The delegation's subsequent meetings in Moscow most likely focused on the urgent military requirements of the regime in Sana, then facing almost overwhelming odds in the struggle against the Royalists. Perhaps the specific details of the Soviet airlift that ultimately saved Sana a few weeks later were also worked out at that time. One indication of the importance attached to the visit by the Soviet side was the fact that both Kosygin and Podgorny received the Yemeni delegation during its stay.

The last year during which the Royalists posed a tenable threat to the YAR was 1968. At least two Yemeni delegations visited Moscow that year, both of which met with Marshal Grechko for talks that almost certainly pertained to military questions. The first was headed by the Yemeni defense minister and arrived in mid-February, only four days after the siege of Sana had been broken; a Soviet military delegation visited Yemen eight weeks later to assess its defense requirements firsthand. The second YAR delegation, headed by the Yemeni premier, was in Moscow October 1–3 and was received by Kosygin as well as by Grechko.[19] It is likely that these meetings resulted in an additional arms agreement of modest size, though they may have concerned continuing assistance under the earlier agreements.[20]

Throughout the three stages of the Soviet Union's involvement in the Yemeni civil war the regime in Sana felt repeatedly constrained by pressing exigencies of survival to petition the Kremlin for military assistance, despite the fact that such petitions often had to be made over the objections of another ally, Egypt. The diplomatic relationship that developed between the USSR and the YAR under these circumstances was characterized by a recurrent pattern: Whenever negotiations pertaining to the civil war opened between Saudia Arabia and Egypt, a Republican delegation would usually be sent to

[18] *Pravda*, August 8, 1967; *Pravda*, November 6, 7, and 11, 1967; *Pravda*, November 25, 1967. SIPRI, *The Arms Trade with the Third World*, 568, claims that a Soviet-Yemeni arms agreement was signed November 16, 1967, just two days before the first known shipment of MiG fighters to Sana. This seems unlikely, however, because no known high-level exchange took place on that date.

[19] *Pravda*, February 13, 1968; Central Intelligence Agency, *Appearances of Soviet Leaders, January–December 1968* (Washington: CIA, 1969); *Mizan* 10(March/April 1968):77.

[20] The arms that were shipped to the Republicans during the siege of Sana were not the last they received from the Soviets. Additional arms agreements, probably mostly for small arms, were reported to have been negotiated in August 1968 and sometime in 1969. The fact of Soviet "material support" having been rendered to the YAR during the civil war is admitted, without any details being offered, in E. K. Golubovskaya, *Revolyutsia 1962g. v Iyemene* (Moscow: Nauka, 1971), 179.

Moscow to appeal for direct military aid as a substitute for an anticipated loss of Egyptian support. This pattern arose from the reality
that any reconciliation between Riyadh and Cairo would necessitate
an Egyptian withdrawal, and that in turn would pose a grave threat
to the survival of the YAR. Sana's acute dependence on Soviet largess,
however, did not give the USSR more than modest leverage over the
young regime, because the Soviet commitment to the YAR arose not
so much from the bilateral relationship involved but from the larger
regional context of the civil war and particularly from Moscow's all-
important relationship with Nasser. The Soviet-Yemeni relationship
during the war was a classic instance of a small client state deriving
considerable advantage from a great power mentor, even while maintaining a considerable measure of independence vis-à-vis that mentor,
because of the great power's preoccupation with a larger strategic
context.

Weapons shipments and other military aid

It is difficult to assess the level of the USSR's military involvement
in Yemen prior to December 1967. Undoubtedly, thousands of Soviet
small arms and ammunition flowed to the Yemeni army via Cairo, but
such transfers cannot be traced or even estimated accurately. Egypt
apparently transferred none of its own heavy Soviet weapons to the
YAR, but the Egyptian expeditionary force itself was very dependent
on Soviet arms, and it is believed that Moscow essentially underwrote
Cairo's intervention. Jacob C. Hurewitz cited one estimate that the
USSR cancelled $460 million of Cairo's indebtedness early in 1966 to
compensate for the high cost of Egypt's participation in the war.[21]
The debt cancellation was probably intended to bolster Egypt's support of Sana, which was faltering in the aftermath of the Haradh
conference; it occurred at the same time that small shipments of
Soviet arms first began going directly to the YAR.

Little information is available about the quantity of Soviet weapons that flowed into Egypt between 1962 and 1967 as a result of the
war in Yemen. According to *New York Times* correspondent Dana
Schmidt:

> In 1963 and 1964 the Egyptians had five squadrons of aircraft
> at airfields near Sana and Hodeidah. They were using Yakovlev
> 11 piston-engined fighters, MiG 16 [sic] and 17 jet fighters, Il-

---

[21] Jacob C. Hurewitz, *Middle East Politics: The Military Dimension* (New York: Praeger, 1969), 259. Despite the subsidy, the cost to Cairo of participating in the war
must have been very great. The costs of maintaining the expeditionary force are
variously estimated to have ranged from $350,000 to over $1 million per day. Even
if the lower estimate is taken as an average, the total cost to Egypt from October
1962 to December 1967 would have been approximately $660 million, $200 million
more than Moscow's subsidy. Egyptian casualties were also high, averaging 24
fatalities per day between October 1962 and June 1964 (over 15,000 total).

yushin 28 twin-engined bombers, Ilyushin 14 twin-engined transports and Mi-14 transport helicopters. In addition they were flying four-engined Tupolev bombers from bases in Egypt, such as Aswan.[22]

Egypt had received most of these weapons from the Russians before the Yemeni conflict began, but some of the Tu-16 bombers arrived in Egypt during 1962 and may have been sent with the conflict in mind. Fifty MiG-21C fighters were shipped to Egypt during 1963–4, and though they were not used in Yemen, they may have freed MiG-15 and MiG-17 planes for combat. Approximately 150 T-54/55 Soviet tanks were also delivered to Egypt in 1964. This marked increase in Soviet arms deliveries to Cairo coincided with the most prolonged period of intensive combat during the entire civil war. Forty thousand Egyptian troops were in Yemen by 1964, and at least some of the new arms were probably intended for their use. Soviet-supplied tanks, armored personnel carriers, and heavy artillery guns played a decisive role in the Haradh offensive. Likewise, early in 1965, when the Royalists were preparing a major counteroffensive, shipments of weaponry from Egypt to Yemen were stepped up considerably.

Despite repeated denials from Cairo, there is also considerable evidence that Egypt employed poison-gas bombs during several air raids over Yemen and Saudi Arabia.[23] These gas bombings, which were fatal to hundreds of villagers, first took place during 1963 and were resumed during 1966–7. Soviet-supplied bombers undertook the raids, and it is possible that Moscow provided the poison-gas weapons also. If so, the USSR may have allowed Egypt to use the weapons in order to test their effectiveness in combat; otherwise it is puzzling why they would have been used, because their military value in the Yemen was not substantially greater than that of conventional bombs.

Perhaps because of Nasser's objections, the direct shipments of Soviet and Czechoslovak weapons to the YAR that began late in 1965 were modest in volume and consisted largely of small arms. Royalist sources reported that two shiploads of Soviet arms arrived in late December; one month later, 22 Soviet transport planes carried weapons and ammunition to Sana and Hodeida.[24] It is not known how much equipment the USSR supplied to the Republican army during this period, although Kosygin's much-inflated claim to al-Amri of having sent the YAR enough arms to equip an army of 5 million does suggest that more than token deliveries were made. Direct Soviet shipments

---

[22] Dana Adams Schmidt, *Yemen: The Unknown War* (London: The Bodley Head, 1968), 168.

[23] The evidence is summarized in Schmidt, *Yemen: The Unknown War*, 257–73. *Izvestia*, December 19, 1967, called the reports of gas bombings a "fabrication." Desmond Stewart "Whose Poison Gas?" *The Spectator* (July 12, 1963):73–4, argues that Egypt may have made the bombs itself.

[24] *The Times* (London), January 13 and February 21, 1966.

Table 5.2. *Register of estimated Soviet arms deliveries to Republican government in Sana, November 1967 to end of 1969*

Type of weapon	Estimated quantity delivered
MiG-17 fighters[a]	12
An-2 transport planes	2
Il-28 bombers	12
T-34 combat tanks	50–75
P-4 patrol boats	5
Bombs, 120-mm mortars, and ammunition	?
Small arms (especially 7.62-mm Kalashnikov rifles)	?
Spare parts and replacement components for tanks and aircraft	?
Armored personnel carriers (BTR-40 and BTR-152)	70
SU-100 self-propelled guns	50
76-mm guns	Some
122-mm guns	Some
Light antiaircraft guns	Some

[a]Some sources list MiG-19s instead of MiG-17s. The *Military Balance 1969–70* states that an agreement for MiG-21 deliveries was signed in 1969, but no other source confirms this.

Sources: SIPRI, *Arms Trade Registers*, 67; SIPRI, *The Arms Trade with the Third World*, 568; *Military Balance 1967–68*, 58; Joshua and Gibert, *Arms for the Third World*, 27; Michael L. Squires and Ann R. Patterson, "Soviet Naval Transfers to Developing Countries," in MccGwire and McDonnell, eds., *Soviet Naval Influence*, 537; Richard R. Nyrop, *Area Handbook for the Yemens*, 1st ed. (Washington: USGPO, 1977), 229–30.

declined during the year beginning October 1966, when Egypt increased its own commitment once more.

In late 1967, when the Soviet Union replaced Egypt as the first-line arms supplier of the beleaguered YAR, it rapidly transferred several thousand tons of modern weapons to the Sana regime. Table 5.2 is a register of estimated arms shipments during the two-year period beginning November 1967. The actual deliveries were probably somewhat higher than indicated. The weapons began arriving during the final withdrawal of Egyptian forces in November and December 1967, when Sana was besieged by a full-scale Royalist offensive that completely cut the city off from outside ground traffic and that most observers expected would easily capture Sana. Edgar O'Ballance claimed that Brezhnev even postponed a planned visit to Cairo in January 1968 "because he did not wish to be in the UAR when (as was then hourly expected) Sana fell to the Royalists."[25]

[25]O'Ballance, *War in the Yemen*, 197.

The first consignment of Soviet weapons is believed to have arrived by air on November 18, 1967, shortly before the ring around the city was closed.[26] Additional shipments arrived by air during the siege, and some seaborne shipments, principally tanks, were received at Hodeida. It was from Hodeida that a Soviet-armed relief column set out in January 1968 to break the cordon around the city on February 8. Additional tanks were delivered by sea to Hodeida in February, around the time that Saudi Arabia, concerned about the growing Soviet presence, decided to renew its own support of the Royalists. Finally, in August 1968, when a new Royalist offensive was anticipated, Soviet transport planes airlifted "large quantities of small arms, mortars, artillery, tanks and components for fighter and bomber aircraft" to Sana.[27]

In addition to providing military assistance, the USSR undertook an extensive economic aid program, some projects of which were of limited military value. The foremost example was the airfield at Al-Rawda, north of Sana, completed with Soviet help in September 1963. The only international-class airport in the country, its 11,500-foot runway was capable of handling four-engine jet aircraft.[28] It provided a crucial transportation link and an indigenous base for bombing missions against the Royalists. Another Soviet project of potential military significance was a road built between Hodeida and Taiz; however, it was not completed until 1969, when the civil war was already cooling down. Special Soviet assistance is said to have been granted in August 1966 when the authorities in Aden cut off fuel shipments to Sana in retaliation for an alleged raid by Egyptian planes. "On the request of the Yemen government, the Soviet Union quickly began supplying fuel, and at drastically cut prices."[29] Outside the realm of economic support, a small Soviet naval task force visited Hodeida in January 1969, a militarily insignificant but politically valuable show of support for the Republicans.[30]

In analyzing the mix of weapons sent to the YAR, notice should be taken of Yemen's very limited capacity to utilize large amounts of

---

[26] SIPRI, *The Arms Trade with the Third World*, 568; *New York Times*, November 23, 1967. In the latter source, correspondent Thomas F. Brady and a Reuter's colleague both saw partly assembled MiG planes at the Sana airport on November 20, just as they were being expelled from Yemen. They also observed a "big-bellied Antonov transport" that apparently had carried in the MiGs.

[27] SIPRI, *The Arms Trade with the Third World*, 568.

[28] Correspondence: Manfred W. Wenner; Goldman, *Soviet Foreign Aid*, 152. During the siege of Sana, a heavy Royalist bombardment made this airfield useless, but airlift shipments were still possible using a smaller airstrip southwest of the city.

[29] Stephen Page, *The USSR and Arabia* (London: Central Asian Research Centre, 1971), 89.

[30] Michael MccGwire, "The Pattern of Soviet Naval Deployment in the Indian Ocean, 1968–71," *Soviet Naval Developments: Capability and Context*, 433.

modern military equipment.[31] This accounts for the relatively modest sizes of the shipments. There is no indication that the Egyptian expeditionary force, for its part, ever suffered from a shortage of weaponry, and it is doubtful the Yemeni Republican army could have handled many more planes or tanks than it received following Cairo's withdrawal. Moscow's failure to supply more sophisticated weaponry was likely a consequence of the generally low technical level of fighting feasible for both the Republicans and the Royalists, not a sign of uncertainty or partial commitment on the part of the Kremlin. The volume and mix of Soviet shipments proved adequate to the task of saving the YAR. During the siege of Sana, the superior firepower and control of the air that the weapons gave the Republicans enabled them to defend the open plain between the city and the superior Royalist forces in the surrounding hills. The Yemeni civil war, in fact, is one case in which Soviet arms shipments reversed a local balance of power and achieved a decisive political outcome in a Third World conflict.

Participation by Soviet and East European advisers

Soviet and East European personnel played a modest role in aiding the Republican regime during the civil war. Hostilities had scarcely begun when Soviet advisers began to arrive in Yemen in November 1962, joining a number of advisers already there in connection with economic assistance projects initiated under the imam. Harold Ingrams estimates that about 400 Russian technicians and advisers entered Yemen in November. In the course of the civil war, Soviet advisers directed the port at Hodeida, supervised the main Republican ammunition depots, directed several construction projects, taught schools, and provided medical care. Five hundred Soviet technicians assisted in the construction of the Al-Rawda airfield near Sana, completed in September 1963.[32] Schmidt estimated that there were about 700 Soviets in Yemen in March 1967, more than half of them military, and that their numbers increased greatly later:

> At Hodeidah the Soviet impact could readily be felt. Many Yemenis were learning Russian, Russian and East European goods were in shops, and Russians and East Europeans walked in the streets.[33]

[31] Les Aspin, U.S. representative from Wisconsin, commented on this in 1979 when the United States decided to send large amounts of sophisticated weapons to Sana to aid it against a Soviet-backed attack by South Yemen: "We are delivering $540 million in sophisticated weaponry to an army with fewer than 1,000 soldiers who can read or write." *New York Times*, March 20, 1979.

[32] Harold Ingrams, *The Yemen: Imams, Rulers, and Revolutions* (New York: Praeger, 1963), 136; *New York Times*, July 30, 1963.

[33] Schmidt, *Yemen: The Unknown War*, 289–90; Macro, *Yemen and the Western World*, 131, also puts the figure at 1,000 prior to 1967.

The Soviets maintained active military training programs at Sana and Taiz, and it is likely that some technical personnel stationed with various construction projects were also involved in the maintenance of military equipment.

Even more significant than the extensive involvement of Soviet personnel as technical advisers and military instructors were the instances of Soviets and Czechoslovaks assisting in military transport, tactical planning, and actual combat. Schmidt noted that the Tupolev bombers used in strategic bombing missions were "thought to have mixed Egyptian and Russian personnel," and he stated flatly that "the Ilyushin transports flying between Egypt and Hodeidah did have Russian crews."[34] Unfortunately, he gave no source for this information. Following the first direct shipments of Soviet and Czechoslovak arms to Sana late in 1965, a group of 12 Czechoslovak experts on guerrilla warfare was sent to assist the Republicans.[35] The relief column that moved from Hodeida toward Sana to break the Royalist siege in February 1968 was at least partially planned and supported by Soviet advisers.

In August 1967, Prince Hassan al-Hussein, a Royalist commander, charged that Russians wearing Egyptian uniforms were in Yemen manning artillery. He claimed that several Soviets had been killed.[36] In early December, when the siege of Sana was beginning, the Royalists claimed to have shot down a red-headed Russian air force captain flying a MiG-17 and possessing instructions from the Soviet Ministry of Defense.[37] The U.S. Department of State reported that the claim appeared to be "substantially correct," although the YAR and the USSR promptly denied it. According to some reports, the Soviet pilots were quickly replaced with Syrian and other Arab pilots, including some Yemeni pilots who had been training in the Soviet Union.[38]

One aim of the Soviet advisers may have been to discourage attempts at negotiation that might have led to a settlement with the Royalists; a settlement could only have reduced Republican dependence on the USSR (which is indeed what took place after the war ended). Early in 1966, when the Jeddah agreement was on the verge of falling apart, *The Times* reported that Soviet advisers in Yemen were urging the regime not to compromise with the Royalists.[39] Again,

---

[34] Schmidt, *Yemen: The Unknown War*, 168–9.
[35] *The Times* (London), January 26, 1966, citing "intelligence sources." The experts were said to have arrived January 12, 1966.
[36] *International Herald Tribune*, August 3, 1967.
[37] *New York Times*, December 13, 1967. American officials reported on December 12 that a Russian had been shot down. Royalists and European mercenaries, some of whom knew Russian, claimed to have found the documents and Russian maps on his person. The pilot was killed when the plane crashed.
[38] *Washington Post*, February 22, 1968; Schmidt, *Yemen: The Unknown War*, 296; O'Ballance, *War in the Yemen*, 191.
[39] *The Times* (London), January 26, 1966.

in February 1970, when the Royalists captured Sada in their last attack of the war:

> Soviet advisers in Sana urged the regime to act forcibly; this advice was rejected in favor of negotiations because it was felt that such a policy would lead to a breakdown in developing relations with Saudi Arabia and to deeper dependence on the Soviet Union.[40]

Evidently the advisers were not in Yemen simply to provide "disinterested support." Rather, they acted fully cognizant of the larger political aims of the Soviet Union.

Soviet-American interactions

Given the strategic location of Yemen and the extent of Soviet involvement in the country both before and after the 1962 coup, U.S. involvement in the Yemeni civil war was remarkably restrained. Although the Soviet press continually asserted that the United States was the prime mover behind the Saudi intervention, there was little evidence to bear this out. In fact, it is fair to say that at the time of the coup the United States had virtually no permanent or valuable interests in Yemen proper and little immediate concern about who ruled its primitive tribes and villages. Washington's primary concern was that the war not widen into a Saudi-Egyptian conflict that might threaten the stability of Saudi Arabia and Jordan and the security of the petroleum fields of the Middle East. Government officials also voiced some concern about the future of Bab el-Mandeb and who would control it.[41]

The United States recognized the YAR on December 19, 1962; the Kennedy administration took the step in the context of a multilateral negotiation with Egypt, Saudi Arabia, and Jordan intended to enable Nasser to withdraw his forces if the Saudis agreed to cease aid to the Royalists. The USSR branded the American recognition a "change of tactics" and declared that it represented no change in the basic U.S. strategy of supporting the monarchists in order to defend the oil monopolies in Saudi Arabia.[42] However, the U.S. recognition failed to achieve the administration's goal of encouraging Egypt and Saudi Arabia to withdraw from the conflict. A second effort was made in the spring of 1963, when Kennedy sent Ambassador Ellsworth Bunker to the Middle East as a special presidential emissary to mediate a disengagement agreement between the Saudi and Egyptian leaders. The United States also prodded the UN into sending its own emissary, Ralph Bunche, the UN undersecretary for special political affairs.

[40] Page, *The USSR and Arabia*, 110.
[41] Correspondence: Manfred W. Wenner.
[42] *Pravda*, December 22, 1962.

Bunche was able to win an agreement from Nasser and Faisal on mutual withdrawal, which eventually led to a UN Yemen Observation Mission (UNYOM) being formed and sent to Yemen in July 1963 to oversee a withdrawal that did not take place. The USSR opposed the mission but abstained when the proposal came to a vote in the Security Council. For a number of reasons the agreement broke down; the UNYOM accomplished little, and it was terminated in September 1964.

From the time this UN initiative failed until the effective end of the civil war – a time roughly corresponding to the Johnson administration – U.S. involvement in the Yemeni conflict was minimal.[43] American foreign policy was preoccupied with Vietnam; little attention could be devoted to an obscure and stalemated war in a tiny Middle East country. The State Department confined itself to issuing occasional statements deploring the Egyptian attacks on Saudi villages, and American policy remained unchanged in favor of withdrawal by all outside powers. When the Soviet involvement increased in December 1967 and reports of Russian pilots flying combat missions were received, the State Department confirmed the reports and condemned the intervention as "only likely to increase tension in the region."[44] There is no public record of any diplomatic contacts between Washington and Moscow pertaining to the conflict.

The China factor

The Yemeni civil war offers an interesting example of Sino-Soviet competition for influence with a newly-established nationalist regime. Charles McLane observed that "Yemen was one of the few states in the Middle East where Chinese activity posed a persistent problem to the Russians in the 1960s.... If Peking sought its 'Albania' in the Arab world, Yemen for some years was a leading candidate."[45] China's ties with Yemen had been established prior to the revolution, when Sana and Peking agreed to open relations in August of 1956. Chinese missions opened at Sana and at Taiz the following year, and in January 1958 the imam signed a treaty of friendship with Peking. In February an agreement on trade and economic aid was negotiated, and by the end of 1958 approximately 1,000 Chinese were in Yemen, most of them at work on a hard-top road between Hodeida and Sana.

---

[43] In 1965, an American-built road between Sana, Taiz, and Mocha was completed, and in 1966 the John F. Kennedy memorial water system was installed in Taiz, the first truly functional water-pipe system in Yemen. The costs of these projects totaled $31 million.

[44] Schmidt, *Yemen: The Unknown War*, 296.

[45] Charles B. McLane, *Soviet–Third World Relations*, vol. 2, (London: Central Asian Research Centre, 1973), 112. McLane adds: "The magnitude of the Chinese threat to Soviet policies, however, should not be exaggerated. Chinese aid and technical assistance were small compared to Russian and trade remained negligible."

After Crown Prince Muhammad al-Badr visited the Soviet Union in January 1958, he also visited Peking, where Yemen was offered unequivocal support for its territorial claims on Aden. By the time of the Yemeni revolution, the Sino-Soviet split had emerged into the open, and China and the Soviet Union found themselves competing for influence with the leaders of the YAR. The USSR's superior resources and geographical proximity, as well as its vastly greater influence with Nasser, gave it the edge in this competition, though the presence of China was evident throughout the civil war and must have been an important factor in Soviet policymaking.

In June 1964, two months after Sallal's visit to the USSR and the renewal of the Yemeni-Soviet friendship treaty, the YAR president traveled to Peking, where on June 9 he signed a 10-year friendship treaty. Agreements on technical and cultural cooperation were also signed. By the middle of the decade, Chinese aid projects totaled over $40 million. They included a large educational center and a modern textile mill in Sana, a highway from Sana to Sada, and a coastal road in the south. Unlike most Soviet aid, China's economic assistance circumvented Nasser's control. China is not known to have transferred any heavy weapons to the Republican regime during the conflict; Royalist sources claimed that some 50,000 Chinese automatic weapons were delivered by ship to the YAR during the Haradh conference, but this cannot be confirmed.[46] Because China and the USSR both supported the Sana government, their efforts to ensure its survival sometimes created the illusion of Sino-Soviet cooperation. For example, during the siege of Sana, the Soviet-armed relief force from Hodeida, apparently conceived and planned by the Russians, "was accompanied by Chinese personnel, who repaired the road as it moved forward and erected a vital bridge near the capital which allowed the armor to cross a ravine and take part in the fighting outside the city."[47] Each side tried to outbid the other in showing its support for the Republican cause. Peking, for example, maintained its diplomatic mission in Sana during the siege, when all other foreign delegations, including the Soviet, had evacuated to Hodeida. As the war progressed, severe tensions are said to have developed between the Chinese and Soviet communities in Yemen.[48]

Had the USSR concluded that the YAR was on the verge of becoming an Arabian Albania, it conceivably could have withdrawn all military aid from the Republicans, almost certainly bringing to pass the regime's collapse. That Moscow did not do so is evidence that it had the upper hand, or at least believed it did, throughout the war. There is no reason to believe that the USSR was involved in the Yemeni

[46] *The Times* (London), January 13, 1966.
[47] O'Ballance, *War in the Yemen*, p. 197.
[48] John Barron, *KGB: The Secret Work of Soviet Secret Agents* (New York: Reader's Digest Press, 1974), 31.

conflict principally to counter the influence of China, but China's presence seems to have been a stimulus to Soviet action and a factor in the Kremlin's policymaking.

The outcome

The war in Yemen was perhaps the only conflict in the Third World during the 1960s in which Soviet arms shipments transformed certain defeat into a definite, if not total, victory for the USSR's client. The Soviet Union's arms shipments to the YAR during the siege of Sana decisively altered the local balance of forces, helped convince Saudi Arabia that the Royalists could not win the war, and laid the foundation for an eventual political settlement on terms highly favorable to the Republicans. Furthermore, by stepping in to rescue the YAR after Nasser withdrew the Egyptian expeditionary force, the USSR strengthened its reputation in the Middle East as a reliable and powerful ally. This perception may have been of long-term value to the Soviet Union's position in the region, but it did little to establish for Moscow a relationship of enduring influence with the Yemeni regime itself.

The YAR began taking steps to reduce its dependence on the Soviet Union even before the war had ended. In July 1969 it resumed diplomatic relations with Bonn at a time when most Arab countries recognized only East Germany. The Kremlin attempted, unsuccessfully, to forestall the action by threatening to cut off arms and assistance and by hinting to the Republicans that in the future, equipment and spare parts would be available only through East Germany. In 1970, France, Britain, and the United States recognized, or reestablished relations with, the YAR, which began to manifest pronounced pro-Western leanings in its foreign policy. In the meantime, Moscow began to turn its attention to South Yemen, where the British withdrawal in August 1967 had led to the establishment of the People's Democratic Republic of Yemen (PDRY), perhaps the most radical regime in the Middle East and a more promising prospect than Yemen for fulfilling the Soviet Union's long-term ambitions on the Arabian peninsula.

Soviet appraisals of the YAR nonetheless remained generally positive as late as 1971, but in the latter part of that year, negotiations on a new arms deal apparently broke down.[49] Sana also became concerned about the USSR's increasingly close ties with the PDRY when Soviet-Yemeni relations worsened further in consequence of a border clash between Sana and Aden in 1972. From then until the end of the decade, Soviet-YAR relations oscillated up and down, but Moscow

[49] L. N. Kotlov, *Iemenskaya Arabskaya Respublika (Spravochnik)* (Moscow: Nauka, 1971), 214–17; Nimrod Novik, *On the Shores of Bab Al-Mandab: Soviet Diplomacy and Regional Dynamics* (Philadelphia: Foreign Policy Research Institute, 1979), 5–6.

was never able to maintain influence in Sana for long because of its close ties with the PDRY. Riyadh and Moscow both supported the growing movement for unification of the two Yemens, but each sought to ensure that the eventual political settlement would be favorable to its own interests. Saudi-Soviet competition over the future of the two Yemens was a constant theme during the decade. The Soviet Union offered Yemen arms in 1975, only to have its advisers expelled from the country the following year. In May 1978, President al-Ghashmi of Yemen was killed by a bomb planted in the briefcase of a messenger from the PDRY; it turned out that the bomb had been planted by the pro-Soviet faction of the South Yemeni regime, the UPONF. That faction used the incident to dispose of President Rubayyi and establish its own firm control in South Yemen; Soviet complicity in the whole affair was widely suspected. In March 1979, South Yemen attacked Yemen, triggering a brief conflict that saw the United States transfer some $400 million of arms to Yemen to counter Soviet and Cuban support being given to the PDRY; Sana nevertheless continued to accept some arms transfers from Moscow. The Soviet invasion of Afghanistan at the end of that year served to cut short a growing Soviet-Yemeni rapprochement when Saudi Arabia succeeded in convincing the Yemeni leaders to curtail, though not break, their military relationship with Moscow in response to the invasion.

Over the long run, the USSR's involvement in the Yemeni civil war yielded it few enduring political advantages, despite the high cost of its military commitment. The Kremlin's unremitting determination to establish a foothold on the Arabian peninsula made it possible for the YAR to influence and manipulate its powerful mentor to a degree far surpassing its relative power vis-à-vis that mentor. The tenacity of the USSR's effort during the civil war says something about the value the Soviet leaders attached to achieving certain broader strategic aims in a crucial region of the world.

6
THE NIGERIAN CIVIL WAR

Another power which is supporting the Federal Government in a very substantial way is, of course, the Soviet Union...her motivations are similar to those which propelled the colonial aspirations of Bismarck's Germany in the last century – *to have a place in the sun.*

Raph Uwechue, *Reflections on the Nigerian Civil War*

The Soviet Union's involvement in the Nigerian civil war began in the late summer of 1967. In many ways it was not a propitious time for the USSR to get involved in another local war. The preceding June, Soviet arms had suffered a devastating defeat in the six-day war, and a massive commitment of military aid to the Arabs was required in order to salvage the Soviet Union's prestige and position in the Middle East. Nasser's impending withdrawal from Yemen meant that Moscow would also be forced to increase its military commitment there if the YAR was to be saved. Nigeria's military regime did not appear to offer particularly great promise as a Soviet client, and meeting its weapons requirements would mean the diverting of resources from the priority struggle for influence in the Arab world. The Kremlin went ahead, nonetheless, deterred neither by the prospect of overcommitment nor by sobering memories of its Congo fiasco and other Soviet setbacks in Africa – in Guinea, Ghana, and Mali. Perhaps the Kremlin leaders felt that demonstrations of Soviet largess and capabilities were badly needed and that the Nigerian civil war offered safe and certain victory, given Britain's pro-Federal position, U.S. neutrality, and the Federal army's quantitative superiority over the Biafran forces. Perhaps the opportunity of penetrating previously aloof Nigeria was too tempting to pass up. Whatever the rationale, the Kremlin's support for Lagos proved to be a highly successful vindication of the pragmatic diplomacy of Brezhnev and Kosygin – the USSR greatly strengthened its ties with Africa's largest nation, nudged Nigeria toward a foreign policy of nonalignment, and won widespread favor in Africa. The new leadership's willingness to back a conservative military regime was one signal of the end of Khrushchev's foreign policy and the dawn of a more calculated *Realpolitik* in the Soviet Union's foreign affairs.

The war began on May 30, 1967, when Lieutenant Colonel Emeka Ojukwu, the 33-year-old military governor of eastern Nigeria, announced that eastern Nigeria was seceding from the Federal Republic of Nigeria to become independent "Biafra." The secession was the culmination of a long period of internal strife and disunity in Nigeria. Following Ojukwu's declaration, the head of state of the Federal military government (FMG), Lieutenant Colonel Yakubu Gowon, publicly stated his "irrevocable decision to crush Ojukwu's rebellion in order to reunite Nigerians resident in the three Eastern States with their brothers and sisters in other parts of Nigeria."[1] Hostilities began on July 6, when the Federal army began a four-front offensive against Biafra.

Despite widespread expectations that the war would end quickly, it lasted for two and a half years, becoming "the biggest, best-weaponed, and bloodiest war in the whole history of Black Africa."[2] By the time Biafra surrendered early in 1970, perhaps a million people had perished as a result of the conflict, most of them from starvation.[3] The conflict consisted of a series of Federal offensives against Biafra, combined with an ever-tightening land and sea blockade. No single Federal attack gained much ground against the smaller but well-commanded and highly motivated Biafran forces,[4] but the cumulative effect of several offensives reduced Biafra from an initial 30,000 square miles with a population of 14 million to under 3,000 square miles and roughly 3 million inhabitants by the end of the conflict. Early in the war Biafra was able to undertake a few offensives of its own, even capturing a portion of the midwest region in August 1967, but as the fighting progressed, the Ibos were forced to devote most of their resources to keeping their shrinking enclave intact. Federal troops captured Port Harcourt in May 1968, cutting Biafra's last direct link with the outside world and compelling it to rely on dangerous night flights for arms and food supplies. The final Federal offensive began mid-November 1969; by early January it became a rout. Biafran resistance collapsed, as starvation, lack of certain supplies (though not of arms), and a sudden loss of will made further fighting impossible. Ojukwu fled Biafra two days before the last surviving airfield at Uli was captured. His successor, Major General Philip Effiong, formally surrendered to Gowon on January 15, 1970.

The war elicited a unique international alignment. Great Britain and the Soviet Union were the foremost diplomatic supporters of the Federal government, while France, Spain, Portugal, South Africa, Israel, and the People's Republic of China offered various degrees of support, though not diplomatic recognition, to Biafra. The United States remained technically neutral throughout the conflict, though it supported mediation and relief efforts to Biafra, and many American leaders sympathized with the fledgling

---

[1] Federal Ministry of Information press release No. 1295/1967, in A. H. M. Kirk-Greene, *Crisis and Conflict in Nigeria: A Documentary Sourcebook 1966–1969*, vol. 1 (London: Oxford University Press, 1971), 453–4.

[2] Kirk-Greene, "Epilogue," *Crisis and Conflict*, vol. 2, 462.

[3] Estimates of the war's toll vary widely, because neither side kept accurate records or published official figures. Estimates range from 0.5 million to 3 million. The figure given is an average of more conservative sources.

[4] *Strategic Survey* (1969):69.

republic. When the eastern region first seceded, no African nation extended recognition, but in April 1968 Tanzania became the first foreign power to do so, followed shortly by Gabon, the Ivory Coast, and Zambia. The Organization of African Unity (OAU) came down on the side of the Federal government, reflecting the vested interest of its members in preserving the existing borders in Africa. The OAU, Britain, and other outside powers made numerous attempts to resolve the conflict through negotiation, but though numerous peace conferences were held, every one eventually broke down.

Despite repeated statements by British officials that London was providing only 15 percent of Federal Nigeria's war materials, every evidence indicates that London actually provided a much higher percentage and was by a large margin the principal arms supplier to Lagos.[5] Britain refused, however, to provide the FMG with certain offensive weapons, such as fighter planes and bombers. In order to appease the demands of his own officers for creation of a strategic air force, and in order to pressure London into being more forthcoming, Gowon turned to the Soviet Union for assistance. An arms agreement was worked out early in the war, and in August 1967 the first Soviet weapons, including several MiG fighters, arrived at Lagos by sea and by air. Nearly three dozen additional aircraft were sent to Lagos in the fall of 1968, including a few Ilyushin bombers. The Soviet planes gave the FMG tactical control of the air and also enabled it to undertake numerous strategic bombing missions, killing hundreds of Biafran civilians. Late in the war, when several months of fighting had failed to take Biafra's small enclave, Moscow transferred additional weapons to Lagos, including bombers and heavy artillery guns.

The USSR's involvement in the civil war marked an important turning point in Soviet policy toward black Africa, the beginning of a more pragmatic and calculated approach to winning influence in the sub-Saharan region.[6] Neither Marxist ideology nor the USSR's previous African policy gave grounds to suppose that the Kremlin would assist a conservative, pro-Western military government against the more progressive Ibo state, yet the shift in policy proved to be strategic and sensible for at least four reasons. First, by filling a crucial gap in Nigeria's military inventory, the USSR was able to expand its influence in a nation previously cool to its overtures; second, by demonstrating its willingness to take the "correct"

---

[5] Nigeria's official *Trade Summary* recorded that Britain's share of arms imports was 47.84% in 1967, 79.19% in 1968, and 97.36% in 1969. The figures do not include Soviet imports, which are estimated as worth only a small fraction of the value of British arms shipments (perhaps 3–5%). For more on the controversy, see Suzanne Cronje, *The World and Nigeria: The Diplomatic History of the Biafran War, 1967–1970* (London: Sidgwick & Jackson, 1972), 54–8, 385–93; Zdenek Cervenka, *A History of the Nigerian War, 1967–1970* (Ibadan: Onibonoje Press, 1972), 93–8, 131–2.

[6] The significance of the war as a turning point in Moscow's African policy is elaborated in Robert Legvold, *Soviet Policy in West Africa* (Cambridge: Harvard University Press, 1970), 311–30; Arthur J. Klinghoffer, "The USSR and Nigeria: The Secession Question," *Mizan* (March/April 1968):64, 69–70; Angela Stent, "The Soviet Union and the Nigerian Civil War: A Triumph of Realism," *Issue* 3 (Summer 1973):43–48.

position on African issues, the Kremlin's support of the FMG favorably impressed the majority of OAU-affiliated nations; third, the policy shift undercut Western interests by demonstrating to Lagos the advantages of a nonaligned foreign policy; fourth, even if Biafra had won the right to secede, Nigeria would have remained the largest and most important African state, so the Soviet effort would not have been wasted.

The USSR's small investment yielded it substantial returns. During the course of the war, Soviet ties with Nigeria in every area – diplomacy, culture, trade, economic assistance, and military cooperation – multiplied dramatically, reversing the trend toward diminished Soviet influence in West Africa that was evident in the years just before the war. Although Britain's support of Lagos and America's neutrality made it politically feasible for Gowon's government to lessen its dependence on the USSR soon after the war ended, Nigeria kept open the channel to Moscow and never returned wholly to a pro-Western alignment.

The local dispute

The Nigerian civil war was a classic case of the problems bequeathed to the Third World by irrational colonial borders, a fact not overlooked by Soviet commentators.[7] When Nigeria became independent in October 1960, it was a federation of three regions, each with a distinct ethnic composition: a northern region controlled by the Hausa-Fulani, a western region where the Yorubas were a majority, and the eastern region, homeland of the Ibos. The federation's constitution provided for considerable regional autonomy, but the northern region dominated national politics, partly because of its larger size and population, partly because colonial policies had favored it. The other regions resented its domination.

In addition to these ethnic divisions, the northern and southern halves of the country were divided along religious and economic lines. The north was primarily Moslem and agrarian, whereas the south was more industrial and predominantly Christian. The northern region was decidedly the most backward of the three, containing less than 17 percent of Nigeria's primary schools but half its population. The Ibos, on the other hand, colloquially known as "the Jews of Africa," had one of the highest literacy rates on the continent, and over one-third of the nation's primary schools, with only 25 percent of the population. During the nineteenth and twentieth centuries, substantial numbers of Ibos emigrated northward, where

---

[7] The impact of the colonial legacy is analyzed in Onyeabo Eze, *Social, Political and Economic Background of the Immediate Events Leading to the Nigeria-Biafra Conflict* (Basel: author-published doctoral dissertation, 1971), 99–119, 16–25. See also Cronje, *The World and Nigeria*, 1–10. These analyses give some credence to Soviet observations such as this: "The fundamental cause of all recent events in Nigeria is to be found in the heavy burden of the legacy left by colonialism. These vestiges are like delayed-action landmines." V. Kudryavtsev, *Izvestia*, January 22, 1970. See also K. Geivandov, *Pravda*, October 21, 1966; Kudryavtsev, *Izvestia*, March 21, 1967; Gerasimov, *Izvestia*, January 9, 1969.

they achieved a disproportionately large role in the commerce of the region. By the 1960s, roughly 2 million Ibos were employed in the north; many of them also occupied prominent positions in the national bureaucracy and educational system. Their very success and influence made them subjects of resentment and hatred among the Hausa.

Racial tensions and interregional political disputes placed strains on the Nigerian federation following independence. In 1963 there was bitter controversy over a census, which showed that the north had increased its population vis-à-vis the southern regions; with some justification the south charged that the census had been fixed so as to maintain northern domination of the legislature. In 1963, a fourth region, the midwest, was carved out. The national elections in 1964 were marred by such widespread fraud and illegal practices that the UGPA, a coalition of eastern parties, boycotted them. The western regional elections in 1965 reflected in their anarchy and intraparty antagonism the general political chaos threatening to engulf Nigeria.

On January 15, 1966, a group of officers staged a coup in which the prime minister, two regional premiers, and several other officials and army officers were killed. Most of the officers behind the coup were Ibos (about half of all army officers were then Ibo). The coup failed when Major General Aguiyi-Ironsi, general officer commanding, managed to escape assassination and rally enough force to arrest the plotters. But Ironsi, too, was an Ibo, and when he was asked to assume power by the remaining members of the Nigerian cabinet, the whole affair came to be viewed in the north as an Ibo plot. Ironsi appointed military governors over Lagos and the four regions. Ojukwu became the military governor of eastern Nigeria; Gowon was appointed army chief of staff. In May, Ironsi announced that he was suspending the constitution and abolishing the regions. Immediately riots broke out in the north, where the proposal was considered tantamount to an Ibo takeover of the country. An estimated 2,000 to 3,000 Ibos living in the north were massacred, and thousands more began fleeing to their tribal homelands in the east. Ironsi withdrew his plan, but on July 29, northern elements in the army revolted, killing Ironsi. Gowon announced that he was taking control of the government, but Ojukwu refused to recognize his authority.

It appeared at first that the north, not the east, might secede from Nigeria. Gowon himself declared that "the basis for unity is not there."[8] But civil war might still have been averted had it not been for the anti-Ibo pogroms that occurred in the north in the last months of 1966. Between September and January, several thousand Ibos were killed, and many more were injured, mangled, and robbed in an orgy of racial violence that brought Ibo-Hausa hatred to a white heat and made some kind of conflict

---

[8] *BBC broadcast ME/2229/B/1*, from Lagos, August 1, 1966, in Kirk-Greene, *Crisis and Conflict*, vol. 1, 197. According to Cronje, *The World and Nigeria*, 17, Gowon was pressured by the British high commissioner not to turn the speech into a declaration of Nigerian dissolution.

inevitable, even had Biafra not seceded. Some 2 million Ibos fled the north for their homeland. A series of negotiations in the latter part of 1966 and early in 1967 failed to resolve the differences between Gowon and Ojukwu. When on May 27 Gowon announced a plan to divide Nigeria into 12 regions, the east viewed it as an attempt to dismember the eastern region and deprive it of its oil revenues. Ojukwu rejected the plan, and three days later the eastern region seceded.

The Nigerian-Biafran war was a coalescence of three conflicts. It was foremost a political conflict that began as a struggle over which region would dominate Nigeria and increasingly became a war over the issue of Biafra's right to secede. Even after the formal secession, Ojukwu entertained hopes of capturing Lagos and winning control of the political center; only after his forces were expelled from the mid-west region did it become evident that secession and sovereignty were the most the east could hope to obtain. Second, the conflict was a race war, fueled by intense Ibo-Hausa hatred. Ibo fears of genocide accounted for the fierceness of Biafra's resistance, though in the end Gowon's statesmanship alleviated the worst of the tensions and averted postconflict racial recriminations. Finally, it was an intramilitary dispute, a war of rivalry between various officers and factions in the Nigerian army. Although it was true that the army "was as nearly a non-tribal force as any in Africa," it was also the case that

> the military and political problems had by the middle of 1966 become inextricable the one from the other . . . The integration of the nation depended in the last resort upon the cohesion of the army: when the latter was lost the nation was on the verge of disintegration.[9]

All three issues – secession, race, and military authority – worked to exacerbate the conflict; none assuaged it. The result was a very intense war, with abundant opportunity for exploitation by an outside power such as the Soviet Union. The secession issue meant that Moscow's backing of Nigeria would be viewed favorably in most of black Africa; the intensity of the conflict made the FMG willing to set aside past inhibitions and seek arms from the Russians in order to pressure Britain into more active support; the central role of the military in the conflict created ideal conditions for translating arms shipments into political influence.

Notwithstanding that the internal dynamics of the conflict created an almost ideal venue for Soviet involvement, a rather tortuous ideological road had to be traveled in order to justify that involvement. Prior to the July 1966 coup against Ironsi, Soviet writers had deplored

---

[9] The quotations are respectively from *Strategic Survey* (1967):42, and Robin Luckham, *The Nigerian Military: A Sociological Analysis of Authority & Revolt 1960–67* (Cambridge University Press, 1971), 298. See also N. J. Miners, *The Nigerian Army 1956–1966* (London: Methuen & Co., 1971), 155–234.

the domination of the "feudal," reactionary north, which was seen as representing British interests, whereas the Soviets spoke favorably of the progressive Ibo people in the east. For this reason the January coup was viewed with some favor. But once Gowon assumed power and the imminence of Biafra's secession was apparent, Soviet commentary on the FMG became increasingly favorable. Ironsi's role was criticized in retrospect, and Ojukwu was seen as falling increasingly under the influence of the imperialist powers, led by the international oil monopolies. The initial criticism of Ojukwu was guarded, however, and Moscow's position was articulated with unusual care, as though the Soviet Union were hedging against the possibility that the eastern region would indeed capture Lagos and control of the central government.[10] The outbreak of the civil war was blamed on Western oil interests, who were allegedly conspiring to divide and rule Nigeria, according to one interpretation, or competing with one another for dominance, in a somewhat different version.[11] The attack on the oil monopolies and the Western powers was a principal refrain of Soviet commentators throughout the war, but as the inevitability of Biafra's defeat became clear, Soviet attacks were directed more pointedly at the Biafran regime and at Ojukwu himself.[12] The ideological difficulties encountered in attempting to portray the conflict as a war of national liberation can be seen in the following excerpt from V. Kudryavtsev (*Izvestia*, October 11, 1968):

> If one approaches the events in Nigeria from a strictly formal standpoint, i.e., from the standpoint of the "absolute inviolability of the principle of national self-determination," then it would seem that the right of the Ibo people to exercise this self-determination in practice should be recognized . . . before the colonialists intruded into Africa the Ibo people . . . had character-

[10] The evolution of the Soviet position may be traced in K. Geivandov, *Pravda*, October 21, 1966; "Soviet Views on Nigeria," *Mizan* 9(March/April 1967):71–2; A. Tryasunov, "Voina ili mir?" *Mezhdunarodnaya zhizn'* (July 1968):119; "Soviet Thoughts on Nigeria's Crisis," *Mizan* 9 (July/August 1967):174. See also Stent, "The Soviet Union and the Nigerian Civil War," 44; Klinghoffer, "The USSR and Nigeria," 64–5.

[11] The first interpretation is found in *Pravda*, October 21, 1966; V. Sidenko, "Voina v Nigerii," *Novoe Vremya* (September 6, 1968):11–12; *Izvestia*, March 21, 1967; *Izvestia*, January 9, 1969; *Izvestia*, May 8, 1969; *Izvestia*, January 14, 1970; *Literaturnaya Gazeta*, October 2, 1968. The second interpretation can be traced in V. Maevskii, *Pravda*, January 26, 1969; V. Makarov, "Konets Krizisa?" *Mezhdunarodnaya zhizn'* (December 1967):152; *Izvestia*, October 11, 1968; *Izvestia*, November 15, 1969.

[12] A. Tryasunov, "Ot vouny k miry," *Mezhdunarodnaya zhizn'* (November 1968):124, accuses Ojukwu of having plotted the secession with leading officials under Ironsi. See also the examples cited in D.L.M., "The USSR and the War in Nigeria," *Mizan* 11(January/February 1969):31–38. Soviet writers were careful not to attack the Ibos *as a people*. Sympathetic accounts of the suffering were sometimes given in the Soviet press, with the blame put on the imperialists who caused the war. See *Izvestia*, January 9, 1969.

istics that brought it close to the concept of a nation...

The principle of the self-determination of nationalities even to the point of secession is not an absolute one, and it is wrong to be believed that it should be applied in all conditions. No, it is subordinated to the tasks of class struggle and social liberation...If one approaches the present situation in Nigeria from the only correct standpoint, then one must say in all certainty that Biafra's secession is advantageous only to the imperialists.

Kudryavtsev's argument provides an excellent illustration of how the concept of a war of national liberation can take on highly expedient hues in its actual application. Kudryavtsev essentially acknowledges that it is not the structure of a local conflict per se that determines what constitutes "national liberation." Rather, it is the place of the conflict in the international class struggle – in the inexorable conflict between the social systems of socialism and capitalism.

The emphasis in some Soviet commentaries on the role of oil in the conflict may have stemmed from the fact that right up to the outbreak of the war, American and British oil companies were competing for drilling rights in the oil fields of eastern Nigeria. Nigeria's oil production had increased in importance following the disruption of supplies caused by the six-day war, and issues of oil and oil revenues did play a modest role in the conflict during its early months. When Port Harcourt was captured by Federal forces in May 1968, all oil production fell under the control of Lagos, and production and exports soon rose to normal levels. From that time on, oil ceased to be even a minor factor in the local dispute, in the hostilities themselves, or in the foreign policies of the major powers, but by continuing to cast the conflict in terms of an imperialist struggle for resources, Soviet theorists managed to salvage a measure of ideological respectability from what appears to have been a *Realpolitik* decision by the Soviet leadership to take sides in the war.

The diplomatic relationship between the USSR and its client

Prior to the civil war, Moscow had been able to make only token progress in advancing relations with Nigeria, one of the most pro-Western anti-Communist regimes in Africa, and a solid member of the British Commonwealth. An agreement on opening diplomatic relations was reached in April 1961, but the Soviet ambassador did not arrive until October, and Nigeria did not open a permanent mission in Moscow until 1964. A trade agreement was signed in July 1963, and various Soviet missions visited Nigeria in connection with economic aid projects, medical collaboration, commerce, and cultural exchanges. Radio Moscow reported that 300 Nigerians were studying in the USSR in June 1965. That was the same month that Soviet

Deputy Foreign Minister Yakov Malik spent three days in Lagos; he was the highest Soviet official to visit Nigeria prior to the civil war.

There was nothing in the Soviet-Nigerian relationship during the prewar years that could serve as a foundation for military cooperation. Britain and West Germany were Nigeria's principal arms suppliers, and Lagos had no reason to turn elsewhere. The situation changed after Biafra's secession. The Nigerian armed forces brought pressure to bear on Gowon to procure fighter planes, apparently because of intelligence reports indicating that Biafra had acquired at least one B-26 bomber from Europe. Despite Gowon's threat to "deal with the devil" if they would not sell him the fighters, Great Britain and the United States refused to provide them. Only then did Gowon turn to the Soviet Union.[13]

Preliminary negotiations on the Soviet-Nigerian arms deal took place in Lagos, where General Gowon and his inner circle of military advisers met with Soviet Ambassador Alexander Romanov. According to John Stremlau, "there was never any suggestion of outright Soviet assistance, and the Nigerians resisted proposals for long-term bartering arrangements." While these negotiations were under way in July, the FMG made further efforts to determine the extent of London's willingness to provide arms. Edwin Ogbu, permanent secretary of the Nigerian Foreign Affairs Ministry, traveled to Moscow on July 29, where he was joined two days later by Chief Anthony Enahoro, the Nigerian minister of information and labor. Enahoro had been in London and met with Harold Wilson less than two weeks previously. According to *Pravda*, Enahoro met "at his own request" with Kirill Mazurov, first deputy secretary of the Council of Ministers, and their visit resulted in the signing of a cultural agreement initialed the previous March in Lagos. However, Soviet aircraft and military equipment began arriving in Nigeria within two weeks of the visit, and Enahoro and Gowon later admitted that the main purpose of the Enahoro-Ogbu mission had been to finalize the military agreement. Radio Biafra broadcast full details of the agreement on August 11, including the names and passport numbers of the Russian advisers who were to accompany the MiG fighters to Lagos.[14]

---

[13] In mid-June 1967, a four-man delegation left Lagos for Moscow, headed by Edwin Ogbu. Several academic sources suggest that this visit was related to arms purchases. See Stent, "The Soviet Union and the Nigerian Civil War," 44; Klinghoffer, "The USSR and Nigeria," 66–7; Peter Schwab, ed., *Biafra* (New York: Facts on File, 1972), 25; Cronje, *The World and Nigeria*, 31–2. This version appears to be inaccurate. John Stremlau learned in interviews with Gowon, Ogbu, and Peter Onu, political officer of the Nigerian Embassy in Moscow, that the main purpose of the trip was to reorganize the embassy staff "in the wake of an internal crisis precipitated by the abrupt departure of Ambassador C. O. Ifeagwu, an Ibo who...threw an Independence Day celebration for Biafra at the Nigerian embassy." John Stremlau, *The International Politics of the Nigerian Civil War 1967–1970* (Princeton University Press, 1977), 79–80.

[14] Stremlau, *International Politics of the Nigerian Civil War*, 80; Cronje, *The World and Nigeria*, 26–30, 32; *Pravda*, August 3, 1967; Schwab, *Biafra*, 25.

The FMG publicly acknowledged on August 23 that it had obtained Soviet equipment and technical assistance "strictly for cash on a commercial basis."[15] The Soviet Union did not confirm the transaction publicly, but in October, Kosygin sent Gowon a letter of support that was released to the press:

> The Soviet people fully understand the desire of the Nigerian Federal Government to preserve the unity and territorial integrity of the Nigerian state and to prevent the country from being dismembered. The Soviet Union has tried to help African states in every way in their noble desire to strengthen their political and economic independence.[16]

It may be significant that Kosygin's letter was not released until October 17 – after the United States had reaffirmed its official neutrality in the war, despite the increasing Soviet involvement, and after the Federal government had recaptured the midwest region (taken by Biafra in August) and won other telling successes on the battlefield.

As noted earlier, Lagos claimed that the arms purchases were strictly for cash. Some cash may have been involved in the agreement, but Suzanne Cronje has offered solid evidence that a barter agreement was also involved in which 7,000 tons of Nigerian cocoa beans were delivered to the USSR in partial exchange for the weapons.[17] It also appears that financing was arranged for some of the purchases made later in the war. Somewhat over a year after the first arms arrived, an eight-man Soviet economic mission toured Nigeria from November 10 to 21, 1968. The delegation was headed by A. I. Alikjanovy, deputy chairman of the State Committee on Foreign Economic Relations, and the visit culminated in the signing of an economic and technical assistance pact with an estimated value of $140 million. This credit quite possibly included financing for additional weapons deliveries. B. Pilyatkin hinted as much when writing of the agreement in *Izvestia*:

> Soviet-Nigerian cooperation on a mutually beneficial basis is called upon to contribute to the successful fulfillment of these tasks.
>
> They are especially complex at the present time for Nigeria, *being in need of war materials to defend its unity and territorial integrity* [italics added].[18]

---

[15] *New York Times*, August 24, 1967.

[16] *Soviet News*, November 7, 1967; *Lagos Daily Times*, October 17, 1967.

[17] See Cronje, *The World and Nigeria*, 264–5, 392. The USSR had been in need of a cocoa supplier since the fall of Nkrumah in Ghana. Nigerian cocoa exports to Russia shot up and remained high throughout the war.

[18] *Izvestia*, November 24, 1968. See also *Izvestia*, November 16, 1968, and *New York Times*, November 22, 1968.

It was widely assumed in Africa and elsewhere that the agreement was related to the financing of weapons. Noticeable increases in Soviet arms shipments occurred in November.

In 1968 the USSR is reported to have broadened its contacts with two left-wing groups in Nigeria: the Socialist Workers' and Farmers' Party (SWAFP) and the Nigerian Trade Union Congress (NTUC). Moscow had developed ties with both groups prior to the civil war. Considerable trade union activity erupted across Nigeria in 1968, a phenomenon that many Western observers and Nigerian officials attributed to increasing Soviet influence. The USSR was reported to be financing the NTUC with "at least £30,000 a year," underwriting the influential radical newspaper *Advance*, and contributing to the Nigerian-Soviet Friendship Society that grew substantially during the war.[19] The FMG yielded little ground to the trade unions and radical parties, maintaining tight censorship and control on labor throughout the war, but it refrained from any major crackdown on either NTUC or SWAFP. Its restraint may be attributed partly to concern that suppression of the left would lead to curtailment or termination of Soviet arms deliveries.

During the last year of the conflict, numerous firsthand diplomatic contacts took place between Nigeria and the USSR, including two Soviet port calls at Lagos, a visit in March of a friendship delegation, and a visit in July by Soviet Deputy Foreign Minister Leonid Ilichev.[20] It seems likely that some of these visits included further discussion of Nigeria's military needs, particularly because the war was then stalemated and the FMG was searching for the proper strategy and weapons to invade Biafra's small enclave successfully. The arrangements for the 122-mm guns that arrived in October 1969 may have been discussed during the latter of these visits. It is curious, however, that the guns did not arrive until October, though the final Nigerian offensive began the previous June. One reason for the apparent delay may have been an incident involving Dr. Tunji Otegbeye, a Yoruba Marxist who headed the SWAFP. In June 1969, Otegbeye attended the International Conference of Communist and Workers' Parties in Moscow. At a press conference there he expressed gratitude to the CPSU and the Soviet people "for their big contribution to the Nigerian people's struggle for the unity of the country against capitalism's intrigues." He also expressed hope that a united Communist party

---

[19]"Nigeria: Russia's Economic Grip," *Intelligence Digest* 31(February 1969):14–15. A later article, "The Real Masters of Nigeria," *Intelligence Digest* 31(April 1969):7–8, claimed that a Soviet-sponsored clandestine group known as the Committee of Ten had been set up to promote revolution in Nigeria. Further information on SWAFP and NTUC during the war and their ties with the USSR may be found in Cronje, *The World and Nigeria*, 265–73.

[20]"Foreign-Port Visits by Soviet Naval Units," in MccGwire et al., eds., *Soviet Naval Policy*, 404; *Izvestia*, March 13, 1969; *Pravda*, July 23, 1969.

dedicated to revolution could emerge in Nigeria.[21] Otegbeye was arrested on his return to Lagos at the end of June. In July the USSR recalled Ambassador Romanov home to Moscow twice for consultations, and Deputy Minister Ilichev made a short visit to Lagos. Otegbeye was freed shortly thereafter,[22] so it is possible that the diplomatic stirrings were connected with his arrest and that Moscow put pressure on the FMG to release him. In October 1969, the same month the guns finally arrived, the NTUC affiliated itself with the World Federation of Trade Unions at the latter's congress in Budapest.[23] Two months later, when it became evident that Biafra's collapse was certain, the Nigerian government introduced the most severe antilabor legislation ever.

A curious twist to the Soviet Union's Nigerian diplomacy surfaces in connection with certain contacts made by the USSR and its Eastern European allies with Nigeria's eastern region just prior to and during the conflict:

1. A team of nine Soviet experts began a tour of industrial establishments in all the regions of Nigeria, including the eastern region, in January 1967. This was several months after Ojukwu had rejected Gowon's authority. Nigeria at the time was in a state of extreme tension because of the anti-Ibo pogroms just ending in the north. Surely, in addition to its economic mission, the Soviet team was sent to assess conditions in the east, Ojukwu's leadership, the chances of secession, and the like.

2. A Hungarian delegation visited the eastern region in April 1967, only a few weeks prior to Biafra's secession. The ostensible purpose of this delegation was to work out an agreement for building a hospital at Enugu, but given the date of the visit and the imminence of war, it was viewed as a diplomatic overture by many. John Stremlau, who learned of this visit, believed that the Soviets wanted to test the waters in the eastern region and that they possibly contemplated supporting Ojukwu even at this late date. But he added: "Ojukwu was very wary of getting involved in anything that would alienate the West."[24]

3. Several of the small arms received by Biafra in the early months of the war were of Czechoslovak manufacture.[25] This was before Dub-

---

[21] *Pravda*, June 14, 1969; Tunji Otegbeye, "Nigeria and the National Question," *World Marxist Review* 12(October 1969):52.

[22] *West Africa*, August 23, 1969.

[23] Cronje, *The World and Nigeria*, 272, believes there was no direct connection between the arrival of the guns and NTUC affiliation with the WFTU, but admits that "the military supplies underlined the fact that the authorities were still under some obligation to Moscow, and could not be too overt in their anti-Communist moves."

[24] Interview: John Stremlau, Rockefeller Foundation.

[25] "The Biafran army was relatively lightly armed, relying on clandestine shipments of weapons many of which came initially from Czechoslovakia." Raph Uwechu, *Reflections on the Nigerian Civil War: Facing the Future*, rev. ed. (New York: African Publishing Corp., 1971), 8. Ojukwu told John Stremlau that Biafra had access to Czechoslovak arms. Interview: Stremlau.

cek came to power. Czechoslovakia denied it was supplying arms to Biafra.

4. Paul Nwokedi, a Biafran Marxist, visited the Soviet Union in the spring of 1969 in order to discuss a memorandum he had submitted to Moscow on behalf of the Biafran government detailing the charge of genocide. This, in turn, led to a secret visit by a Biafran delegation to the Soviet Union in July 1969. Gordon Brock-Shepherd, a British newspaper correspondent, learned that the Biafrans were in Moscow and published a story claiming that the delegation was making an "appeal for arms." Biafra admitted that a delegation was in Moscow but denied that it was seeking arms. The delegation was asked to leave the USSR, and the Soviet press, neither confirming nor denying that the visit had taken place, denounced Brock-Shepherd's story as a "vicious falsehood."[26]

What is to be made of these events? Perhaps little. The Czechoslovak arms used by Biafra, for example, may have been purchased on the private world market. That is SIPRI's explanation for their presence: "The Czech denial has been confirmed by reliable sources who explain the reports by reference to the large amounts of Czechoslovak World War II equipment circulating on the black market."[27] The events leading to the Biafran delegation's visit to Moscow in 1969 do suggest that its purpose was to argue a moral case, not to seek arms. But taken together, the incidents give reason to believe that the Soviet leaders were hedging in the early months of the war, waiting to see where each side stood and which would put together the military-political combination necessary for victory. The later contacts with Biafra may then have been an attempt at partial reconciliation, a search for political contacts in eastern Nigeria that could be useful after the war was over. Less likely, but not unthinkable, is the explanation that the Soviet Union was attempting to influence the course and duration of the war by making an opening to Biafra.

Weapons shipments and other military aid

The Nigerian civil war marked the USSR's first significant military involvement in a sub-Saharan conflict. During the two and a half years of the civil war, Nigeria was the foremost recipient of Soviet weapons in all of black Africa. The decision as to what types of weapons to send seems to have been carefully considered by the Soviet Union and it allies, with weight given to political as well as military factors. Table 6.1 is a register of weapons known to have been transferred to Lagos by the USSR or its allies during the war. Three of the Ilyushin bombers and some of the MiG-17s that arrived in Nigeria in 1968 were sent directly from Algeria and/or Egypt. Whether these transfers were made in consultation with Moscow and with its financial backing or

[26] *Izvestia*, July 9, 1969.
[27] SIPRI, *The Arms Trade with the Third World*, 633.

Table 6.1. *Transfers of Soviet weapons to Federal Nigeria during the Nigerian civil war, July 1967 to January 1970*

Year	Weapons transferred	Country of origin
1967	10 MiG-17s	USSR/Czechoslovakia
	12–15 L-29 Delfin trainers	Czechoslovakia
	6 MiG-15 UTI	Poland (?)
	3 torpedo boats	USSR
	Bombs, ammunition, small arms	
1968	4 Il-28 bombers	USSR, Algeria & Egypt
	31 MiG-17s	USSR, Algeria & Egypt
	Approximately 80 jeeps and command cars	USSR
	Small arms	
1969	1 Il-28 bomber	USSR
	122-mm howitzers	USSR
	(4–5 Su-7s)	(USSR/Egypt)
	(2 MiG-19s)	(USSR/Egypt)
	Small arms	

Sources: SIPRI, *The Arms Trade Registers*, 82; Cronje, *The World and Nigeria*, 57, 268, 279; de St. Jorre, *The Brothers' War*, 181–4, 395; Peter Schwab, *Biafra*, 26, 70; *Keesing's Contemporary Archives* (*KCA*), September 9–16, 1967, p. 22243. The sources differ somewhat as to the number of aircraft transferred; the foregoing figures are the more conservative estimates.

whether they were independent transfers by the governments in Cairo and Algiers is not known. A few Su-7 fighters and MiG-19s may also have been transferred from Egypt in 1969.

The first shipments – two Czechoslovak fighter planes sent to Lagos through Ghana – arrived on August 8, less than a week after Enahoro had left Moscow. Additional shipments arrived by sea during the following week, and on August 18 several Antonov transport planes landed at Kano airport. The torpedo boats arrived from the USSR in mid-November.

The weapons shipments in the fall of 1967 included several jet trainers and fighters from Czechoslovakia. In January 1968, Alexander Dubcek came to power in Prague and initiated a series of startling reforms, among which was a reassessment of Czechoslovakia's arms export policy. In April 1968 the Czechoslovak Foreign Ministry announced that the government would cease sending war material to Nigeria, a step that won immediate praise from Biafra. Tanzania's recognition of Biafra less than two weeks earlier may have contributed to Prague's decision, which represented one of the few historical instances of a Warsaw Pact member differing publicly with Moscow on military assistance policy.[28]

[28] Another example would be Romania's provision of arms to the FNLA early in the Angolan civil war.

The next major shipments of Soviet arms arrived around the end of October 1968. The FMG was then in the middle of a difficult "final offensive" and may well have made a special appeal for help. It is interesting that the deliveries were not made earlier – say in August, when the offensive began – for by the end of October it was evident that the offensive would not be victorious and that a new influx of weapons could not change the outcome. Perhaps Lagos wanted to make its final push without additional outside help and turned to Moscow only when the offensive faltered. Or, conceivably, the Kremlin was not overanxious to see Biafra fall just then; a more prolonged war, after all, would mean expanded Soviet influence. The fact that the next major Soviet arms deliveries did not take place until October 1969 is compatible with this latter conjecture; it is, of course, impossible to do anything but speculate on this point.

It seems that the Soviet weapons shipments were intended principally to create a small Nigerian air force that could undertake strategic strikes against Biafra. By providing fighters, bombers, and bombs, the USSR filled the key gap in Nigeria's offensive capabilities that Britain had refused to fill. The situation was different with other types of equipment. London provided the FMG with five warships and over 50 tanks, while the Soviet Union supplied three patrol boats and no tanks. Britain was also the main supplier of Nigeria's antiaircraft guns, in accordance with London's announced policy of providing weaponry "as defensive as possible."[29] (It is unclear why Britain considered tanks defensive, but aircraft offensive.) The 122-mm artillery guns provided by the USSR in the fall of 1969 had extremely high accuracy and a range of over 20 kilometers. They were clearly intended to enable the Federal army to knock out the stubborn Uli airfield, which had defied numerous attempts to capture or destroy it during the year after it had become Biafra's only major link to outside supplies. As it was, the Biafran army collapsed so rapidly under the final Federal offensive that the 122-mm guns saw little action, though they were given an inordinate amount of credit for the victory.[30]

The tiny contingent of aging Western planes that Biafra managed to assemble for its own air force was no match for sophisticated MiG fighters, and the Federal air force commanded the skies during most of the conflict. The Soviet aircraft were used in several bombing missions, striking Port Harcourt, Aba, Owerri, and other cities in addition

[29] Statement of Commonwealth Relations Office, August 10, 1967, in Schwab, *Biafra* 24. The information on British ships and tanks is from SIPRI, *The Arms Trade Registers*, 82–83.

[30] Oye Ogunbadejo, "Nigeria and the Great Powers: The Impact of the Civil War on Nigerian Foreign Relations," *African Affairs* 75 (January 1976):24; Walter Schwarz, "Foreign Powers and the Nigerian War," *Africa Report* 15 (February 1970):14; John de St. Jorre, *The Brothers' War: Biafra and Nigeria* (Boston: Houghton Mifflin, 1972), 317.

to military targets. The bombing, however, was of marginal military value.[31] Biafra charged that Nigeria was deliberately attacking civilian targets, including a Red Cross hospital; Lagos denied the charge and attributed any evidence of such strikes to inexperienced pilots. John de St. Jorre, a war correspondent, reported that the MiG fighters and Ilyushins were too swift for effective use against Uli, because pinpoint night bombing was the only way to strike effectively against the well-disguised airfield.[32] Given the weakness of Biafra's air defenses and the small size of the enclave it held during the last year of the war, it is interesting that Nigeria did not seek to obtain more effective weaponry from the USSR. The right combination of low-flying bombers, ground-to-ground missiles, and helicopters might have rapidly ended the war. The USSR had transferred such equipment to other Third World countries before, and Moscow was reportedly willing to provide it to Nigeria. The Nigerians, however, were interested only in inexpensive, early generation weapons. Western diplomats in Lagos during the war indicated that the Soviets were as frustrated as the British about the incompetence of the Federal army in translating new weaponry into battlefield victories.[33]

The Soviet intervention was a test of Moscow's ability to transfer weapons over longer distances and under circumstances more difficult than those it had faced in most previous local conflicts. Many of the fighters were brought by sea, but a substantial number were airlifted in on Antonov transports, which flew via Anaba, Algeria, to the Kano airport in Lagos. The war thus demonstrated the USSR's increasing airlift capabilities and its potential to translate a military assistance relationship with one Third World country into temporary base rights for distant military operations in another.

Soviet war vessels visited Lagos twice during the war, once in March 1969 and again the following September. Although the visits came late in the war, when there was little doubt that the FMG would win, Gowon welcomed them as a sign of Soviet support.[34] Like the

---

[31] John Oyinbo, *Nigeria: Crisis and Beyond* (London: Charles Knight, 1971), 82–9, offers a thoughtful analysis of the military aspects of the war. He writes: "The supply of Russian MiG fighters and fighter-bombers to the Federal airforce had no strategic effect on the war and proved a costly way of raising Federal morale" (p. 85).

[32] de St. Jorre, *The Brothers' War*, 317–18. He suggests that the mercenary pilots in some cases colluded to avoid destroying Uli in order to prolong the war and their own salaries. Stremlau disagrees, believing that Gowon deliberately did not knock out Uli from the air because he knew that a much greater toll by starvation would result if the relief planes were cut off before the ground war was won. Interview: Stremlau. See also Stremlau, *International Politics of the Nigerian Civil War*, 283–4.

[33] Interview: Stremlau.

[34] The first squadron arrived March 6 and consisted of two destroyers, a submarine, and an oil tanker. *Krasnaya Zvezda*, March 27, 1969, contains a lengthy article about the visit. Gowon is reported to have told Second Captain Radchenko of the *Boiki* that "the visit of the Soviet warships would be perceived by the capital's public as moral support for the healthy forces which are fighting for the unity of the country."

provision of the long-range artillery, the naval calls were a prime example of the Soviet Union gaining significant political mileage by offering insignificant but well-publicized military support.

Participation by Soviet and East European advisers

Approximately 170 Soviet technicians and advisers arrived at Kano airport in August 1967 along with the first shipments of Soviet weapons. Most of them were mechanics who came to assist in assembling the jet aircraft and who left shortly thereafter. An unknown number stayed on, some to service the weaponry, others apparently to provide military expertise. Very little is known about what influence these advisers exerted on the strategy and tactics of the FMG, but their role seems to have been quite limited.[35] It is known that early in 1969, when a new Federal offensive was about to be launched, Colonel Mikhail Medvedev, a Russian expert on armored warfare with experience in China, Egypt, and Sudan, arrived in Lagos as the new military attaché to the Soviet Embassy.[36] Although his arrival may have been connected with the upcoming offensive, it is doubtful that he played an effectual advisory role, because armored warfare was secondary in the conflict, and Soviet armored fighting vehicles were never sent to Nigeria. The Soviet MiG fighters and Ilyushin bombers are believed to have been flown largely by Egyptian mercenaries, but it is possible that at least some pilots from East Germany were also employed in combat.[37] If so, their involvement on a small scale would have foreshadowed the USSR's more extensive use of proxy combatants from among its allies in the 1970s.

Soviet-American interactions

As in the Yemeni civil war, diplomatic interaction between the United States and the USSR over the Nigerian civil war was minimal. As in Yemen, this was because Washington decided against any direct involvement in the conflict. In September 1968, Dean Rusk revealed that prior to the war the United States had counseled both sides against secession and civil war and made efforts to forestall a resort to arms.

---

[35] Nigeria is a larger and more modern country than Yemen, and although its army was backward by Western standards, it did possess a small elite of very capable officers trained at British academies. See Luckham, *The Nigerian Military*, 94–101. They were capable of their own military planning and may have regarded advice from Soviet advisers with suspicion.

[36] *The Listener*, January 30, 1969, cited in Cronje, *The World and Nigeria*, 268.

[37] Several Nigerian sources mentioned this to Stremlau; Ojukwu also told him that at a certain point in the war there was a sudden improvement in the accuracy of the MiGs. Interview: Stremlau. The British, anti-Communist *Intelligence Digest* 31(April 1969):7 claimed that "East European" pilots were manning Soviet bombers against Biafra.

Following Biafra's secession, Washington continued to recognize unified Nigeria and "affirmed its strong hope that a settlement would be negotiated which would preserve a single, democratic Nigeria." The Johnson administration supported efforts by the OAU and others to mediate the conflict as an internal one, an African problem to be solved by Africans. The State Department disclosed on July 10, 1967, that it had turned down a request for military aid from the Nigerian government and that it would not sell arms to either side. The statement also observed that Nigeria fell within Britain's traditional sphere of influence, thus essentially abdicating the great-power role to London.[38]

Shortly after the Soviet arms deliveries began, the State Department issued a statement deploring the Soviet involvement:

> Neither the United States nor the Soviet Union has in the past been an important supplier of arms to Nigeria... In these circumstances, it is a matter of regret to the United States that the Soviet Union has not shown the same forbearance, but, on the contrary, has decided to engage in the supply of arms in this internal conflict.[39]

This statement was reaffirmed by American spokesmen a number of times during the war, but Washington seems to have taken no further political or military actions to discourage the Soviet shipments, and concern about the Soviet role played a distinctly secondary part in U.S. policy toward Nigeria during the war years. Preoccupied with its own political problems and the looming challenge of Vietnam, the Johnson administration was not inclined to spend time worrying about Soviet military assistance granted to an ally of Great Britain. Because Moscow was arming the same side as London, it was believed that Soviet gains would be limited by the British involvement. Washington's official neutrality, its unusually passive attitude toward the Soviet effort, and its refusal to consider Nigeria's requests for arms unquestionably facilitated the USSR's own diplomatic and military initiatives during the conflict. It is conceivable, though by no means certain, that had the United States been willing to assist Nigeria militarily, or had it taken firmer steps to protest and complicate the Soviet involvement, the USSR's involvement in the conflict might have been more limited and Nigeria's subsequent drift from its pro-Western alignment might have been averted. Britain's failure to resist

---

[38] The quotation in this paragraph is from Roy M. Melbourne, "The American Response to the Nigerian Conflict," *Issue* 3(Summer 1973):33. Melbourne chaired the U.S. interagency task force on Nigeria during the civil war. Other information in the paragraph is from the following: "Address by Secretary Rusk," September 12, 1968, in *DOSB* LIX(October 7, 1968):353; State Department press release F-347, LRS-12, July 10, 1967.

[39] *DOSB* LVII(September 11, 1967):320. Nigerians were angered by the American protest. See *New York Times*, August 24, 1967.

Moscow's involvement in the Commonwealth affair more vigorously also contributed somewhat to the Soviet Union's success.

As the war progressed, a vigorous pro-Biafran lobby arose in the United States, organized by American churches and students and by the more than 1,700 Nigerians – largely Ibo – studying in the United States. Partly because of this lobby, Washington provided some financial aid to the International Red Cross and other international organizations that were providing relief to Nigerians on both sides of the conflict. Some of the food flown into Biafra was purchased with U.S. money, a fact that irritated the FMG. Most Nigerians became convinced that the United States was pro-Biafra, neutral only in the formal sense. Gowon and other Nigerians worked to persuade the United States that Nigeria's turning to the Soviet Union for arms was a decision of expediency, not one with long-term political ramifications. As Gowon told *Time* magazine, "Going to the Soviet Union, I assure you, was just a way of dealing with Ojukwu's threat. After all, Ojukwu started the air war. Even Abraham Lincoln went to Russia for help to win his own civil war."[40]

In September 1968, Richard Nixon's campaign office issued a statement urging greater U.S. involvement in the Biafran relief effort. The statement hinted that the FMG was guilty of genocide. Nixon's election a few months later was hailed in Biafra, but aside from the somewhat more publicized attention the new administration gave to humanitarian relief, U.S. policy toward Nigeria did not shift significantly under Nixon. The United States maintained its position of tacit support for Nigerian unity and formal neutrality in the war.

Despite the U.S. position of neutrality, the Soviet news media criticized Washington throughout the war, charging that the United States was the principal cause of Biafra's secession and the head of a league of imperialist powers hoping to dismember Nigeria.[41] The United States was allegedly interested in Biafra's secession because Shell-B.P. dominated Nigerian oil extraction, whereas the largest U.S. concern, Gulf Oil, controlled only 10 percent:

> Some people would like to change this state of affairs.
>
> The main oil wells are situated in the Eastern province, and it is not surprising that the State Department showed reserve in its relations with Lagos during the crisis, while the CIA forecast early recognition of Biafra.[42]

This article asserted that Ojukwu's primary encouragement was from the United States and that the CIA was providing most of the rebels' arms.

On January 27, 1969, the Soviet ambassador to Nigeria, Alexander Romanov, made a statement warning all foreign powers to "steer clear of

---

[40] *Time*, July 4, 1969.
[41] See, for example, *Izvestia*, March 21, 1967; *Pravda*, October 21, 1966; *Izvestia*, November 24, 1968; *Izvestia*, January 22, 1970.
[42] V. Makarov, "Konets Krizisa?" 117.

Nigeria's internal affairs or face the consequences."[43] He charged that certain powers, particularly the United States, were responsible for prolonging the conflict. This statement came after Nixon's inauguration and only a few days after the president ordered a major review of American aid to Nigerian war victims. Romanov's warning was more or less gratuitous, but it was a politic gesture of support for the FMG, then about to begin another offensive against Biafra.

Had Great Britain not entered the war as the chief arms supplier of Lagos, the United States might have felt obliged to do so in order to prevent Soviet influence from increasing too much. It is doubtful, however, that Washington would ever have backed Biafra outright; so the possibility of the superpowers confronting one another on opposite sides of the conflict was at all times fairly remote, and their interaction remained rhetorical to the end.

The China factor

Diplomatic relations did not exist between Peking and Lagos at the time the civil war broke out, but Nigeria was China's third largest trading partner in Africa, and the Chinese had connections with political leaders in both the north and the east. So reluctant was Peking to take a position on the dispute that the Chinese news media maintained complete silence on events in Nigeria for over two years, from the July 1966 coup to September 1968. Eventually the Chinese leadership came down on the side of Biafra, apparently because they believed that doing so would serve to counter rising Soviet influence in Nigeria.[44]

Biafra sent a delegation to China in October 1967, possibly more with the intent of prodding Washington into some kind of action than in expectation of assistance from Peking. No public support was forthcoming, but from that time, rumors of Chinese weapons and personnel arriving in Biafra caused a number of minor Chinese "scares" in Federal Nigeria "which sent the small Formosan-oriented Chinese community at Lagos . . . scuttling about to declare its undying loyalty to the Federal cause."[45] Not until September 1968 did China make its support for Biafra official. Chinese Foreign Minister Chen Yi made the following statement at a banquet for the visiting foreign minister of South Yemen:

> In Africa, Soviet revisionism, in league with U.S. and British imperialism, is even openly supporting the military government of Federal Nigeria in massacring the Biafran people in a vain

---

[43] Schwab, *Biafra*, 109.
[44] Alaba Ogunsanwo, *China's Policy in Africa 1958–71* (Cambridge University Press, 1974), 233–4.
[45] de St. Jorre, *The Brothers' War*, 185.

attempt to squeeze into Nigeria and enjoy an equal share with imperialism there.[46]

A few days later, the New China News Agency issued a lengthy dispatch denouncing "collusion" between U.S. and British imperialists, on the one hand, and Soviet revisionists, on the other, "to redivide the sphere of influence in Africa." The statement accused Moscow of supporting a war of genocide.[47] The expressions of support for Biafra made it clear that Peking was primarily concerned with the Soviet presence and Nigeria's strategic importance, not with the niceties of local politics.

China's statements on the war led Ojukwu to write a carefully tailored letter to Mao Tse-tung in September 1968 seeking assistance "in our struggle against Anglo-American imperialism and Soviet revisionism."[48] The letter was a calculated gamble, for Biafra was trying to avoid doing anything that would alienate the Western powers – it was the only official Biafran document ever to use the word "socialist" in reference to Biafra's revolution. A large number of press reports indicate that Peking responded to Ojukwu's request and transferred a number of small arms to Biafra via Tanzania.[49] Ojukwu admitted as much in an interview with Stremlau.[50] The volume of arms transferred was no doubt small. The Tanzanian route would suggest that China was drawn into support of Biafra partly through its close ties with Tanzania and Zambia, both of which had recognized the Ibo republic earlier in the year. In 1968, China was assisting in the construction of the Tanzania-Zambia (Tanzam) railway, one of the largest economic aid projects in all Africa. President Nyerere of Tanzania had visited the CPR for five days in June 1968, only a few weeks after his recognition of Biafra, and his deep personal concern about the war may have led him to raise the issue while there. There were numerous other Chinese-Tanzanian contacts that summer, including a visit by China's Minister of Communications to Dar es Salaam in September, the month Peking announced its support of Biafra. Thus, China's support for Biafra may have arisen as much from its close ties with Biafra's African supporters as from its opposition to the Soviet Union's role in the conflict. In any event, it is clear that China's action followed the Soviet involvement by several months; so the USSR cannot be said to have been responding to China by its support

[46] National Chinese news agency (NCNA), September 18, 1968. The choice of occasion was ironic, because South Yemen probably supported the FMG.

[47] NCNA, September 22, 1968.

[48] *Sunday Sun* (Biafra), September 29, 1968, reprinted in full in Appendix 1 of Cronje, *The World and Nigeria*, 382–3.

[49] *Pravda*, January 28, 1969; *West Africa*, September 6, 1969; *Financial Times*, October 31, 1968, cited in Schwab, *Biafra*, 74; Radio Nigeria, February 10, 1969, and *San Francisco Chronicle*, October 30, 1968, quoted in Bruce D. Larkin, *China and Africa 1949–1970* (Berkeley: University of California Press, 1971), 186.

[50] Stremlau, *International Politics of the Nigerian Civil War*, 237.

to Lagos. Nor did China's minimal involvement in the war exert any visible influence on Soviet policy at any level other than the rhetorical.

The outcome

As the civil war progressed, the Soviet leadership seems to have become concerned about the length and extent of its commitment in Nigeria. *The Economist*, on January 11, 1969, recorded the following from a Soviet contact discussing the war:

> "We thought we were supporting a short, sharp police action," he says. He adds, "It is a quicksand; we could win the war for them, and they might break off relations a year later on some excuse. But what can you do?"

Such fears, if real, proved unfounded, for the Soviet Union did end up winning substantial diplomatic gains because of the assistance it provided Federal Nigeria. Less than a week after the war had ended, the Nigerian ambassador to Moscow, Brigadier Kurubo, was quoted as saying that Soviet support was "responsible for the Federal victory more than any single thing, more than all other things put together."[51] Given the ambassador's position, the statement is most politic, but it hardly accords with the facts of the Nigerian victory. As was pointed out earlier, analysis of Nigeria's *Trade Summary* reveals that Britain supplied the overwhelming majority of the FMG's weapons during the war, including well over 90 percent of the arms received in 1969. The Soviet contribution was largely in creating an offensive air force for Nigeria, but the air force was so small and the pilots so poor that the FMG could not put a single, poorly defended airfield out of commission in over a year of bombing missions. The 122-mm artillery guns that received so much attention were not even put into operation until late December 1969, when the Biafran collapse was well under way, and according to de St. Jorre, they "were never close enough to do any serious damage."[52] From a military point of view, the Soviet contribution must be rated as a decidedly secondary factor in the Nigerian victory.

The real victory was the Soviet Union's enhancement of its image and influence in West Africa. The Lagos *Sunday Post* wrote that the Federal victory "was accomplished by the efforts of the country's patriotic forces and the constant support of true friends, above all the Soviet Union, the United Arab Republic, Algeria, and other friendly countries of Asia and Africa."[53] A goodwill mission headed by Federal Commissioner Aminu Kano went to Moscow in March 1970 to discuss expanded Soviet-Nigerian ties. Those ties had already increased ma-

---

[51] *The Times* (London), January 21, 1970.
[52] de St. Jorre, *The Brothers' War*, 317.
[53] Quoted in *Pravda*, March 11, 1970.

nyfold during the war. In 1967, Avtoeksport purchased an 80 percent interest in the Nigerian West African Automobile and Technical Company, and by 1968, "Moskovitch" passenger cars were being vigorously marketed in Federal Nigeria. The $140 million economic assistance agreement signed in November 1968, in addition to paying for weapons, contributed to the financing of several projects: the development of Nigeria's steel industry, an 800-bed hospital at Enugu, and an oil production training center at Warri. During the civil war, dozens of Soviet delegations visited Nigeria, Nigerian-Soviet chambers of commerce opened in Lagos and Benin, air service was established between the USSR and Nigeria, and the number of Nigerian students in the USSR increased to 1,000. Soviet-Nigerian trade grew rapidly during the conflict; by 1970 the volume of trade was 30 million rubles, 30 times what it had been in 1963, and by 1971 Nigeria was the USSR's largest trading partner in Africa.

Although it was inevitable that Nigeria would turn back toward the West somewhat after the war ended, Soviet-Nigerian ties continued to make progress throughout the 1970s. Numerous technical and economic aid agreements were signed with the USSR and with other COMECON nations, so many, in fact, that the Nigerian government more than once felt obliged to deny reports that the Russians were involved in certain projects. In May 1974, General Gowon visited the USSR, the first such visit ever made by a Nigerian head of state. In the course of a lengthy joint communiqué issued May 28, Gowon expressed his gratitude for "the moral, political and material support provided by the Soviet Union in the period of struggle to safeguard the unity and integrity of Nigeria."[54] Several cooperative agreements were signed at the time of Gowon's visit. During the Angolan civil war several months later, Nigeria's new leaders eventually came down on the side of the MPLA and declared that Moscow's involvement was justified because of South Africa's intervention.

The Soviet involvement in the Nigerian civil war opened the door to influence in Africa's largest nation after previous attempts had failed to make headway. Although in 1978, after President Jimmy Carter's visit to Nigeria, Lagos warned the USSR and Cuba not to overstay their welcome in Africa, there is no doubt that the USSR's earlier involvement in the civil war served to shift Nigerian foreign policy from its unwavering pro-Western stance in the 1960s to a more ambiguous stance in the 1970s, closer to the nonalignment that Moscow evidently values as a midway point to a pro-Soviet policy. The low risks, low costs, and substantial political rewards reaped by Moscow as a result of its involvement made the affair a high point of Soviet foreign policy in Africa.

[54] *Pravda*, May 29, 1974. See also Gowon's speech quoted in *Pravda*, May 22, 1974. For a good review of Soviet-Nigerian relations after the war, see Oye Ogunbadejo, "Ideology and Pragmatism: The Soviet Role in Nigeria, 1960–1977," *Orbis* 21(Winter 1978):819–26.

7
THE YOM KIPPUR WAR[1]

Even Israeli Prime Minister Golda Meir explains her troops' heavy losses as . . . the consequence of the growing might of the Arab forces, in whose training Soviet military specialists participated, and of the high quality of the Soviet weapons with which the Arabs are equipped.
Krasnaya Zvezda, October 20, 1973

The Yom Kippur War was a watershed in world politics. Although the hostilities lasted only three weeks, the war profoundly affected the subsequent course of the Arab-Israeli dispute, altered the regional balance in the Middle East, damaged relations between Washington and Moscow, and traumatized the international economy by catalyzing OPEC's transformation into a potent and determined cartel. The war also underscored the USSR's maturing stature as a global power – it was the Soviet Union's first *massive* intervention during the postwar era on behalf of a non-Communist client engaged in all-out conflict and the first historical instance of its taking definite escalatory steps in a regional conflict central to U.S. interests. The unprecedented level of Soviet involvement must be attributed not only to the USSR's determination to maintain influence with the Arab states but also to advances during the 1960s in its military capabilities: the achievement of strategic parity with the United States, the expansion of airlift and sealift capacity, and the logistical experience gained in previous regional conflicts. The war, in effect, inaugurated a new and more turbulent stage of Soviet military activism in the Third World.

By choosing to back the Arabs with massive arms shipments during the conflict, the Soviet leadership struck a serious blow at the relationship of détente that the superpowers had painstakingly cultivated during the preceding few years. The peculiar relationship known as détente that flowered between the USSR and the United States in the early 1970s had been codified in agreements signed at the Moscow summit meeting in May 1972 and the Nixon-Brezhnev summit in Washington in June 1973. The United States and the USSR agreed formally that certain basic principles would govern their relationship: Each side promised to prevent conflicts that would

---

[1] The war began on the Jewish holy day of Yom Kippur, the day of atonement. The Arabs sometimes refer to it as the Ramadan war, because it occurred in the Moslem holy month of Ramadan. It is also widely known as the October war.

increase international tension, to avoid military confrontations, and to refrain from threat or use of force against the other side or its allies. Soviet behavior in October 1973 violated enough of these principles, at least in the view of policymakers in Washington, to raise serious doubts about the underlying premises of détente. In this sense, the conflict was a harbinger of the progressive deterioration and virtual demise of détente that occurred between 1973 and 1980, partly as a result of the USSR's involvement in local conflicts.

The war began at 1:55 p.m. on October 6, when 150 Egyptian planes launched a surprise attack on Israeli positions in the Sinai, and more than 1,000 artillery guns opened a barrage along the entire front. Waves of infantrymen crossed the Suez Canal in boats, established themselves on the opposite bank, and rapidly erected Soviet-supplied pontoon bridges for bringing heavy equipment across the canal. To the north, Syrian forces carried out a massive assault on Israeli fortifications in the Golan Heights. Within 24 hours of the onslaught, Egypt had established three large bridgeheads on the east bank of the Suez, sustaining only minimal casualties, while Syria had employed vastly superior numbers of tanks and troops to achieve a breakthrough on the southern flank of the Golan front. Israel could slow the Syrian breakthrough only by throwing most of its air force into battle against the advancing tank columns; this, in turn, freed Egypt to consolidate its bridgeheads on the east bank and to fortify them with SAM batteries.

The war evolved through three main stages, corresponding to phases of Soviet and U.S. involvement in the conflict. During the first stage, October 6–10, Washington and Moscow refrained from military involvement in the conflict. After the initial Egyptian and Syrian attacks, Israel, on October 8, attempted a large counterattack in the south that failed to dislodge the well-positioned Egyptian forces, though Israel suffered heavy losses in troops and tanks. In the north, on October 8–9, Syria pressed its initial attack and nearly made further breakthroughs before Israel stemmed the offensive and began a counterattack that in one day recaptured most of the territory lost in the first three days of fighting.

By the end of the fifth day, all three armies were exhausted, with supplies of ammunition and equipment running low. Israel had lost over 500 tanks; Syria had lost 900, but more significantly had exhausted most of its stock of SAM-6 missiles, crucial for checking Israeli air superiority. None of the combatants was in condition to fight much longer without outside arms supplies. The time was ripe for a cease-fire, and a coordinated initiative by the United States and the USSR might well have achieved one. Israel had regained the Golan Heights, but Egypt still held its Sinai bridgehead; so those two combatants would have profited. On October 10, however, Soviet arms began arriving by air in Syria and Egypt, and seaborne shipments followed shortly behind. Thus began the second stage of the war, October 10–22, during which the battle continued with weapons supplied by Washington and Moscow. The U.S. airlift to Israel followed slightly behind the Soviet shipments, with modest quantities of ammunition and missiles transported by air on October 10, and a large-scale airlift beginning October 14.

On October 11, Israel's high command attempted to turn its counterattack in the Golan into a major offensive against Syria, hoping to eliminate Damascus from the war before the Soviet resupply effort could make a difference. That would free Israeli forces for use in the south. The strategy was only partly successful. Reinforced by crack armored divisions from Iran and Jordan, the Syrian army resisted valiantly and was pushed back only slowly and at great cost. Air strikes against selected targets in and around Damascus merely strengthened the Syrian resolve, and on October 13 the SAM batteries began firing again, replenished by the Soviet airlift. Israel decided to halt the offensive, having pushed the front 10 miles back from its prewar position. From then until the end of the war the Golan front was relatively quiet, and the center of war shifted to the south.

Under the pressure of the Israeli onslaught, President Assad of Syria had urged Egypt to open an offensive in the south, and President Sadat had agreed. Egypt prepared for an offensive by transferring most of its armor to the east bank of the Suez in what eventually proved to be a costly mistake. The Egyptian attack began early on October 14 and resulted in one of the largest tank battles in history. Israel repulsed the attack decisively, destroying nearly 500 Egyptian tanks while losing less than 30 of its own. On the next day, the Israeli army put into action a bold plan to recover the initiative in the war. Taking advantage of a small gap between the Egyptian Second Army and Third Army, Israel managed to wedge a corridor to the canal, construct bridges, and transfer large forces to the west bank. The operation was well under way before the Egyptians realized it was not just a diversionary maneuver. Against fierce opposition, Israel secured and widened the corridor, and by October 18 three Israeli tank divisions (several hundred tanks) had crossed the canal and were beginning a two-pronged drive to surround the Egyptian army by cutting off the Cairo-Ismailia road to the north and the Cairo-Suez road to the south.

Kosygin flew to Cairo (October 16–19) in order to convince Sadat that an immediate cease-fire was in the Arabs' interest. Sadat did not agree to a cease-fire initiative until October 18, when the seriousness of the Israeli action on the west bank of the Suez became apparent. On Kosygin's return, the Kremlin invited Henry Kissinger to Moscow for urgent consultations. The U.S. secretary of state arrived on October 20. Even as the negotiations were under way, the Israeli army pressed to cut off the roads between Cairo and the canal. The Moscow talks rapidly resulted in an agreement, and just after midnight on October 22 the UN Security Council passed Resolution 338, jointly sponsored by the United States and the Soviet Union, calling for a cease-fire in place 12 hours later.

The third stage of the war began when the cease-fire broke down less than half a day after it had begun. The two sides evidently shared responsibility for violating the cease-fire, but once hostilities resumed, Israel sought to exploit its superior position to maximum advantage. Two Israeli tank divisions pressed southward, cutting off the Suez-Cairo road and surrounding the Egyptian Third Army completely. The Israeli advance could not be halted, and it threatened to turn the war into a resounding victory for Israel, an outcome that Moscow could hardly tolerate.

On the evening of October 24, Brezhnev sent a message to the White House that threatened unilateral Soviet action against Israel if Washington did not agree to join the USSR in sending troops to enforce the cease-fire. The United States reacted with a worldwide alert of American military forces early on the morning of October 25, and Kissinger indicated to the USSR that Washington would not tolerate unilateral military action on Moscow's part. The next afternoon in the UN Security Council the governments agreed to a proposal for a peacekeeping force that excluded troops from the permanent members of the council. Under heavy pressure from the United States, the Israeli government ceased military operations on the west bank and reluctantly allowed the Third Army to be supplied with food and water. This marked the practical end of hostilities, though several weeks of negotiation followed, with the United States as the ascendant mediator, before Egypt and Israel signed a disengagement agreement in January that extricated the Third Army and left Cairo with net territorial gains. Syria and Israel, after much thornier negotiations, signed a disengagement agreement four months later.

The local dispute

The substance of the Arab-Israeli dispute is so generally familiar as to require only a brief review. In November 1947, the UN General Assembly voted to partition Palestine, then under a British mandate, into separate Arab and Jewish states. Arab opposition to the partition triggered widespread hostilities between the indigenous Arab and Jewish populations. On May 15, 1948, one day after the British mandate expired, the state of Israel was proclaimed, and in effect the conflict assumed the form of an interstate war between Israel and the surrounding Arab states. It was the beginning of a protracted state of war that amounted to an unending, bitter truce between sworn enemies, punctuated by brief periods of actual conflict: the Suez war in the fall of 1956, the six-day war in June 1967, the war of attrition, 1969–70, and the October war. Each successive conflict witnessed an increasing level of involvement on the part of the major powers; each conflict was characterized by short, intense battles followed by an internationally sponsored cease-fire; each war altered the local balance of power and transfigured the political dynamics of the region; and each war failed to settle the fundamental issues at stake in the clash between Arab nationalism and Jewish Zionism.

Prior to the June 1967 war, the immediate goal of the Arab states had been to annihilate Israel as a political state. After the war – which resulted in an overwhelming victory for Tel Aviv, and Israeli occupation of the Sinai, the West Bank of the Jordan, and the Golan Heights – the Arabs were forced to limit their struggle, at least for the time being, to the more urgent task of retaking the occupied territories.

Between 1967 and 1973 the Arab states pursued numerous strategies for regaining the territories short of all-out war, but little progress was made, and pressures grew to seek by means of war a restoration of some measure of the national pride lost in 1967. Sadat wrote of the decision to go to war:

> The basic task was to wipe out the disgrace and humiliation that followed from the 1967 defeat. I reckoned it would be 1,000 times more honorable for us ... to be buried crossing the Canal than to accept disgrace and humiliation.[2]

According to Mohammed Heikal, editor of the semiofficial Cairo newspaper *Al Ahram*, considerations involving Egypt's chronic economic problems and the domestic troubles of the regime also created pressures to go to war. If even a small strip of the Sinai could be won, the Suez Canal could be opened to provide much-needed revenue, the government would gain legitimacy at home, and the oil-rich Arab states would be more inclined to aid Egypt. The Egyptians also believed that if the U.S.-Soviet rapprochement developed much further, the superpowers might collude to prevent another Middle East war.[3] Convinced that time was on the side of the Israelis, and seeing no other recourse, the Arab leaders decided to turn to armed force. This was the immediate cause of the Yom Kippur war.

Like the Arab-Israeli wars that preceded it, the October conflict offered in some respects an ideal opportunity for the Soviet Union to seek influence by offering military assistance to its clients. The Arab states were totally dependent on outside sources for arms, and the Soviet Union was the only power able and willing to provide arms of sufficient quantity and sophistication to make war against Israel feasible. The frustrated aspirations of Arab nationalism were easy to exploit, and Moscow could rightfully claim that since 1967 it had unwaveringly supported the Arab position regarding the occupied lands. However, the local dispute was fraught with potential difficulties for the Soviet position in the Middle East. If war broke out, it would almost certainly slow the progress being made with Soviet-American relations, no matter what the outcome. If the Arabs began to win decisively, the United States would certainly intervene, and the possibility of a superpower confrontation would then arise. If the Arabs began to lose

---

[2] Anwar el-Sadat, *In Search of Identity: An Autobiography* (New York: Harper & Row, 1977), 215; see also pp. 181 and 244.

[3] Mohammed Heikal, *The Road to Ramadan* (New York: Quadrangle, 1975), 203–5. In a speech in Alexandria on April 3, 1974, Sadat observed that "June came, and with it the second summit conference between Nixon and Brezhnev ... That meeting resulted in military relaxation. This meant that everything must stop and that Israel would remain superior and that we would remain in our position.... They agreed that nothing should happen anywhere in the world." Cairo Radio, April 4, 1974. See also Sadat, *In Search of Identity*, 213–15, 228–9.

decisively – and Moscow probably viewed this as the most likely outcome – they would put great pressure on the USSR to intervene directly and would blame Moscow for the loss if it did not respond. After the debacle in June 1967, the USSR had been able to maintain favor with the Arabs only by responding immediately with massive arms shipments and diplomatic support. Although that event served to vastly increase the Russian presence in the Middle East, such an outcome probably would not be possible a second time. An Arab loss would almost certainly mean expulsion of the Soviet Union from the Arab world. The high risks associated with involvement in the conflict, weighed against the uncertain benefits, seem to have made the Soviet leadership rather hesitant about the plans of Egypt and Syria to go to war.[4]

The Soviet Union's view of the Arab-Israeli dispute differed in at least one fundamental respect from that of its Arab clients in 1973: The USSR did recognize Israel. When the first Arab-Jewish war broke out in Palestine, Moscow had leaned to the side of the Jews and had even allowed a consignment of Czech arms to be sent to the Jewish Haganah. When Israel announced its independence, the USSR was one of the first nations to recognize the new state, apparently viewing the establishment of Israel as a blow to the British position in the Middle East and therefore as an integral part of the worldwide national liberation movement. Although Soviet-Israeli relations soon cooled, and Moscow seems to have begun to view Arab nationalism as a more potent lever for penetrating the Middle East, the Soviet Union never withdrew its recognition of Israel. Diplomatic relations were cut off in the dark days that followed the 1967 defeat, but despite Arab pressures, Moscow's recognition of Israel was not withdrawn. Even at the height of the October war, when the tide was turning against the Arabs, *Pravda* declared (inaccurately) that "no state in the world, including neighboring Arab states, has any question about the state of Israel's right to sovereign existence."[5] If only because the existence of Israel created the very issues and tensions that made Soviet advances in the Middle East possible, Moscow had a certain vested interest in seeing Israel survive. This policy placed the Soviet Union in a rather difficult position of striving to win favor with the Arabs by backing their demands against Israel even to the point of military action, while withholding from them the capacity to threaten Israel mortally, so as to ensure its continuing existence and to avoid confrontation with the United States. It was one of the most insoluble contradictions of Soviet foreign policy from 1955 onward.

---

[4] According to Sadat, the possibility of military action was discussed with the USSR several months before the war, "but the USSR persisted in the view that a military battle must be ruled out and that the question must await a peaceful conference." Cairo Radio, April 4, 1974.

[5] *Pravda*, October 17, 1973; see also Radio Moscow, October 15, 1973.

Soviet ideologists naturally interpreted the Arab-Israeli dispute in the larger context of the national liberation movement:

> . . . the Arab-Israeli conflict arose as a result of the policy pursued by the imperialist powers in the Arab East, utilizing the Zionists as their tool in the fight against the national liberation movement of the Arab peoples. This conflict was aggravated as Israel's rulers, encouraged by the imperialist circles, particularly of the US, pursued their expansionist policy.[6]

This concept of the Arab national liberation movement being the central target of Israeli-Western aggression had been voiced even before the Arab lands were occupied in 1967. In 1956, Gromyko declared that the Suez war had been a French-British conspiracy to crush the national liberation movement in the Middle East and to reimpose imperialist domination. After the June war, a plenum of the Central Committee of the CPSU declared that "the aggression by Israel is a result of a conspiracy of the most reactionary forces of international imperialism, above all of the United States, directed against a contingent of the national liberation movement – the leading Arab states."[7] Brezhnev was more explicit in a speech delivered a few days later:

> The main reason for Israel's aggression against the Arab countries is the aspiration of American and British imperialists to inflict a blow on the national liberation movement in the Middle East, to stop the movement of peoples along the path of social progress at any cost.[8]

The same themes surfaced again in the October war. On October 8, an official government statement charged that responsibility for the war and its consequences rested entirely with Israel "and the foreign reactionary circles that constantly indulge Israel in its aggressive actions."[9] The statement repeatedly condemned Israeli aggression and expansionism and called for immediate return of the Arabs' occupied lands. A few days later, a *Pravda* commentator outlined the alleged imperialist plan:

> . . . acting together with imperialist forces and internal Arab reactionaries, Tel Aviv planned to compel Egypt and Syria to abandon their progressive path of development, their social transformations in the interests of the working people, and their cooperation with the socialist states.[10]

[6] E. Dmitryev, "Blizhnii Vostok: likvidirovat' opasnuyu napryazhennost'," *Mezhdunarodnaya zhizn'* (June 1973):37.
[7] *Pravda*, June 22, 1967.
[8] *Pravda*, July 6, 1967.
[9] *Pravda*, October 8, 1973.
[10] *Pravda*, October 12, 1973.

The argument that Israel and its international allies were responsible for frustrating social progress and national liberation in the Arab nations was one sure to strike a responsive chord with Arab regimes swamped by insoluble problems.

The diplomatic relationship between the USSR and its client

In order to understand the USSR's relations with the Arabs during the Yom Kippur war, it is necessary to go back more than a year to July 8, 1972, when Sadat announced the nationalization of the air bases and other military facilities constructed by the Soviet Union in Egypt following the June war. At the same time, he ordered the withdrawal of thousands of Soviet military advisers, a surprise move that brought Soviet-Egyptian relations to their lowest nadir in nearly two decades and led some Western observers to believe that the USSR could not recover its position in the Middle East for years to come, if ever. In fact, only seven months after the expulsion order, a partial Soviet-Egyptian rapprochement had occurred, and Soviet weapons were flowing into Egypt at an unprecedented pace. A further eight months passed and the October war took place, marking the Soviet Union's most extensive involvement in any Third World conflict up to that time. The rapid – though not full – recovery of Soviet influence after the events of July 1972 suggests that the break was not as final or as deep-seated as it appeared to be. Sadat knew that his only po-litically feasible recourse against Israel was military action; he also knew that only the USSR was willing and able to provide him the military wherewithal to conduct a war. The expulsion of the Soviet advisers was a tactical maneuver on his part, a kind of diplomatic shock treatment meant to force Moscow into greater concessions. The real split with the USSR did not – indeed, could not – take place until after the Yom Kippur war had fundamentally altered the political order in the Middle East. This may explain why the Egyptian presi-dent did not at the time of the expulsion abrogate the treaty of friend-ship and cooperation Egypt had signed with the USSR in May 1971. It was a signal, perhaps, that he did not want to precipitate a total break with Moscow.

Only five days after Sadat announced the expulsion of the Soviet advisers, he sent Prime Minister Aziz Sidqi to Moscow "with instruc-tions to do what he could to soothe the Russians' ruffled feelings and, if he could, arrange for the purchase of more equipment." Sadat also declared publicly that the termination of the military mission was "only aimed at getting Soviet-Egyptian friendship back to its normal atmosphere" and that it would "in no way prejudice the substance of Egyptian-Soviet friendship." Frustrated by delays in weapons ship-ments, broken promises, and the Soviets' unwillingness to provide certain types of weapons, Sadat wanted to dramatize Egypt's determination to remain independent from the USSR. His action was meant to show the Kremlin that it must either pay up – with more and better arms deliveries – or lose its privileged position in the Middle East. To emphasize the point, Sadat made several contacts with Washington during this period, though they led to no significant shift in the U.S. position.[11]

Early in August, Brezhnev sent Sadat a personal letter criticizing the decision to send the advisers home. In an aloof and frigid tone the letter recounted all the USSR had done for Egypt and contrasted Soviet policies with those of the imperialist states. As to the expulsion:

> We cannot be indifferent to the policy which has been adopted by the Egyptian government, which is objectively and subjectively contrary to the interests of our two peoples. It is a policy resulting from the intrigues of rightist elements directly or indirectly allied with imperialism to halt Egypt's march along the progressive road and turn it back.[12]

Insulted by the letter, Sadat told the People's Assembly on August 17 that it was "totally unacceptable," but that "I do not want to sever relations; I want to get them back on a healthy line."[13]

Knowing he could not wage war without Soviet help, Sadat soon took steps to restore the relationship with Moscow. On August 30 he sent Brezhnev a letter with detailed complaints about Soviet military assistance and Soviet policy toward the Arabs. The letter implied that if the Soviets did not respond by October 31, a further deterioration of relations would follow.[14] Early in October, Assad visited Moscow, and on his return home traveled via Cairo with a Soviet invitation to send an Egyptian delegation to Moscow for talks. Aziz Sidqi visited the Kremlin from October 16 to 18, accompanied by the commander of the air force and other military leaders. Sadat later said of this visit:

> Our relations with the USSR were frozen throughout the summer – until October, when our brother President Hafez Assad went to Moscow and raised the question again. Dr. Aziz Sidqi went there on October 16, and when he returned it seemed that

[11] Quotations are from the following: Mohammed Heikal, *Sphinx and Commissar: The Rise and Fall of Soviet Influence in the Arab World* (London: Collins, 1978), 244; *Arab Report and Record*, August 16–31, 1972; Sadat, "Speech to the National Conference of the Arab Socialist Union, July 24, 1972," *Journal of Palestine Studies* II(Autumn 1972):176. See also Sadat, *In Search of Identity*, 225–31; *New York Times*, July 25, 1972; Sadat address to a student conference in Alexandria, April 3, 1974, in *Journal of Palestine Studies* III(Summer 1974):216.

[12] The letter is quoted at length in Heikal, *Sphinx and Commissar*, 244–6.

[13] *Arab Report and Record*, August 16–31, 1972.

[14] Sadat's letter to Brezhnev is reproduced in full in Appendix I of Sadat, *In Search of Identity*, 317–24; see also p. 234.

relations had started to improve. But it was only on the surface; in fact relations hadn't improved at all.[15]

A trickle of spare parts and ammunition began to come from the USSR, but the basic rift remained unhealed. The Soviet leaders well understood the game Sadat was playing and may have been holding back to demonstrate that they could not be manipulated so easily. In accordance with an agreement reached with Sidqi, an Egyptian military delegation visited Moscow from November 16 to 29, 1972, but no visible evidence of success came from the talks.[16]

At this point Sadat made a conciliatory gesture. He informed the Soviet Union that a five-year agreement concluded in 1968, giving the Soviet fleet access to Egyptian port facilities in the Mediterranean, would be renewed for five additional years in March 1973 when it was due to expire. "My object was to show the Russians that in spite of my decision to expel the Soviet military experts, I did not wish to break with them altogether."[17] The action seems to have served to mollify Moscow, for shortly afterward the Politburo of the CPSU Central Committee was reported to have ordered a review of the full scope of Soviet relations with Egypt. On January 24, 1973, the Soviet ambassador to Cairo, Vladimir Vinogradov, met with Sadat for the first time in several months, and arrangements were made for a Soviet military delegation to visit Cairo and for Hafiz Isma'il, Sadat's adviser on national security affairs, to visit Moscow.

The military delegation arrived in Egypt on February 1, the first such visit after July 1972.[18] However, the real breakthrough in relations took place as a result of Isma'il's visit to Moscow from February 7 to 10, 1973. Isma'il met with Brezhnev and other top leaders, and the visit received lengthy coverage in the Soviet news media. The joint communiqué issued February 10 noted that the talks had taken place "in a friendly atmosphere" and affirmed the determination of each party to strive for a Middle East settlement on the basis of Security Council Resolution 242. Particularly significant were two statements by the Soviet side that "the Arab governments have the complete right to use *any form of struggle* in the liberation of their occupied territories" and that the Soviet side "will continue its political and economic support of Egypt, and *will make possible the strengthening of its military potential*" (italics added).[19] Relations were back on course.

---

[15] Sadat address, *Journal of Palestine Studies* III(Summer 1974):216.
[16] *New York Times*, November 12 and December 4, 1972.
[17] Sadat, *In Search of Identity*, 238.
[18] *The Times* (London), February 2, 1973.
[19] *Isvestia*, February 11, 1973. The Soviets had suggested in two early communiqués that the Arabs had the right to employ "other means" (April 27, 1972) and "diverse means" (October 18,1972) to liberate their territory, but this was the strongest statement yet. Sadat later said that "from February 1973 our relations began to return to normal." Cairo Radio, April 4, 1974. He met with the visiting Soviet military delegation the day after the communiqué was issued.

General Ahman Ismai'il 'Ali, Egypt's minister of war and commander in chief of the armed forces, went to Moscow from February 26 to March 2. According to Sadat, "the biggest arms deal ever to be concluded (either with Nasser or myself) was the result of his visit. For the first time, too, shipments started promptly." Sadat told Heikal that "they are drowning me in arms," and in a *Newsweek* interview he stated that the Russians "are providing us now with everything that's possible for them to supply. I am now quite satisfied."[20] New arms also poured into Syria during the months preceding the outbreak of the war. Sadat's gamble had paid off – the USSR was forced to raise the ante of its commitment in order to salvage its influence in the region.

The Soviet-Egyptian relationship remained strained, however, despite the new arms. Sadat claimed that the decision to go to war against Israel was made in April, "but the USSR insisted that military battle must be avoided and that the problem must await a military solution." Early in June, Vinogradov told Sadat that Moscow wanted to send President Nikolai Podgorny to Cairo on June 11. Sadat refused to see him on the grounds that Podgorny harbored anti-Egyptian sentiments. Muhammad Hasan az-Zayyat, Egypt's foreign minister, visited Moscow May 27–29 and met with Gromyko and other Soviet officials. The communiqué simply reaffirmed the relationship established during Isma'il's visit in February. A number of further exchanges at various levels took place during June, including a trip to Moscow by the commander of the Egyptian navy.[21]

The summit meeting between Nixon and Brezhnev in June 1973 seriously concerned the Arabs. Cairo's leaders suspected the superpowers would agree to "a policy of military balance" in the Middle East that would leave the Arab-Israeli problem unresolved. Disappointed by the scanty attention given to the Middle East in the summit communiqué, Egypt went so far as to recall its ambassador in Moscow for consultations. Hafiz Isma'il flew to Moscow in mid-July to smooth over the friction and to hear the Soviet version of the summit meeting. Sadat reported on this visit to the Central Committee of the Arab Socialist Union and the People's Assembly, stating that it reassured him that Soviet support would continue.[22]

Egypt's preparations for war intensified in August and September. On August 28–29 Sadat visited Assad in Damascus, where the two leaders settled on October 6 as the day to begin the war against Israel. On September 10, Assad, Sadat, and King Hussein met in Cairo to

[20] The Sadat quotations are from the following: Sadat, *In Search of Identity*, 238; Heikal, *The Road to Ramadan*, 181; *Newsweek*, April 9, 1973.
[21] Sadat speech, April 4, 1974, *Journal of Palestine Studies* (Summer 1974):217; Sadat, *In Search of Identity*, 242–3; Radio Moscow, May 30, 1974.
[22] Radio Cairo, June 26, July 23, August 16 and 21, 1973. Rubinstein considers the ambassador's recall part of Sadat's campaign to deceive Israel into thinking that his relations with Moscow were worse than they in fact were.

coordinate their efforts against Israel. Less than two weeks after this meeting, Sadat and Brezhnev exchanged messages on the "international situation," and on September 23 Sadat met privately with Vinogradov. The timing of these exchanges is cited by some analysts as evidence of direct Soviet complicity in the Arab war plans.[23] This seems unlikely, however. The contacts took place at the initiative of Sadat, who quite probably only wanted general reassurances about Soviet support in the event a war broke out. Heikal even asserted that the Soviet leaders preferred not to know the details or timing of the attack. According to Sadat – and his account is substantially confirmed by Heikal and Vinogradov – Moscow was not informed until October 3 that military operations were about to commence, and the exact date and time of the attack were first communicated on October 4, when Assad told the Soviet ambassador in Damascus, Nuritdin Mukhitdinov, the details.[24]

On the basis of intelligence data and reports from the Soviet advisers in Syria and Egypt, it is possible that the Kremlin had surmised much earlier that an Arab attack was approaching. One reason that U.S. and Israeli intelligence did not draw that conclusion is that they lacked information about Arab intentions and assumed that Cairo and Damascus were not ready for war. Throughout the summer the Soviet news media had published regular warnings that Israeli provocations were bringing the Middle East to the brink of conflict and that the tensions in the Middle East were becoming serious.[25] Once Moscow knew of the timing of "Operation Badr," it was possible to publish a more unambiguous warning in the morning edition of *Pravda*, October 6: "Tension on the ceasefire line between Syria and Israel is height-

[23] Jon Glassman, *Arms for the Arabs: The Soviet Union and War in the Middle East* (Baltimore: Johns Hopkins University Press, 1975), 120–4; Foy Kohler et al., *The Soviet Union and the October 1973 Middle East War: The Implications for Détente* (Coral Gables: University of Miami, 1974), 32–50; Walter Laquer, *Confrontation: The Middle East War and World Politics* (London: Wildwood House, 1974), 71–5; Rubinstein, *Red Star on the Nile*, 251–62. One of the key arguments used to build the case for Soviet complicity is that the Kremlin must have known the date of attack in order to have made the necessary preparations for the airlift and sealift, and for launching a reconaissance satellite over the Middle East on October 3. In fact, though some seaborne weapons shipments took place very early in the war, they apparently were previously scheduled transfers that would have occurred even in the absence of a conflict. Not until October 11 was there a definite increase in the number of ships passing through the Bosporus. As to Cosmos 596, its launching proves only that the Soviets wanted more information about a very troubled region in which they knew war might shortly break out. An intelligence-gathering initiative is no proof of foreknowledge; it is just as likely to be the opposite.

[24] Sadat, *In Search of Identity*, 242, 246; Heikal, *Road to Ramadan*, 21, 34–5; V. Vinogradov, "October War Counter-Claims," *al-Safir* (Beirut), April 16, 1974; reprinted in *Journal of Palestine Studies* III(Summer 1974):161–3; Heikal, *Sphinx and Commissar*, 256.

[25] E. Dmitryev, "Blizhnii Vostok," 35, 40–2; D. Volsky, "Novye vozmozhnosti i starye nomekhi," *Novoe Vremya*, No. 32(August 1973):14; Radio Moscow, September 15, 1973; *Tass*, September 16, 1973.

ening. The Egyptian press assumes that Tel Aviv is preparing a massive attack.... In the light of recent provocations, yesterday's threats from Israeli Chief of Staff Elazar ... are a signal for the preparation of new aggression."

After Moscow was informed officially of the war plans, Vinogradov was instructed to tell Sadat that "the decision to make war was an Egyptian decision, and that the USSR would fulfill all its obligations and would support Arab rights by all means ... military, political, and economic." The Kremlin then complicated matters by requesting permission to land aircraft in order to evacuate Soviet dependents in Egypt. Sadat assented, but he was left troubled by the meaning of the Soviet evacuation. He wondered if it was a sign that the Soviets might not give him the support he expected.[26]

The evacuation of the Soviet dependents is a puzzling move that has never been explained satisfactorily. The notion that Moscow withdrew the civilian families out of fear for their welfare is not tenable – Moscow had never taken such a move before unless lives had been immediately threatened by actual hostilities.[27] The early evacuation was detected by Western and Israeli intelligence – as both Egypt and the USSR knew it would be – and was taken by Cairo as a sign of poor confidence in the Arabs. One possible explanation is that the Kremlin wanted to put subtle pressure on Sadat and Assad to reconsider their decision, but wanted to do so in a manner that would still leave open the option of supporting them militarily. In the days just prior to the war and just after its outbreak, the Soviets were balanced on a fine wire between wanting to restrain the Arabs and yet being compelled to support them lest the Soviet Union lose face and influence.

Shortly after the outbreak of the conflict, Soviet-Egyptian communications nearly broke down over a Syrian proposal that the USSR introduce a cease-fire resolution in the UN Security Council. Exactly what occurred is not clear, but by piecing several accounts together, the following picture emerges:

1.   Just before the hostilities began, Assad suggested to Mukhitdinov that no harm would be done if a resolution calling for a cease-fire was put forward in the Security Council after the war commenced. Apparently he felt that "if the fighting was going Syria's way the resolution would not matter; if the fighting went Israel's way the resolution might come in useful."[28]

2.   Mukhitdinov relayed the request to Moscow. After Operation Badr had begun, Moscow telephoned Vinogradov in Cairo; he, in turn, requested an urgent meeting with Sadat. They met on the evening of

---

[26] Vinogradov, "October War Counter-Claims," 161–2; Heikal, *Road to Ramadan*, 34; Sadat, *In Search of Identity*, 246–7.

[27] Rubinstein, *Red Star on the Nile*, 259–61. As Rubinstein notes, evacuation is always a political act, no matter what its intent.

[28] Heikal, *Road to Ramadan*, 209.

October 6, shortly before 8:00 p.m. Vinogradov gave Sadat official congratulations on the crossing of the canal and told him that Syria had requested the USSR to obtain a UN cease-fire resolution within 48 hours of the start of the fighting. Sadat did not believe that Assad had made the request, and he refused to consider a cease-fire.

3.   Sadat sent Assad a coded telegram regarding the Soviet message, and Assad replied, assuring Sadat that he had said nothing of the kind to the Soviet ambassador.[29]

4.   On the evening of October 7, Vinogradov again asked to see Sadat. Sadat told him of Assad's denial, but Vinogradov said that he had received another message from Moscow indicating that Syria had repeated its cease-fire request. Sadat was angered, and he informed Vinogradov that the subject was closed.

5.   Vinogradov claimed that Syria requested a cease-fire yet again on October 9, when the Israeli counterattack had turned the battle on the Syrian front; once again Sadat was consulted, and he refused to contemplate a cease-fire.[30]

What was involved apparently was a somewhat clumsy Soviet attempt to get Egypt and Syria to agree to an early cease-fire. Most likely Syria did discuss the possibility of having the USSR introduce a cease-fire resolution early in the war, but only so that it could be invoked if needed. The Soviets then may have tried to use this request to put pressure on Sadat, but without success. Sadat wrote that Vinogradov was in touch with him every day during the first stage of the war, to exchange information and to urge Egypt to consider a cease-fire. If this is true, and all the accounts seem to agree on the general outline, it suggests that Moscow made a serious effort to contain the conflict in its first four days, before concluding that a military supply bridge would be necessary.

Once the initial Soviet attempt to convince the Arabs to seek a cease-fire had failed, and once it became clear that the Arabs were performing respectably on the battlefield, the Soviet approach began to change. Heikal wrote that Vinogradov informed Sadat on October 8 that an airlift of arms would shortly begin and that Sadat was delighted and told the ambassador to inform Brezhnev that Soviet arms had made the canal crossing possible. Sadat told Heikal and Vinogradov that the Arab victory would restore the prestige of Soviet arms in the Middle East. The airlift actually began on October 9. Then, according to Vinogradov, "on the morning of October 10 the Soviet command gave its approval to Sadat's plan to recover the Mitla and

[29] Heikal claims that Sadat contacted Assad on October 7 and received his reply on October 8. Sadat and Vinogradov agreed that their second meeting was on October 7, Sadat having contacted Assad immediately after the first meeting on October 6.

[30] The sources dealing with this account are the following: Sadat, *In Search of Identity*, 252–4; Heikal, *The Road to Ramadan*, 208–9, 212–17; Vinogradov, "October War Counter-Claims," 161–3.

Gidi passes and stated that if Egypt wanted to develop the attack so as to recover the passes, this should be done immediately without delay."[31] Vinogradov's account, written after the war, must be viewed with some skepticism, but it does not contradict the general thrust of the accounts of Sadat and Heikal. These accounts suggest that Moscow had made a decision to give at least a certain degree of support to the Arab offensive – rather than seeking to halt it outright – by October 9.

This conclusion is strengthened by the fact that on October 9 the Kremlin opened a diplomatic campaign to encourage other Arab nations to give active support to Egypt and Syria. Brezhnev sent a personal message to President Boumedienne of Algeria on October 9, urging him to support the frontline combatants; Soviet ambassadors in several other Arab countries delivered similar messages urging all-out support for the Egyptian and Syrian forces.[32] Boumedienne visited Moscow October 14–15, where he met with Brezhnev, Kosygin, Podgorny, and Marshal Grechko, reportedly offering to pay $200 million for further arms shipments to Cairo and Damascus.[33].

Moscow's enthusiasm, such as it was, for continuation of the hostilities did not last long, for the battle soon turned in Israel's favor. When Kosygin arrived secretly in Cairo on October 16, his main purpose was to convince Sadat that the time had come to seek a cease-fire. The Soviet premier's cease-fire proposal reportedly called for an Israeli withdrawal to the pre-1967 boundaries, with "some corrections" and, most important, an international guarantee of the resulting frontiers that would be policed by a peacekeeping force including Soviet and American troops. Kosygin and Sadat met in five separate sessions during the visit, usually in the evenings; Kosygin stayed at the Soviet Embassy during the day. Sadat pressed for more weapons, while Kosygin insisted that a cease-fire was imperative. On October 18, Kosygin produced satellite photographs flown in from the USSR that convinced Sadat that the bridgehead established by Israel on the west bank of the canal was a serious threat. Sadat still refused to approve Kosygin's cease-fire proposal formally, but he did give tacit approval for a Soviet initiative in that direction. Satisfied, Kosygin returned to Moscow early on the morning of October 19. During

---

[31] Vinogradov, "October War Counter-Claims," 162. General Shlomo Gazit, former director of Israeli military intelligence, questions Vinogradov's account, because Israeli intelligence obtained Egypt's battle plans and found no mention of occupying the passes. Interview: Gazit.

[32] *New York Times*, October 10, 1973; *Arab Report and Record*, October 1–15, 1973. On October 11, Gromyko received the ambassadors of Egypt, Syria, Iraq, Algeria, and Jordan, who expressed their "heartfelt gratitude" for Soviet assistance to the Arab cause. *Tass*, October 11, 1973.

[33] *Tass*, October 15, 1973; Sadat, *In Search of Identity*, 263–4. Sadat claims that Boumedienne left convinced that the Soviets wanted an Egyptian defeat, because Brezhnev had lost his temper and stormed about Sadat's foolishness in going to war.

that day, Egypt's tactical position worsened, and in the evening Sadat summoned Vinogradov and told him that Egypt would accept the cease-fire proposal. At that point the diplomacy of the war became elevated almost totally to the superpower level.

Weapons shipments and other military aid

Given the devastating defeat suffered by Soviet arms in the June war of 1967, Moscow's overriding concerns in the Yom Kippur war were undoubtedly to vindicate the performance of Soviet weapons and to prove the USSR's value as an ally. Another total Israeli victory would have discredited Soviet power in the eyes of many Third World leaders. It is not surprising, therefore, that the Soviet news media were quick to attribute the early Arab victories to the arms and training provided by the USSR. *Krasnaya Zvezda*, the official organ of the Ministry of Defense, wrote on October 13 that "the Western press is unanimous in noting the great effectiveness of the anti-aircraft defenses of the ARE and the Syrian Arab Republic," and it quoted the Israeli commander of the air operation against Syria in support of this claim. When Golda Meir blamed Israeli losses on Soviet weapons and training, her comment was quoted at length in *Krasnaya Zvezda* and *Izvestia*.[34]

The weapons inventories of the Arab states had been built up steadily by the USSR since June 1967; indeed, almost all of their weapons were of Soviet manufacture. Table 7.1 is a register of the arms holdings of Egypt and Syria just prior to the October war; it also presents what data are available on the influx of weapons during the year preceding the war. These latter shipments are particularly significant, as they took place after it should have been increasingly evident to Moscow that the Arabs were planning for war. Iraq also received substantial numbers of Soviet weapons in 1972–3, many of which saw action in the latter half of the Yom Kippur war. The SAM-6 missiles and the Sagger antitank missiles were extremely valuable additions to the Arab weapons stocks. One source indicates that of the 120 aircraft lost by Israel in the war, 80 were brought down by SAM-6 missiles, which are both radar-guided and heat-seeking.[35] However, the SAM-2, SAM-3, and hand-held SAM-7 missiles were relatively ineffective. The Sagger missiles and the RPG-7 rocket launcher took a heavy toll of Israel's tanks; Israeli tank personnel found that the weapon was much more potent than they had believed prior to the war, but as the conflict progressed, they were able to take measures that reduced its kill ratio considerably. Despite the Arab stocks of

[34] *Izvestia*, October 16, 1973; *Krasnaya Zvezda*, October 20, 1973. See also D. Volsky and A. Usvatov, "Proschet izrail'skikh ekspansionistov," *Novoe Vremya*, No. 42(October 1973):10, and Georgi Mirskii, "Novoye faktory na Blizhnem Vostoke," *Novoe Vremya*, No. 48(November 1973):18.
[35] Glassman, *Arms for the Arabs*, 127–8.

antitank weapons, Israel destroyed over twice the number of tanks that it lost – 2,000 to somewhat over 800 – and in the massive tank battle on the Egyptian front that began October 14, Egypt lost 500 tanks to Israel's 30. Israel's superiority in the tank battles is largely attributable to the superior ability of its tank crews and to its control of the air, but the U.S. tanks were technically superior in many respects to the Soviet T-54/55 tanks – their range was greater, they possessed sophisticated range finders, they did not overheat in the desert as did the Soviet tanks, their shells had greater penetrative power, and they had more maneuverable turrets.

The T-62 tanks provided to Egypt before the war (and to Syria during the war) were first-line Soviet tanks, but the USSR was not as forthcoming with aircraft, perhaps because of the shortage of trained Egyptian pilots. MiG-23 and MiG-25 fighters were not provided to the Arabs before the war. Tu-22 medium bombers were provided to Iraq, but they remained under Soviet control and were not used during the war. However, the Tu-16 medium bombers delivered to Egypt proved to be of some military value. Armed with *Kelt* stand-off missiles, they enabled Egypt to launch missile strikes at a safe distance from Israeli interceptors, and though their percentage of successful strikes was not high, they did score some important hits in the Sinai. The transfer of the Su-20 ground-attack aircraft was particularly significant, because these aircraft had not yet been deployed in the Soviet air force. An important indicator of Soviet intent is the fact that Moscow steadfastly refused to provide the Arabs with long-range heavy bombers that could have undertaken strategic missions against Israel's heartland. The Soviet Union apparently did not want the war to escalate to that level, though such a destructive level of combat, if sustained, would have worn Israel down more quickly than Egypt. Perhaps Moscow feared that a conflict of that nature would have increased the probability of direct U.S. intervention.

The closest the USSR came to providing the Arabs with a long-range strike capability was the provision of FROG-7 surface-to-surface missiles to Syria and Egypt, and the provision of SCUD missiles to Egypt. The FROG-7 can deliver 1,100-pound warheads over 40 miles. Between October 6 and October 9, Syria launched at least 16 FROG missiles against Israel, some of which caused massive damage in civilian settlements. It was the first use of surface-to-surface missiles in Middle East warfare and an illustration of how vulnerable Israel would be to such weapons. Israel responded by air strikes against Damascus. The approximately 30 SCUD missiles transferred to Egypt before the war were of even greater significance. Although the SCUDs apparently remained under partial Soviet control, Moscow may have provided them in order to signal to Tel Aviv that concessions at the negotiating table would be preferable to the kind of war the USSR could potentially make possible. On October 16, when events on the battlefield were beginning to turn against Egypt, Sadat addressed the

Table 7.1. *Weapons deliveries and inventories prior to the Yom Kippur war*

Type of weapon	Number delivered		Number available by 10/73	
	Egypt 3–9/73	Syria 8/72–9/73	Egypt	Syria
Tu-16 medium bombers	7	—	25	—
Su-7 fighter-bombers	—	?	80	80(?)
Su-20 ground-attack aircraft	A few	—	A few	—
Il-28 light bombers	—	?	5	16
MiG-15/17 fighter-bombers	—	?	100	80(?)
MiG-19 fighters	—	?	—	—
MiG-21 fighters	—	100	210	200
Mi-1, Mi-4, Mi-6, Mi-8 helicopters	—	—	190	<50
SAMLET missiles	75	—	100	—
FROG-3 missiles	—	?	24	?
FROG-7 missiles	Some	30	Some	30
SAM-2 launchers	?	?	780	12 batteries of missiles
SAM-3 launchers	?	?		
SAM-6 launchers	Numerous	Numerous	Numerous	Numerous

Artillery guns	150	—	1,690	Numerous
AT-1 "Snapper" antitank missiles	Several hundred	?	Some	Several
AT-3 "Sagger" antitank missiles	Several thousand	Thousands	Several thousand	Several thousand
PT-76 light tanks	—	?	75	100
IS-111 & T-10 heavy tanks	—	?	30	30
T-34 medium tanks	150	?	100	240
T-54/55 medium tanks	90	?	1,650	90
T-62 medium tanks		Some	100	Some
Osa-class patrol boats		4	12	4 to 6
Komar-class patrol boats			7	6
Skory-class destroyers			4	—
Styx missiles		48	Some	At least 48
SCUD missiles	30 or more		30	—
SAM-7 missiles	?	500	?	500

Notes: A dash indicates no known deliveries. The first two columns show known Soviet weapons shipments to Egypt (March 1973 to September 1973) and Syria (August 1972 to September 1973) during the year preceding the conflict. The third and fourth columns show their total inventories of Soviet weapons on the eve of the conflict.

Sources: Glassman, *Arms for the Arabs*, 112–16, 105–6; SIPRI, *The Arms Trade Registers*, 44–6, 54–65; *The Militaryt Balance* (1972–3):82–3; *The Military Balance* (1973–4):89–90; *Arab Report and Record*, October 1–15, 1973.

People's Assembly. He declared that Egypt had rockets that could reach the farthest depths of Israel, but so far had not used them because "we realized the responsibility of using some types of weapons, and we refrained from using them. But we must remember what I once said: an eye for an eye, a tooth for a tooth, and depth for depth."[36] On October 22, just before the cease-fire went into effect, two SCUD missiles are believed to have been fired at Israeli troops on the west bank salient, on orders from Sadat: "I wanted Israel to learn that such a weapon was indeed in our hands and that we could use it at a later stage of the war."[37] At least one Western analyst considered the firing of the SCUDs to have been "an event of extreme significance," because it was the first time a long-range offensive weapon with assured penetrability had been used by the Egyptians – or by any Third World client of the USSR.[38] But, in fact, the SCUDs could not reach Israeli cities, because they were deployed deep inside Egypt in order to avoid preemption. Cairo had no means of responding to an Israeli air strike against Egyptian cities.

More significant was the beginning of the Soviet supply bridge to the Arabs – historically the first massive resupplying by the USSR of any non-Communist combatant engaged in full hostilities. The Soviet airlift began late on October 9, with the first planes arriving in Syria on October 10.[39] The airlift was of modest dimensions at first, but on October 12 the number of flights went up dramatically – a fact recorded by the air traffic controllers at Belgrade and Cyprus. By midnight, October 12, 18 flights an hour were passing over Cyprus. An-12 and An-22 transport planes provided the bulk of the transport, but Il-62s, Il-18s, and Tu-154s were also alerted for use. The large freight planes reportedly flew 934 round trips, carrying some 12,500 tons of military equipment to the Arabs from October 10 to 23. The equipment was apparently acquired by drawing down the large reserve stocks of equipment in the Warsaw Pact. Flights originated primarily in Kiev and Budapest, though many of the Kiev flights made refueling stops in Budapest (a necessity for the An-12s). Turkey apparently allowed some overflights within the framework of Soviet-Turkish civil aviation agreements. One source claimed that Romania refused transit rights, but that the Soviet planes were able to fly over Yugoslavia, Greece, and Cyprus. The sealift, orginating in Odessa and other Black Sea

---

[36] *The Times* (London), October 17, 1973. Sadat bluffed that the missiles were Egyptian-made Zafirs.
[37] Sadat, *In Search of Identity*, 265. Sadat does not identify the type of missiles fired in this account.
[38] Glassman, *Arms for the Arabs*, 136–8.
[39] This is the most common version of when the airlift began, but the *New York Times*, October 11, 1973, reported that Soviet planes began landing in Syria on the afternoon of October 9. Other versions are reviewed in William B. Quandt, *Soviet Policy in the October 1973 War* (Santa Monica: Rand, 1976), 19.

ports, involved some 30 freighters that delivered approximately 85,000 tons of equipment.[40]

The rapidity of the Soviet shipments and the fact that they occurred during a war in which huge amounts of arms were destroyed made it difficult for Western analysts to estimate what actual weapons were involved. In the beginning, the primary purpose of the resupply effort was to replace Syria's dangerously depleted stocks of SAM-6 missiles and to replace other ammunition losses. Eventually the supply bridge began to bring in tanks to replace the massive losses on the battlefield. Egypt received at least 250 tanks from the Russians and another 140 from Tito. Syria was reported to have received 850 replacement tanks, including 700 T-62s. Syria was also reported to have received MiG-21s, and Israeli sources reported that MiG-25 aircraft were introduced into Egypt at the end of the war, though not employed in battle.

The supply effort continued after the cease-fire, into November, building the Egyptian and Syrian stocks back up to a sizable level. Sadat claimed that much of the equipment given to Egypt during the war was agreed on as early as April 1971, but was delivered only after the conflict broke out. The Egyptian president was not fully satisfied with the performance of Soviet weapons, nor the speed with which they were delivered, nor the USSR's refusal to grant Cairo everything it wanted.[41]

Apparently sensitive to the possibility of a Soviet-American confrontation, and aware of the potential influence of passive external forces on a local conflict, Moscow increased its Fifth *Eskadra* in the Mediterranean from 60 ships on the eve of the conflict to a peak of 96 ships on October 31. The buildup of naval forces was particularly rapid following the U.S. military alert on October 25. According to Admiral Worth Bagley, then commander in chief of U.S. naval forces in Europe, the Fifth *Eskadra* acted with restraint and avoided incidents, but "they deployed their ships and submarines so that our forces were targeted for instant attack from multiple points."[42] The *Eskadra* managed to reconnoiter all four of the main U.S. task forces in the Mediterranean during much of the conflict. Soviet warships also

---

[40] Information on the airlift and sealift is from the following: Quandt, *Soviet Policy in the October War*, 18–27; *The USSR and the Third World* 4(1974):560; Kohler et al., *The Soviet Union and the October War*, 64–5; "The Middle East War," *Strategic Survey* (1973):29; Glassman, *Arms for the Arabs*, 130–1, 145–6; London Sunday Times, *The Yom Kippur War* (London: Andre Deutsch, 1975), 276–9. Quandt, pp. 25–6, offers the following breakdown of the tonnage delivered by air: Egypt, 6,000 tons; Syria, 3,750 tons; Iraq, 575 tons. He sets the sealift at 63,000 tons carried on 25 freighters, but this covers only the period October 7–23. The figure is based on Soviet declarations when transiting the Bosporus; the actual capacities of the cargo ships were much greater.

[41] Sadat, *In Search of Identity*, 221, 247, 259, 267, 292.

[42] *U.S. News and World Report*, December 24, 1973. The best and most detailed analysis of Soviet naval diplomacy during the October war is Stephen S. Roberts, "The October 1973 Arab-Israeli War," in *Soviet Naval Diplomacy*, 192–210.

(1) gathered intelligence off the Syrian coast, (2) provided a protective umbrella for the Soviet sealift of arms and the evacuation by sea of some Soviet personnel from Latakia and Alexandria, and (3) maneuvered off the Egyptian coast October 24–26 in a manner that bolstered the credibility of Brezhnev's intervention threat. The USSR's naval involvement in the conflict greatly surpassed its small efforts to shadow the Sixth Fleet during the June war only six years earlier and was a potent testimony to the rising importance of the Soviet navy in the USSR's foreign policy.

The role of Soviet and East European advisers

An estimated 3,000 to 4,000 Soviet advisers were in Egypt and Syria when the war began. A number of other advisers and technicians flew in during the war to assist with various aspects of the supply effort. Soviet personnel participated in an extremely broad range of non-combat operations: Plainclothes Russian air force technicians reassembled the MiG-21s that were shipped to Syria in the airlift; Russians drove tanks from Latakia and Tartous to Damascus; air traffic controllers flew to Egypt and Syria to operate radar equipment that was flown in; Soviet engineers repaired military equipment damaged in the fighting. The available accounts suggest that the Soviet advisers performed their technical and military tasks skillfully, but that they alienated many Egyptians by their personal manners and behavior. They won a reputation for being rude, arrogant, and brusque.

There is no evidence that any Soviet troops or advisers participated in military operations on the front, but there was some secondary involvement in combat. Soviet advisers accompanied Syrian air-defense units and ground units everywhere except on the front line, and Soviet advisers were reported to have been assigned to Syrian command posts, from the battalion level up, at a ratio of one per post. Soviet soldiers actually controlled and operated air-defense systems at Latakia and Damascus, apparently to deter Israeli air strikes against the resupply operation. It is possible that Soviet personnel also assisted in the firing of the SCUD missiles on October 22.[43]

The USSR was not the only Communist country to support the Arabs with military personnel. Some 20 to 30 North Korean pilots flew passive air-defense missions over the Egyptian heartland, freeing Egyptian pilots for forward combat. After the hostilities ceased, Cuba sent an armored brigade of roughly 500 men to Syria; it was deployed

[43] "The Middle East War," *Strategic Survey* (1973):25; Galia Golan, *Yom Kippur and After: The Soviet Union and the Middle East Crisis* (Cambridge University Press, 1977), 89; Glassman, *Arms for the Arabs*, 134, 137–8. Glassman suggests that the six-day delay between Sadat's public warning that he had long-range rockets and their firing indicates that permission had to be obtained from the Soviets to fire them. A simpler explanation is that Sadat waited until just before the cease-fire in order to avert possible Israeli retaliation.

on the front during the war of attrition that smoldered from October to April.[44] Although the military contribution of the Cuban troops was minute, their deployment in Syria was of considerable political significance. It not only somewhat appeased the Arab demand for direct involvement of Soviet troops but also offered Moscow an opportunity to test Western and Third World reactions to the use of Cubans as Soviet proxies in a local conflict. It was a portent of Cuba's vastly larger involvement in Angola two years later.

Given the large numbers of Soviet advisers involved in the intense combat of the October war, it was perhaps inevitable that some casualties took place among them. *Tass* announced that Soviet civilians had been killed in an Israeli air raid on Damascus, October 9, in which the Soviet cultural center was destroyed. Radio Moscow acknowledged two deaths, while the director, Mr. Hakimov, said six persons had been killed. This incident, together with the sinking of the Soviet cargo ship *Ilya Mechnikov* by rockets fired from an Israeli patrol boat, led *Tass* to release an official statement condemning the Israeli actions and warning Israel that punishment would follow: "The Soviet people resolutely condemn the barbarous bombing and strafing of civilian targets and civilian population... The continuation of criminal acts by Israel will lead to dire consequences for Israel itself." The Soviet representative to the UN walked out of a Security Council session in protest of the Soviet casualties.[45] After the war, in July 1974, Israeli Defense Minister Shimon Peres revealed to the Knesset that high-ranking Soviet officers had been killed on the Golan front during the war.

Soviet-American interactions

On the day following the outbreak of hostilities, the United States requested that the Security Council convene to consider steps toward an immediate cease-fire. When the council met on October 8, the U.S. representative, John Scali, urged that all belligerents return to the positions they held prior to the war. The Soviet representative, Yakov Malik, and the Arab representatives opposed the U.S. position and called for implementation of Resolution 242. Soviet opposition to the U.S. proposal could not have stemmed from confidence that the Arabs would prevail on the battlefield, for the Kremlin was at that very time seeking approval from Sadat and Assad to introduce its own cease-fire proposal in the Security Council. Rather, the USSR could not afford to support the U.S. proposal without an explicit nod from the

[44] *Arab Report and Record*, October 16–31, 1973; *The Jewish Chronicle*, October 9, 1973, cited in *The USSR and the Third World*. Interview: Major General Shlomo Gazit, director of Israeli military intelligence, 1974–9.
[45] *Arab Report and Record*, July 1–5, 1974; Radio Damascus, October 9, 1973; Radio Moscow, October 12, 1973; *Tass*, October 12, 1973; *New York Times*, October 10, 1973.

Arab leaders – to do so would have invited their wrath and disfavor. On October 8, Nixon and Brezhnev exchanged messages on the war, and Brezhnev reportedly said that he "shared the American desire to limit the conflict in the Middle East."[46] That same day, Kissinger addressed the Pacem in Terris conference in Washington and alluded to the conflict as a test of détente:

> We will react if relaxation of tensions is used as a cover to exacerbate conflicts in international trouble spots. The Soviet Union cannot disregard these principles in any area of the world without imperiling its entire relationship with the United States. . . Détente cannot survive irresponsibility in any area, including the Middle East.[47]

During the first week of the conflict, the United States unsuccessfully attempted to reach an agreement with the USSR, Israel, and Egypt on the terms of a cease-fire in place.[48]

Shortly after the Soviet airlift commenced, the United States began resupplying Israel with small quantities of arms and ammunition. El Al planes flew to the Oceana naval station near Norfolk, Virginia, to pick up cargoes prepared and awaiting them. Kissinger claimed that at this early stage of the resupply operation the United States made a diplomatic effort "to bring about a moderation in the level of outside supplies that were introduced into the area."[49] On Saturday, October 13, after it became evident that the combatants would not agree to a cease-fire, and the day after the Soviet arms transfer suddenly accelerated to a massive level, President Nixon gave approval for the United States to begin an overt, large-scale resupply effort. Even as this decision was being implemented, the United States informed Moscow that it was still willing to work out an acceptable solution and to discuss mutual limitation of arms supplies into the area. Kissinger, however, reportedly wanted the United States to deliver 25 percent more arms than the USSR every day until the cease-fire in order to demonstrate to Moscow the superiority of American arms and transport capabilities.[50]

From October 13 to 19, the Soviet and American arms shipments continued, with negotiations deadlocked. On October 19, Kosygin returned from Cairo, having finally convinced Sadat of the urgency of the situation and the importance of undertaking cease-fire negotiations immediately. The Sadat-Kosygin proposals were relayed to

[46] *New York Times*, October 9, 1973.
[47] Kissinger, *Pacem in Terris III*. The last line of this quotation was omitted in the transcript of the speech that appeared in *DOSB* LXIX(October 29, 1973): 528.
[48] Kissinger, "News Conference of October 25," *DOSB* LXIX(November 12, 1973):586; William B. Quandt, *Decade of Decisions: American Policy toward the Arab-Israeli Conflict, 1967–1976* (Berkeley: University of California Press, 1977), 170–83.
[49] Kissinger, "News Conference of October 25," 586.
[50] Quandt, *Decade of Decisions*, 187–8.

Washington the same day, but the United States found them unacceptable. Later that day, a message was relayed to the White House on the hot-line telex inviting Kissinger to come to Moscow for urgent consultations. He embarked from Washington with a large entourage at 1 a.m. on Saturday morning, October 20, and arrived in Moscow about 7:30 p.m., local time. Gromyko met him at Vnukovo airport and insisted that the talks begin immediately.[51] Kosygin was conspicuously absent, and several newspapers reported that he was back in the Middle East visiting Baghdad, Damascus, and perhaps Cairo, secretly.[52]

The Saturday evening talks made no progress. Brezhnev repeated the standard demands for an immediate return to the pre-1967 lines, and the United States offered only to take note of the Soviet position. When discussions resumed the next morning, Kissinger offered a new cease-fire proposal, which the Russians accepted as a starting point for the negotiations. By early Sunday evening the two sides had reached agreement on a cease-fire proposal to be submitted to the Security Council as a joint resolution. Egypt, Syria, and Israel were immediately notified of the terms of the resolution, and Kissinger left Moscow, flying to Tel Aviv to discuss the proposal with Golda Meir.

The Security Council convened late on Sunday and after brief debate passed Resolution 338 shortly after midnight. It had three points: All combatants should cease fire and terminate military activity within 12 hours in their current positions; after the cease-fire, all parties should begin implementation of Resolution 242 "in all its parts"; immediate negotiations should be opened between the parties concerned "under appropriate auspices" to seek a just and durable peace.[53] The very ambiguity of the resolution made it barely acceptable to all parties. The Israeli cabinet agreed to the cease-fire early on the morning of October 22, and Cairo announced its acceptance a few hours later. Damascus did not follow until the next day, and then only under great pressure from the Soviet ambassador.[54] The cease-fire became official at 6:52 p.m., October 22, (local time), exactly 12 hours after the Security Council resolution was passed.

[51] The highest officials on the American side were Henry Kissinger, Joseph Sisco, Helmut Sonnenfeldt, and Winston Lord. On the Soviet side were Leonid Brezhnev, Andrei Gromyko, Anatoly Dobrynin (who flew in with the Americans), A. M. Aleksandrov, and G. M. Kornienko. *Pravda*, October 21, 1973.

[52] *Arab Report and Record*, October 16–31, *Al-Anwar* (Beirut), October 22, 1973, *Financial Times*, October 23, 1973, and the Iraqi News Agency all carried reports of his alleged visit that are cited in *The USSR and the Third World* 3(October–December 1973):548.

[53] The text of this resolution and the texts of Resolutions 339 and 340 are in *DOSB* LXIX(November 12, 1973):604–5.

[54] Mukhitdinov ordered a temporary halt to the airlift, except for ammunition; he sent a Soviet cargo ship away without unloading; he threatened to send home the technicians helping at the SAM sites. London Times, *The Yom Kippur War*, 399–400.

Had the cease-fire taken hold at that time, it would have been a remarkable example of the speed with which international conflicts can be resolved by joint U.S.-Soviet agreement, but the cease-fire broke down a few hours after it started, and Israel decided to press its operations on the west bank of the Suez. Moscow issued a statement charging Israel with flagrant violations of the armistice and demanding an immediate withdrawal to the cease-fire line: "The Soviet government warns the government of Israel of the most grave consequences which the continuation of her aggressive actions against the Arab Republic of Egypt and the Syrian Arab Republic will entail."[55] Moscow also notified Washington of its concern. A second joint resolution was rushed through the Security Council; it urged the sides to return to their cease-fire positions and requested the secretary-general to dispatch a UN observation team to supervise the cease-fire.

Events on the battlefield moved a step ahead of diplomacy. The fighting continued, to Israel's advantage, and the UN mission found it impossible to establish itself between the two armies. On the afternoon of October 24, Sadat contacted both Washington and Moscow and requested that they form a joint U.S.-Soviet peacekeeping force to police the cease-fire by compelling Israel to withdraw to the October 22 line. He also requested an urgent meeting of the Security Council. When it convened on the evening of October 24, Egyptian Foreign Minister Zayyat requested that the council call on the United States and the USSR to send forces to patrol the cease-fire. Malik stated that "in the light of the continuing Israeli aggression the Egyptian proposal for sending Soviet and U.S. troops to the area of conflict is fully justified and accords with the U.N. charter."[56] Dobrynin had communicated to Kissinger earlier that the USSR would support the proposal.

This surprise move by the USSR possibly was intended as a test of the U.S. reaction to the introduction of Soviet troops into the region. Most probably the Soviet Union very much wanted to send a small contingent of troops to Egypt, but hesitated to do so without assurances as to the likely response by Washington. A small number of troops would have placated Arab demands for greater support, forced Israel to think seriously about the wisdom of continuing the offensive, and improved the bargaining position of the Arabs. The Kremlin would lose none of these advantages if U.S. troops were also sent under a joint agreement, but the risk of unmanaged escalation would diminish, and the USSR would appear as a superpower equal to the United States. However, Kissinger firmly rejected Sadat's proposal; Scali told the Security Council that involvement of the superpowers' armed forces would not promote peace.

[55] Radio Moscow, October 23, 1973.
[56] *Tass*, October 24, 1973.

As the Security Council debated late into the night, evidence began to accumulate in Washington that Moscow might actually be preparing to take unilateral military action. Around 7:30 p.m., Kissinger called Dobrynin, who told him that the USSR might itself introduce a resolution in the Security Council calling for a joint U.S.-Soviet peacekeeping force. At 9:25 p.m., or thereabout, Dobrynin called Kissinger with an urgent message from Brezhnev to Nixon. It was this message that precipitated an international crisis. The third paragraph read as follows:

> I will say it straight, that if you find it impossible to act together with us in this matter, we should be faced with the necessity urgently to consider the question of taking appropriate steps unilaterally. Israel cannot be allowed to get away with the violations.[57]

Kissinger, Secretary of Defense Schlesinger, and certain staff members of the National Security Council considered the message in the light of intelligence reports on Soviet military movements: Seven Soviet airborne divisions had been placed on alert status after the cease-fire; an air transport unit in Prague had been moved to southern Russia; most of the Soviet transport aircraft in the Middle East had been returned to the USSR and were available as troop carriers; a task force of several Soviet warships, including *Alligator* troop carriers, was approaching the Egyptian coast. The intelligence was not conclusive, but it demonstrated that the USSR was in a position to lift airborne troops rapidly into Egypt. To complicate matters, reports indicated the possibility that tactical nuclear warheads had been introduced into Egypt.[58] Kissinger and Schlesinger agreed that the best response would be an alert of U.S. military forces. At 11:35 p.m., Schlesinger ordered all U.S. commands to assume "Def Con 3," an alert status one step above the normal peacetime status. It was a comprehensive alert that included the nation's nuclear forces. Kissinger drafted a reply to Brezhnev stating that the United States would not tolerate unilateral action in the Middle East, and President Nixon ratified the actions of his two cabinet members at 3 a.m.

At a press conference the next morning, Kissinger publicly stated the American position:

> The United States does not favor and will not approve the sending of a joint Soviet–United States force into the Middle East . . .

---

[57] Marvin Kalb and Bernard Kalb, *Kissinger* (Boston: Little, Brown, 1974), 490.
[58] Neutron emissions had been detected from a Soviet cargo ship as it passed through the Bosporus; the shapes of certain warheads associated with the SCUD missiles and the handling procedures used with them were similar to those used with tactical nuclear warheads. However, according to Galia Golan, the White House did not receive the report on nuclear materials until after the alert. Golan, *Yom Kippur and After*, 123.

It is inconceivable that we should transplant the great-power rivalry into the Middle East, or, alternatively, that we should impose a military condominium by the United States and the Soviet Union. The United States is even more opposed to the unilateral introduction by any great power, especially by any nuclear power, of military forces into the Middle East in whatever guise those forces should be introduced.[59]

The U.S. alert rapidly led to a compromise resolution in the Security Council. Moscow clearly did not desire a confrontation. Malik obtained Kremlin approval of the compromise shortly after Kissinger's press conference, and Resolution 340 passed without dissent. The resolution provided for a special UN emergency force (UNEF) "to be composed of personnel drawn from States Members of the United Nations *except the permanent members of the Security Council*" (italics added).[60] The UNEF would join the UN observers already in the field in policing the cease-fire. The passing of this resolution defused the crisis, though the U.S. alert continued for a few more days. The UNEF was able to establish itself between the armies, and the cease-fire took hold, though Israel did not withdraw from its commanding position.

Was the Soviet Union actually prepared to intervene unilaterally with its own troops? Probably not. It is more likely that the Soviet leaders calculated that the appropriate diplomatic messages and military actions would signal to Washington the importance of stopping Israel's offensive. Brezhnev's ultimatum accomplished that end. Washington let Israel know of the Soviet threat and insisted that the Egyptian Third Army not be attacked; if Israel persisted, American shipments would cease, and U.S.-Israeli relations would be damaged severely. However, it is just conceivable that if Washington had not voiced its opposition to unilateral action, and if Israel's advance had not halted, Moscow might have introduced forces, perhaps a token number, into the Middle East. This would have cast the USSR in the role of savior of the Arabs and done much to win their forgiveness for past hesitancies and blunders. In 1956 and 1967 the Russians had turned down urgent requests from the Arabs for direct military intervention; the temptation to make some show of force in 1973 must have been very great indeed. Vinogradov even claimed that "the vanguard actually arrived in Cairo,"[61] possibly referring to a contingent of 70 Russian observers who landed in Egypt on October 26.

The Soviet Union made cautious and calculated responses to U.S. actions throughout the conflict. There is every evidence to indicate that the Kremlin wanted to contain the conflict and to avoid an overt confrontation with Washington. However, this does not mean that Brezhnev's threat was mere posturing or propaganda. Some analysts have

[59] Kissinger, "News Conference of October 25," 587.
[60] "Resolution 340," *DOSB* LXIX(November 12, 1973):604.
[61] Vinogradov, "October War Counter-Claims," 163.

oversimplified its meaning by comparing it to previous Soviet threats to intervene in the Suez war and the June war, threats made only after the danger of East-West confrontation had passed. Those threats were neither serious nor credible. Brezhnev's communications to the White House arrived while confrontation was still a possibility, and the USSR had the necessary forces in readiness to carry it out. It was a credible threat, adroitly employed as an instrument of diplomatic pressure.

The China factor

The PRC exerted no significant influence on the course of Soviet policy during the Yom Kippur war, but Peking's virulent rhetoric and its actions in the Security Council constituted a small thorn constantly in Moscow's side, and it felt obliged to respond to the Chinese accusations.

Shortly after the conflict began, China's foreign minister, Chi Peng-fei, made an official statement to the Egyptian and Syrian ambassadors and the head of the PLO mission in Peking. He expressed unqualified support for the struggle against Israel and pledged that China would stand firmly by their side in "the sacred cause of recovering the lost territories and restoring the national rights to Palestine."[62] The Chinese position on the Soviet role in the conflict was elaborated in detail in a *People's Daily* article by Jenmin Jih Pao:

> Even though Soviet revisionism has given some weapons to the Arab countries, it has restrained them from recovering their lost land and used all possible means in an attempt to tie the hands of the Arab countries and people. Soviet revisionism and US imperialism are colluding, as well as contending with each other in the Middle East.[63]

The Chinese position was carefully tailored to take advantage of Arab fears about U.S.-Soviet détente damaging their cause. It also exploited their dissatisfaction with the level of Soviet support and Moscow's attempts to restrain them from going to war.

On October 11, Chou En-lai sent messages to Sadat and Assad asserting that Israel's aggression was caused by "the support and connivance of the super-powers." Moscow replied to the charge, accusing Peking of "trying to drive a wedge in Arab-Soviet relations" and of offering only lip service, not material aid, to the Arabs. China's charges were "a ridiculous lie." The Soviet-Chinese rhetoric reached a peak during the Security Council debates on the cease-fire resolutions. When Resolution 338 came up, the Chinese representative, Huang Hua, stated

[62] NCNA, October 8, 1973.
[63] *People's Daily*, October 8, 1973, in *The USSR and the Third World* (October–December 1973).

that it was further proof of superpower collusion and of the superpowers' attempt to impose a "no war, no peace" situation on the
Arabs. When China abstained from voting, Moscow criticized the ab-
stention as showing a lack of interest in settling the conflict. The session
on Resolution 339 was much stormier and had to be recessed temporarily after a shouting match developed between Hua and Malik.
When the meeting resumed, Hua opened the debate by asking if Russia
and America owned the world. *Tass* later accused the Chinese delegate
of helping the Israeli aggressor prolong its cease-fire violation by
delaying the vote on the resolution.[64] In the end, China abstained from
voting on this resolution and on Resolution 340. Peking could hardly
veto resolutions designed to prevent Israel from achieving a total
victory.

There is some evidence that Sadat sought military assistance from
China shortly before the October war. He met with the Chinese ambassador on September 1, and then sent Vice-President Husayn ash-
Shaf'i to Peking along with Egypt's minister of war production. They
arrived in Peking on September 21 and met with Chou En-lai and
several high-level defense officials. Mao met with them two days later.
If any arms purchases took place, they were insignificant compared
with the amounts being received from Moscow, but the Kremlin surely
took notice of the visit. Sadat later thanked Chou En-lai for China's
"firm stand" during the October war.[65]

China's involvement in the Yom Kippur war was too peripheral to
have been a major factor in Soviet policymaking, but Moscow could
not afford to ignore Peking entirely. Although the PRC could not deliver weapons in anywhere near the same volume or class as the USSR,
China's willingness to lend unqualified rhetorical support to the Arab
cause – going even somewhat beyond Moscow – could embarrass the
USSR and lead the Arabs to question its sincerity and resolve. It
undoubtedly increased the Kremlin's determination to demonstrate
commitment and generosity to the Arab war effort.

The outcome

The historical record argues that the Soviet leadership did not want
the October war. When it nonetheless came, the Russians were remarkably successful in preventing a disastrous Arab defeat, on the
one hand, and in avoiding a direct confrontation between Soviet and
U.S. military forces, on the other. The ambiguous military outcome
of the war was probably as favorable as any scenario the Kremlin
could have hoped for, but the political ramifications of Egypt's canal

[64] NCNA, October 11, 1973; *Tass*, October 17, 1973; *Pravda*, October 21, 1973; *The USSR and the Third World* 4(1974):549; Radio Moscow, October 22, 1973; *Daily Telegraph*, October 24, 1973; *Tass*, October 24, 1973. See also NCNA, October 24, 26, 27, and 31, 1973, and the lengthy commentary on April 29, 1974.
[65] NCNA, September 3 and 21–24, 1973; NCNA, October 20, 1973.

crossing proved to be far less positive. With inexorable logic, the October war brought to an end the very circumstances that had invited the massive Soviet entry into Egypt after June 1967 and even partly unraveled the web of diplomatic events and calculations that had drawn the USSR into the region in the first place. The Yom Kippur war was the beginning of the end of what Mohammed Heikal called "the great Soviet offensive" in the Arab world. Perhaps any military outcome that left Egyptian forces on the east bank of the canal would have led to the same consequence.

To begin with, the war created a sudden fluidity in the political alignment of the Arab nations, thereby achieving Cairo's goal of ending the political stalemate that had existed since 1967. As Sadat had expected, the war forced the United States to undertake diplomatic initiatives it had previously shunned; only one month after the canal crossing, Washington and Cairo restored diplomatic relations. Once galvanized into action, the United States became the ascendant mediator of the dispute, outflanking Soviet diplomatic efforts with little problem. Because of its enormous influence in Tel Aviv, the United States simply had more to offer the Arabs in peacetime than did the Soviet Union. Kissinger could shuttle to Israel; Gromyko could not.

Furthermore, by demonstrating that armed force alone could not retake the occupied lands, the war rendered a diplomatic solution more attractive to the Arabs. By restoring a measure of national pride to Egypt, the canal crossing also forged the necessary political conditions for the Egyptian-Israeli negotiations that later took place. Sadat's decision to pursue a "political option" greatly lessened the significance and diplomatic weight of arms shipments into the region, undercutting the Soviet Union's main lever of influence over the Arabs. Sadat's personal disaffection with the Russians also contributed to the decline in Soviet influence.

Finally, the war triggered the oil embargo and accelerated the rise of Saudi Arabia as a world financial power. Saudi wealth offered Egypt an alternative to dependence on the Soviet Union, and Saudi oil increased the incentives for the United States to pursue an even-handed approach vis-à-vis the Israelis and Arabs. Egypt's desire to curry favor with the anti-Communist Saudis was an important factor encouraging Cairo's turn from Moscow. Sadat apparently even promised King Faisal that he would limit Soviet influence in Egypt after the war if Faisal would support the war effort by employing the oil weapon.

Once these factors coalesced, the downward trend in Soviet-Egyptian relations was steady: The Kremlin found itself virtually excluded from the disengagement negotiations and unable to exert much influence on the process; in April 1974, angered by Moscow's insistence on full payment plus interest for the arms delivered during the war, Sadat began publicly criticizing the Soviet Union; on April 18 he announced that Egypt would diversify its arms-supply sources and pursue a nonaligned foreign policy. During 1975, Cairo deliberately downstaged the Soviet role in the opening of the Suez Canal, friction developed over the issue of debt repayments and the cancellation of a planned trip to Cairo by Brezhnev, and Sadat complained that the Soviets were pressuring him by denying spare parts. In March 1976, the Egyptian president abruptly announced that the 1971 treaty of friendship and cooperation with the USSR would be terminated. Three weeks later, Moscow's access to Egyptian naval facilities was cancelled. The Soviet Union's loss of influence in Egypt was almost total.

The complex chain of events that followed the conflict elicited widely differing scholarly interpretations of its meaning for the USSR. William Griffith referred to the USSR's loss of influence with Egypt as "Moscow's greatest political defeat, and Washington's greatest political victory, since the Sino-Soviet split." Rubinstein saw a quite opposite outcome:

> The subsidizing of Arab surrogates has been a small price for the havoc they have wreaked on the Western world and the American alliance systems. In the jargon of Marxism-Leninism, the October War, subjectively speaking, was unanticipated, but objectively speaking, it produced Moscow's greatest triumph since 1945.[66]

Griffith, of course, was exaggerating the magnitude of Moscow's regional losses, and Rubinstein was referring only to the global, strategic consequences of the conflict. A balanced assessment of Soviet gains and losses requires that the two be evaluated separately.

Regionally, it is important to recall that Soviet losses were confined largely to Egypt. It is true that the Kremlin lost some of its standing in Damascus and Baghdad during the peak period of Kissinger's shuttle diplomacy. But only the break with Egypt proved lasting. Once Cairo turned toward genuine reconciliation with the West, Moscow's influence began to rise once again in the more militant Arab countries. Libya, Syria, and Iraq received large quantities of Soviet arms, and Soviet influence remained strong. When Sadat visited Jerusalem in November 1977 and began the process that led to an Egyptian-Israeli peace treaty, the militant Arab states turned even more sharply toward Moscow. This development could not possibly compensate for the loss of Egypt, but it meant that the USSR remained a key actor in the region.

Looking to the future, it seems clear that unless the Egyptian-Israeli rapprochement is expanded into a genuine regional settlement – an exceedingly chancy prospect, at best – Moscow's influence in the rest of the Arab world will likely remain substantial. Because an Arab-

---

[66] William Griffith, "The Decline of Soviet Influence in the Middle East," in Lawrence L. Whetten, ed., *The Political Implications of Soviet Military Power* (London: Macdonald & Jane's, 1977), 81; Rubinstein, *Red Star on the Nile*, 287.

Israeli war is ruled out so long as Egypt and Israel are at peace, the USSR's overall military presence in the region may not become as great as before 1973, but it should remain a constant factor in the equation. Nor can the possibility of a renaissance of Soviet influence in Egypt be ruled out. Even an optimist would have to grant that the peace treaty signed in 1978 may well break down, tied as it is to the reigning governments and specific leading personalities of Egypt and Israel. Any turn toward militance in Egypt will increase the likelihood of a Soviet comeback there, for in the 1980s, no less than in the preceding two decades, the Soviet Union will be the only arms supplier the Arabs can rely on for a major campaign against Israel.

The regional setback suffered by Moscow in the Middle East must be weighed against the strategic and global consequences of the Yom Kippur war. First, the war demonstrated beyond question that the Soviet Union had achieved the standing of a global power, one capable of exerting massive conventional force in distant regions. Although the USSR became involved in the war reluctantly and only because of a lack of alternatives, its performance was undeniably impressive. It gained valuable experience in conflict intervention, and it demonstrated its superpower status by negotiating with Washington almost continuously during the conflict. The Kremlin crossed many new thresholds during the war, doing things it had never dared do before, and displaying military capabilities and a political will that neither the West nor the Third World will soon forget.

Second, Soviet arms received favorable publicity because of the war. The 1967 defeat was at least partly reversed for the Soviet Union as well as for the Arabs. In particular, the performance of the SAM-6 missile and the Sagger antitank missile led military experts around the world to reconsider the implications of precision-guided weapons for modern warfare. In actual fact, the contribution of the antitank missiles was less than is often realized, for Soviet tanks proved decidedly inferior to Western models. But the weaknesses of Soviet weapons were largely overlooked in most commentaries on the war; so Soviet prestige received a needed boost.

Third, and most important, the war furthered the USSR's global interests in an indirect way by triggering the Arab oil embargo and giving impetus to OPEC's emergence as a powerful economic cartel. The embargo and the quadrupling of oil prices that followed wreaked havoc on the economies of the Western industrial nations. Soviet doctrine on wars of national liberation holds that any conflict that inflicts damage on capitalism is just and is a success; official and unofficial commentaries in the Soviet press expressed unqualified satisfaction with this aspect of the war's outcome. A related outcome that was favorable in the Soviet zero-sum view of events was the strain placed on the cohesiveness of the NATO alliance and the EEC by the new-found oil power of the Arabs. Nor could the USSR be displeased by the vast sums of hard currency it subsequently earned by exporting its own oil at the higher price – Soviet petroleum earnings went from $580 million in 1972 to nearly $4 billion in 1974. Yet the emergence of OPEC and the subsequent price increase for petroleum were not entirely favorable for the Russians, because the development magnified the influence of Saudi Arabia and led to an increased U.S. stake in the region. On balance, however, the USSR benefited.

Against the strategic gains reaped by the Soviet Union, one significant loss should be noted. The war upset the delicate structure of détente that the Soviet leadership valued so much. Both sides tried to downplay this development after the war, with Brezhnev claiming that without détente, "the clash in the Middle East might have become much more dangerous," and Kissinger declaring that détente had made possible a rapid settlement of the conflict.[67] In fact, détente continued in letter but was almost mortally wounded in spirit. It remained for the Angolan civil war to strike a coup de grace.

[67] *Pravda*, November 30, 1973; *DOSB* XLB(December 10, 1973):716.

8
THE ANGOLAN CIVIL WAR

It was an improbable locus for a superpower collision.

John A. Marcum

The Angolan civil war marked the USSR's debut as a major power in Africa. Although the Soviet Union had been involved as an arms supplier in African conflicts before – the Nigerian civil war being a prominent example – never had Soviet arms shipments to any black African country reached the massive levels that were attained in Angola. Nor had large numbers of Cuban troops ever before intervened directly in a Third World country. From the point of view of Washington, the Soviet-Cuban intervention in Angola was a dangerous and unprecedented power play, an offensive thrust that went beyond the traditional geographical perimeter of Russian interests and beyond the accepted postwar "rules of the game" for international behavior. From Moscow's point of view, the war evidently was seen as an opportunity to maintain the global strategic and diplomatic momentum that had been gained with the Communist victory in Vietnam. A massive Soviet-Cuban intervention in sub-Saharan Africa would have been unthinkable only a few years earlier and highly improbable even a year earlier, before Saigon fell. But Hanoi's conquest of the south, by arousing isolationist sentiment in the United States, created the very condition that made the USSR's involvement in the Angolan conflict both feasible and ultimately successful. As a result of the victories in Vietnam and Angola, Brezhnev was able to enter the twenty-fifth congress of the CPSU in February 1976 atop a crest of impressive foreign policy successes.

The civil war took place in consequence of Portugal's precipitous withdrawal from Angola following the demise of the Marcello Caetano regime in 1974. Already by November 1975, when the Portuguese commissioner in Luanda declared Angola independent, a bitter struggle was raging among three contenders for power: the *Movimento Popular de Libertação de Angola* (MPLA), the *Frente Nacional de Libertação de Angola* (FNLA), and the *União Nacional para a Independência Total de Angola* (UNITA). These three liberation movements had a long history of acrimony and mistrust among them, and their divergent aims and ideologies, as well as their differing territorial-ethnic bases, had rendered futile all Portuguese efforts in 1974 and 1975 to establish some kind of coalition government to which power could be ceded.

Dr. Agostinho Neto's MPLA was Marxist in orientation, dominated by an elite leadership of urban intelligentsia, most of whom were in exile outside Angola at the time of the April 1974 coup in Lisbon. The MPLA was the best organized of the movements, finding its natural support among the Mbundu people of Central Angola, where Luanda, the capital city, was located. In 1970, the publication *Strategic Survey* of the London-based International Institute for Strategic Studies rated the MPLA as the liberation movement offering the most effective guerrilla resistance to the Portuguese. It had allies in all of Angola's major urban centers, and it maintained the most extensive international contacts of any of the movements: It had a long history of close ties with the Portuguese Left; it maintained valuable contacts in Sweden; it was recognized as the leading Angolan nationalist party by FRELIMO and the PAIGC, the liberation movements of Mozambique and Guinea-Bissau; for several years it had received material aid from the Soviet bloc and from the PRC.

The FNLA, led by Holden Roberto, was thought to have the largest guerrilla forces of any of the groups, but its political organization was sorely deficient. The FNLA's political base was among the Bakongos of northern Angola and in the large community of Bakongo refugees living in Zaire. Roberto had close ties with President Sese Seko Mobutu of Zaire, from whom he received substantial military and financial support, and the goals of the FNLA were hardly distinguishable from the foreign policy aims of Zaire. The United States offered the FNLA a modest amount of clandestine financial support beginning in mid-1974, and some arms beginning in mid-1975. Peking also provided Roberto with modest arms shipments.

Jonas Savimbi was a close associate of Roberto at one time, but he broke with Roberto in 1964 to found UNITA. He was the only nationalist leader who led his movement from within Angola, supplying it by capturing weapons from the Portuguese. UNITA's territorial base was among the Ovimbundu population of southern Angola, the largest tribal group in the country. UNITA had the least developed external ties and the most poorly armed forces of any of the groups, but Savimbi's personal charisma and the widespread support he commanded among the Ovimbundu made him a major contender for power. Had national elections been held, it is possible that he would have received a plurality of the votes.

During the decade prior to independence, the three movements had devoted as much of their energy to fighting one another as to resisting the Portuguese. Nevertheless, the constant harassment inflicted by these increasingly strong guerrilla forces, combined with the resistance of allied movements in Mozambique and Portuguese Guinea, had put a burdensome strain on the resources and will of Lisbon. Widespread domestic opposition to the African wars was a principal factor in bringing about the military coup that toppled Caetano in April 1974. Within less than six months the new provisional government of Portugal underwent three leadership changes, with each succeeding administration taking a more liberal position on Angola. By October, Lisbon had signed cease-fire agreements with the FNLA and MPLA (UNITA was not then offering serious resistance) and had formally acknowledged Angola's right to independence.

In January 1975, the leaders of the three liberation movements met at Mombasa, Kenya, in order to work out a united front for negotiations with the Portuguese. Neto, Roberto, and Savimbi pledged their respective parties to a common negotiating platform and to cooperation "in all spheres" relating to decolonization and reconstruction. Ten days later, near Alvor in the Portuguese Algarve, they signed an accord with Portugal that recognized them as "the sole legitimate representatives of the people of Angola" and that provided for a transitional government to be formed. The Alvor agreement stipulated that elections would be held before the end of October, shortly before the date set for independence, and that the rival guerrilla armies and the Portuguese army in Angola would be integrated into a single national security force.[1]

The Alvor accords broke down within a few weeks, when violence erupted between the MPLA and FNLA in Luanda. Attempts by the Portuguese and the OAU to bring an end to the fighting resulted in three paper truces (May 12, June 8, and June 21) that collapsed almost as rapidly as they were signed. By August 1975, the MPLA had taken advantage of Soviet arms shipments (which had been resumed late in 1974, after a break) and its natural base in the west to win firm control of Luanda, and it had begun to press its offensive into the rest of Angola. By the end of August it controlled 11 of 15 provincial capitals, including the oil-rich enclave of Cabinda. Its success forced Savimbi and Roberto into an uneasy coalition. In October their forces undertook a series of attacks against key MPLA positions, with little success. The military situation was rapidly transformed, however, when an armored column of 1,500 to 2,000 South African troops crossed the Namibian border on October 23 and joined the FNLA-UNITA offensive.[2] The South African intervention enabled the coalition to recapture five provincial capitals, including the port cities of Novo Redondo and Benguela, within less than three weeks. By mid-November, virtually the entire southern half of Angola was retaken, and the offensive was still being pressed.

By the date set for independence (November 11), over 10,000 Angolans had perished in combat during 1975 alone, more than had died in two previous decades of anticolonial warfare.[3] On Portugal's departure, Neto immediately declared the establishment of the People's Republic of Angola (PRA); it was recognized by the Soviet Union and its East European allies, Yugoslavia, Cuba, Vietnam, Brazil, Portugal's former African colonies, and

---

[1] "The Mombasa Agreements," *Africa Contemporary Record* (*ACR*) (1975–6):C78–9; "The Alvor Agreement," *ACR* (1974–5):C221ff.

[2] Regular South African troops had already occupied a narrow strip of southern Angola in order to protect the hydroelectric facilities at Ruacana Falls and the Calueque Dam. South Africa did not admit its involvement until December, when the defense minister claimed that Pretoria was involved because of Russia's "campaign of militaristic imperialism." *The Times* (London), December 11, 1975.

[3] *Africa* No. 51(November 1975):14. Some estimates of the toll in 1975 were much higher.

six other nations, all African. The rival regime established in Huambo by Savimbi and Roberto received no diplomatic recognition, though it had the support of the United States, South Africa, Zaire, and Zambia, and the sympathy of China and several conservative African nations. The MPLA's relatively superior diplomatic standing contrasted notably with its crumbling position on the battlefield. During the first 10 days in December, the South African forces pushed to within 150 miles of Luanda, while from the north and the east, FNLA troops closed in on the capital, strengthened by U.S. arms shipments and tactical advice. The MPLA was forced to consider the possibility of evacuating Luanda and establishing a stronghold in Cabinda.

Beginning in late October, in anticipation of the upcoming departure of the Portuguese and in response to the South African intervention, Soviet arms shipments had increased dramatically. Substantial numbers of Cuban troops were deployed in Angola around this time; their numbers grew rapidly, reaching approximately 12,000 in February. The Cuban troops and the Soviet arms deliveries enabled the MPLA to stabilize the three battlefronts and save Luanda. The MPLA then turned to the offensive once again. The war assumed a dual nature: In the countryside it was a guerrilla struggle; in the cities and along the highways it was a conventional conflict.[4] Control of the cities and highways counted most in winning meaningful political control over the country, and it was there that the Soviet-Cuban intervention turned the tide. In the north, where the FNLA faced the onslaught alone, the MPLA made rapid advances. Ambriz, Carmona, and Negage – respectively the military headquarters, the political center, and the main airbase of the FNLA – fell by early January. On the southern and eastern fronts the situation remained more fluid during December, with counterbalancing gains and losses made by each side.

In December, the U.S. Senate voted to terminate all military aid to Angola, effectively ending the CIA's program of support for the FNLA and UNITA. The Senate vote also discouraged South Africa, which was already suffering severe diplomatic censure and modest military losses because of its intervention. In January, Pretoria began to withdraw its troops, and the MPLA commenced advancing in the south. Novo Redondo fell on January 24, Huambo by February 9, Lobito and Benguela by February 10, and Silva Porto by February 12. In the north, the FNLA disintegrated, retreating in confusion across the Zairian border. Although fighting continued through February and March in the south, the MPLA's victory was assured, and it began to receive rapid recognition: from the OAU, Portugal, the EEC nations, and dozens of Third World parties. In April it was admitted to the UN. Savimbi's UNITA has, however, with South African support, continued to wage a guerrilla struggle against the new government in Luanda, a conflict still under way at the end of 1983.

---

[4] *Strategic Survey* (1975):32–6. "Most of the fighting during the civil war consisted of advances and retreats to and from the main urban centers and occurred along the main lines of communication" (p. 35).

The local dispute

Although the MPLA, FNLA, and UNITA each possessed a distinct tribal and territorial base, their conflict was never simply an ethnic one. Racial antagonism contributed to the fighting that regularly broke out in Luanda under the transitional government, but it was not the only cause. All of the leaders stressed the multiracial composition of their memberships and the nationalist aims of their movements. They all agreed on certain key principles of Angolan nationalism: that the territorial integrity of the nation should be preserved, that Cabinda was an integral and inseparable part of Angolan territory, that independent Angola would be a unified society without ethnic, racial, or other forms of discrimination. Separatist tendencies never arose in any of the groups – none of them wanted to create another Biafra. Nonetheless, there is no question that the MPLA was the group least dependent on a single tribe for support, because of its predominant influence with the urban population of Angola. Its links with that "central society" of city-dwelling blacks and Portuguese *assimilados* gave it perhaps the most broadly based claim to being a legitimate representative of Angolan nationalism.[5]

The hostility and deep mistrust that divided the movements stemmed from a long history of conflict among them. The armed struggle against Portuguese rule in Angola had started explosively in 1961, when the country was rocked by an MPLA-led revolt in Luanda and a surprise FNLA invasion from the north, the latter of which killed over 1,000 Portuguese nationals. The Portuguese repression that followed was as brutal as the atrocities that had been committed by the FNLA, but more widespread: Portuguese troops killed several thousand Africans that year, many of whom had not been involved in the revolt at all. But even in the face of their common enemy's offensive, the nationalist movements found themselves unable to forge a united front: "As 1961 progressed and fighting in northern Angola continued, a struggle for revolutionary leadership developed as an increasingly central motif of Angolan nationalist politics."[6]

As time passed, the MPLA-FNLA rivalry grew increasingly bitter and came to overshadow the liberation struggle. The MPLA considered Rob-

[5] See Franz-Wilhelm Heimer, "Der Entkolonisierungsprozess in Angola: Eine Zwischenbilanz" (Arnold-Bergstraesser-Institut, February 1976).

[6] John A. Marcum, *The Angolan Revolution: The Anatomy of an Explosion (1950–1962)* (Cambridge: M.I.T. Press, 1969), 200. This book and a second volume – John Marcum, *The Angolan Revolution: Exile Politics and Guerrilla Warfare (1962–1976)* (Cambridge: M.I.T. Press, 1978) – are excellent histories of Angola's nationalist movements. See also Basil Davidson, *In the Eye of the Storm: Angola's People* (London: Longman, 1972), 141–340. On the history and legacy of Portuguese colonialism, see James Duffy, *Portuguese Africa* (Cambridge: Harvard University Press, 1961); David Abshire and Michael Samuels, *Portuguese Africa: A Handbook* (New York: Praeger, 1969); Davidson, *Eye of the Storm*, 47–140; Gerald J. Bender, *Angola under Portuguese Rule: The Myth and the Reality* (London: Heinemann, 1978). On the early roots of the divisions between Angola's nationalists, see Antoine Matumona, "Angolan Disunity," in Institute of Race Relations, *Angola: A Symposium. Views of a Revolt* (London: Oxford University Press, 1962), 120–9.

erto's movement to be tribalistic; after Mobutu came to power in Zaire and became Roberto's foremost supporter, Neto also branded the FNLA an agent of a foreign leader. Roberto, in turn, distrusted the radical orientation of the MPLA. The feud became trilateral when Savimbi broke with Roberto in 1964, charging that he was "flagrantly tribalist" and in the control of American advisers and interests. He eventually set out to build his own movement from within Angola, providing an indigenous alternative to the "hotel nationalists." At an early stage of the FNLA-MPLA rivalry, Roberto's troops began to inhibit the movements of MPLA patrols trying to infiltrate the country from the north. They were killed or captured, and those captured were invariably killed later, often cruelly. The MPLA responded in kind. Over time, each of the three movements made a standard practice of massacring or capturing any soldiers from the other movements who happened to stray into its territory.

Given such a legacy, it is understandable why the Alvor agreement broke down. The only conceivable basis on which the three movements might have been unified was their shared opposition to Portuguese rule, but with independence in sight, this had little effect. Shortly after the Nakuru agreement (a reaffirmation of the Alvor agreement) was signed in June, Neto gave an interview in which he several times attacked both the FNLA and UNITA and declared that the MPLA "is the only party devoted to genuine independence."[7] Roberto and Savimbi were equally self-righteous about their respective parties. In retrospect it is clear that the three leaders never expected the unity agreements to hold and signed them only for tactical purposes.

From Moscow's viewpoint the war was never a dispute between competing national liberation movements. The official Soviet position held that the MPLA was the only genuine liberation movement. Oleg Ignatyev, writing from Luanda in the fall of 1974, branded FNLA and UNITA as "organizations which call themselves champions of national liberation but which were actually knocked together by antipopular forces mainly for the purpose of fighting the country's real patriots united in the MPLA."[8] Ignatyev charged that UNITA was a front organization of the Portuguese secret police and hinted that it might have CIA support; the FNLA was allegedly backed by the CIA and by Maoist China. The MPLA, on the other hand, fulfilled the Kremlin's key criterion of a genuine liberation movement: "An inalienable part of the MPLA's democratic policy is its determination to cooperate with the progressive forces of the world, above all the countries of the socialist community."[9] The USSR did not recognize the MPLA as

---

[7] *Afriscope* (August 1975):6–11. The prognosis for undisciplined troops is found in *Africa Report* 20(May/June 1955):31, and *Africa*, No. 43(March 1975):37.
[8] Oleg Ignatyev, "Angola v predverii peremen," *Novoe Vremya* No. 46(November 1974):15–16. See also *Izvestia*, August 4, 1975; *Pravda*, September 9 and November 28, 1975; *Literaturnaya Gazeta*, December 10, 1975.
[9] Radio Moscow, March 31, 1975.

a full-fledged Communist party, however, but as a "revolutionary democratic party" with a leadership whose views "approximated" Marxist-Leninist ideology.[10]

From January to March 1975, the Soviet news media refrained from attacks on the FNLA and UNITA; it was during this period that the movements were pledged to cooperation, and a strong international effort was being made to ensure the success of the Alvor agreement. When the agreement began crumbling in March, Radio Moscow obliquely criticized both the FNLA and UNITA, declaring that, "unlike certain tribal organizations, which are narrowly nationalist, the MPLA does not speak for one tribe or ethnic group but for the whole Angolan people." When the fighting in Luanda intensified in June, the MPLA's rival movements again came under open criticism from the Soviet news media, and following the breakdown of the Nakuru agreement in July, the Soviet commentators' attacks on the FNLA and UNITA became open and frequent.[11]

The conspiratorial influence of imperialism was a constant theme in Soviet commentary. When the Alvor agreement first began to break down, the resulting clashes in Luanda were blamed on "the ill-doing of imperialist provocateurs who are trying to transform the liberation struggle into an internecine one." The subsequent escalation of the fighting prior to independence was blamed on imperialist intervenors attempting to restore the Western position in Angola.[12] South Africa's intervention in the war lent credibility to the Soviet viewpoint and was a propaganda boon:

> One can say with full justification that what is now happening in Angola is not a civil war but a full-scale intervention against the Angolan people...Troops of the South African Republic and units of former agents of the PIDE, the Portuguese secret police...acting in close contact with...UNITA, are operating in Angola's southern provinces.[13]

After Portugal left Angola and the Soviet Union recognized the PRA, the conflict was portrayed as the struggle of a legitimate government against foreign aggression. The Soviet news media offered the stan-

---

[10] V. L. Tyagunenko, ed., *Voorzuhennaya bor'ba narodov Afriki za sovbody i nezavisimost* (Moscow, 1974), 337–8. The MPLA delegation to the twenty-fifth party congress was not seated with the visiting Communist parties, but with "national-democratic parties and organizations with which we maintain friendly ties." *Pravda*, February 25, 1976. Neto himself made conflicting statements on the MPLA's ideological stance. See *Afriscope* (August 1975):9, and *Africa*, No. 64(December 1976):36.

[11] Radio Moscow, March 31, 1975; Radio Moscow, June 11, 1975; *Pravda*, July 13, 17, and 24, 1975; Radio Moscow, July 16 and 18, 1975; *Izvestia*, August 4, 1975.

[12] *Izvestia*, May 22, 1975; *Pravda*, July 13 and September 22, 1975.

[13] Ignatyev, from Luanda, in *Pravda*, October 30, 1975.

dard Marxist interpretation that economic considerations were motivating the imperialist intervention.[14]

The Soviets were unusually meticulous in justifying their own involvement in the conflict, probably because by shipping arms to the MPLA during the transitional period before independence and by recognizing the PRA immediately following its founding, Moscow was openly defying the authority of the OAU and potentially jeopardizing its standing in Africa. The invasion by South Africa served to soften African criticism of the USSR's subsequent massive arms shipments and the Cuban intervention, but Soviet writers were still careful to outline a precise rationale for assisting the MPLA. Three principal arguments were developed:

1.   Soviet assistance to the MPLA was said to be a continuation of aid given during the colonial period at the request of the OAU:

> ... the Soviet Union [has] for many years given and continues to give political, moral and material support to the armed struggle of national liberation movements in Africa, including the [MPLA] ...
>
> This support is given at the request of both the movements themselves and the OAU, which is unable to give them great aid and which has repeatedly made such a request to all countries of the world in its documents and via special missions.[15]

At the time of this statement, the OAU was in fact officially opposed to all outside involvement in Angola, but by mentioning earlier OAU requests and by lumping Angola together with other African liberation movements, the USSR's actual divergence from the OAU position was obscured.

2.   The Soviet Union claimed not to be intervening at all. Rather, it was helping a legitimate government defend itself against foreign intervention. Three legal scholars detailed this position in an *Izvestia* article:

> The Western press is trying to present matters as though a civil war were underway or continuing in Angola. In fact, there can be no question of any civil war in Angola. Foreign military intervention is being undertaken against the young republic's legal government, employing, as a cover-up, misled Angolans under the influence of factional groups. The unquestionable aim of this intervention is to overthrow the legal government of ... Angola.[16]

---

[14] *Pravda*, December 18, 1975; Radio Moscow, December 2, 1975; *Tass*, December 29, 1975.

[15] A. Klimov, *Izvestia*, December 26, 1975.

[16] Kozhevnikov, Ushakov, and Blishchenko, *Izvestia*, January 11, 1976. See also A. Klimov, in *Izvestia*, December 26, 1975; K. Uralov, "Angola – Torzhestvo pravogo dela," *Mezhdunarodnaya zhizn'* (April 1976):54–60; Radio Moscow, December 17, 1975; *Izvestia*, January 29, 1976; *Tass*, February 3, 1976.

The article then described the alleged foreign intervention, emphasizing the role of South Africa. By defining the PRA as a legally recognized government and the other movements as instruments of foreign intervention, the USSR's own involvement acquired a measure of arguable, albeit self-defined, international legality.

3. The USSR's actions were claimed to be in accordance with the UN declaration on the granting of independence to colonial countries and peoples. This declaration called for universal implementation of the right to national self-determination and urged governments to render moral and material assistance to peoples seeking independence from colonial domination. K. Uralov asserted that the Soviet aid to the MPLA was "in complete accord with the well-known decisions on decolonization taken by the United Nations and the Organization of African Unity." It followed that the intervention of other outside powers was "a flagrant violation of the norms of international law, a flouting of the U.N. Declaration on the Granting of Independence to Colonial Countries and Peoples, U.N. decisions, and the U.N. Charter."[17]

Although the USSR's ideological justifications for its involvement in Angola were patently self-serving, the fact remains that the Soviet viewpoint came to be at least partially acceptable to many member states of the OAU, and the Soviet-Cuban intervention came to be accepted in much of black Africa as a necessary counterweight to South African involvement. It is doubtful that the USSR would have been quite so successful, at least diplomatically, had Pretoria refrained from involvement in the conflict.

The diplomatic relationship between the USSR and its client

The Soviet Union's relationship with the MPLA and eventual intervention on its behalf stemmed from a long history of Soviet aid to the exiled party. "The Soviet people . . . began to render the patriotic forces of Angola moral and material help nearly two decades ago, from the very establishment of the MPLA," wrote a Soviet journalist in 1976.[18] Exactly when Soviet arms first began to be shipped to the MPLA is uncertain. One source pieced together Western intelligence estimates and set the value of Soviet arms shipments from 1960 to 1964 at £27 million; a State Department source estimated Soviet as-

---

[17] K. Uralov, "Angola – Torzhestvo pravogo dela," 58; *Pravda*, November 8, 1975.
[18] K. Uralov, "Angola: K. Novym Rubezham," *Mezhdunarodnaya zhizn'* (July 1976):85. What little is known about the Soviet connection in the years prior to 1974 is traced in Marcum, *The Angolan Revolution*, vol. I, 27–30, 133, 175–6, 200, and vol. II, 157, 168, 171–2, 201–4, 229. See also Colin Legum, "Foreign Intervention in Angola," *ACR* (1975–6):A5–6, A11–14, and Jiri Valenta, "The Soviet-Cuban Intervention in Angola, 1975," *Studies in Comparative Communism* XI(Spring/Summer 1978):4–9.

sistance prior to the April coup in Lisbon at approximately $63 million.[19] This aid was occasionally disrupted when factional splits in the MPLA made it unclear who was in charge, and the aid did not always go to Neto's faction.

One such shuffle occurred in 1972–3, when Moscow suspended its support to Neto and offered it instead to an MPLA faction led by Daniel Chipenda. Neto's leadership was evidently viewed as failing to convert the MPLA into an effective fighting force, and the Kremlin found the proud and introverted poet a difficult man to work with, despite a lengthy history of contacts with him (Neto first visited Moscow in 1964). But despite his flaws, Neto proved to be a more tenacious leader than Chipenda, and he maintained the upper hand within the party. In January 1973, he was invited to Moscow for talks intended to heal the rift. He met with Boris Ponomarev, a Central Committee secretary and candidate member of the Politburo, who assured him that "the USSR would continue to support the MPLA against the Portuguese," meaning, no doubt, Neto's wing of the party.[20] When the April coup in Lisbon found Neto and the MPLA unprepared and still wracked by internal disputes, the Kremlin again withheld its assistance for a few months while the situation sorted itself out. Arms and assistance began to flow again in August 1974, after Neto had strengthened his position by moving from Lusaka into eastern Angola and reorganizing the MPLA's guerrilla forces. In December 1974, some 250 MPLA cadres traveled to Moscow for military training.

There is little information on Soviet-MPLA diplomatic relations from this time until November 1975, the crucial period prior to independence, perhaps because the Alvor and Nakuru agreements made any overt contacts with the Soviet Union extremely sensitive. No visits of Angolan delegations to Moscow are known to have taken place, and official Soviet visits to Luanda consisted of but two delegations from the "Committee of Afro-Asian Solidarity," the first in February and the second in April.[21] Yet Moscow needed regular, close contacts with the MPLA in order to coordinate the several large arms packages delivered directly to Luanda during this time and to make the necessary arrangements for still larger shipments in November. It is possible that Brazzaville, in the Congo, became the main center for contact with the MPLA. The government of Marien Ngouabi supported Neto, and Congo-Brazzaville was the main transit point for Soviet

---

[19] Brigadier W. F. K. Thompson, *Daily Telegraph* (London), April 11, 1975, cited in Legum, "Foreign Intervention in Angola," A13; Marcum, *The Angolan Revolution*, vol. II, 229, 417. These figures should be taken only as rough estimates; their closeness does not confirm their accuracy but may indicate that the State Department figure was derived from Thompson.

[20] *Tass*, January 24, 1973.

[21] Radio Moscow, February 5, 1975; *O'Seculo* (Lisbon), April 17, 1975. The latter delegation discussed the question of "specific material aid."

arms shipments to the MPLA.[22] It seems logical that the Soviet Embassy in Brazzaville would have maintained regular contact with Neto and his representatives.

Ngouabi visited Moscow with a delegation in late March and met with Soviet leaders Leonid Brezhnev, Nikolai Podgorny, Kirill Mazurov, and Andrei Gromyko. A major topic of discussion was "the struggle of the African countries and peoples for complete liberation from colonialism." The Soviet ambassador to the Congo, Yevgeny Afanasenko, was present at some or all of the meetings. The joint communiqué on the visit committed the two sides to giving "all-around support to peoples struggling for their freedom" and noted the upcoming independence of the Portuguese colonies. It seems possible that details of the arms shipments to Angola were discussed at this time, for it was already apparent that the Alvor accords were disintegrating, and Soviet arms had already been flown from Brazzaville to Luanda that very month. In September, Ngouabi visited Cuba, where he and Castro issued a joint communiqué supporting the MPLA, and in late October and early November, when the South African intervention was beginning and the MPLA was losing ground, three separate Congolese delegations visited the Soviet Union.[23] The last arrived November 14. It included Congolese Politburo member Pierre Nze and Deputy Premier Charles Ngouoto, both of whom had been with Ngouabi's delegation in March. They met with Kirilenko, Ponomarev, Ulyanovsky, and representatives from the State Committee on Foreign Economic Relations and from the Foreign Ministry. Again, given the tense situation in Angola and the flood of Soviet arms passing through Congo-Brazzaville at the time, it seems probable that some details of payment and logistics were worked out in this visit.

A Soviet delegation attended Neto's inauguration as president of the PRA on November 11, the same day the USSR announced its recognition of the new republic and expressed readiness to open relations at the embassy level.[24] This enabled Moscow to place an ambassador in Luanda, where the MPLA was in firm control, to coordinate the multiple aspects of the rapidly increasing Soviet assistance. Soviet-MPLA relations seem to have been cordial. Near the end of December, President Neto praised the Soviet assistance in lavish terms and declared that "from the outset of our just struggle we have had

[22] On the MPLA's relations with Brazzaville, see Charles K. Ebinger, "External Intervention in Internal War: The Politics and Diplomacy of the Angolan Civil War," *Orbis* (Fall 1976):677–82, 689.
[23] The quotations and information in this paragraph are from the following: *Tass*, March 25, 1975; Radio Moscow, March 29, 1975; *New York Times*, November 21, 1975; Radio Moscow, October 20 and 29 and November 12, 1975; *Tass*, November 14, 1975.
[24] *Pravda*, November 12, 1975.

very good relations with the Soviet Union."[25] It is, of course, difficult to see how Neto could have felt otherwise, given that the Kremlin was insuring the survival of his regime.

On January 22, 1976, Jose Eduardo dos Santos, the foreign minister of the PRA, arrived in Moscow with at least three other Angolans. It is interesting to note that among those who met him at the airport was the Congolese ambassador to the Soviet Union.[26] The next day he met with Ponomarev, Deputy Chairman of the Council of Ministers Ivan Arkhipov, Deputy Foreign Minister Leonid Ilichev, and other Soviet officials. The CPSU and the MPLA reaffirmed their desire to continue expanding relations. Seven weeks later, when the civil war had been virtually won, Neto was able to reaffirm Angola's solidarity with the other power that had intervened on his side: Cuba. Fidel Castro traveled to Conakry, Guinea, and Neto flew to meet him to discuss the future of the 12,000 or more Cuban troops then still in Angola.[27]

This summarizes most of what is known about Soviet-MPLA relations from April 1974 to April 1976. During that period, Moscow also mounted a diplomatic effort to win the OAU's backing for its client – and its forgiveness for the Soviet intervention. One example of this was a 15,000-ruble gift presented to the OAU secretary-general in Addis Ababa on May 28, 1975.[28] After the date for the OAU emergency summit on Angola was set (January 10–13, 1976), the Soviets employed what few diplomatic tools they could summon to encourage African states to support Neto's new government. During December and early January the USSR undertook a major propaganda campaign in preparation for the summit; the Russian and Cuban delegations were present at Addis Ababa as observers. When the conference resulted in a 22-22 deadlock on whether to recognize the MPLA or to continue seeking a government of national unity, the Soviet news media blamed the outcome on "feverish diplomatic activity" and intense pressure from the United States.[29]

A few weeks earlier, the Soviet Union had been caught applying diplomatic pressure of its own. On November 9, 1975, the Soviet ambassador in Kampala, Andrei Zakharov, had met with Idi Amin, chairman of the OAU. Zakharov complained about Kampala Radio's reporting of Zairian criticisms of the Soviet intervention in Angola, and he urged Amin to recognize the MPLA when Angola became in-

---

[25]*Tass*, December 27, 1975; Neto was obviously tailoring his words for the *Tass* correspondent, but in fact none of the foreign correspondents in Luanda and none of the analysts who have written on the war, so far as I can determine, ever suggested that there were rough spots in Moscow's relations with the MPLA during this period.

[26]*Pravda*, January 23, 1976; *Tass*, January 23, 1976, reports the visit in detail.

[27]*The Economist*, March 20, 1976.

[28]*Tass*, May 28, 1975.

[29]*The Economist*, January 17, 1976; *Tass*, January 13 and 29, 1976.

dependent in two days and to use his position as OAU chairman to win its recognition in the rest of Africa.

> Amin retorted that OAU policy was to recognize all three Angolan liberation movements; he was not accepting Soviet dictation on such a matter; he was not a puppet leader, and was neither a Communist nor a capitalist; the USSR should not involve itself in matters such as Angola; the Ambassador's attitude showed no respect either for a sovereign state or for the decisions of the OAU.[30]

Amin gave the Soviet Union an ultimatum to send a high official to explain the ambassador's conduct or Uganda would break off relations with the USSR in 48 hours. Moscow broke off relations on its own two days later. Relations were restored only six days later, but the incident cast the Soviet Union in a bad light. Zaire also complained of being put under great pressure from the Soviet Union.[31]

In the end, Moscow's diplomatic efforts to pressure the OAU accomplished little for Angola and somewhat tarnished the Soviet image in Africa. Fortunately for the Kremlin, it was weapons, rather than diplomacy, that counted in Angola. The Soviet Union's superb performance in transferring large volumes of arms to the MPLA more than compensated for its clumsy diplomacy, and South Africa's intervention in the war deflected black African criticism of the Soviet Union's involvement.

Weapons shipments and other military aid

The covert nature of arms transfers to Angola, especially in the early stages of the conflict, and the small number of Western correspondents who initially covered the war firsthand make it somewhat difficult to estimate accurately what weapons the USSR shipped to the MPLA. Table 8.1 lists known arms deliveries, with estimates of quantity, where available. The figures are at best approximations, but it is virtually certain that all the various types of weapons listed did appear in Angola as a consequence of the Soviet intervention. Dr. Neto himself confirmed in a radio interview that the Soviet Union supplied him with MiG-21s, T-34 and T-54 tanks, armored personnel carriers,

[30] *The Times* (London), November 10, 1975; see also David L. Morison, "The Soviet Union's Year in Africa," *ACR* (1975–6):A108; Radio Moscow, November 11, 1975; Kampala Radio, November 11, 1975; the latter is a lengthy account of the Ugandan side of the story. Amin claimed he did not take more drastic steps because the ambassador may have taken "an overdose of vodka" before they met. Kampala Radio, November 10, 1975, hinted that the Russians were putting pressure on Uganda in connection with receiving arms and spare parts it had ordered.
[31] According to Kampala Radio, November 6, 1975, Zaire received a note from the Soviet Union containing "threats and accusations," which Zaire rejected, threatening to cut off relations over it.

Table 8.1. *A register of Soviet-bloc weapons deliveries to the MPLA during the Angolan civil war: August 1974 to April 1976*

Type of weapon	Quantity
Helicopters	?
MiG-17 fighters	10(?)
MiG-21 fighters	12
PT-76 light tanks*a*	50(?)
T-34 tanks	70(?)
T-54 tanks	200(?)
Armored personnel carriers*b*	300(?)
SAM-7 missiles and launchers	?
Wire-guided missiles (antitank)*c*	?
BM-21 rocket launchers	Several
122-mm rockets	Large quantities
Bazookas	Large quantities
Ak-47 rifles, machine guns, etc., with ammunition	Thousands
Field artillery	?
120-mm mortars	?

*a*Some sources list as APCs; some refer to PT-76 amphibious tanks.
*b*Apparently Czech-made Tatar armored troop carriers.
*c*Probably AT-3 Sagger antitank missiles.
Sources: New York Times, September 25 and November 21, 1975; *Strategic Survey* (1975):31; Marcum, *The Angolan Revolution*, vol. II, 274; *SIPRI Yearbook*, 1976, 55–56; Institute for the Study of Conflict, *Angola after Independence*, 10–14; *Newsweek*, December 1, 1975, and February 2, 1976; *Washington Post*, November 15, 1976, and January 11, 1977; *The Guardian*, November 26, 1975, Foreign Broadcast Information Service (FBIS); *Time*, January 19, 1976; U.S. Senate Committee on Foreign Relations, *Angola*, Hearings, 94th Congress, 2d sess. 1976, 19, 184.

antitank missiles, SAM-7 missiles, rocket launchers, and Ak-47 automatic rifles.[32] The volume of small arms and equipment provided was no doubt enormous, for they were the primary weapons of the war until the Cuban forces arrived in large numbers. Official U.S. estimates put Soviet arms shipments between April and October 1975 – a period before the massive introduction of heavy weapons – at 27 shiploads and 30 to 40 air supply missions by An-22 cargo planes. Between November 1975 and March 1976, at least 19 shiploads and 70 flights took place. The heavier reliance on airlift beginning in November reflects both the escalation of the conflict that month (with the ensuing urgent need for weapons) and the beginning of direct flights by VTA, the Soviet air transport corps, into Luanda.

The Soviet Union and the MPLA devised numerous methods for

[32] Agostinho Neto, Vienna Radio, January 29, 1976, cited in Legum, "Foreign Intervention in Angola," A13.

delivering and receiving the required weapons. At least five separate supply routes can be identified:[33]

1. An-22 transport planes flew their cargoes to Maya Maya, near Brazzaville, where they were unloaded and shipped in smaller planes to various airfields in MPLA-controlled areas, particularly Barra do Dande north of Luanda, Cela, and Henrique de Carvalho.

2. Direct flights of An-22 transports went from the Soviet Union to Luanda or Henrique de Carvalho, refueling in Guinea, Algeria, or Mali. These direct flights to Angola did not begin until late October. Measured in ton-miles, this stage of the airlift was roughly equivalent to the Soviet airlift during the October war; the latter effort required many more flights (over 1,000), but the flight distance from the USSR to Angola via the various refueling stops in Africa was some six times the flight distances to Egypt and Syria. Therefore, total ton-miles involved probably reached 18 million.

3. Arms were carried by cargo ships to Dar es Salaam, Tanzania, and then carried by air to the MPLA at Serpa Pinto, by sea to various collection points on the Angolan coast (including Luanda), or overland, making use of the Benguela railroad. Nearly $6 million worth of arms were reported to have passed through Dar es Salaam alone.

4. Arms were delivered by cargo ships to Pointe Noire, Congo, or to Guinea, and then ferried to collection points on the Angolan coast.

5. Some cargo ships docked directly at Luanda. This was possible even before the Portuguese withdrawal, because the Portuguese authorities in the capital city generally did not interdict arms being shipped to the MPLA.[34] In April 1975, however, the Yugoslav freighter *Postoyna* began unloading a cargo of trucks and military equipment in Luanda and was prevented from fully unloading by the National Defense Council of the provisional government. It later finished unloading its cargo at Pointe Noire, Congo. The merchant vessels that delivered Soviet arms included Soviet, Yugoslav, and East German ships. Greek and Algerian vessels are also known to have unloaded arms at Luanda, but they may have been connected with private arms dealers rather than with the Soviet supply effort.

The weapons provided the MPLA by the USSR were well suited for winning the war, though this would not have been the case if Cuban troops had not been available to handle the more sophisticated weap-

---

[33] *Strategic Survey* (1975):31; Institute for the Study of Conflict, *Angola after Independence: Struggle for Supremacy* (London: ISC, 1975), 10, 13–14; *The Economist*, November 22, 1975; Charles C. Petersen and William J. Durch, "Angolan Crisis Deployments (November 1975 to February 1976)" in *Soviet Naval Diplomacy*, 144–5.

[34] The FNLA and UNITA charged that the Portuguese authorities were biased in favor of the MPLA. There is considerable evidence that this may have been true, though the Portuguese and the MPLA denied it. One source even asserts that in mid-July 1975, Portuguese army units helped transport Soviet arms from the port at Luanda to MPLA headquarters. Institute for the Study of Conflict, *Angola after Independence*, 14. See also Valenta, "The Soviet-Cuban Intervention," 16–18.

ons. The BM-31 "Stalin organ" rocket launchers proved to be particularly devastating. Each one is a grouping of 122-mm rocket launchers
mounted on a truck. These rockets have powerful explosive charges
and a range of 12 kilometers (the best FNLA mortars had a range of
8 kilometers). These truck-mounted launchers fire a deafening volley
of 20 rockets at once. Their first major appearance in combat took
place in mid-November, when a number of the Stalin organs deci-
mated the FNLA army advancing on Luanda in an exposed column
from Caxito. It was later termed the "Battle of Death Road." American
observers estimated that 2,000 rockets fell on the FNLA column,
which "broke and fled in panic, scattering across the valley in aimless
flight, abandoning weapons, vehicles, and wounded comrades alike."[35]
This was a key turning point in the war, "the beginning of the end of
the National Front in the north."[36] These rockets are too inaccurate
for use against disciplined and well-trained troops, however, and in
the south the South African/UNITA column was able to evade and
capture or destroy several 122-mm cannon of even greater accuracy
and longer range than the Stalin organs. The South Africans nevertheless found themselves greatly outgunned, and outnumbered in both
tanks and soldiers, and they proved unwilling to commit the forces
that would have been necessary to match the Cuban soldiers, with
their abundant stocks of Soviet weapons. Moscow provided everything necessary for the MPLA victory, and for good measure added
weapons not even needed and little used, such as the MiG-21 fighters.

The USSR was the first non-African nation to transfer arms to
Angola after the April 1974 coup in Lisbon. Soviet weapons deliveries
can be divided into three major stages. The first arms shipments took
place in August 1974.[37] That was 11 months before any U.S. arms
shipments took place, though the CIA had begun funding the FNLA
the previous July. Military supplies flowed to the MPLA throughout
the fall of 1974, largely via Congo-Brazzaville. The State Department
estimated that by January 1975, sufficient Soviet arms had been delivered to equip an MPLA force of 5,000 to 7,000. A second stage of
arm shipments began in March 1975, when Moscow substantially increased the volume of weapons moving to Angola. This was also prior
to the first U.S. arms shipments, and it was most likely in response
to signs that the Alvor agreement was falling apart, not a reaction to
China's modest effort to aid the FNLA, as Colin Legum has suggested.
The arrival of these shipments may have contributed to the collapse
of civil order in Luanda that began in late March. The next major

[35] John Stockwell, *In Search of Enemies: A CIA Story* (New York: W. W. Norton, 1978),
214; see also pp. 162–3 and 215; Marcum, *The Angolan Revolution*, vol. II, 274–5.
[36] David B. Ottaway, *Washington Post*, February 19, 1976. "To the bitter end, the 122
mm. rocket, a noisy but relatively ineffectual weapon, sowed panic in the ranks
of the [Roberto's] troops, who never became accustomed to conventional warfare."
[37] U.S. Congress, Senate, Committee on Foreign Relations, *Angola*, Hearings, 94th
Congress, 2d sess., 1976, 184.

acceleration of arms shipments began late in October, when the MPLA had begun to lose the war as a result of the South African offensive. Only during this third stage did the Soviet Union undertake its own direct airlift of sophisticated weapons to Angola. The bulk of the heavy weapons, such as tanks, arrived during this third period.

There is no evidence that the USSR at any time delayed arms deliveries in order to influence or exert pressure on the MPLA leadership. In July 1975, interruptions in the transshipment of supplies from Congo-Brazzaville to Luanda led Neto to visit Brazzaville in order to urge the Congolese to expedite the shipments. Apparently this delay was not caused by the Soviets, but by Ngouabi, who had wavered in his commitment to the MPLA because of its opposition to the separatist FLEC movement in Cabinda, which he supported. The only other significant break in the Soviet arms shipments took place from December 9 to 24, when the Soviet airlift was halted entirely. Again, however, this was not an attempt to influence the MPLA, but evidently was a pause for consideration of a formal U.S. proposal on mutual superpower withdrawal. The cessation of deliveries did not last long, and it was, at any rate, of little military importance, because the MPLA-Cuban forces were already amply equipped for waging an offensive, which they did throughout that period.

The MiG-21 fighters that Moscow sent to Angola reportedly arrived in the Congo as early as October 1975. They were later moved to Luanda, but they were not used in combat until March 1976, after the war was virtually won. It is possible that the Soviet Union restricted their use in the belief that the introduction of advanced fighters would give Washington a justification for shipping more advanced weapons, but this would only explain why they were not used before December 1975, when the U.S. Congress voted to cut off American aid to the FNLA and UNITA. Perhaps there was a delay while pilots were being trained, but Cubans could have flown the planes; so a more likely explanation is that the Soviets believed that the fighters would contribute only marginally to the war effort, but would attract considerable attention to the Soviet involvement at a time when the MPLA was seeking diplomatic recognition from the more conservative African states.[38]

During the war the Soviet Union deployed a small naval task force off the West African coast, consisting at its peak of an *Alligator*-class tank landing ship, a *Kotlin*-class guided-missile destroyer, a *Kresta-II* guided-missile cruiser, and a companion oil refueler. It is also highly likely that a *Juliett*-class submarine accompanied the surface

---

[38] Savimbi first charged that the MiGs were in the Congo in the *Zambia Daily Mail*, October 30, 1975 (cited in *SIPRI Yearbook*, 1976, 56). *Newsweek*, December 1, 1975, learned of the MiGs also. The CIA received unconfirmed reports from its agents in the field, but did not acquire absolute confirmation of their presence until they attacked a UNITA supply base in eastern Angola on March 13, 1976. Stockwell, *In Search of Enemies*, 182–3, 242–4.

vessels during a portion of their voyage. The *Alligator* LST carried a
detachment of naval infantry. The task force was apparently deployed
in order to deter any potential threats to the Soviet and Cuban merchant vessels involved in the sealift of troops and arms to Angola.
Patrol boats from the Zairian navy that arrived off northern Angola
in November posed the most immediate threat; in late November the
LST traveled southward from Conakry, paid a port call at Pointe Noire
during the first week of December, and then assumed a patrol off the
West African coast. The destroyer and cruiser arrived in the region
in January. In addition to protecting the sealift, the naval deployment
demonstrated Moscow's commitment to the MPLA and served as a
passive deterrent to any U.S. counterintervention by naval forces.[39]

The role of Soviet and East European advisers and Cuban troops

Aside from the Soviet crews who manned some of the gun-bearing
vessels that docked in Angola in the spring and summer of 1975, there
was little direct participation by Soviet advisers in the civil war before November 1975. No more than a handful of Russians, mostly
correspondents, are known to have been in Luanda prior to the day
Angola attained its independence. After the People's Republic of Angola was declared, there were widespread reports that hundreds of
Soviet advisers and technicians had begun arriving in Luanda. Estimates of their number ranged from 170 to 400.[40] Little is known
about what role they played, but it is likely they helped plan the
MPLA's military strategy and provided instruction and servicing related to the Soviet arms shipments. There was some friction right at
the beginning, when the MPLA rejected a Soviet demand that military
personnel from the USSR have charge of securing the airport near
Luanda where Soviet transports were to land. The problem must have
been resolved rapidly, for there were no significant delays in the
airlift.[41]

Far more significant than the participation of Soviet advisers was
the direct intervention in the conflict by Cuban troops, eventually num-

[39] The information in this paragraph is largely from Petersen and Durch, "Angolan
Crisis Deployments," 144–53. See also *Facts on File*, January 10,1976. The White
House made public the fact of the Soviet deployments on January 7, 1976. *Tass*
denied the report in a statement published in *Pravda*, January 9, 1976. According
to Peterson and Durch, the denial was "technically correct," for the vessels moved
away from the coast shortly following the White House announcement.
[40] *Strategic Survey* (1975):32; *Newsweek*, December 1, 1975 and January 19, 1976;
Washington Post, February 18, 1976. Stories that earlier appeared in the world
press about Soviet advisers assisting the MPLA as early as September, and a
Washington Post report (November 22, 1975) that UNITA had captured 20 Soviet
advisers – the latter denied by *Tass* – proved to be propaganda plants by the CIA.
See Stockwell, *In Search of Enemies*, 194.
[41] *Washington Post*, November 15, 1975.

bering over 20,000. This was several times the number of Cuban soldiers ever sent abroad before. Cuba had established contact with the Portuguese African liberation movements, including the MPLA, as early as 1961, and Cuban advisers had been present at various times thereafter in Congo-Brazzaville and in Angola to assist in training guerrilla soldiers. Some of the more promising insurgents had been sent to Cuba (as well as to Algeria, Tanzania, Guinea, and the USSR) for training, and there are some reports that Che Guevara visited the MPLA in Cabinda briefly while on an African tour in 1965. It is certain that Neto met with him in Brazzaville that year, and Neto is also said to have met Castro in Havana in 1966.[42] Cuba's history of contacts with the MPLA facilitated transition to a much broader relationship in 1975.

In 1977, Gabriel Garcia Marquez, a Colombian novelist with close ties to Castro, published a semiofficial version of the Cuban involvement in the Angolan civil war.[43] His account, reports by Castro and others in the official Cuban newspaper, *Granma*, and information from Western correspondents make it possible to piece together a fairly accurate picture of Cuba's intervention. According to Garcia Marquez, Cuban commandant Flayio Bravo met with Neto in Brazzaville in May 1975. "Neto requested help with shipment of arms and asked about the possibility of further more specific aid." Neto was particularly interested in having military instructors sent. The MPLA made a formal aid request on July 16, 1975. Garcia Marquez stated that the first delegation of civilian instructors, led by Raul Diaz Arguelles, arrived in Luanda three months later, in August. This accords with Castro's later claim that there was not a single Cuban instructor in Angola until August. Cuban Deputy Premier Carlos Rafael Rodriguez, however, admitted to a group of correspondents in January 1976 that Cuba had sent 230 military advisers to Angola in the spring of 1975 to train MPLA forces. They arrived sometime in May. This was before any South African military involvement and before any U.S. arms shipments had taken place.[44]

The decision to escalate Cuba's involvement was apparently made sometime in August, for troop-carrying merchant ships embarked for Angola early in September. Further, according to Jorge Dominguez,

[42] Marcum, *The Angolan Revolution*, vol. I, 261, vol. II, 172, 225; Nelson P. Valdes, "Revolutionary Solidarity in Angola," in Cole Blasier and Carmelo Mesa-Lago, eds., *Cuba in the World* (University of Pittsburgh Press, 1979), 95–6; Gabriel Garcia Marquez, "Cuba in Africa: Seed Che Planted," *Washington Post*, January 12, 1977.

[43] His account is serialized in three issues of the *Washington Post*, January 10–12, 1977, which is the source used in this chapter. The original work, "Cuba en Angola: Operacion Carlota," was published in *Proceso*, January 1977, 6–15, an official Cuban publication.

[44] *Washington Post*, January 12, 1977; *Granma Weekly Review*, May 2, 1976; *Facts on File*, January 17, 1976; Interview: David Smith, U.S. State Department; Barry A. Sklar, "Cuba: Normalization of Relations," Issue brief No. IB75030, Congressional Research Service, Library of Congress (March 3, 1976), 23.

"Sometime between August 20 and September 5, 1975, the Chairman of the Joint Chiefs of Staff, the chiefs of the three armies and of the air force, and other vice ministers of the Armed Forces Ministry were temporarily relieved of their posts." They were back at their posts by July 1976; it is believed that in the interim they were assigned to oversee the Angolan operation. Western intelligence sources later confirmed that Major General Zenen Casa Regueiro, chief of the General Staff, was serving as commander of the Cuban expeditionary force in Angola, and four of the other missing generals held command positions under him. On October 4, the Cuban ship *Vietnam Heroico* arrived in Puerto Amboim; it was followed by *Coral Island* on October 7 and *La Plata*, which docked at Puerta Negra, on October 11. These ships carried hundreds of Cuban military personnel, and according to Garcia Marquez, "They docked without anyone's permission – but also without anyone's opposition." The Cubans immediately set up four training centers – at Delatando, Benguela, Saurime (Henrique de Carvalho), and Cabinda.[45]

The large South African military incursion that began on October 23 soon threatened the MPLA with sudden and irreversible defeat. Some South African troops had entered Angola as early as July, but this operation was the beginning of a major commitment by Pretoria. On November 3, a South African column attacked the Cuban training camp at Benguela. According to Castro, it was this attack, in which Cubans first perished in Angola, that led to the decision to send combat troops to assist the MPLA. He asserted that "on November 5 the Revolutionary Government of Cuba decided to send the first military units to Angola, to support the MPLA."[46] The effort was given the name "Operation Carlota," after a slave woman who led a black uprising in Cuba in 1843. It began with the sending of a reinforced battalion of special forces, 650 elite fighters from the Ministry of the Interior, rather than Cuba's Revolutionary Armed Forces. The first contingent of 82 men, dressed in civilian clothes and carrying luggage full of small arms, left from Jose Marti airport in Havana on November 7. Three ships left the next day carrying an artillery regiment and a mechanized battalion; they landed on November 27.

From November 7 to December 9, a total of 70 air trips from Havana to Luanda were made, with stops in Barbados, Guinea-Bissau, and the Congo. From December 9 to 24 the flights apparently were discon-

[45] Jorge I. Dominguez, *Cuba: Order and Revolution* (Cambridge: Belknap Press of Harvard University Press, 1978), 354–5; *Newsweek*, December 19, 1975, citing American intelligence analysts; Gabriel Garcia Marquez, *Washington Post*, January 12, 1977.

[46] Fidel Castro, speech at Conakry, Guinea, *Granma Weekly Review*, March 28, 1976. See also Barbara Walters, "An Interview with Fidel Castro," *Foreign Policy* 28(Fall 1977):22–51 (p. 39), and *Granma Weekly Review*, May 2, 1976.

tinued.[47] This was the same period in which Soviet arms shipments ceased, evidently in response to a U.S. diplomatic initiative, and it would seem to be evidence of the close coordination that took place between Havana and Moscow during the Angolan intervention. The flights resumed with some difficulty, because Barbados in the meantime had denied landing rights to the Cubans. Various routes were then tried: Cuban planes refueled in Guyana a few times, but the runway proved too short, and Texaco cut off fuel supplies to the Cuban planes that landed there; pressure from Washington resulted in a ban on refueling stops at Trinidad and Tobago; a number of stops were made in the Azores, despite Portuguese objections, but on January 21, 1976, the authorities in Lisbon cracked down and refused to allow Cuban planes to refuel; a few flights were made via the Gander International Airport in Newfoundland, but Canada quickly forbade landings by Cuban planes bound for Africa. The Canadian and Portuguese actions followed formal U.S. protests. A number of flights were made from Holguin in eastern Cuba to Cape Verde, but this route left fuel supplies dangerously low at the end of every flight. Finally, a number of transport planes were modified with supplemental gasoline tanks, which allowed nonstop flights from Holguin to Brazzaville, but with a reduced number of passengers.[48] Most of the transport planes used by the Cubans were Air Cubana planes of Soviet manufacture. In early January 1976, the USSR dispatched two Il-62 transport planes to Havana to assist the ailing airlift. Castro later acknowledged that the USSR "collaborated with our efforts when imperialism had cut off practically all our air routes in Africa."[49] Converted cargo ships also carried soldiers to Angola; Garcia Marquez wrote that they usually were crowded well beyond their intended capacity and that at one time as many as 15 Cuban vessels were en route to Angola.[50]

The Cuban expeditionary force expanded rapidly, as illustrated by the following Western intelligence estimates of the number of Cubans in Angola at various stages of the war:[51]

> November 15, 1975 2,000
> November 20, 1975 3,000

[47] Valdes, "Revolutionary Solidarity in Angola," 104. Garcia Marquez, *Washington Post*, January 10, 1977, asserts that 101 flights were made during the war. Petersen and Durch, "Angolan Crisis Deployments," 145, estimate that 50 Air Cubana flights and 40 Aeroflot flights took place from Cuba to Angola.

[48] Garcia Marquez, *Washington Post*, January 10, 1977; *Washington Post*, January 31, 1976; Valdes, "Revolutionary Solidarity in Angola," 103–5; *Facts on File*, January 24 and February 14, 1976.

[49] Fidel Castro, speech of April 19, 1976, in *Granma Weekly Review*, May 2, 1976.

[50] Petersen and Durch, "Angolan Crisis Deployments," 145, estimate arrivals of Cuban shipping vessels as follows: September 1, October 2, November 2, December 6, January 8, February 15, March 4.

[51] *New York Times*, November 21, 1975, December 21, 1975, January 17, 1976, May 1, 1976; Valdes, "Revolutionary Solidarity in Angola," 106.

November 30, 1975   3,000–5,000
December 20, 1975   4,000–6,000
January 6, 1976   9,500
February 3, 1976   12,000–14,000
Late April 1976   15,000

If anything, these figures are low as a result of the consistent under-estimation of Cuban military strengths by Western intelligence agencies prior to 1976.[52] And more individual Cubans served in Angola than even the highest estimates reveal, because of a policy of rotating troops between Angola and Cuba during the war.

Havana is said to have used special procedures in selecting the troops who went to Angola, so that approximately half of them were blacks, well above the black representation in the army and nearly twice their proportion in the general population. However, this assertion has never been proved. The Cubans found the climate and society in Luanda to be well suited to their tastes, and they are reported to have become somewhat popular with the Angolans, at least more so than were the Soviets. Castro claimed that the Cuban fatality rate was relatively low, especially considering the vast territory the Cubans won for the MPLA. There were, however, some cases of discontent and desertion in the ranks, a fact admitted in the Cuban military press. Two American writers who visited southern Angola in the fall of 1976 cited UNITA sources to the effect that on December 21, 1976, 142 Cuban soldiers defected in military vehicles to Zambia and requested asylum.[53] However, there is no independent confirmation of this claim.

Little is known about the Soviet-Cuban relationship during the war. Many American journalists and Western analysts assumed that Cuba entered the war on instructions from Moscow and that the Cubans were little more than Soviet surrogates. The correlation between the two governments was unquestionably very close (else one ends up with more tanks than tank crews), but there is reason to believe that the decision to send combat troops was a Cuban decision. Sensitive to the prevailing opinion in the West that the Soviets had planned and directed Operation Carlota, Castro made this statement in April 1976:

> Cuba alone bears the responsibility for taking that decision. The USSR ... never requested that a single Cuban be sent to that

[52] Interview: Jorge I. Dominguez, Harvard University. In his book, *Cuba* (p. 354), Dominguez places the peak total of Cuban troops at around 20,000.

[53] On the recruiting of black troops and the problem of discontent in the military, see Dominguez, *Cuba*, 353–6; on the Cuban experience in Luanda, see Gerald J. Bender, "Angola, the Cubans, and American Anxieties," *Foreign Policy* 31(Summer 1978):10–11; Castro's appraisal of Cuban losses is in *Granma Weekly Review*, May 2, 1976; the report on the mass defection to Zambia is R. Bruce McColm and David Smith, "The Other Angola," *National Review* XXIX(January 21, 1977):86.

country. The USSR is extraordinarily respectful and careful in its relations with Cuba. A decision of that nature could only be made by our own party.[54]

A Soviet official confirmed this view to an African journalist. "We did not twist their arms," he said. "The Cubans wanted to go for they are more radical than we are."[55] These statements may be deliberate distortions, but virtually all accounts of the Cuban involvement stress that Cuba's motivation to enter the war arose independent of Soviet pressures or inducements.

Nevertheless, Castro could not have acted in Angola without the full approval and support of the Soviet Union. As Zdenek Cervenka noted,

> While there is no doubt that the decision to send troops, as well as the whole planning of the operation, initiated from Havana, Moscow's consent was essential for the simple reason that the Russians were paying for the whole exercise. Besides, its success also depended on the timing of the arrival of Soviet heavy arms.[56]

The complexities of the military operation undoubtedly required constant consultation between the Soviet and Cuban military commands. It seems logical that the necessary coordinating mechanisms were set up sometime between early September, when the top-ranking Cuban military leaders were freed from their duties at home in order to plan the Angolan operation, and late November, when the Cuban chief of staff arrived in Angola. This supposition is strengthened by the fact that Cuban Deputy Premier Rodriguez was in Moscow for a week in mid-September, where he met with several Politburo members and candidate members, including Kosygin. An economic protocol was signed that may have been related to the financing of the Angolan intervention; it provided for coordination of economic planning between the USSR and Cuba and for continuing Soviet assistance to Havana. Beginning September 30, a week of solidarity with Angola was declared in the Soviet Union, and in October, Cuban Vice-Premier Bravo visited Moscow. The timing and nature of these events suggest that a definite decision to escalate Cuba's involvement may have been made in September and that Moscow both knew of and supported the decision.[57]

There is some evidence to suggest that Moscow rewarded Cuba financially as compensation for its role in Angola. Jorge Dominguez

[54] *Granma Weekly Review*, May 2, 1976; see also Castro's speech to the party congress, *Granma Weekly Review*, January 4, 1976.
[55] "The Latin African Connection," *Africa* No. 57(May 1976):81.
[56] Zdenek Cervenka, "Cuba and Africa," *ACR* (1976–7):A87–8.
[57] Central Intelligence Agency, *Appearances of Soviet Leaders, January 1975–December 1975* (Washington: CIA, 1976), 216–17, 230; *Pravda*, September 20, 1975; *Tass*, September 29, 1975.

suggested that two tacit payoffs may have taken place: a large-scale replenishment of Cuba's military inventory, and a Soviet offer to purchase Cuban goods that could not be sold on the world market. The offer to replenish military stocks was not unusual, and the transfers may have been scheduled before the war, but the offer to buy unmarketable Cuban goods was unprecedented.[58]

Soviet-American interactions

In early November 1975, when the Cuban cabinet faced the decision whether or not to escalate its Angolan commitment into a massive intervention, a major consideration was whether or not the United States would intervene openly. A "rapid analysis" concluded that Washington was unlikely to do so – the fall of Saigon, the Watergate scandal, Ford's status as an unelected president, the CIA's current disrepute with the public, and black hatred for South Africa all made a major commitment by the United States unthinkable.[59] The Cubans were correct, and the Soviet leadership no doubt made a similar assessment. In retrospect, given the intense isolationist sentiment that reigned in the United States shortly after Vietnam, it is remarkable that the Ford administration made any attempt to resist the Soviet involvement in Angola by military means.[60]

Kissinger himself admitted that "America's modest direct strategic and economic interests in Angola are not a central issue."[61] Gulf Oil operated a good-size petroleum field in Cabinda, and the United States consumed some $100 million worth of Angolan coffee beans each year, but these interests did not provide a rationale for American involvement. The secretary of state, then the preeminent architect of American foreign policy, viewed the conflict in a more global perspective as a test of America's will vis-à-vis the Russians after Vietnam. He was also concerned that equilibrium be maintained between the great powers:

> When one great power tips the balance of forces decisively in a local conflict through its military intervention – and meets no resistance – an ominous precedent is set, of grave consequence even if the intervention occurs in a seemingly remote area.[62]

[58] Interview: Dominguez; Dominguez, "Cuban Foreign Policy," *Foreign Affairs* 57(Fall 1978):97–8.

[59] Garcia Marquez, *Washington Post*, January 12, 1977.

[60] One motivation had nothing to do with foreign policy. Ford was then facing a major challenge from Ronald Reagan for the 1976 Republican nomination, and Reagan was portraying the president as "soft on the Soviets."

[61] Kissinger, statement before the Subcommittee on African Affairs of the Senate Foreign Relations Committee, *DOSB* (February 16, 1976):175.

[62] Kissinger, address in San Francisco on February 3, 1976, *DOSB* (February 23, 1976):209.

The USSR's own immediate interests in Angola were also subordinate to larger issues: the Sino-Soviet rivalry, the long-term future of southern Africa, and what the Soviets no doubt saw as a choice opportunity to once more humiliate a weakened America by doing what Kissinger always believed was so important – "delivering the goods" to an ally. The South African involvement was a boon to Moscow in that it enabled the Soviets to cast the American intervention as a pro-apartheid action and to maneuver the United States one step nearer the distant but not inconceivable day when Washington would face the unenviable choice of assisting South Africa militarily, or watching it fall to Soviet-supported black nationalism. Given that the actions of the superpowers in Angola were intimately connected with the central goals of their respective foreign policies, it was inevitable that the conflict expose the fundamental fragility of détente.

The coup that toppled Caetano caught the Nixon administration by surprise. With Nixon fighting to retain the presidency and Kissinger preoccupied with the Middle East, Washington was hardly in a position to adjust its foreign policy to cope with the coup's implications for both Europe and Africa. Two months after it took place, the CIA resuscitated a covert channel to Holden Roberto that had been active during the sixties.[63] From July to December 1974, the FNLA received small amounts of financial assistance from the CIA in a program devised and approved entirely within the agency itself. In a piecemeal and haphazard fashion, this channel evolved into a major covert operation that was the main instrument of U.S. policy in Angola throughout the civil war period. The CIA eventually appropriated over $32 million from its FY 1975 contingency reserve fund to support the Angolan operation, dubbed IAFEATURE. The funds were approved and expended as follows:[64]

January 22, 1975	The "Forty Committee" of the NSC approves $300,000 of financial support for the FNLA.
July 16, 1975	President Ford and the Forty Committee approve $6 million in financial aid and arms shipments for the FNLA.
July 27, 1975	Ford approves an additional $8 million for arms and aircraft.
August 20, 1975	Ford approves $10.7 million for arms, ammunition, and mercenaries' salaries for both the FNLA and UNITA.

[63] The CIA provided Roberto limited financial and material assistance during 1962–9, thereafter retaining him as an intelligence agent. See *New York Times*, September 25, 1975.

[64] Stockwell, *In Search of Enemies*, 55, 67, 162, 206–7. John Stockwell was chief of the CIA Angolan Task Force during the civil war. In addition to the funds shown, some money was drawn from the CIA's operation budget. Also, a great amount of U.S. military assistance to Zaire in 1975–6 went to support the FNLA and Mobutu's own troops in Angola.

November 27, 1975   Ford approves $7 million for arms, mercenaries, and the leasing of a C-130 transport plane.

The Soviet involvement in Angola was not a response to IAFEA-TURE, as some critics have suggested, for most of the $32 million was not approved until after the acceleration of Soviet arms deliveries in March 1975. The first planeload of American arms left the United States on July 29, 1975; the first shipload, aboard the *American Champion*, left Charleston, South Carolina, on August 29 and arrived in Matadi, Zaire, on October 7.[65] Washington's ability to respond to the USSR's involvement ran up against a sharp limit in November, however, when the CIA exhausted its contingency reserve fund, and no spare resources could be found in the Pentagon's budget. When the massive Soviet-Cuban intervention commenced in November, the White House found itself unable to match the raised ante without congressional authorization and additional funds. Needless to say, six months after the fall of Saigon, the mood of Congress and of the nation was strongly opposed to escalating U.S. involvement in another local war.

The Senate voted 54-22 on December 19, to approve the Tunney amendment to the FY 1976 defense appropriations bill, cutting off all funds for CIA assistance to the nationalist movements in Angola. The Senate's action reflected the national disillusionment with brushfire wars in the Third World, and the debate revealed a polity bitterly divided about the meaning of Soviet interventionary actions and the instruments the United States should use in response. Division had already been manifested within the administration itself when the State Department's assistant secretary for African affairs, Nathaniel Davis, quietly resigned in August because of disagreement over the policy of covert action in Angola.[66]

Soviet intelligence had likely learned of IAFEATURE well before it became public knowledge in the United States,[67] but it seems to have been a minor factor in the Kremlin's decision making. The increases in Moscow's involvement at various points during the war did not coincide with any U.S. actions. This may have been partly because Washington made little effort to couple the covert operation with a diplomatic initiative – at least not until it was too late. Kissinger later explained to a Senate committee that although the United States had desired a political solution, it initiated the covert operation because "the Angola situation is of a type in which diplomacy

[65] U.S. Congress, House, Commission on International Relations, *United States–Angolan Relations*, Hearing. 95th Congress, 2d sess., 1978, 16.
[66] Nathaniel Davis relates the story of his resignation and the events leading up to it in "The Angola Decision of 1975: A Personal Memoir," *Foreign Affairs* 57(Fall 1978):109–24.
[67] Leslie Gelb broke the story in the *New York Times*, September 25, 1975.

without leverage is impotent."[68] But, in fact, the military leverage provided by the CIA was not linked with the requisite diplomacy. According to Kissinger's own timetable, the United States did not raise the issue of Angola with the Soviets until late October, long after both superpowers were deeply involved militarily.[69] Superpower consultation on the prevention of local conflicts was presumably one of the cornerstones of détente – and one of its alleged advantages for the United States – yet, inexplicably, Kissinger delayed opening "the channel" to the Soviets until much too late in the crisis. Twice more in November the secretary of state discussed Angola with the Soviet Union, but not until December 9 did President Ford make a formal proposal through the Soviet Ambassador Dobrynin on mutual withdrawal from Angola and support of OAU mediation of the dispute. This proposal was made only after the CIA exhausted its working funds, after the Cuban-MPLA forces regained the offensive, and after it became obvious that U.S. arms shipments were amounting to a fraction of Soviet shipments – in short, after American leverage had all but disappeared.

Despite its late date, Ford's proposal was apparently taken seriously in Moscow, for the Soviets halted their airlift from December 9 to 24. Cuba's airlift of soldiers to Angola also ceased over the same period. The Senate vote came on December 19. However wise it may have been for the United States to avoid entanglement in another war, the timing of the vote was diplomatically disastrous. Only five days later the Soviet and Cuban airlifts resumed, presumably just enough time having passed for the Kremlin to evaluate the significance of the Senate decision and to organize new arms deliveries:

> After the Senate vote to block any further aid to Angola, the Cubans more than doubled their forces and Soviet military aid was resumed on an even larger scale. The scope of Soviet-Cuban intervention increased dramatically; the cooperativeness of Soviet diplomacy declined.[70]

Deprived of military leverage, the Ford administration clung to the hope that the leverage of rhetoric might restrain Soviet behavior. The USSR was warned repeatedly that its intervention in Angola would threaten the entire spectrum of Soviet-American relations and might spell the end of détente. *Izvestia* may have been referring to the U.S. warning when it wrote the following:

[68] *DOSB* XLVIII(February 16, 1976):181.
[69] U.S. Congress, *Angola*, Hearings, 52.
[70] *DOSB* XLVIII(February 16, 1976):178. The Senate vote was probably not the only factor that reassured the Soviets and encouraged their deeper involvement. In an effort to win congressional support, Ford and top administration officials had openly stressed that the United States was not contemplating direct combat intervention. *New York Times*, December 17, 1975.

Some of the leaders of the United States and other imperialist powers are attempting to exert pressure on the Soviet Union, are shifting onto the USSR responsibility for the conflict's emergence, and are accusing it of disrupting the "balance of forces" in southern Africa and of pursuing a policy "contradictory" to the process of détente.[71]

The prospect of détente being damaged seems to have had only a minimal effect on Soviet behavior in the conflict. The Soviet press argued that Moscow's involvement was perfectly consistent with détente, indeed that "détente by no means signifies – nor can it signify – freedom from action for aggressors."[72]

Although Ford and Kissinger invoked the specter of détente's demise, they deigned to apply the leverage provided by two of its central achievements: the 1975 U.S.-Soviet grain agreement and the upcoming negotiations on a new strategic arms limitation treaty (SALT). When the Kremlin issued a statement declaring that the Soviet Union "comes out firmly for the termination of foreign armed intervention in Angola,"[73] the White House took it as a promising gesture, evidently not realizing that Soviet terminology does not allow for the USSR's own actions to be considered "intervention." Partly because of optimism generated by this statement, and influenced also by the upcoming elections and the farm vote, Ford declared in Iowa in mid-January that linking grain exports to the Angolan situation would not serve "any useful purpose whatsoever."[74] A few days later, Kissinger announced that he would soon fly to Moscow for SALT negotiations despite the Soviet intervention in Angola. On his return from the USSR, he told a Senate committee on January 29 that the SALT talks were too important to be linked to other issues. By this time the United States had renounced or been denied every instrument it could have used to resist the Soviet-Cuban intervention, and it was only natural that the intervention proceeded without impediment.

As a final observation, it is interesting that the United States made no significant effort to counteract the modest Soviet naval buildup that took place off the Angolan coast at the peak of the war. John Herzog noted that the Soviet navy had advanced from playing the

> ... role of a spectator in the Suez crisis to a viable deterrent force in the 1967 and 1973 Israeli-Arab conflicts to the only major nation active as a participant in the Angolan affair. Conversely,

[71] *Izvestia*, December 26, 1975.
[72] Aleksey Ionov, "Angola i Razryadka," *Za Rubezhom* No. 2(January 8, 1976). See also *Izvestia*, December 26, 1975, *Tass*, January 29, 1976, and especially K. Uralov, "Angola – Torzhestvo pravogo dela," 59–60.
[73] *Pravda*, January 3, 1976.
[74] *Newsweek*, January 19, 1976.

by 1976 the United States had given up its place of naval dominance and had assumed the role of spectator.[75]

In such trends the evolution of the international order can be seen.

The China factor

Of the major outside powers in Angola, the PRC played the most diplomatically correct – and perhaps, for that reason, the least influential – role in the civil war. Although China, much like the United States, was concerned about advancing Soviet influence, it never denounced the MPLA, and throughout the war it maintained an official policy of recognizing and supporting all three liberation movements. However, Peking's military involvement in the conflict was extremely minimal.

Before the outbreak of the civil war, China had developed and maintained ties with the leaders of all of the three national liberation movements. The MPLA, in fact, was the first liberation movement with which China had had contact. Table 8.2 is a register of known diplomatic contacts between the PRC and the Angolan movements before and during the civil war.[76] The competition for Chinese support became particularly intense during the spring and summer of 1975, when the Alvor accords were breaking down. The MPLA, the FNLA, and UNITA all sent delegations to Peking seeking favor and material assistance. In addition to the political contacts listed in the table, all of the movements received financial or military aid from Peking. In the case of UNITA, modest financial sums, but no arms, were received from China during the late 1960s and early 1970s.[77] In mid-July 1975, Peking authorized Zaire to release Chinese military equipment to UNITA, apparently because of concern about the volume of Soviet arms going to Neto. Chinese arms intended for UNITA were also shipped directly to Dar es Salaam, but President Julius Nyerere of Tanzania prevented their further passage. The FNLA fared somewhat better. A group of roughly 120 Chinese military advisers headed by a major general arrived at the FNLA base in Kinkuzu in 1974 to train Roberto's soldiers in guerrilla warfare. They remained over two years. In August 1974 the FNLA received some 450 tons of small arms and explosives from Peking, and additional armaments are reported to have arrived as the civil war heated up in 1975. Finally, it is known

[75] John J. Herzog, "Perspectives on Soviet Naval Development: A Navy to Match National Purposes," in Paul J. Murphy, ed., *Naval Power in Soviet Policy* (Washington, D.C.: U.S. Air Force, 1978), 41–42.

[76] See V. Sofinsky and A. Khazanov, "Angolskaya khronika pekinskogo predatel'stva," *Mezhdunarodnaya zhizn'* (July 1978):68–77, for a lengthy Soviet attempt to explain China's contacts with all three movements as part of a grand Peking conspiracy.

[77] Marcum, *The Angolan Revolution*, vol. II, 229–30; Fritz Sitte, *Flammenherd Angola* (Vienna: Kremayr and Scheriau, 1972), 149. See especially Sitte's interview with Savimbi (pp. 139–59).

Table 8.2. *Known diplomatic contacts between the PRC and the three major Angolan liberation movements, 1960 through 1975*

MPLA	
August 1960	MPLA delegation visits China
April 1965	Lucila Neto leads MPLA women's delegation to China
July 1971	Neto and MPLA delegation visit Peking, meet with Chou En-lai and chief of general staff
May 29–June 3, 1975	High-level MPLA delegation visits Peking, meets with vice-foreign-minister and vice-premier
FNLA	
December 1963	Holden Roberto meets with Chinese Foreign Minister Chen Yi at Nairobi, Kenya
December 1973	Roberto and FNLA delegation visit Peking and confer with the vice-foreign-minister and vice-premier Teng Hsiao-ping
June 1974	First contingent of Chinese advisers arrives at Kinshasa headquarters of FNLA; others follow
July 1975	FNLA representatives meet with Teng Hsiao-ping in Peking
UNITA	
Summer 1964	Savimbi visits China and confers with Mao Tse-tung and Chou En-lai; he seeks aid in establishing UNITA
March 1975	Samuel Chiwale leads UNITA delegation to Peking; talks with Teng Hsiao-ping and other officials

Sources: Mizan Newsletter (May 1964):6; NCNA, December 4, 6, and 18, 1973; NCNA, March 20 and 28, 1975; Radio Clube Portuguese, June 4, 1964; Marcum, *The Angolan Revolution*, vols. I and II.

that the MPLA received some assistance from China as late as the summer of 1975 in what may have been a Chinese attempt to counteract Soviet influence with Neto. Dr. Neto stated in an *Afriscope* interview granted after the Nakuru agreement that the Sino-Soviet conflict had not hindered Peking from supporting any of the liberation movements. He acknowledged China's aid to UNITA and the FNLA and stated flatly that "we also get some aid from China, but we do not make much propaganda about it." He insisted that the MPLA's relations with Peking were cordial.[78]

China attempted to maintain an evenhanded stance toward all three movements during the civil war. After the Alvor agreement, Chou En-lai sent identical messages to Neto, Roberto, and Savimbi, congrat-

[78] Ebinger, "External Intervention in Internal War," 689; *UNITA's Official Position on the War in Angola* (UNITA Information Office, December 1975), a document cited in Legum, "Foreign Intervention in Angola," A6-7; Marcum, *The Angolan Revolution*, vol. II, 246; *Afriscope* (August 1975):10.

ulating them and assuring them of China's support for their "just struggle." At the end of August, when it became obvious that only a military struggle could decide the internal dispute, China blamed the breakdown of unity on Soviet imperialism and observed that Peking had always been friendly with all three liberation movements.[79] On the day Angola attained its independence, the Chinese Ministry of Foreign Affairs issued a statement:

> The Chinese Government and people extend their warm congratulations on this victory to the Angolan people and all the three Angolan liberation organizations.
> ... an unfortunate situation of division and civil war has appeared in Angola after independence. This is entirely the result of the rivalry between the two Super-powers, and particularly the undisguised expansion and crude interference of the Soviet Union.[80]

The statement charged that the Soviet Union "single-handedly" had provoked the war; it called for the three movements to settle their differences in accordance with OAU policy.

Two weeks earlier the Chinese had withdrawn all military advisers from Angola, effectively ending China's direct involvement in the war. Peking's withdrawal was a hasty one, triggered by the intervention of South Africa on the side of the FNLA and UNITA, and by an OAU statement urging outside powers to end their involvement in the war. President Kenneth Kaunda of Zambia, speaking at the OAU summit meeting on Angola, praised China in profuse terms for being willing to support national liberation movements and for not attempting to impose its will on Africa. He noted that China was the only great power to obey the wishes of the OAU with respect to withdrawal and nonintervention.[81]

China and the Soviet Union waged a vitriolic propaganda battle over Angola, with Peking accusing Moscow of hegemonism and "meddling," and the Soviets charging the Chinese with supporting separatism and reaction, and of backing the same camp as South Africa and the imperialist powers.[82] Despite such histrionics, there is good reason to doubt the assessment of Colin Legum and others that Sino-Soviet rivalry was a greater influencing factor on Soviet behavior in

---

[79] NCNA, January 27, 1975; NCNA, August 30, 1975.
[80] PRC Ministry of Foreign Affairs, Peking, NCNA, November 15, 1975.
[81] *Afriscope* (March 1976):32.
[82] See *Tass*, July 17, 1975, and November 13 and 17, 1975; Radio Moscow, December 13, 1975, December 19, 1975; *Tass*, December 23, 1975; Radio Moscow, January 5, 1976; *Tass*, January 27, 1976. On China's view, see NCNA, August 30, 1975, October 15, 1975, November 14, 1975, and December 31, 1975.

the crisis than was the U.S. involvement.[83] Peking's military assistance to all three liberation movements was small compared with the U.S. involvement and minute compared with the Soviet-Cuban effort. Furthermore, its commitment was terminated well before the escalation of the war in November. It is simply not tenable to suppose that Moscow would arm and help transport 20,000 Cuban troops to Angola principally in order to compete with a small body of Chinese military advisers who had already left the country.

Although Peking's role in Angola seems to have been a secondary factor in the Soviet decision to intervene, the USSR did recognize that the conflict provided an ideal opportunity to score a propaganda victory over the PRC in their ongoing ideological struggle over the correct line to be taken toward the developing world. A commentary in the Soviet newspaper *Izvestia* stressed this point with reference to the Angolan conflict:

> The African and nonaligned countries have also had an opportunity to see for themselves the groundlessness of the Maoist allegations that, under the influence of a normalization of relations with the capitalist countries and of an international détente, the Soviet Union "will not want" to defend the interests of the peoples of young states.[84]

China, in fact, did lose some influence in southern Africa as a result of the Soviet victory in Angola. Prior to the war, Peking had exerted a certain ideological influence on the liberation movements in Mozambique, Namibia, and Rhodesia, as well as in Angola; it also enjoyed a high standing in Zambia and Tanzania because of the Tanzam railway it had helped to construct, and its relations with Zaire and the Congo were friendly. Although nothing China did or said during the war particularly offended these governments and liberation movements, neither were they very impressed with Peking's influence on the outcome of the war. The conflict revealed that China could bring very little political or military influence to bear on a distant crisis. Angola caused the Kremlin's star in southern Africa to rise dramatically, as some of the black leaders of the region came to view the Soviet Union as a potential ally. China's ideological fervor simply could not compensate for the Soviet Union's capacity to deliver military equipment. Nevertheless, China's standing with some nations was enhanced as a result of its evenhanded policy during the war, and Peking had reason

[83] Colin Legum, "The Soviet Union, China, and the West in Southern Africa," *Foreign Affairs* 54(July 1976):745–62; Legum, "Angola and the Horn of Africa," in Stephen S. Kaplan et al., *Diplomacy of Power: Soviet Armed Forces as a Political Instrument* (Washington: Brookings Institution, 1981) 573; William Griffith, "Soviet Policy in Africa and Latin America: The Cuban Connection," in Griffith, ed., *The Soviet Empire: Expansion and Detente* (Lexington, Mass.: Lexington Books, 1976), 337, 342.

[84] *Izvestia*, December 26, 1975.

to be pleased that the conflict damaged détente and widened the distance between Washington and Moscow. The convergence of the Chinese and U.S. positions on the situation in Angola became apparent within a year after the war, when virtually every government in the world, except the PRC and the United States, had recognized the MPLA government in Luanda.

As for the Soviet Union, although its rhetorical fire may have been directed quite fiercely at China, there is little doubt that its primary adversary in Angola was the United States. The massive Soviet-Cuban commitment took place well after China was out of the conflict. Throughout the civil war, the only conceivable obstacle to a Soviet victory would have been a major U.S. military effort. From November to the end of the war – the period of most intense fighting – the Kremlin was clearly more concerned about Washington's actions than about Peking's propaganda.

The outcome

The Soviet Union yielded a high return from its investment in the Angolan civil war. To begin with, by proving that the fall of South Vietnam was not an anomaly, the war fostered a diplomatic climate in the Third World that was highly conducive to Soviet political and military initiatives. The MPLA's victory created the impression in Africa and elsewhere that the USSR was riding a tide of victory, that its military power was overtaking that of the United States, that the world's future lay with the East rather than with the West. The war proved that Moscow was as capable of delivering a military victory to a liberation movement in Africa as in Asia; the USSR thereby strengthened its claim to being the "natural ally" of the Third World. Although it is difficult to measure, this may have been the greatest reward reaped by the Kremlin from the war.

In a more regional context, the war was a debacle for black Africa, a tragic event that underscored the political weakness of the OAU and the great extent to which Africa was still a province of European powers. But despite the deep divisions that the war unveiled, it proved that there was one cement capable of firmly uniting the black nations: opposition to South Africa. It was that very opposition that eventually exonerated the Soviet intervention in African eyes. The USSR's violation of the OAU resolutions on noninterference in Angola was largely forgotten once Pretoria entered the war. Nyerere even called openly for the Soviet Union to send the MPLA the arms necessary for fighting South Africa.[85] In the course of the war, several African nations adopted the Soviet line that Moscow's involvement was not intervention, but support of a legitimate government against foreign intervention. Con-

[85] *Tass*, December 3, 1975.

versely, the United States lost face and influence in Africa because of its involvement on the same side as Pretoria.

The intervention also prepared the way for a greatly enhanced Soviet role in determining the future of southern Africa. The victory gave the Soviet Union direct geographical access to SWAPO guerrillas in Namibia, increased Soviet influence in the Congo and Zambia, and enhanced Soviet prestige (already high) with the new revolutionary government in Mozambique. Soviet influence with the front-line guerrilla army of Joshua Nkomo in Zimbabwe also increased noticeably, although another Zimbabwean guerrilla leader, Robert Mugabe, leaned more toward Peking than Moscow.

The war saw the forging of a new kind of Soviet-Cuban military cooperation, a seemingly accidental development that proved to be a propitious advance in Soviet interventionary capabilities. In the past, the USSR had often been forced to entrust Soviet arms in large quantities and of high sophistication to untrained and unstable armies in the Third World. The Kremlin had been reluctant to commit its own troops in local wars; yet arms shipments without trained soldiers had usually proved ineffectual. Now, with Cuban cooperation, the advantages of having experienced combat troops could be enjoyed without the high risks.

Finally, the Soviet-Cuban intervention in Angola brought to power a firm Soviet ally in west-central Africa. Angola's new government was effusive in its praise of Soviet assistance during the war. Neto visited Moscow for a week at the end of May, where he met with Kosygin and signed a "Declaration of the Principles of Friendly Relations and Cooperation between the USSR and the PRA," preparatory to the signing by Neto and Brezhnev of a "Twenty-Year Treaty of Friendship and Cooperation" in Moscow on October 8, 1976. Castro and Neto are said to have reached an agreement on slow withdrawal of Cuban troops (200 per week) when they met at Conakry in March, but the Cubans proved too important in defending Neto's government against the continuing guerrilla incursions of UNITA in the south and against possible coup attempts from factions within the MPLA,[86] and the withdrawal did not take place. Neto visited Cuba for a week in July and again in December, signing a total of ten cooperative agreements on Cuban aid to Angola. The closeness of the PRA's ties to the Soviet bloc was demonstrated following the Vietnamese invasion of Cambodia, when Angola joined the Soviet bloc in recognizing the new

---

[86] The number of Cubans in Angola actually increased after the March agreement, rising to 19,000 soldiers and 4,000 civilians. *Africa Report* (January-February 1978):24. In May 1977, a faction within the MPLA staged an abortive coup against Neto, killing 7 of 33 Central Committee members. There may have been some Soviet complicity in the coup, but Cuban troops are reported to have assisted in defending Neto. Gerald Bender, "Angola, the Cubans, and American Anxieties," 23–6.

regime before any other Third World country had done so. Even Romania was not so pliant.

Nevertheless, it is possible that Moscow will yet experience troubles maintaining the high degree of influence with the MPLA that it enjoyed through 1980. Neto declared at the peak of the civil war that "the government and people of the Popular Republic of Angola will never be enslaved to any foreign country, be it the USSR or any other power. Never!"[87] The Soviets have not been granted their own naval facilities in Angola as compensation for their intervention in the civil war; in fact, Article 16 of the PRA constitution expressly prohibits "the installation of foreign military bases." In December 1978, Neto dismissed a cabinet minister for signing an agreement with Cuba for an additional 6,000 Cuban technicians to come to Angola. He warned of the need "to defend the independence of the Party" and made overtures for better relations with Western nations and for the opening of relations with the United States.[88] Also, Angola's economy has stagnated badly in the years since the war, forcing the government to search about for Western assistance and credits.

As was the case with the Yom Kippur war, one loss experienced by the Soviet Union as a result of its intervention in Angola was a further deterioration in its relations with the United States. Although the SALT talks continued and the Soviet-American grain agreement was not rescinded, the Angolan civil war marked the end of the euphoric period of Soviet-American détente engineered by Henry Kissinger. President Ford even made a point of dropping that term from his vocabulary in the 1976 presidential campaign. Moscow learned that however plainly it had always stated its position that détente did not preclude supporting wars of national liberation, that argument could not be made popular in the United States. That the Soviet Union went ahead in Angola anyway is evidence that its leaders considered the value of peaceful coexistence to be waning as compared with the fruits of revolutionary activism abroad.

[87] "Let the Struggle Continue," *Afriscope* (December 1975):62.
[88] Zagoria, "Soviet Alliances in the Third World," 748.

9
THE OGADEN WAR[1]

Russia is outmaneuvering America. Soviet leaders have convinced the Carter Administration not to react to the biggest Soviet airlift in history. Bigger than the October War. Bigger than Angola ... Moscow has hoodwinked you.

President Siad Barre

The nagging question is why anyone covets this bleak place at all.

Elizabeth Peer, *Newsweek*

The Somali flag is a five-pointed white star set in a field of azure blue. The star is a proud symbol of irredentist nationalism, its five points representing the five territories in the Horn of Africa that are principally inhabited by Somali peoples: former British Somaliland, former Italian Somalia, Djibouti, the northeastern region of Kenya, and the Ogaden desert of Ethiopia. The first two of these territories together constitute the sovereign territory of the Somali Democratic Republic; annexation of the other three has been that republic's central foreign policy aim since it achieved independence in 1960. During the summer of 1977, smoldering guerrilla activity in the Ogaden desert erupted into an interstate conflict between Somalia and Ethiopia. President Siad Barre of Somalia, aware of the turmoil and internal divisions rending Ethiopia, had evidently concluded that the time was ripe to attach a third point to the Somali star – the Ogaden. Equipped with modern Soviet weapons, thousands of regular Somali troops invaded the Ogaden in July, joining forces with the Western Somali Liberation Front (WSLF), a guerrilla army supported by Mogadishu that already controlled parts of the eastern Ogaden.[2] Ethiopia's ruling council, the Dergue, was at the time handicapped by widespread

---

[1] This chapter draws heavily on information given the author by reliable Ethiopian and other sources who had firsthand knowledge about the Soviet arms deals made with Ethiopia. These sources have asked to be kept strictly confidential.

[2] Until February 1978, Somalia steadfastly maintained that its regular troops were not involved, though it acknowledged that aid was being rendered to the WSLF. Somali officials would admit only that regular troops on leave were allowed to "volunteer" for the WSLF. *ACR* (1977–8):B374. There is, however, abundant evidence that regular Somali troops were involved beginning in July; see dispatches by Elizabeth Peer and James Pringle from opposite sides of the conflict, *Newsweek*, September 5 and 26, 1977, respectively.

domestic opposition to its regime and by the necessity of devoting substantial military resources to the northern province of Eritrea, where guerrilla armies were waging a determined struggle for secession. By mid-September, the fall of the entire Ogaden to the pan-Somali forces appeared imminent, and many observers saw the breakup of Ethiopia as the inevitable outcome.

Six months later, Somalia's offensive had collapsed, and its devastated army was in full retreat, the victim of a massive Soviet-Cuban intervention on behalf of Ethiopia. Once again the Soviet Union had engineered large-scale air and sea shipments of weaponry, roughly comparable in volume to the arms shipped to the MPLA during the Angolan conflict. Some 15,000 Cuban troops had joined the Ethiopian offensive, providing the technical skill and trained manpower necessary for employment of the Soviet weapons, and, in an unprecedented step, a top-level command group, headed by at least two ranking Soviet generals, was sent to Ethiopia to help plan and direct the Ogaden campaign. The Soviet-Cuban intervention proceeded smoothly, almost unimpeded by international constraints – it was the first time that a large Soviet military operation had taken place outside Eastern Europe without any other major power becoming involved militarily.

This is not to say that Soviet involvement in the Ogaden was without risk. The stakes were in fact very high. Moscow had devoted nearly 15 years to cultivating a loyal client regime in Somalia. Economic and military assistance totaling over $285 million had been extended to Mogadishu, and the USSR had almost entirely supplied and trained the Somali armed forces. Approximately 1,700 Soviet advisers were stationed in Somalia as of 1977, and the Soviet fleet enjoyed access to naval facilities at Kismayu, Mogadishu, and Berbera. The latter port – strategically located directly across the Gulf of Aden from South Yemen (the PDRY), another Soviet client – was the site of extensive docking, communications, and missile support facilities constructed entirely by the USSR. It was the closest thing to a full-scale, Western-style military base that the Soviet Union possessed anywhere in the Third World. By choosing to offer its support to Ethiopia, Moscow faced the prospect – which ultimately became a fact – of losing all of this.

When the conflict initially broke out the USSR perhaps hoped that by supplying arms to both sides it could act as mediator in the dispute and prod Ethiopia and Somalia into joining South Yemen in a federation of Socialist Red Sea states. When this scenario shattered against the strength of pan-Somali feeling in Mogadishu, the Soviet Union opted for the larger power. Ethiopia has nearly nine times the population of Somalia, a GNP eight times larger, twice the area, much greater natural resources, and greater influence in Africa. Nevertheless, by choosing to support the unstable and unpopular Dergue, Moscow took the risk of possibly finding itself entrenched on the side of a disintegrating regime unable either to conduct the war or to unify the nation. In that event the USSR might have lost all it had gained in Somalia in return for little in Ethiopia. Also, given the Angolan experience and the fact that the policies of the new Democratic administration in Washington had not yet been defined, the Kremlin could not be totally confident that its intervention would proceed without triggering some kind of U.S. response. Ethiopia had been linked closely with Washington as late as 1976, and its future was surely more pertinent to American interests than the future of Angola had been. Despite the risks, Moscow seems to have concluded that the opportunity presented by the conflict was too promising to pass up in the name of prudence.

The first report of a direct Ethiopian-Somali clash in the Ogaden was dispatched from Nairobi in February 1977.[3] No doubt Mogadishu, with the WSLF as its main tool, hoped to take advantage of the bitter internecine violence that had erupted in Addis Ababa a few days earlier following the self-appointment of Colonel Mengistu Haile-Mariam as chairman of the ruling Provisional Military Administrative Council (the PMAC or Dergue). From February to July, the WSLF's guerrilla forces captured dozens of villages in the western Ogaden, destroyed five crucial bridges on the Addis Ababa-Djibouti railway, and claimed to have won control of 60 percent of the disputed territory. The fighting escalated sharply beginning in July. Ethiopia charged that a full-scale Somali invasion had taken place on July 23, and numerous sources confirmed this, though it was officially denied in Mogadishu. Jijiga, the easternmost stronghold of the Ethiopian army, was soon under siege, and by the end of the month Radio Mogadishu was reporting WSLF claims that over 100 villages had been taken, some over 150 miles inside Ethiopia. In mid-August, Mengistu ordered nationwide mobilization in order to check the Ogaden invasion, and on September 7 Ethiopia broke off diplomatic relations with Somalia. Mogadishu followed suit the next day, but neither side made a formal declaration of war. Jijiga finally fell to the Somali forces on September 12, giving them undisputed control of over four-fifths of the Ogaden. Morale in the Ethiopian ranks was so low that many soldiers mutinied, abandoning large stocks of American weapons as they retreated westward. Somalia pressed its offensive further in October, besieging the walled city of Harar and threatening Diredawa, respectively the fifth and third largest cities in Ethiopia. Both cities lay outside the predominantly ethnic Somali area of the Ogaden, but they fell within the scope of an ambitious vision of Greater Somaliland and were essential for defending the Ogaden against anticipated counterattacks.

As the conflict progressed, the Soviet Union gradually abandoned its stance of studied neutrality and began to lean distinctly toward the Ethiopian side. On August 14, *Pravda* published a *Tass* statement referring to "hostilities between regular Somali army units and Ethiopian troops" and to "the invasion of one country's territory by the armed forces of the other."

---

[3] *Washington Post*, February 22, 1977. The dispatch reported that 1,500 Somali troops had raided into the Ogaden. For several months prior to that time, Somalia had waged a small and ineffectual guerrilla campaign in the southeast Ogaden and in northern Kenya.

An even more direct condemnation of Somalia appeared in the August 17 issue of *Izvestia*, though arms shipments continued arriving from the USSR at Mogadishu until at least the end of the month.[4] President Siad flew to Moscow at the end of August but was unable to resolve the growing impasse with his erstwhile allies. In mid-October the Soviet ambassador to Ethiopia, Anatoly Ratonov, stated that the USSR "officially and formally" had ceased arms shipments to Somalia. The inevitable break occurred on November 13, 1977. Following a 10-hour meeting, the Central Committee of the Somali Socialist Revolutionary party, the ruling party, ordered all Soviet and Cuban military advisers to leave the country within a week, banned the Soviets from access to military facilities in Somalia, and abrogated the treaty of friendship and cooperation signed with Moscow in 1974. Diplomatic relations with Cuba – but not with the USSR – were severed. It was a stunning setback for Moscow.

Within two weeks a massive Soviet airlift of arms into Ethiopia began. The commencement of the arms shipments coincided with the peak of the Somali attack on Harar. Although outnumbered nearly 3 to 1, some of the Somali forces were able to breach the walls of the city and engage the defenders in street fighting. At one point the WSLF claimed absolute control of the city, but Ethiopian air superiority, increasing Soviet support, superior numbers, and the overextended supply lines of the Somalis prevented its fall. By the end of November the Somali forces had been forced to retreat a few miles from Harar. Fighting on the ground died down in December, but Ethiopia made a number of air strikes against border cities in northern Somalia.

Throughout December and January, arms from the Soviet Union poured into Ethiopia at a pace rivaling the intensive deliveries of the October war. Significant numbers of Cuban troops also entered Ethiopia during this period, though a massive buildup of the Cuban military presence did not occur until February. The Ethiopian counteroffensive was triggered by a second Somali attempt to take over Harar that reached its peak on January 22, 1978. Reinforced by Cuban units, Soviet T-54 and T-55 tanks, and MiG fighter-bombers, the Ethiopians repulsed the attack and began a four-pronged drive from Harar and Diredawa toward Jijiga and along the railway toward Djibouti. Early in February the Somali government announced a national mobilization to meet "an invasion mounted by the allied Russian and Cuban forces" and publicly committed its regular army to the war. In mid-February, some of the Ethiopian forces crossed the Ahmar Mountains between Jijiga and the Somali border, bypassing the heavily defended Gara Marda Pass, while Soviet Mi-6 helicopters airlifted tanks, two at a time, around the back of the mountains to a point near Genasene, north of Jijiga. The maneuver enabled the Ethiopians to threaten the Somali rear in heavy fighting on February 28. The battle of Jijiga was

[4] *Newsweek*, September 5, 1977. The dispatch refers to a secret shipment of spare parts for military equipment. Confidential sources confirm that arms shipments were sent to Somalia until the end of August.

the largest and most decisive action of the war. The Somalis suffered terrible casualties, including the destruction of a complete armored brigade, and on March 5 the city fell to the attackers. The routed Somali forces rapidly retreated across the border, and within a week the Ethiopians had recaptured all of the Ogaden save Kelafo and Mustahil in the southeast corner. On March 9, President Siad announced that all Somali troops were being withdrawn from the Ogaden, bringing the war to a de facto end.

The local dispute

The Ogaden dispute was a rivalry involving the aspirations and claims of two very different types of nationalism. Unlike most African countries, Ethiopia and Somalia each possessed strong nationalist roots predating the colonial era. Ethiopia's nationalism was fundamentally political, based on the legacy of the Ethiopian Empire as the oldest independent country in Africa, whereas the nationalism of Somalia was largely ethnic and cultural in origin, based on the homogeneity of the Somali people. The impetus of the dispute came from Somalia. Truncated colonial borders frustrated its nationalist aspirations, which took the form of irredentist claims on neighboring territories.

The Somalis are a Moslem, Cushitic-speaking people with a historical identity nearly 1,000 years old and a traditional sense of independence. Out of a total of roughly 4 million Somalis, less than 3 million live within the republic proper. Pan-Somali feelings run deep:

> The Somalis are as culturally uniform as the Ethiopians are mixed. From Djibouti in the north to Kenya's Tana River in the south, they speak a common language, enjoy a rich oral literature centered on poetic forms, organize communal life around similar, egalitarian social institutions, distinguish themselves from their Bantu and Nilotic neighbors by emphasizing a genealogy stretching back to an original Arab ancestor, and manifest a powerful devotion to Islam.[5]

Somalia lacked the communications infrastructure necessary for true national integration, and it suffered from certain tribal divisions, particularly between the Samaale and Sab tribes, but "these fissures do not snap a deep underlying spirit of national unity."[6] The chief weakness of Somali nationalism was that it never developed the political forms of modern nation-building prior to the time that the colonial scramble for Africa left the Somali people divided among

---

[5] Tom J. Farer, *War Clouds on the Horn of Africa: A Crisis for Détente* (New York: Carnegie Endowment for International Peace, 1976), 50.

[6] John Drysdale, *The Somali Dispute* (London: Pall Mall, 1964), 165. On the nature and origin of Somali nationalism, see Saadia Touval, *Somali Nationalism: International Politics and the Drive for Unity in the Horn of Africa* (Cambridge: Harvard University Press, 1963), especially Chapters 3–6.

five separate political entities. Not until 1960 did the first Somali state come into existence.

Ethiopia's sense of nationhood was not based on cultural and ethnic unity, as was Somalia's, but on territorial proprietorship and the early development of a state: "As in the case of agricultural populations settled around permanent supplies of waters in Iraq and Egypt, the inhabitants of the Ethiopian plateau far back in history developed a cultural identity, reinforced and sustained by a written language and literature and by aristocratic and monarchial traditions."[7] Ethiopia's constant military struggle for territorial integrity also contributed to the emergence of a strong binding force of political nationalism. As far as the Ogaden was concerned, Ethiopia based its claim on the simple fact that its emperors had generally held suzerainty over the area, on boundary agreements signed with the Italians and the British, and on the thousands of casualties suffered by Ethiopia in defending the Ogaden against Italy's offensive in 1935. From the viewpoint of Addis Ababa, the Somalis were merely one of the many minority communities in Ethiopia.

The fundamental Ethiopian-Somali dispute, then, arose from equally ardent but differently based claims to the Ogaden. At least four other factors aggravated the conflict. First, both nations lay claim to French Somaliland, the tiny territory of the Afars and the Issas wedged between them at the strait of Bab el-Mandeb. Ethiopia's foreign trade was highly dependent on the port of Djibouti; yet a majority of the local population was Somali. In an effort to blunt Somalia's claim, Addis Ababa had relinquished its own claim on the territory in 1975 and challenged Mogadishu to do the same. Somalia had refused. When this territory became independent Djibouti in June 1977, just as the Ogaden war was heating up, it was feared that it might be engulfed in the conflict; however, the presence of a French garrison and the combatants' greater concern with the Ogaden averted that possibility. Second, the antagonism between Addis Ababa and Mogadishu was heightened by a long history of warfare between the Moslem and Christian peoples of the Horn of Africa. In 1973, Somalia underlined its Islamic identity by joining the Arab League, which organization lent support to the Greater Somaliland concept and tried to weaken Ethiopia and cut off its Red Sea littoral by supporting the Eritrean rebels. This factor made the dispute as much a Middle Eastern one as an African one. A third factor contributing to tension was added when Tenneco drillers discovered a natural gas deposit in the Ogaden just 30 miles from the Somali border. The find immediately

---

[7] John H. Spencer, "A Reassessment of the Ethiopian-Somali Conflict," *Horn of Africa* I(July–September 1978):23. Spencer disputes the validity of Somalia's claims on the Ogaden and analyzes the role of foreign powers in aggravating the local dispute. For a very different viewpoint supporting self-determination in the Ogaden, see W. Michael Reisman, "The Case of Western Somaliland: An International Legal Perspective," *Horn of Africa* I(July–September 1978):13–22.

led to a small buildup of forces on each side of the frontier and added an element of economic avarice to what had formerly been a conflict over nomadic people and desert territory. Finally, completely aside from pan-Somali claims on the Ogaden, a complex legal dispute remained unresolved as to the correct placement of the *colonial* borders dividing Ethiopia and Somalia.[8] The boundary dispute was an irritant between the two governments, though in fact Mogadishu's plans for a Greater Somaliland would have pushed the Somali border far beyond anything at issue in the more technical border dispute.

The multiple tensions between Ethiopia and Somalia were a source of constant friction along the border from 1960 onward, often resulting in small skirmishes and once exploding into a brief armed conflict between regular troops in 1964. The seeming intractability of the dispute had proved an ideal lever for the Soviet Union to enter the Horn, signing its first arms agreement with Somalia in August 1963. During the 1960s and early 1970s, the USSR had exploited Mogadishu's military dependence and nationalist aims in order to establish a Soviet presence in Somalia second in the Third World only to the Soviet base complex in Egypt. After U.S-Ethiopian military ties were dissolved in 1977, Moscow sought to use the dispute to its advantage from the other side as well. The Dergue's desperate military position and its radical orientation inclined it naturally toward Moscow. The OAU's steadfast stance on the inviolability of the existing borders in Africa made Soviet involvement in this instance easy to justify. The USSR was defending the territorial integrity of a black nation against an Arab ally – something few Africans could argue with – and could be assured that if Washington intervened on behalf of Somalia it would lose stock in black Africa.

In the case of the Ogaden war, Soviet theorists invoked the theme of national liberation far less than in any other conflict studied herein. One reason may have been that the Somalis themselves had raised the banner of national liberation as the rallying point of their campaign.[9] Moreover, in the early stages of the war the Soviets did not want to suggest that either side had become a tool of the imperialists. Rather, both combatants were "progressive" nations, and both were victims of imperialist intrigues:

> By fanning an armed conflict in the Horn of Africa, imperialism and reactionary regimes want to undermine the progressive re-

---

[8] On the colonial border dispute, see the following: Mesfin Wolde Mariam, *The Background of the Ethio-Somalia Boundary Dispute* (Addis Ababa: Berhanena Selam, 1964); Sven Rubenson, "The Genesis of the Ethio-Somali Conflict," paper presented at Fifth International Conference on Ethiopian Studies, April 13–16, 1978; Touval, *Somali Nationalism*, 154–63; Drysdale, *The Somali Dispute*, 88–9.

[9] *Zarya Vostoka*, January 10, 1978, scored the alleged hypocrisy of the West for advocating "national liberation" only in the case of Somalia, while fighting national liberation movements everywhere else in the world.

gimes in Somalia and Ethiopia and to distract the Africa peoples from their fundamental task – eliminating remaining colonial and racist regimes, strengthening new progressive regimes, and liberating the continent completely.[10]

Africa's foremost task, in the Soviet view, was national liberation; the conflict in the Horn was not the central arena of the struggle but only a diversionary maneuver of imperialism. The Western powers and reactionary Arab regimes had "instigated" and "incited" the conflict, hoping to "destabilize" the continent and thus plunge Africa into wars that would divert resources from the struggle for national independence and against apartheid.[11]

By downplaying Somalia's responsibility for causing the conflict, Soviet theorists effectively placed the war in the category of "military conflicts between developing countries . . . provoked by the imperialist and domestic reactionaries."[12] In the Soviet taxonomy of wars, this put the Ogaden war in much the same category as the Indo-Pakistani conflict of 1965–6, in which the USSR had also actively sought to maintain good relations with both combatants. After Mogadishu expelled the Russians in November, Soviet criticisms of Somalia became more pronounced, but it was emphasized that the Soviet people still entertained "sentiments of friendship" toward the people of Somalia.[13]

Soviet writers perceived a broad-ranging Western and conservative Arab conspiracy in the Horn of Africa:

> There is no longer the slightest doubt that the present events in the Horn of Africa are the direct result of a compact between the imperialist powers, primarily the United States, and the reactionary Arab regimes – a compact spearheaded against the progressive forces in the Red Sea basin. The area has been allotted an exceptionally important place in the imperialist strategic plans because of its geographical location at the junction of two continents . . . its first-class ports in the Gulf of Aden and

[10] A statement by the Soviet Committee for Solidarity with Afro-Asian Countries, *Izvestia* and *Pravda*, August 7, 1977.

[11] Radio Moscow, July 27, 1977; *Izvestia*, August 2, 1977; *New Times*, No. 1(January 1978):14; *Za Rubezhom*, No. 7(February 9, 1978):1; *Sovetskaya Belorussiya*, February 17, 1978; *Tass*, January 31, 1978; *Selskaya Zhizn*, January 28, 1978; *Pravda*, July 16, 1977.

[12] *Marxism-Leninism on War and Army* (Moscow: Progress Publishers, 1968), 70; See Chapter II for an outline of a general Soviet taxonomy of wars and further discussion of this type of war.

[13] Radio Moscow, November 16, 1977. After the expulsion, Soviet commentators stressed that the Soviet Union had been in Somalia at the request of the Somali government, which had often expressed its gratitude for the Soviet assistance. Moscow's only purpose had been to assist the building of Somalia's defensive capabilities on a basis of equality and mutual trust. See *Pravda*, November 16 and 20, 1977; Radio Peace and Progress, November 15, 1977; Radio Moscow, November 16 and 18, 1977; *Tass*, November 22, 1977.

the Indian Ocean, and, above all, its proximity to key sea lanes linking oil-producing countries with America and Europe.[14]

Imperialism's chief motive was "to strike a blow at advanced positions of African revolution," referring to Somalia as well as Ethiopia.[15] Radio Moscow observed that the United States had opposed pan-Somali aims only so long as Ethiopia was "America's stronghold," and Sofinsky and Khazanov, in *Novoe Vremya*, suggested that Western backing of Somalia's aggression began only after the revolution in Ethiopia. Although one writer noted that "Ogaden is said to have oil resources," and a *Za Rubezhom* editorial asserted that the imperialists wanted to exploit the Horn countries in order to obtain "superprofits," the economic motives of the Western powers were in fact rarely mentioned during the crisis. One commentary asserted that the United States was arming Somalia in order to test its weapons in actual field conditions.[16]

Three stock arguments were used to justify Soviet intervention in the conflict: (1) The Soviet Union did everything possible to prevent the conflict from breaking out. (2) The Soviet Union always takes the side of the victim of aggression. (3) The USSR and Cuba were not seeking any gains for themselves. To these familiar themes a new and more timely argument was added: Somalia had "flagrantly violated the basic principle of the established borders in Africa and observance of the territorial integrity of states, a principle laid down in the Charter of the Organization of African Unity." The OAU's position was stressed repeatedly, as it provided a certain legal underpinning for the Soviet effort on behalf of Ethiopia. A *Tass* commentator defended the intervention as compatible with détente, but in general the question of détente received much less attention than in the Angolan crisis, perhaps because of the lesser U.S. involvement in the Ogaden war.[17]

[14]Vsevolod Sofinsky and Anatoly Khazanov, "The Imperialist Design for the Horn of Africa," *New Times* No. 7(February 1978):4. On the conspiracy theme, see also Y. Tsaplin, "Reaction at Work," *New Times* No. 1(January 1978):14–15, and P. Menzentsev, "Covering up the Tracks," *New Times* No. 11(March 1978):12.

[15]Radio Moscow, July 27, 1977, *Pravda* and *Izvestia*, August 14, 1977, stated that reactionary forces sought to strike a blow "against the progressive revolutionary regimes first of Ethiopia and then of Somalia." After the expulsion of Soviet advisers, a Radio Moscow broadcast to Somalia, November 18, 1977, asserted that reactionary forces wanted to "divert the Somali people from the progressive path they are now following."

[16]Radio Moscow, January 28, 1978; Sofinsky and Khazanov, "The Imperialist Design," 5; *Sovetskaya Belorussiya*, February 17, 1978; *Za Rubezhom* No. 7(February 9, 1978):1; V. Simonov, *Zarya Vostoka*, January 10, 1978.

[17]Radio Moscow, January 19, 1978; *Tass*, January 18 and 30, 1978; *Pravda*, March 19, 1978; Radio Moscow, November 22, 1977, January 18 and 28, 1978; *Tass*, November 23, 1977, January 17 and 31, 1978, and February 6, 1978; Y. Babenko, *Tass*, February 14, 1978.

The diplomatic relationship between the USSR and its client

Ethiopia was the one country in Africa that had had significant ties with Imperial Russia, principally because of its adherence to Eastern Orthodox Christianity. Nevertheless, prior to the revolutionary events of 1974 and the fall of Emperor Haile Selassie, relations between Ethiopia and the Soviet Union had been relatively low-key and lack-luster. Shortly after World War II, the USSR opened a diplomatic mission in Addis Ababa and undertook a small medical assistance program. In 1948, Addis Ababa signed an agreement with Czechoslo-vakia for assistance in the construction of Ethiopia's first munitions factory (completed in 1953).[18] This was a few years prior to the time that Czechoslovakia, with Soviet encouragement, signed an arms agreement with Egypt. Soviet relations with Ethiopia did not subsequently blossom, however, as they did in Egypt.

Haile Selassie became the first African head of state to visit the USSR when he made a highly publicized two-week tour in 1959 and signed a $100 million credit agreement, at that time one of the largest Soviet loans ever extended to a Third World country. The emperor's opening to Moscow was partly motivated by the approaching inde-pendence of Somalia and an awareness of the high likelihood of future conflict over the Ogaden, but despite additional visits by the emperor in 1967 and 1971, and a number of Soviet economic aid projects, Moscow and Addis Ababa never grew much closer than they had been in 1959. Ethiopia's many links with the United States, the Soviet Union's military links with Somalia, clandestine Cuban and Soviet arms shipments to the Eritrean rebels, and Haile Selassie's conserv-atism all precluded warmer relations. Ethiopia's armed forces were largely equipped by the United States and Western Europe; Soviet military supplies were limited to two jet aircraft and two helicopters.

The Soviet news media devoted almost daily coverage to the tide of dissent and unrest that rose in Ethiopia during 1974. The situation was described as a struggle between the forces of progress and re-action, as a struggle of the masses for democratic reforms, and as a deepening of the class struggle.[19] When the PMAC deposed the em-peror on September 12, imprisoning him in the Grand Palace, the act was hailed as "a landmark in the revolution."[20] Soviet and East Eu-ropean delegations began to appear in Ethiopia with greater fre-quency than before, and throughout 1975 the relations between the Dergue and the Kremlin slowly became warmer, helped, no doubt, by the PMAC's declaration in December 1974 that Ethiopia would be

---

[18] V. S. Yagya, *Efiopiya v 1941–1954 gg.* (Moscow: Nauka, 1969), 175.
[19] *Izvestia*, March 13, 1974; Radio Moscow, March 12, 1974; *Pravda*, March 17, 1974; Radio Moscow, May 7, 1974, and April 27, 1974.
[20] Georgii Tanov, Radio Moscow, October 5, 1974.

a Socialist state. But the USSR moved cautiously during this stage of the revolution:

> Through mid-1976, at least, the Soviets appear to have followed essentially a spoiling policy in Ethiopia: they encouraged revolutionary zeal and ferment, they encouraged and probably funded a wide variety of groups and individuals, but they avoided putting all their cards on any one element. The situation was too confused.[21]

The USSR's initial caution toward the revolution is illustrated by an incident that occurred shortly after the military government came to power. The Soviet ambassador in Addis Ababa, Anatoly Ratonov, indicated to the PMAC that the USSR would be amenable to requests for military purchases. In doing so, he apparently stepped beyond his authority, for when such requests were made, no response was forthcoming, placing the ambassador in an awkward position vis-à-vis the Ethiopian government for some months.[22]

In the spring of 1975, the Dergue sent a secret mission to Moscow, consisting of both military personnel and civilians, to explore the possibility of military assistance. At that time the PMAC had not become disillusioned with Washington as an arms supplier, as would later be the case, but it had decided to pursue a deliberate policy of diversifying its arms sources. The delegation met with Grechko, Kosygin, and a number of lower-level officials. According to a source familiar with the negotiations:

> The Soviets asked numerous questions about Ethiopia's defense needs and about the revolution. They did not seem enthusiastic about supplying arms, but they did express interest in exploring the subject further. They were particularly concerned about the future direction of the revolution, intimating that the presence of a number of pro-Western people in the government made it difficult for them to provide many weapons. But it was not an outright rejection. [Confidential source.]

Another source, also familiar with the situation, described the Soviet approach in these terms:

> The year 1975 marked the beginning of the Soviet involvement in Ethiopia. The Russians began by carefully planting a small bait, hinting that large numbers of weapons would be available as the revolution progressed. They very cautiously and diligently followed this initiative up. The Soviets are exceptionally dextrous at using armaments for leverage. [Confidential source.]

---

[21] Paul B. Henze, "Russians and the Horn: Opportunities and the Long View," unpublished manuscript. This manuscript was published by the European American Institute for Security Research (Marina del Rey, California) in 1983. References in the text are to the unpublished version.

[22] Confidential sources provided this information and the quotations following it.

Although the Kremlin agreed to send a military delegation to assess Ethiopia's needs firsthand, several members of the Ethiopian mission returned deeply disappointed by the evident reticence of the Soviet leadership.

The promised military delegation did not arrive until September. The visit was a secret one. The delegation's only immediate response to a detailed Ethiopian request for arms was that "it is on the big side." The question of payment for the arms was not discussed. Once again the Soviet leaders created the impression that the presence of "certain elements" in the military inhibited their ability to respond with arms. Ambassador Ratonov continued to propagate this line in Ethiopia after the delegation had returned. The enthusiasm of the military for a turn to Moscow was not dampened by the visit, but no response was received from the USSR for several weeks, despite "constant prodding" from Addis Ababa. During this period of waiting, Gromyko told the Ethiopian ambassador in Moscow that the USSR would be put in a difficult position if by shipping arms to Ethiopia it created problems for Somalia. When the Soviets finally replied to the Ethiopian request early in 1976, they offered only to provide certain types of equipment useful for both civilian and military purposes, such as earth-moving equipment and small transport planes. Moscow asked that a delegation be sent for further negotiations. The PMAC was incensed by the response: "We communicated our displeasure to the Russians in no uncertain terms, and refused to send the delegation."[23] Relations stagnated for some time while Addis Ababa sought to make arms purchases from France, Yugoslavia, on the open market, and from the United States.

Although the Soviets left open the possibility of supplying arms, their failure to do so at that time was a source of frustration to the Dergue's leadership. Mengistu is reported to have explained Ethiopia's dependence on American arms to disaffected leftist elements at Debre Zeit air base in June 1976 by saying, "What else can we do, the Soviets will not provide them!"[24] Gradually, however, progress was made. A PMAC delegation headed by Captain Moges Wolde Makael visited the USSR from July 6 to 12, 1976. Soviet Prime Minister Alexei Kosygin received the delegation, which then held talks with Andrei Gromyko, Boris Ponomarev, and Ivan Arkhipov. A communiqué stated that the talks were held "in a friendly atmosphere and in a spirit of mutual understanding." The Soviet side expressed sympathy with the reforms of the revolution and agreed to "expand the training of Ethiopian national cadres in various fields and specialties" by admitting Ethiopians to Soviet educational institutions and by sending Soviet instructors to Ethiopia.[25] However, sources familiar with the visit

---

[23] Confidential sources.
[24] Henze, "Russians and the Horn," 21.
[25] *Pravda*, July 14, 1976.

reported that no discussion of military assistance took place, though the Soviets did hint that their earlier communication was not an outright rejection and that discussion on arms purchases might be revived.

Mengistu and other leftist officers in the Dergue were determined to explore the military potential of the Soviet connection further. Although the events of the next few months are somewhat obscure, it seems that the numerous hints and remarks of the Soviets regarding the obstructing presence of pro-Western elements in the leadership and the need for "progress" in the revolution began to take hold with Mengistu. He began to establish contact with revolutionary groups outside the military, including *Meison*, a Marxist-Leninist party that maintained ties with the Soviets. *Meison* took the position that the revolution would be incomplete so long as strong ties with the West persisted, and Mengistu edged toward that view himself. The lines of a confrontation within the Dergue developed. Before it exploded, however, the Soviets finally agreed to make available certain weapons to Ethiopia. Additional negotiations on possible arms purchases had begun not long after the Moges mission in July, and on December 14, 1976, a secret arms agreement was signed in Moscow by the head of the Defense Committee of the Dergue. The agreement, valuing nearly $100 million, was largely for defensive weapons: antiaircraft guns, artillery, antitank missiles, and so forth. The visiting delegation met with Soviet Defense Minister Ustinov and other top officials and attempted to determine where the Soviet Union stood with respect to Ethiopia's overall, long-term defensive needs. Mengistu was invited to visit Moscow in January, but the visit was later postponed by the Kremlin.

Less than two months after the signing of the agreement, the growing confrontation within the Dergue erupted, and Mengistu came to power in a bloody shoot-out at the Grand Palace. The speed with which he was congratulated by the Soviet, Cuban, and East European governments after the coup suggests that "it was an outcome which they had both hoped for and expected."[26] It may even have been a condition linked to actual delivery of the arms, which did not begin arriving until March. Whatever the level of direct Soviet complicity, Moscow's long and careful effort to encourage leftist elements in Ethiopia at the expense of pro-Western officers proved successful, for not long after Mengistu's accession to supreme power, the pro-Western elements in the Dergue were purged.

A political delegation from Cuba headed by Division General Arnaldo Ochoa Sánchez arrived in Ethiopia sometime in February or early March, 1975, shortly after the secret Ethiopian mission to Moscow. The timing of the visit, which led to the establishment of diplomatic relations in July, suggests a close coordination of policies

[26] Henze, "Russians and the Horn," 24.

between Havana and Moscow. The Cubans eventually came to play an intermediary role between Mengistu and the USSR. Cuba's commitment in Ethiopia seems to have increased noticeably at about the same time as the December arms agreement. In mid-November, the *Ethiopian Herald* had given prominent coverage to a *Granma* article praising the Ethiopian revolution. On December 15 (the day after the arms agreement was signed to Moscow), Raul Castro and Cuban Foreign Minister Rodriguez met with Brezhnev and Chernenko in the Kremlin to discuss "the state of affairs in the international arena."[27] Given the timing of this meeting, it seems likely that the situation in the Horn was discussed and the possible consequences of deeper Soviet-Cuban involvement considered.

At this early stage, however, Moscow was still more interested in sponsoring a détente between Addis Ababa and Mogadishu than in intervening on either side should conflict break out. Fidel Castro set about promoting just such a reconciliation when he visited the Horn of Africa in March 1977, in connection with an extended tour of several African countries. From March 12 to 14 he was in Mogadishu, where he received a warm reception; he traveled on to Addis Ababa on March 15, and the next day he and Mengistu traveled secretly to Aden, where they met with Somali leader Siad Barre and with Salem Rubayi Ali, the leader of South Yemen. According to Siad, who revealed the fact of the meeting in May, Castro proposed "some kind of federation between two Marxist states."[28] In an interview with the newspaper *al-Ahram*, Siad later disclosed that Castro's plan had been an ambitious design for the federation of Red Sea Marxist states embracing Ethiopia, Somalia, Eritrea, Djibouti, and South Yemen.[29] Siad had flatly rejected the proposal, stating his viewpoint that the Dergue did not consist of Marxists at all, but of "fascist imperialists." Castro left convinced that the Ethiopians were the truer ideologues.[30] Arab diplomatic sources revealed that for several weeks following the March meeting, the Soviets conducted a "very active" diplomatic campaign to bring about such a federation in the Horn.[31] The Somalis, however, would not compromise.

With hopes for a Soviet-sponsored settlement in the Horn fading, Moscow moved still closer to Mengistu. Even as the first Soviet arms were arriving in the spring of 1977, negotiations were taking place

---

[27] *Ethiopian Herald*, November 20, 1976; *Pravda*, December 16, 1976. See also Teferi's message to Fidel Castro, *Ethiopian Herald*, December 7, 1976.

[28] *Washington Post*, May 17, 1977.

[29] Zdenek Cervenka and Colin Legum, "Cuba: The New Communist Power in Africa," *ACR* (1977–8):A106–8; see also *ACR* (1977–8):B379–80.

[30] However, confidential sources say the following of Ethiopia's accession to the proposed agreement: "What the Soviets were doing was very clearly transparent. Ethiopia 'agreed' in order to expose the Soviet cover. We knew that Somalia had first proposed the confederal agreement at the OAU meeting on Angola in 1976."

[31] *Washington Post*, May 26, 1977.

on the details of the December agreement and on additional weapons purchases. These negotiations took place entirely in Addis Ababa and were headed on the Ethiopian side by the defense minister, Ayalew Mandefro. In April, the two sides signed a number of protocols detailing the December agreement. In early May, Mengistu finally paid the long-postponed state visit to the USSR. On May 4 he was honored at a dinner in the great Kremlin Palace at which Soviet head of state Nikolai Podgorny spoke of strengthening Soviet-Ethiopian cooperation, and Mengistu declared the goal of the Ethiopian revolution to be the laying of "a firm foundation for the transition to socialism" and "the establishment of the people's democratic republic." Two days later, Mengistu and three accompanying PMAC members discussed "the international situation" with Brezhnev, Gromyko, and Ustinov.[32] The arms agreement that was signed later in the week may also have been discussed at that meeting.

This was one of the largest single arms agreements ever negotiated between the USSR and a Third World nation. Western sources estimated its value at $350 to $450 million, but a knowledgeable Ethiopian source placed it much higher.[33] The May agreement was to run four years and included a definite delivery schedule of armaments laid out to the year 1981. The majority of weapons later involved in the USSR's emergency airlift was included in this agreement, but in the event, the 1979 deliveries were speeded up and were made in 1978. No restrictions were placed on the use of the weapons, outside a routine provision that they could not be transferred to another nation without permission. According to a source familiar with the May negotiations in Moscow:

> The Soviets would not sign the arms agreement until after certain political documents were signed, including a Declaration of Friendship. Although the Soviets resisted, the Ethiopian side insisted on including a provision on nonalignment. The conditions of payment were very stiff in our view, especially the definition of ruble exchange and the grace period of payment. The Soviets claimed that the MiGs were half-price, but it was a meaningless claim. [Confidential source.]

The "political documents" referred to were a joint communiqué, a protocol on economic and technical cooperation, an agreement on cultural and scientific cooperation, a consular convention, and a declaration on principles of friendly relations and cooperation. The communiqué noted that the talks had taken place in an atmosphere "of

---

[32] *Pravda*, May 5, 1977; *Pravda* and *Izvestia*, May 7, 1977. Ethiopian sources report that Brezhnev did not meet personally with Mengistu, but only spoke with him by telephone. This displeased the Ethiopian delegation.

[33] Colin Legum and Bill Lee, "Crisis in the Horn of Africa: International Dimensions of the Somali-Ethiopian Conflict," *ACR* (1978–9):A43; confidential sources.

friendly and complete mutual understanding"; it condemned imperialist intrigues designed to stir up tension in northeast Africa and
affirmed opposition to any attempts to establish control over the Red
Sea. The declaration of principles reflected unqualified support of the
Ethiopian position on the Ogaden by stressing the importance of "the
territorial integrity of states and the inviolability of state
boundaries."[34]

One objective of Mengistu's visit was to persuade the Soviet leadership to restrain Somalia from attempting to carry out its designs
on the Ogaden. He received assurances that Moscow would exert its
still substantial influence in Mogadishu toward that end. The Kremlin,
of course, did not deliver on this promise, either from inability to do
so or because it knew that a Somali invasion of the Ogaden would
increase Ethiopia's dependence on the USSR. As the principal arms
supplier for both sides, from May to September 1977, the Soviet Union
would hold most of the diplomatic cards in the Horn and be in a
position to exercise great influence over the unfolding events. The Soviet leaders also attempted to influence Ethiopia's internal political
evolution by extracting a promise from Mengistu during his visit that
he would forge the five pro-Dergue Marxist-Leninist parties in Ethiopia – the "Union of Five" – into a single "revolutionary democratic
party." Such a party would have played a role similar to that of the
MPLA in Angola, giving Moscow an eventual institutional alternative
to the PMAC. Mengistu did not carry through with this pledge, despite
prodding from the Kremlin, recognizing, perhaps, that the Soviet
Union could use such a party to undermine his own power base in
the military.

Broken promises notwithstanding, Mengistu's visit was a definite
watershed in the political alignments of both Ethiopia and Somalia.
Mogadishu did not at first officially protest the Soviet military support being offered to Addis Ababa, but Siad made it clear in separate
interviews with *Newsweek* and the Kuwaiti *al-Yaqza*, published in late
June, that the arms shipments were a major irritant in Mogadishu's
relations with Moscow. As the Ogaden fighting heated up that summer, attempts were made to heal the growing Soviet-Somali rift. Podgorny had already visited Somalia for two days early in April. Three
weeks after Mengistu's visit to Moscow, General Mohammed Ali Sa-
matar, the Somali Vice-President and Defense Minister, visited Moscow, probably seeking reassurances about Soviet intentions and
continuing willingness to aid Somalia militarily. President Siad himself made a quiet trip to Moscow at the end of August, which apparently achieved nothing. The only word on the meeting was a brief
Tass statement that he had met with three members of the Politburo
– Alexei Kosygin, Andrei Gromyko, and Mikhail Suslov – to discuss
subjects of common interest. Soviet arms, meanwhile, continued to

[34] *Pravda*, May 9, 1977.

arrive in Ethiopia. On October 21, the eighth anniversary of the 1969 revolution in Somalia, Brezhnev and Kosygin sent Siad a message of congratulations, expressing confidence that Soviet-Somali relations would continue to develop fruitfully; however, the Somali president used the occasion to warn "that Moscow's 'frantic one-sided support' for Ethiopia could jeopardize relations between Somalia and the USSR."[35] On November 13, the expulsion of the Soviet advisers from Somalia took place, as described earlier.

In the meantime, the stage was being set for the massive Soviet-Cuban intervention that began in November. A medium-level Soviet military delegation visited Addis Ababa in mid-September, probably to assess Ethiopia's weapons requirements. A number of Western sources have asserted that an additional arms deal was signed around this time, but confidential Ethiopian sources indicate that the September negotiations resulted only in a protocol within the framework of the larger agreement signed the previous May. No additional credit was extended at that time. On October 15, the Ethiopian foreign minister, Felleke Gelde-Giorgis, traveled to Havana for four days of meetings with the Cuban leaders. The Cuban foreign minister offered Havana's "total support" for the Ethiopian revolution and Ethiopia's defense against "external aggression."[36] There were already Cuban advisers in Ethiopia at the time, but subsequent events suggest that the meeting may have dealt with the possibility of a larger Cuban commitment. Mengistu himself went to Havana at the end of October. A few days later, Raul Castro was in Moscow to attend the ceremonial session of the CPSU Central Committee and Supreme Soviet, convened to celebrate the sixtieth anniversary of the Russian revolution.[37] According to Paul Henze, a U.S. official at the time, he was accompanied by "the same Cuban generals who later figured prominently in operations in Ethiopia."[38] A high-level Ethiopian delegation headed by PMAC member Berhanu Bayeh was also present, so the opportunity for trilateral talks existed. The presence of the Cuban generals is circumstantial evidence that at least the possibility of a large-scale intervention was considered at that time, over a week before the Somalis' expulsion of the Soviets and Cubans. The timing

[35] *Washington Post*, May 17, 1977; *Newsweek* and *al-Yaqza*, June 27, 1977, cited in ACR (1977–8):B380; *Pravda*, October 1, 1977; Radio Moscow, October 21, 1977; ACR (1977–8):B381.

[36] Henze, "Russians and the Horn," 27; *Ethiopian Herald*, October 29, 1977.

[37] *Pravda*, November 5, 1977.

[38] Henze, "Russians and the Horn," 27. Henze also states that Mengistu flew to Moscow after his trip to Havana, but this is not confirmed in the Soviet press. Ethiopia was represented at the anniversary celebrations by Major Berhanu Bayeh, a top-ranking PMAC member who spoke at the ceremonial session (*Pravda*, November 7, 1977; *Ethiopian Herald*, November 16, 1977); if Mengistu had been in Moscow, protocol would have demanded that he attend the session and speak. Secrecy need not have been a concern, because the occasion offered the perfect justification for his presence in Moscow.

even suggests that Somalia may have been aware of the talks in Moscow and that they were a factor in Siad's decision to curtail relations.

When the Soviets and Cubans were expelled from Somalia, the Soviet ambassador in Mogadishu is reported to have said of the Somalis, "We will bring them to their knees." Only four days later, General Vasilii Petrov arrived in Ethiopia and became the senior Soviet commander in charge of the operation. Nine days after his arrival, the massive weapons airlift began. The sequence of these events leaves no doubt that the expulsion was the final act that triggered the Soviet airlift of arms to Ethiopia. By January, some 2,000 Cuban troops had been airlifted to Ethiopia, most of them deployed on the Ogaden front. Raul Castro arrived in Ethiopia early in January and spent several days in Haile Selassie's former palace residence. Probably he was there to review the current deployment of Havana's soldiers, make preparations for the thousands who would yet arrive, and review the plans for the upcoming offensive. By February 1 he had left Ethiopia and was in Moscow for a meeting with Brezhnev and Ustinov, where, it is believed, the Ogaden conflict was discussed.[39].

After Moscow had codified its new relationship with Addis Ababa during Mengistu's visit in May, there is every evidence that Soviet-Ethiopian ties were extremely cordial and close. Ethiopian Foreign Minister Felleke stated that there was "complete accord and understanding with the Russians, who know the situation and understand the situation" and insisted that there was no misunderstanding with the USSR or Cuba.[40] Although the USSR had every reason to be satisfied with its new client, Moscow did not abandon efforts to regain influence with the Somalis. During the last week of February 1978, when a Somali defeat appeared certain, President Siad met with Colonel Muammar el-Qaddafi, the Libyan head of state, in Tripoli. Qaddafi presented him with a Soviet peace plan that included, according to Arab and Western diplomatic sources, the following points: a Somali withdrawal from the Ogaden, respect for Ethiopia's recognized boundaries, renunciation of Somali claims on Kenya and Djibouti, regranting of Soviet access to Somali naval facilities, and participation in a political arrangement with Ethiopia and South Yemen. In return for all this, Somalia would receive a promise of eventual autonomy for the Ogaden Somalis, a guarantee of the border with Ethiopia, and a resumption of military aid.[41] Siad did not accept the proposal, but the mere fact that it was made at all demonstrated Moscow's unflagging interest in establishing a Soviet sphere of influence in the Red Sea basin.

---

[39] Henze, "Russians and the Horn," 29; *The Economist*, January 21, 1977; *New York Times*, February 2, 1978.
[40] Ian Goddard, "An Interview with Ethiopia's Foreign Minister," *Horn of Africa* 1(April–June 1978):6. The interview took place in June 1978.
[41] *ACR* (1977–8):B392.

Table 9.1. *Soviet weapons shipments to Ethiopia during the Ogaden war, March 1977 to May 1978*

Types of weapons	Number transferred
T-34 tanks	30–56
T-54/55 tanks	300–400
T-62 tanks	A few
Other armored vehicles, including	200–300
BTR-152 APCs	40
BMP-1 AFVs	Some
MiG-17s	Some
MiG-21s	55–60
MiG-23s	12–20
Mi-4 helicopters	Some
Mi-6 heavy transport helicopters	A few
Mi-8 helicopters	30
SAM-7 missiles	Several hundred
Sagger antitank missiles	Thousands (?)
SAM-3 missiles	Some
BM-21 rocket launchers (Stalin organs)	At least 28 launchers
Artillery guns, 100-mm to 152-mm	Over 300
Artillery guns, 155-mm and 185-mm	Some
Mobile antiaircraft guns, 57-mm	Six
Mortars	Numerous
Small arms	Thousands

Sources: Keesing's Contemporary Archives, October 28, 1977; Legum and Lee, "Crisis in the Horn of Africa," *ACR* (1977–8):A43–5, B235, B379; *Strategic Survey* (1978):94.

Weapons shipments and other military aid

The value of Soviet weapons deliveries to Ethiopia during the Ogaden conflict is generally set in the vicinity of $1 billion. American intelligence sources estimated the volume of war material transferred during the first six months of 1978 as approximately 61,000 tons; earlier weapons transfers would raise the total somewhat, making the arms shipments nearly as large as those undertaken in the October war.[42] Table 9.1 is a register of known arms shipments; the figures have been described as "generally accurate" and "conservative" by sources in the U.S. State Department and National Security Council. An Ethiopian source with firsthand knowledge of the arms agreements would only say that the figures are "very conservative." Some Western analysts expressed the opinion that the volume of weapons far exceeded Ethiopia's actual tactical requirements, but this was discounted by

[42] *The Economist*, January 21, 1978; Kenneth Tomlinson, *Reader's Digest* (September 1978):156; Legum and Lee, "Crisis in the Horn of Africa," A43; *New York Times*, July 5, 1978.

an Ethiopian specialist, who pointed out that by 1979 Ethiopia still had not taken the entire Ogaden or subdued Eritrea.[43]

Thirty Soviet tanks were transferred from South Yemen in early March, shortly after Mengistu's accession to power, and by mid-April over 100 additional tanks and APCs had arrived from the USSR. The first MiG aircraft began arriving at Addis Ababa in September.[44] Late Saturday evening, November 26, American spy satellites and radar stations detected the beginning of a massive Soviet airlift in Ethiopia.[45] Upward of 200 flights were made by several An-22 and Tu-76 transport planes; to ease the strain on VTA, the Soviets employed some planes from their Warsaw Pact allies. Early in January it was reported that at one time transport planes were taking off from airfields north of the Black Sea at intervals of only 20 minutes. An Ethiopian source observed that "once the weapons started rolling, they came fast; there was no Congressional subcommittee to hold things up." An operation of such magnitude required an elaborate communications system: Cosmos 964 was launched into orbit on the day the airlift began and is believed to have played a key intelligence and communications role; in Ethiopia, a large communications complex was set up next to the International Equestrian Club in Addis Ababa. The Soviet aircraft embarked from airfields near Moscow, north of the Black Sea, near Tbilisi, and from Central Asia. Some flights also originated in Hungary. The planes took a variety of air routes and reportedly filed misleading flight plans at refueling stops, such as listing their destination as Mozambique instead of Ethiopia. Overflights of several countries – Yugoslavia, Pakistan, Sudan, Saudi Arabia, Egypt, Iran, Greece, and Turkey – were made, usually after Moscow requested overflight rights in the context of civil aviation agreements. Pakistan, Iran, and Egypt eventually cancelled permission to make overflights. Turkey allowed the flights to continue without exercising its right of inspection under the Montreaux Convention, apparently because of its own dependence on Bulgaria for overflights to Western Europe. Yugoslavia reportedly protested to Moscow that some overflights were made without permission. The chief refueling stops were in Libya, Iraq, and Aden, but Iraq quickly put an end to Soviet access to its Baghdad airfield out of sympathy for the Moslem Somalis. The Soviets unloaded some of the arms at Aden, which were later ferried

[43] *New York Times*, January 8, 1978; interview: Paul Henze, National Security Council.
[44] *Washington Post*, May 25, 1977; Marina and David Ottaway, *Ethiopia: Empire in Revolution* (New York: Africana, 1978), 168; Stephen F. Larrabee, "After the Break: Soviet-Somali Relations," *Radio Liberty Research Bulletin* (January 2, 1978):2–3; *ACR* (1977–8):A43.
[45] Information on the airlift is taken from the following: *The Economist*, January 21, 1978; *New York Times*, December 14, 1977, January 8 and February 18, 1978; Legum and Lee, "Crisis in the Horn of Africa," A43–4; *New York Times*, July 5, 1978; Bonner Day, "Soviet Airlift to Ethiopia," *Air Force Magazine* (September, 1978):33.

to Assab, and the rest at the Addis Ababa airport. Libya also served as a depot for some of the arms.

After their expulsion by the Somalis, the Soviets towed a large floating dry-dock from Berbera to Assab, and it became the main unloading point for armaments delivered to Ethiopia by sea. Between June 1977 and June 1978, over 35 freighters passed through the Turkish straits and the Suez Canal into the Red Sea to Assab or Massawa, many of them escorted by Soviet warships. Armored vehicles delivered at the Red Sea ports were driven directly to the Ogaden across territory held by hostile Eritrean rebels. During the sealift, the port at Assab became so backlogged that civilian vessels, some of them carrying drought-relief grain, had to wait up to three weeks to unload their cargoes. Although accurate figures are not available, the sealift probably accounted for over 75 percent of the total delivered.

Although the USSR sent Mengistu a sizable air force of MiG fighter-bombers, these were much less decisive in the Ogaden warfare than were the battle tanks, armored personnel carriers, and Sagger anti-tank missiles. This was because Ethiopia already possessed an excellent air force of British and American planes; its American F-5Es had almost eliminated Somalia's MiG forces and established air superiority by September.[46] Ethiopia employed its own Soviet-supplied MiGs mainly in air strikes against tank columns. Aside from the carefully engineered attack from the rear at Jijiga, the February offensive consisted largely of slow advances along the entire front, employing artillery barrages and massed columns of armor. It was basically a ground war, and the Soviet arms shipments reflected this. Three types of Soviet equipment deserve particular mention. One was the BMP-1, a "highly mobile armored vehicle with a 73 mm. gun, anti-tank missiles, and heat-seeking anti-aircraft missiles."[47] Never before tested in combat, it had a devastating effect and was described by Somali sources as a "moving castle." Also of considerable help to the Ethiopians were the Mi-6 helicopters, which played a crucial role in the battle of Jijiga by ferrying pairs of tanks around the Ahmar Mountains. It was this maneuver that made possible the surprise attack on the Somali rear. Finally, the Soviets tried to take a chapter from the Angolan civil war by supplying the Ethiopians with a number of Stalin organ rocket launchers, but in this case they proved relatively ineffective against the highly trained and disciplined Somali troops.

Participation by Soviet and East European advisers and Cuban troops

In the fall of 1976 and the spring of 1977, large numbers of Soviet and East European delegations visited Ethiopia, and the Soviet dip-

[46] *Newsweek*, August 29, 1977; Henze, "Russians and the Horn," 26.
[47] *ACR* (1977–8):B379. See also *Jane's Weapons Systems 1979–80* (New York: Franklin Watts, 1979), 339.

lomatic corps increased noticeably. It is not known at what point the
first Soviet military advisers or technicians arrived, but it is probable
that a small group arrived early in the year to make preparations for
the first shipment of tanks from South Yemen. Certainly that shipment, which took place in early March, would have been accompanied
by technicians and military trainers to assist the Ethiopians in deploying the weapons. In mid-May, just a few days after Mengistu had
signed the $400 million arms agreement with the Russians, 50 Cuban
advisers arrived in Addis Ababa, some of whom were apparently
transferred directly to Somalia.[48] From that time on, the Cuban contingent in Ethiopia apparently outnumbered the Soviets. New Cuban
advisers began to arrive in September, and by November some Western diplomatic sources were estimating that 400 Cuban and 100 Soviet
advisers were in Ethiopia.[49] An unknown number of East German
military advisers were also active in Ethiopia by this time; their roles
were principally in military training and in reorganizing Ethiopia's
internal security forces along Soviet and East European lines. The
U.S. State Department received unconfirmed reports of Cuban participation in combat as early as August, but Addis Ababa denied that
Cuban combat troops or even "military specialists" were then in the
country.[50] An Ethiopian source with firsthand knowledge about the
involvement of Soviet and Cuban personnel in Ethiopia observed the
following:

> Ethiopia was required to pay the living expenses of the foreign
> personnel. The Soviets are very condescending, unlike the Cu-
> bans. They expected to live very luxuriously. One of the Soviet
> generals who was coming to Addis Ababa wanted to bring a
> chauffeur for his personal use. The Defense Minister refused un-
> less the chauffeur were also a technical adviser. The general took
> the request to Mengistu who acquiesced. [Confidential source.]

A rapid buildup of the Cuban presence in Ethiopia began late in
December in conjunction with the massive Soviet arms shipments
that were still under way. A top priority in the airlift, in fact, was the
deployment of a 1,000-man Cuban expeditionary force on the Ogaden
front. The Cuban soldiers were first flown to the USSR and then to

[48] *Washington Post*, May 25 and 26, 1977.
[49] *New York Times*, December 15, 1977. The number of Cubans was confirmed by a
confidential source. For a detailed study of the Cuban presence in Ethiopia, see
Nelson P. Valdes, "Cuban Foreign Policy in the Horn of Africa," *Cuban Studies*
10(January 1980):49–80.
[50] Interview: Anne Reid, U.S. State Department; *Tass*, November 4, 1977, and *Pravda*,
November 18, 1977, reported official Ethiopian denials of the presence of Cuban
combat troops in Ethiopia; *Pravda*, November 20, 1977, reported that the Ethiopian Foreign Ministry had rejected as "totally groundless" reports that Cuban
military specialists were in Ethiopia. Addis Ababa denied the presence of Cuban
troops as late as February 18, 1978. See Radio Moscow, January 20, February 8
and 18, 1978; *Pravda*, February 15, 1978.

Ethiopia, where they were supplied with Soviet equipment and rapidly moved into positions near the front. It was a remarkable example of Soviet-Cuban coordination, surpassing in complexity and logistical precision their earlier cooperative effort in Angola. By early January, the number of Cubans in Ethiopia had reached roughly 2,000, a figure that remained fairly constant through the first week of February. Many of the soldiers had arrived from Cuba by sea at Assab, following the initial force that was airlifted in. Hundreds of Soviet advisers had also been sent to Ethiopia, bringing the Soviet presence to some 1,000 persons.[51] Beginning around mid-February, a sudden quantum leap in the number of Cuban troops took place. The Ethiopian civilian airline cancelled many of its flights in order to provide transport for large numbers of soldiers, some of whom came from Angola. By February 17, the State Department and other diplomatic sources placed the Cuban buildup at 3,500 to 5,000 and rapidly expanding. One week later, the U.S. national security adviser, Zbigniew Brzezinski, stated that 10,000 to 11,000 Cuban soldiers and officers were in Ethiopia. By the time of Somalia's withdrawal in early March, some 12,000 to 15,000 Cubans and 1,500 Soviet advisers were in Ethiopia.[52]

Moscow took the unprecedented step of sending to Ethiopia two top-level military officers, who played some sort of command role in the conflict. The senior Soviet commander was General Vasilii Petrov, formerly the deputy commander in chief of Soviet ground forces. The other officer was General Grigory Barisov; his involvement was a cruel irony for Mogadishu, because he had been in charge of the Soviet military aid program in Somalia prior to the expulsion and thus had an intimate knowledge of the Somali armed forces.[53] The Cuban expeditionary force was headed by Arnaldo Ochoa, one of the Cuban generals who had directed the Angola intervention. The involvement of the Soviet and Cuban commanders, who were reported to have assumed most of the command of the counteroffensive, gave Moscow a degree of control over the course of combat not attained in previous local conflicts.

The Cubans, who actually entered combat sometime in January, made an enormous contribution to Ethiopia's success in the war. During the battle of Jijiga, Cuban pilots attacked Somali tanks and provided the main strength of the rear attacks that ultimately broke

[51] *New York Times*, February 10, 1978; Henze, "Russians and the Horn," 27; Legum and Lee, "Crisis in the Horn of Africa," 44.

[52] *New York Times*, February 18 and 25, 1978; Henze, "Russians and the Horn," 29. Many of the Cuban troops were airlifted by Ethiopian Airlines from Angola; some were transshipped from Cuba via Angola. Interview: Henze.

[53] Legum and Lee, "Crisis in the Horn of Africa," 45; *Newsweek*, February 1978. *The Daily Telegraph*, January 17, 1978, claimed that the Soviet minister of defense, Marshal Dmitri Ustinov, had arrived secretly in Addis Ababa to help Raul Castro plan the Ethiopian offensive. *Trud* (Moscow), January 24, 1978, denied the assertion, a denial confirmed by Ethiopian sources.

the Somali resistance. Soviet advisers and a small number of East German technicians played a variety of combat-support roles, including assisting in the construction of military airfields. There were also at least a few casualties, for 18 months after the war had ended, Mengistu publicly acknowledged that "international martyrs" from Cuba, South Yemen, and the USSR had been killed or wounded during the war.[54] American intelligence officials reported that some Soviet pilots and planes were sent to Cuba to assist in providing air defense there in order to free Cuban pilots for combat in Ethiopia, an allegation denied by Soviet Deputy Defense Minister Kirill Moskalenko.[55] If the U.S. sources were correct, it demonstrates the lengths to which the Soviet leadership was prepared to go to avoid committing Soviet troops in combat in supporting a foreign client.

Soviet-American interactions

The Soviet Union's intervention in the Ogaden war occurred at a time when Soviet-American relations were in a state of uncertainty and flux. The Carter administration had hardly entered office when the first hostilities began, and its first year was spent groping for a coherent policy vis-à-vis the USSR, trying to balance the tensions caused by a new human rights campaign with the need to make progress on the permanent issues dividing the two powers: arms negotiations, the European balance, the Middle East, and the appropriate mix of cooperation and conflict. Preoccupied with such concerns, top officials in the administration tended to overlook the significance of events in Ethiopia. The Ford administration, it must be said, had not done any better. The United States simply found it very difficult to court the Ethiopian Dergue. Significant increases in U.S. economic and military aid failed to stem the anti-Americanism of the Dergue and ultimately failed to prevent Ethiopia's turn toward the USSR. During the Ogaden War, Washington made little serious effort – diplomatically or otherwise – to resist the Soviet involvement, with the result that Moscow undertook a large-scale military operation nearly 2,000 kilometers from its borders with an almost totally free hand. Given the experiences of Angola and Vietnam, and Somalia's role as an aggressor in the Ogaden, it is understandable why the United States decided not to become involved militarily. Washington's marginal diplomatic role is less easily rationalized, given traditional U.S. interests in Ethiopia.

Those interests dated from at least 1952, when the United States acquired a major communications base at Asmara. Subsequently named "Kagnew" in honor of the Ethiopian contingent sent to Korea,

[54]*New York Times*, August 25, 1979.
[55]*ACR* (1977–8):B378–9; *New York Times*, July 5, 1978; *New York Times*, February 14 and 17, 1978.

the base was acquired on a 25-year lease, and it became a key component of the strong U.S.-Ethiopian ties that existed for more than two decades thereafter.[56] In May 1953, a military assistance agreement was signed with Addis Ababa, and from then until 1976, over $250 million in aid was provided to the Ethiopian armed forces. This was in addition to $350 million in economic assistance, making Ethiopia the recipient of the largest U.S. aid package in all Africa. By contrast, American ties with and interests in Somalia were less developed, largely because of Somalia's claims on Ethiopian territory. The modest U.S. assistance program that did operate there was ended when the Somalis turned sharply toward the USSR shortly after Siad's military government came to power in 1969.

In January 1974, the U.S. ambassador became ill and departed Ethiopia for America. From then until the summer of 1978, Washington maintained an ambassador in Ethiopia only during a 16-month period in 1975–6. A consequence of the Watergate affair and pressing foreign policy concerns elsewhere, this oversight epitomized the United States' failure to conduct a resourceful and sustained diplomacy in the Horn of Africa at the very time it was most needed. Further contributing to the impression of American disengagement from Ethiopia was a considerable reduction in the number of personnel stationed at Kagnew once the advent of satellite communications had lessened the strategic value of the base. The United States continued to provide military aid to Addis Ababa after the revolution, but as the PMAC grew increasingly radical in its politics and violent in its methods, the U.S. attitude toward Ethiopia became ambivalent. The Dergue's incessant anti-American denunciations did not help the situation.

In the spring of 1975, the Ethiopian ambassador in Washington transmitted a request for nearly $35 million worth of ammunition, needed to combat the insurgency in Eritrea. The State Department was slow to respond to the request, leading to the first doubts in Ethiopia about how much it could rely on the United States as an arms supplier. Ammunition was eventually supplied, but in a smaller amount than had been sought. In the fall of 1975, U.S.-Ethiopian negotiations were renewed on a request for M-60 tanks, F-4 fighters, antitank missiles, radar, and Redeye antiaircraft missiles that had been pending at the time of the revolution. Ethiopia was told that the Redeye would not be available because of formal restrictions on its transfer to non-NATO powers. Washington also ruled out the F-4, insisting on the F-5E in its place, and approved a lower number of

---

[56] At the peak of its operation, the Kagnew facility employed 3,000 Americans. On the acquisition of the base and its strategic significance, see the testimonies of John Spencer, Edward Korry, and William E. Schaufele in U.S. Congress, Committee on Foreign Relations, *Ethiopia and the Horn of Africa*, Hearings, 94th Congress, 2d sess., August 4–6, 1976, 26–7, 35–7, 111–13.

M-60 tanks than requested. A high-level Ethiopian source made the following observation:

> Washington was generally responsive to our requests, but it differed on the types of weapons to be provided. The failure to provide the Phantom-4 was a source of displeasure in the Air Force ... Washington also insisted that the weapons would have to be newly manufactured instead of drawn from existing stocks. This slowed their delivery. The military could not understand the restrictions. The general feeling grew that the U.S. could not be relied on to deliver requested weapons on schedule. This feeling was strongest in certain parts of the military, particularly among the NCOs in the Air Force. [Confidential source.]

The outcome in Washington perhaps strengthened the hand of Mengistu's supporters and other leftist elements in the military who had been pressing for a turn toward the Soviet Union.

At this stage, Ethiopia still had numerous incentives to maintain its quarter-century-old relationship with its principal arms supplier – the volume of arms being obtained from the United States was greater than at any time in Ethiopian history, and the initial contacts with the Soviets were disappointing. However, as 1976 progressed, a variety of events led to a further deterioration in the relationship with Washington: The Senate Foreign Relations Committee held hearings on human rights in Ethiopia; two moderate and reportedly pro-American officers in the Dergue, Majors Sisay Habte and Kiros Alemayehu, were executed because of an internal dispute related to the abortive peasants' march on Eritrea; in the late fall, Ethiopia was informed that the interest rate on future arms purchases from the Pentagon would be raised. Despite these problems, U.S. arms sales to Ethiopia in 1976 amounted to over $135 million, over six times the amount in 1975 and many times higher than the average annual amount of U.S. military grant assistance in previous years.

In December, as noted earlier, the Dergue signed an arms agreement with the Soviet Union, and Moscow "declared itself ready to become Ethiopia's main arms supplier on the condition that the PMAC sever its military relationship with the United States."[57] On February 24, 1977, U.S. Secretary of State Cyrus Vance informed the Senate Foreign Relations Committee that military aid to Ethiopia would be reduced because of human rights violations. The public announcement offended the Ethiopians, who had already privately agreed that the grant portion of the military assistance program be abrogated. The Dergue accused the United States of opposing the revolution in Ethiopia and declared that it would turn to the Socialist bloc for its arms. The fact that it had already done so was, of course, still a secret. In mid-April, Mengistu learned that the United States would shortly

[57] Ottaway, *Ethiopia*, 168.

reduce the 46-man Military Advisory Assistance Group (MAAG) by more than half and would shut down the Kagnew center by September. He decided to upstage the Americans. On April 23 the Dergue ordered the expulsion of the entire MAAG and of all other U.S. personnel outside the embassy staff; Kagnew and the consulate at Asmara were closed. One week later, Mengistu flew to Moscow to formalize the new relationship with the USSR.

For a few months it appeared as though a complete diplomatic revolution might take place in the Horn, with the United States replacing the Soviet Union as the primary arms supplier of Somalia. Even before Mengistu's expulsion of MAAG, President Carter had instructed Vance and Zbigniew Brzezinski, his national security adviser, to "move in every possible way to get Somalia to be our friend."[58] In mid-June, Dr. Kevin Cahill, Siad's personal physician and an American citizen, carried a message to the Somali president that was allegedly from the State Department. Siad was told that the United States was "not averse to further guerrilla pressure in the Ogaden" and was prepared "to consider sympathetically Somalia's legitimate defense needs."[59] Cahill claimed that in return, Washington wanted Mogadishu to drop its claims on the northern territory of Kenya and Djibouti.

On July 1, Vance made a public statement that was viewed as an overture to Somalia. Speaking at an NAACP convention in St. Louis, he said that "we will consider sympathetically appeals for assistance from states which are threatened by a build-up of foreign military equipment and advisers on their borders in the Horn and elsewhere in Africa."[60] On July 26, the State Department announced that it had agreed "in principle" to sell arms to Somalia "for the defense of that country's present territory and not to be used by Somali guerrillas fighting to detach the Ogaden region from Ethiopia." The statement added that Somalia "does not have to depend on the Soviet Union but can obtain arms from other sources."[61] Despite the clear qualifications, the U.S. pronouncement may have encouraged Somalia to press its offensive in the Ogaden.[62]

---

[58] *Time*, April 18, 1977.
[59] *Newsweek*, September 25, 1977. Cahill claimed to have received this message from Matthew Nimetz, State Department counselor and a close adviser to Secretary Vance. Three months after the event, Nimetz denied that he had encouraged pressure in the Ogaden, but admitted that Siad could have received the impression that the United States was unconcerned about the Ogaden.
[60] Cyrus Vance, "The United States and Africa," *DOSB* 77(August 8, 1977):170.
[61] *Keesing's Contemporary Archives*, October 28, 1977, 28637. See also Secretary Vance, news conference of July 29, in *DOSB* 77(August 22, 1977):229.
[62] The Soviets later charged that American promises of aid to Siad had touched off the war. *Izvestia*, January 24, 1978. However, Richard Moose, the U.S. assistant secretary of state for African affairs, stated that the U.S. assurances given Siad had not been "of such a nature that a prudent man would have mounted an offensive on the basis of them." *ACR* (1977–8):B383. Raymond L. Thurston, "The United States, Somalia and the Crisis in the Horn," *Horn of Africa* 1(April–June 1978):11–20, 17, argues that it was not the American assurances that touched off the offensive, but Somalia's perception of Ethiopia's weakness.

Once the fighting in the Ogaden became serious, Washington abruptly reversed its position on arms sales to Mogadishu. A Somali delegation visiting the United States was informed that no weapons could be provided as long as Somali troops were in the Ogaden, and on September 1 the State Department formally stated that Somalia would not receive arms: "We have decided that providing arms at this time would add fuel to a fire we are more interested in putting out."[63] Despite the unwillingness to provide military assistance, it was only natural that Washington should draw closer to Somalia after the Soviets were expelled early in November. Ten days after the expulsion, a large group of congressmen from the House Armed Services Committee visited Mogadishu along with officials from the Pentagon. Moscow definitely viewed the visit as a move to take advantage of the expulsion,[64] but in fact Somalia received little assurance from the visitors, and the U.S. position on arms sales did not change. On December 5, the United States announced that economic assistance to Somalia, cut off in 1971, would be restored. Plans for $25 million of assistance for agriculture and health were unveiled, a gesture of support that Somalia welcomed, but that did nothing to solve its pressing military situation.[65] Washington was in a diplomatic cul-de-sac. Having been kicked out of Ethiopia, the United States retained virtually no influence in Addis Ababa – the chargé d'affaires was unable to arrange even a single meeting with Mengistu[66] – yet it was difficult to create in Somalia a counterweight to the Soviet presence in Ethiopia because of the infeasibility of providing arms to an African nation determined to seize the territory of its neighbors. Once the United States was in this position, the USSR's involvement in the conflict became relatively safe, "a red-carpet operation" in the words of Robert Legvold.[67]

As the massive Soviet intervention unfolded, Washington was reduced largely to rhetoric. At a press conference in mid-January, Carter accused the USSR of having contributed to the hostilities by shipping excessive quantities of arms to both sides: "We have expressed our concern to the Soviets in very strong terms."[68] On February 11, Secretary Vance called on the Soviet Union to bring about a withdrawal of Soviet and Cuban forces from Ethiopia. Three days later, Mengistu pledged at a press conference that his forces would not cross the border; Gromyko also passed on Moscow's assurances to the White House that the border would not be crossed. It seemed reasonable to assume that Moscow would keep the promise, because a crossing of

[63] Quoted in Bruce Oudes "The United States Year in Africa: Reinventing the Wheel," *ACR* (1977–8):A74.
[64] Radio Moscow, November 18, 1977.
[65] *ACR* (1977–8):B384.
[66] Interview: Henze.
[67] Quoted in *Newsweek*, June 25, 1979.
[68] *Presidential Documents*, January 16, 1978.

the border might well have brought the United States into the conflict behind Somalia.

By that time, the State Department was as concerned about the sorry state of American-Ethiopian relations as about the course of the war. President Carter sent Deputy National Security Adviser David Aaron to Addis Ababa as a presidential emissary, accompanied by Paul Henze of the NSC and William Harrop from the State Department. In a meeting with Mengistu, the delegation explained "in very frank terms" the nature of the Soviet campaign and expressed America's strong interest in maintaining good relations with Ethiopia. The meeting was a key turning point, the beginning of a small reversal in the long downtrend of relations between Washington and Addis Ababa. Mengistu again gave assurances that Ethiopia would not cross the Somali frontier nor interfere in the internal affairs of its neighbors. It was also agreed that the White House would appoint and Ethiopia would receive a new ambassador shortly.[69]

In a press conference on March 2, Carter again blamed the Ogaden war on "the fact that the Soviets have overarmed to the teeth the Somalians, who then use the Soviet weapons to invade Ethiopia and now are overarming Ethiopia and directing their military effort."[70] He observed that if the Soviet and Cuban advisers and troops were not removed, that would make it much more difficult to ratify a SALT agreement, not because of an official policy of linkage, but because it would lessen American confidence in the peaceful intentions of the Soviet Union. This was perhaps the closest the United States came to trying to influence Soviet action in the crisis by means of linkage to other issues.[71] One week later, Siad informed Carter that he was withdrawing his forces from the Ogaden, and the president made the news public, stating that once the Somalis had evacuated completely, "withdrawal of the Soviet and Cuban combat presence should begin."[72] Although this did not occur, the termination of the war served to defuse the tension that had been building in Soviet-American relations, which soon returned to a more routinely cantankerous course.

The China factor

In the 1960s and 1970s, China did not choose to compete militarily with the USSR in the Horn of Africa, but its substantial programs of

[69] Interview: Henze; *Presidential Documents*, February 27, 1978.

[70] *Presidential Documents*, March 6, 1978.

[71] Secretary Vance, on February 10, had observed that the Soviet intervention in the Horn would affect the "political atmosphere" of Soviet-American negotiations on arms limitations in the Indian Ocean. *DOSB* 78(March 1978):15. The talks were eventually suspended. The crisis in the Horn of Africa was also a factor contributing to the decision to send U.S. National Security Adviser Zbigniew Brzezinski to Peking for talks with the Chinese leadership.

[72] "The President's News Conference of March 9, 1978," *Presidential Documents*, March 13, 1978.

economic assistance and its ideological appeal made it a factor Moscow was forced to reckon with. The competition was particularly acute in Somalia, where the Chinese made their second largest economic aid effort in Africa, surpassed only by the Tanzam railway. Mogadishu and Peking opened diplomatic relations within six months of Somalia's independence, and Prime Minister Shermarke paid the first high-level state visit to Peking in August 1963, signing agreements for $23 million in loans and grants. Chou En-lai spent three days in Somalia in February 1964, and President Osman visited Peking in July 1965. Although relations cooled somewhat during China's Cultural Revolution, they became very active again following the military's accession to power in Somalia. Numerous exchanges took place, and in June 1971 a Somali economic delegation in the PRC signed an agreement for economic assistance reported at $110 million, the largest single credit ever granted Somalia. Siad visited Peking the next May and signed protocols on hospital and highway construction. A number of Chinese projects were under way when the Ogaden conflict erupted. Peking's assistance was said to be popular with the Somali people, but the government found it less useful than the massive military assistance granted by the USSR. By the time of the Ogaden war, the Kremlin had definitely surpassed Peking in terms of influence with the Somali leadership.

Sino-Soviet competition was more muted in Haile Selassie's Ethiopia because of the dominant American position there. Chou En-lai had visited Ethiopia in 1964 on the same tour that took him to Somalia, but diplomatic relations were not opened until late 1970, partly because of the emperor's concern about Chinese support of the Eritrean Liberation Front. Bilateral relations improved considerably after Haile Selassie's state visit to China in October 1971, which culminated in the signing of an agreement for $84 million in economic credits. As a quid pro quo for Ethiopia's earlier recognition, China agreed to end its support for the Eritreans.

Early in 1976, not long after Ethiopia's initial failure to obtain arms from the Soviets, the PMAC sent a delegation to visit China. It was followed up by a secret mission to Peking in the summer. As far as is known, the only result of these negotiations was a 200-ton shipment of small arms for the peasant militia that arrived in January 1977. Such a small offering could not keep China in the running with the Soviet Union, and its influence in Addis Ababa faded toward zero as 1977 progressed. Peking was careful to refrain from criticizing the Dergue directly, but the Chinese excoriated the USSR for "meddling" and "introducing large amounts of munitions" into the area. As the USSR turned toward Ethiopia, Somalia cultivated its own relationship with China. Vice-President Ismail Ali Abokor paid a highly publicized two-week visit to Peking in June and July 1977.

Mogadishu and Peking drew still closer following the expulsion of the Soviet military advisers from Somalia. China gave great publicity to the event, describing it as "a just action against hegemonism" and "a heavy blow to the hegemonist ambitions of the Soviet Union."[73]

> This decision is a courageous and just measure taken by the Somali government and people in defense of state sovereignty and independence against Soviet social-imperialism and its policy of expansion.[74]

The Chinese news media also published the following observations from the Somali minister of information and national guidance. It was a perfect statement of Peking's position:

> In their liberation struggle the African people, deeply respectful of the homeland of the October Revolution, sought support from the Soviet Union. But, the Soviet Union has gradually changed since the passing away of Stalin and it has become a superpower concerned only with its own self-interests . . . It was China which first exposed the truth about the Soviet Union. Later on countries like Egypt and Sudan became aware of the Soviet schemes. And now it's Somalia's turn.[75]

In a probably fortuitous coincidence, a friendship delegation from China arrived in Mogadishu on the day the expulsion of the Soviets was announced. Two days later, the delegation attended a ceremony in which the PRC turned over a 31,000-seat sports stadium to Somalia, built with Peking's aid. Siad met with the delegation, which expressed its appreciation for the "firm and resolute" abrogation of the Soviet-Somali treaty of friendship and cooperation. Siad spoke favorably of Chinese-Somali friendship and used the occasion to criticize the Soviet Union.[76]

The PRC's limited capability to furnish Somalia with heavy weapons meant that its role in the Ogaden conflict per se was marginal. China was not a significant player during the most intense months of the crisis, and China's policy in the Horn of Africa does not seem to have been a significant factor in shaping the key Soviet decisions on leaning toward Ethiopia, undertaking the airlift of arms, and supporting the introduction of Cuban troops. Whether or not China would have risked its ties with other African countries by outright backing for Somalia's move against Ethiopia is yet another question. Peking did, in any event, reap improved relations with Somalia as a result

---

[73] NCNA, November 14 and 15, 1977. The editorial on November 14 used the word "hegemony" or a derivative eight times. The NCNA issued lengthy articles and editorials on the Soviet expulsion virtually every day for two weeks after it was announced.

[74] NCNA, November 16, 1977. The NCNA, November 21 and 25, 1977, played up Siad's characterization of the Soviet Union as "the number one enemy of the Somali people."

[75] NCNA, February 1, 1978.

[76] NCNA, November 10, 14, 15, and 19, 1977.

of the war. During 1978, there were at least four major diplomatic exchanges beween Somalia and the PRC, including a visit by Siad to Peking in April and the signing of a deal for small arms in November.[77] The signing of the arms agreement reflected Somalia's interest in diversifying its arms sources and China's interest in establishing itself as a genuine alternative to the USSR, though in another sense the limited size of the agreement only underscored Somalia's diplomatic isolation and China's deficiencies in the realm of military assistance.

The outcome

Because of Washington's early decision to avoid military involvement, the Ogaden war did not result in a serious U.S.-Soviet crisis, as almost certainly would have been the case had it occurred five years earlier. Its immediate significance for the Soviet-American relationship was correspondingly less than that of the October war or Angolan war. However, the long-term geopolitical implications of the Soviet Union's involvement were substantial. The victory in the Ogaden sustained the diplomatic momentum the USSR had acquired by its historic successes in Vietnam and Angola, and it opened for the Soviet Union an alternative route of influence into the Middle East and North Africa, compensating partly for the earlier loss of Egypt. The war convinced North African nations and other nations of the Third World that the Soviet Union was riding a tide of power and victory unlikely to cease in the near future, that alliance with the USSR was a key to security. The confidence of Egypt in particular was shaken.

Moscow also won an important new protégé in Africa. In November 1978, Mengistu visited Moscow and signed a 20-year treaty of friendship and cooperation, forging a virtual alliance between the USSR and a former citadel of American influence. Following the war, Ethiopia began to support the Soviet position on virtually every international question, more faithfully even than some of the USSR's East European allies. Addis Ababa's requirement for military assistance in subduing the stubborn Eritrean rebellion ensured its continuing reliance on Moscow. With leftist regimes in Addis Ababa and Aden both heavily dependent on Soviet support, the Kremlin was in a promising strategic position on the strait of Bab el-Mandeb, and there was a good possibility it would yet acquire port facilities at Massawa and Assab equaling in value the one lost at Berbera. From Ethiopia, the USSR could potentially exert strong pressures on Egypt, Saudi Arabia, Sudan, Kenya, and Somalia; its influence in Africa was also enhanced by close ties with a pro-Soviet client who enjoyed far greater influence with the black nations than Egypt or Somalia ever had. By 1979, some

[77] NCNA, February 24, April 14, 17, and 18, July 30, August 4, and November 2–6, 1978; William Ndege, "Barre's Year of Disappointments," *Africa* No. 85(September 1978):96–7; "Somalia Calculates Anew," *Horn of Africa* 2(March 1979):16.

Western intelligence analysts and NATO officers even considered the Soviet presence in Ethiopia to be "the most important strategic development facing the Western alliance," though this was perhaps an exaggeration. Colin Legum likened the Ogaden conflict to the Spanish civil war, when the democracies stood by passively as a totalitarian power engineered the establishment of a dictatorial regime.[78]

In retrospect, it seems possible that Ethiopia had been a major objective of Soviet diplomacy in the Horn long before the 1974 revolution. By building up a powerful client state in Somalia and by extending its military facilities there inland, Moscow put itself in a position to threaten Ethiopia in the Ogaden at any time. The USSR restrained Somalia only until the opportunity arose to replace the United States as the primary arms supplier to Addis Ababa; once the December arms agreement was signed and Mengistu had come to power, Somalia's attack on the Ogaden seems to have served the USSR's interests splendidly. Whether or not the Soviet Union quietly encouraged Somalia to go ahead may never be known, but the fact remains that in a matter of months Ethiopia was transformed into a client state of the Soviet Union, dependent on Moscow for defense against the very force the USSR had built up over nearly a decade.

The Soviet Union no doubt would have preferred to accomplish this end without losing Somalia – hence its long and intense diplomatic effort to create a Red Sea federation of Marxist states that would link Ethiopia, Somalia, and South Yemen. Although Siad upset this part of the Kremlin's plans, it is possible he may yet be forced to acquiesce. Already by the fall of 1978, there were signs that Moscow was wooing Mogadishu vigorously – and not without some success. Brezhnev sent a congratulatory message to Siad on the anniversary of the Somali revolution. It was given prominent coverage in the Somali party newspaper on October 23. In November, a Somali vice-president attended the anniversary celebration of the Russian revolution at the Soviet Embassy. His presence caused a stir in the diplomatic community, for one year earlier, just prior to the expulsion of the Soviets, only the Somali chief of protocol had attended the celebration. In January 1979, at a special party congress, Siad declared that "it is not inconceivable that Somalia and the Soviet Union could cooperate, given mutual goodwill."[79] Somalia has had difficulty finding a reliable outside arms supplier since the war, and it thus stands largely helpless before Ethiopia's new power; sporadic conflict on the two countries' common border has continued during the period

[78] Louis Rapoport, "There's Hope for Ethiopia," *Horn of Africa* 2(January/March 1978):2–6. Colin Legum, "The Horn, but Silence," *New York Times*, December 6, 1978.

[79] "The Horn: Somalia Calculates Anew," *Horn of Africa* 2(January/March 1979):17; *New York Times*, January 11, 1979.

from 1980 to 1983. The rift between Somalia and the Soviet Union has remained wide, but it would be premature to assume that it is permanent or that Moscow will not continue to make efforts to bridge it.[80]

[80] For additional information on events in the Horn of Africa from 1980-83, see the excellent summary articles in *Nene Zürcher Zeitung*, March 10, 1983; March 20–1, 1983; March 26, 1983; and April 13, 1983. See also Paul B. Henze, "Getting a Grip on the Horn: The Emergence of the Soviet Presence and Future Prospects," in Walter Laquer, ed., *The Pattern of Soviet Conduct in the Third World* (New York: Praeger, 1983), 150–86.

10
CONCLUSIONS

> We see, therefore, that War is not merely a political act, but also a real political instrument, a continuation of political commerce, a carrying out of the same by other means.
>
> Karl von Clausewitz, *On War*

Lenin was a devoted reader of the Prussian general Karl von Clausewitz and a firm believer in the dictum that war is but politics by another name. That fundamental tenet continues to hold a prominent place in Soviet strategic and political thinking today. Leonard Schapiro has observed that the Soviet Union always behaves as if it were at war, and although this insight may not apply to all aspects of the Soviet system, it does go far toward explaining some of its peculiarities, both in domestic and in international policies. The Soviet leaders, it would seem, do not view conflict as the breakdown of politics or diplomacy – as it is often seen in the West – but rather as a continuation of the same in another form. This may be particularly true when the Soviet Union becomes involved in local conflicts in which it is not actually at war, but is actively engaged in providing military assistance and support to a regime that is at war.

The preceding five chapters have employed the conceptual framework developed in Chapter 4 to study the USSR's involvement in specific Third World conflicts. This systematic review now makes it possible to outline some of the general patterns and trends of Soviet involvement in Third World conflicts, to analyze the multiple factors that bear on Soviet policy, and to delineate some of the problems, limitations, and strengths of the USSR as an actor in local conflicts. The following analysis is based largely on the material reviewed in the case studies, but it draws also on other relevant historical materials, such as that surveyed in Chapter 2, in order to provide confirming examples or contrasts.

The local dispute

In the postwar period, U.S. foreign policy has often been criticized for typecasting all Third World conflicts as directly related to the larger East-West ideological struggle. American policymakers are also charged with not becoming sufficiently acquainted with the local causes, nuances, and dynamics of specific conflicts. The Soviet leadership might well be accused of the first shortcoming, but never of the second.

On an ideological level, to be sure, the Soviet leadership's interpretation of conflicts in the Third World has invariably been couched in the most stark black-and-white terms. The Soviet news media portrayed each of the conflicts studied as a "war of national liberation," even in cases such as Nigeria's civil war, where the term had to be stretched almost beyond recognition to make it fit. The side opposing the Soviet Union's own client was in each instance characterized as a pawn of imperialism, manipulated and exploited, this despite the fact that in at least three of the five cases (the Yemeni civil war, the Nigerian civil war, and the Ogaden war) the Western powers were either neutral or essentially in support of the same regime being backed by Moscow. The only chinks that appear in this wall of ideological purity are in instances in which the USSR initially hedged somewhat in its commitment to a given side. Thus, in the case of the Nigerian civil war, Soviet commentary on the dispute remained fairly balanced right up to the outbreak of conflict; it turned sharply anti-Biafran only after the Federal Military Government (FMG) had turned to Moscow for assistance. Likewise, in the Ogaden war, Moscow shifted gradually from a position of neutrality in the dispute to a position leaning subtly and then not so subtly toward Ethiopia, then finally to a position in which Somalia was portrayed as the aggressor in a war instigated by imperialism (despite the fact that no Western power supported Somalia in the war).

Although the ideological concept of national liberation may have provided the Kremlin with a convenient moral justification for involvement in local conflicts, it cannot have contributed much to the Soviet leadership's practical understanding of the forces and issues at stake in specific conflicts. The concept was applied too simplistically and too expediently for that. The Soviet leadership nevertheless displayed every indication of being well acquainted, in a most practical way, with the actual dynamics, both military and political, of each conflict. In true Leninist style, ideology was not generally allowed to interfere with the actual implementation of policy.

One clear sign of the care taken by the Soviet leadership to understand the issues and the local balance of forces involved in each conflict was the fact that Moscow did not back a losing side in any of the cases studied. Indeed, throughout the postwar period, the USSR has only rarely been caught supporting a client who has been defeated (the most striking and catastrophic instance was the Arab defeat in June 1967). It is not tenable to suppose that this record of military successes by Soviet-backed clients came about solely because of the USSR's military power or because of the Clausewitzian genius of its leadership. Rather, the USSR seems to have chosen which conflicts to become involved in with considerable care, deliberately avoiding those in which defeat – with its attendant implications for Soviet prestige and influence – was probable. This would suggest that the Kremlin has devoted considerable research and intelligence-gathering resources to studying and comprehending the dynamics of specific local disputes.

This does not mean, however, that the Soviet Union has sought involvement only in conflicts in which there was no probability or little probability of defeat. The nature of conflict is such that few of these instances can be found. In every case studied, there was at least some significant probability that the side backed by the USSR would suffer a military defeat or at least be forced to stop fighting short of victory. In two cases, that probability was quite high: the Yemeni civil war and the October war. In the first instance, Moscow initially transferred most of its arms to the Yemen Arab Republic (YAR) via Egypt, perhaps believing that the use of an intermediary would limit any loss of face if the regime in Sana collapsed. But in 1967, the Soviet Union began transferring arms directly to the YAR, despite the predictions of numerous journalists and outside observers that the regime in Sana was on the verge of collapse. The intelligence available to the Soviet leadership in this case may have been superior to that of most observers, for the siege of Sana was broken without much difficulty, and the breaking of the siege soon led to a winding-down of the conflict. In the case of the October war, Moscow clearly did not want a conflict to break out and tried to take measures to prevent it. The Soviet leadership evidently had no illusions about the local balance of forces and recognized the high probability of a military disaster or at least a diplomatic setback.

Two types of risk confront the Soviet Union each time it becomes militarily involved in a local conflict. One is the risk of a confrontation with the United States. This will be examined in the section on Soviet-American interactions. The second type of risk is the possibility that the local client will be defeated and that this defeat will impact unfavorably on Soviet prestige and standing, both in the region of the conflict and on a more global scale. This latter type of risk is virtually built into every conflict in which the Soviet Union becomes involved, if only because the only regimes open to becoming Soviet clients are generally those that face some risk of defeat and that are at least partly dependent on the Soviet Union for arms. Regimes confident of victory with their own resources do not normally turn to the Soviet Union for assistance. A Third World regime's dependence on the USSR for weapons provides the lever that enables Moscow to intrude itself into a local conflict in the first place, and it constitutes the Kremlin's main source of continuing influence with the client. But dependence cannot arise from situations in which there is little or no risk of military defeat. This makes Soviet successes all the more remarkable.

The dependence of a given Third World regime on the USSR arises not only from its acute need for military supplies but also from the refusal or reluctance of the Western powers to provide the quantity or type of military assistance desired. Non-Communist clients rarely turn to the Soviet Union as a principal source of arms when they are able to obtain what they require from Western countries. Because Western governments are generally not reluctant to sell weapons unless the purchaser is liable to threaten their own interests, virtually every client relationship established between the USSR and a Third World country tends to be in some measure inimical to Western interests. The Nigerian civil war is the only dispute studied in which a Western power and the Soviet Union supplied the same side during the time of actual conflict. In every other instance, the United States and its allies were opposed to providing, or were at a minimum hesitant to provide, arms to the side eventually backed by Moscow. The unique situation in Nigeria came about because General Gowon wanted to pressure Britain to maintain the flow of weapons to Lagos. He also needed to placate the military's demand for combat aircraft, which London refused to supply. But throughout the war, Britain provided the FMG with far greater amounts of military assistance than did the USSR. It is the solitary example among the case studies of the Soviet Union becoming militarily involved in a local conflict when it was not the primary supplier of arms.

Although the logic of the world arms export market meant that the USSR tended to become involved in conflicts in which Western interests would be challenged, the Soviet Union cannot plausibly be accused of having instigated or caused the local conflicts in which it became involved. The deeper one digs into the causes of local disputes, the more plainly do the indigenous roots of conflicts appear. All of the conflicts studied had deep historical origins essentially unrelated to the actions of the Soviet Union. Most of the conflicts would have occurred even had Moscow refrained from involvement; some, in fact, were well under way before Soviet arms began flowing in. The USSR and other outside powers who became involved may have exacerbated or prolonged the conflicts and may have influenced the timing of their outbreak, but they did not outright cause them. Soviet arms shipments to Somalia, for example, certainly emboldened Siad to undertake military action against Ethiopia, but the Ethiopian-Somali dispute existed independent of and prior to the USSR's involvement in the region.

Of the five conflicts studied, three were civil wars, and two were interstate conflicts. The two interstate conflicts – the October war and the Ogaden war – were the two largest conflicts in terms of troops, weapons, and scale of combat. They were also the two most strategically important conflicts and perhaps for that reason the two in which the USSR made the greatest investment. The three civil wars were of somewhat less strategic importance, given that the fate of only one country and regime was at stake and no territorial issues affecting other states were concerned. It is interesting to note that in every civil war, the USSR supported the side that had succeeded in capturing the political center of the country. Perhaps drawing on the experience of the Russian revolution, the Soviet leadership seems to have recognized the significant psychological and political advantages that accrue to whatever side gains control of the capital city and extant organs of power in a country. The USSR shipped some arms to the MPLA prior to Portugal's withdrawal, but it did so clandestinely; Soviet support became massive and undisguised only after Angola was independent and the MPLA entrenched in its historical stronghold, the capital city of Lagos. This would seem to accord with past Soviet policy. While the USSR has supported numerous insurgencies, its support in such instances is usually clandestine, and its foremost aim is to facilitate the capture of the political center of the country over which the struggle for power is being waged. Only then does Soviet support become fully open and direct.

Capture of the political center is also an important element in making any appeal to nationalist sentiments, and in every conflict studied the Soviet Union seems to have been highly sensitive to the potential rallying power of nationalism. This was true of the interstate conflicts as well as the civil wars. The USSR wholly backed the Arabs' fundamentally nationalist claims to the territory Israel had occupied in the June 1967 war, though it stopped short of supporting any threat to Israel's own territorial sovereignty per se. Likewise, in the Ogaden, Moscow never openly backed Somalia's claim to the desert region, but once it had switched sides in the conflict, it recognized the emotive power of Ethiopian nationalism and used it to good advantage.

Ethnic rivalry was an important underlying cause in each of the three civil wars examined, but ethnic issues were strongly downplayed in Soviet commentary, and there is no evidence of the USSR having sought to exacerbate or manipulate this aspect of the local disputes in question. The Soviet media carefully refrained from disparaging the tribal or ethnic groups that opposed its client. Ethnicity in these instances was a force that worked at cross purposes to nationalism; yet nationalism was the force that had to be harnessed in each case if the regime backed by Moscow was to achieve control of the entire country.

It is also interesting to note that all of the civil wars were at least partly intramilitary in nature. In the Yemen, modernist elements in the military provided the core of the Republican revolution in 1962, while more traditional elements opposed it; in Nigeria, Ojukwu's struggle with Gowon originated at least partly as a struggle for power within the Nigerian officer corps; in Angola, three rival liberation armies, all of whom, for a brief period at least, had been officially united, went to war over which would govern the country in the future. It would seem that intramilitary disputes, by their very nature, lend themselves particularly well to being manipulated by an outside power offering military assistance. Even in the case of Ethiopia, Moscow took advantage of the deep intramilitary split in the Dergue to strengthen its links with Mengistu in the months prior to the palace coup that consolidated his power.

The diplomatic relationship between the USSR and its client

As far as can be determined from public sources and (in one case) confidential sources, the initial impetus for Soviet military assistance in each conflict was a specific request from the Third World client, rather than an offer from Moscow. This is a particularly interesting result, for it underscores the essential opportunism of Soviet foreign policy. The USSR has not actively sought opportunities for military involvement in local conflicts so much as it has taken advantage of opportunities as they have arisen.

However, Moscow did, on occasion, take steps that seem to have been intended to increase the likelihood that an opportunity for involvement would develop. In Ethiopia, for example, Ambassador Ratonov hinted that the USSR might consider supplying arms, and this may have influenced the Dergue's decision some months later to send a delegation to Moscow for exploratory talks. Moreover, in this instance, and also in the case of Yemen, the USSR may have been directly implicated in the coup that brought to power the regime (the YAR) or individual (Mengistu) with whom a client relationship was later established. These examples do not change the fact that the Kremlin did not actively solicit arms agreements in any of the cases studied. The Soviet leadership may feel that until a regime itself is actively pursuing military aid, its need is not sufficiently great or its purposes sufficiently serious to warrant consideration as a client.

In two cases – the October war and the Angolan civil war – there was a long history of ties between the Soviet Union and its Third World ally prior to the outbreak of conflict. In the case of the Yemeni civil war, some Soviet military aid had gone to Sana prior to the coup of September 1962, aid that enabled contacts to develop between Soviet officials and at least some of the Yemeni officers who participated in that coup. In the cases of Nigeria and Ethiopia, however, there was virtually no significant history of military links with the USSR prior to the arms agreements signed during or on the eve of the conflicts. Both cases demonstrate that a history of links is not a prerequisite to Soviet military involvement, even massive involvement, in a local conflict. Indeed, the length or extent of past ties did not seem to be a major factor bearing on the course of Soviet involvement in any of the conflicts, save possibly in the October war, in which a long history of disappointments and frustrations had led Sadat to distrust Soviet promises and intentions. There was a limit to how long the USSR could remain Egypt's ally without delivering the military and political prizes its support seemed to promise.

Perhaps the most important question to consider in analyzing the diplomatic relationship between the USSR and client regimes in the Third World is that of who exerted the most influence on whom. Whereas each client's dependence on the USSR for arms obviously gave Moscow a degree of leverage over the client, the influence relationship was by no means always unilateral. In the case of Yemen, the YAR was able to manipulate the USSR considerably by virtue of the latter's preoccupation with a larger strategic context. This was true to an extent during the civil war, and it became an even stronger characteristic of the bilateral relationship after the war had ended. In the late 1960s and throughout the 1970s, the regime in Sana manipulated Moscow's desire for a foothold on the Arabian Peninsula in an almost brilliant fashion, ultimately gaining far more from the relationship than it gave in return.

In the case of Nigeria, the FMG was never really dependent on Moscow for arms; so it retained virtually complete independence from the Kremlin, determining its own weapons requirements with minimal input from Soviet advisers. Because Nigeria was exploiting its ties with Moscow in order to put pressure on Great Britain, the USSR was, in effect, serving Nigeria's purposes as much as or more than Nigeria was serving the Soviet Union's purposes. The USSR did seek opportunity during the conflict to use its new relationship with Lagos in order to establish closer links with left-wing labor organizations in the country, but this effort was not very successful. Once the war was over, Nigeria clamped down on labor more tightly than ever before; any influence Moscow had had in that regard proved to be ephemeral.

As for Egypt, Sadat adroitly exploited Moscow's preoccupation with the larger strategic context of the region and its fear of losing all influence in Cairo to force the Soviet leadership to raise the ante of its support to the highest levels ever. The Egyptian leader's skill in exploiting the USSR's desire for a continuing presence in Egypt was particularly evident in the period from the expulsion of Soviet advisers in July 1972 to the outbreak of war in October 1973. During this period, Egypt, not the Soviet Union, dominated the relationship. Sadat also proved his dominance of the relationship after the war as he gradually reduced and then all but eliminated the relationship with Moscow that had been built up over the years. He thus proved that even by raising the ante of its support to unprecedented heights, Moscow could not prevent Egypt from taking a new course in its own interest – that of turning toward a closer relationship with the United States and away from Moscow.

In the case of Angola, the diplomatic relationship between the MPLA and the USSR seems to have been extremely cordial and close, at least by all outward appearances, both prior to and during the civil war. There had been a brief period in 1972–3 when Moscow had shifted its support from Neto to a different faction within the MPLA, but these differences were patched over well before the civil war heated up in the aftermath of the April 1974 coup in Lisbon. Moscow was forced to act discreetly in providing aid to the MPLA prior to Portugal's withdrawal, and it seems to have used the Congo as a diplomatic intermediary for several months during this sensitive period, but there is little evidence of any discord or struggle for dominant influence having characterized Soviet-MPLA relations in those months. A close working relationship continued to prevail during the months of conflict that followed Portugal's final withdrawal. This close relationship seems to have stemmed both from the MPLA's long dependence on the USSR for arms and support and from the mutually compatible ideological outlooks and commitments of both parties. It is interesting, therefore, to note that in the case of Ethiopia, the diplomatic relationship with Moscow was quite rocky and marred by friction prior to February 1977; but following Mengistu's palace coup that brought radical elements of the Dergue into ascendancy, the relationship went much smoother. The acute threat posed by Somalia's offensive in the summer of that year vastly increased Ethiopia's dependence on Moscow and created conditions that enabled the latter to almost totally dominate the relationship. But once the conflict had ended, the Soviets found it impossible to persuade Mengistu to move ahead with the creation of an actual workers' party. Military dependence tends to become a lesser factor in shaping a supplier-client relationship once a conflict has ended.

Although lasting influence may always be somewhat elusive, it would seem that the USSR's diplomatic influence over a Third World client is apt to be greatest when the client is a radical, left-wing regime intent on establishing a Socialist state. When such a client is also embroiled in a conflict and almost totally dependent on the Soviet Union for its very survival, conditions may be favorable for transforming it into a highly loyal ally. As was noted in Chapter 2, in the 1970s the USSR began to shift away from relying on bourgeois nationalist regimes and toward greater reliance on ideologically motivated regimes and parties in the Third World. In 1974, a team of authors from the Military History Institute of the Soviet Ministry of Defense and from the Moscow Institute for Africa published a lengthy work, *The Armed Struggle of the Peoples of Africa for Freedom and Independence*, in which African wars and insurgencies were classified in ascending order. The fourth and highest category of wars was

> national liberation wars headed by revolutionary-democratic parties with a relatively high level of political and military leadership, strong links with the masses (PAIGC in Guinea-Bissau, FRELIMO in Mozambique, the MPLA in Angola, the NAC in South Africa, and ZAPU in Rhodesia). The military capability of these parties is in substantial measure determined by the closeness of their leadership's views to Marxist-Leninist ideology and by their cooperation with communist parties and Marxist-Leninist groups.[1]

The Soviet leadership evidently realizes that this type of war and client affords it the greatest possible likelihood for political success in a local conflict. It seems to be the key to a close and productive diplomatic relationship.

In the majority of the cases studied, the Soviet Union had no known diplomatic contact whatsoever with the side opposing its client. In at least one case, that of the October war, Moscow's lack of diplomatic

---

[1] V. L. Tyagunenko et al., eds., *Vooruzhennaya borba narodov Afriki za svobodu i nezavisimost* (Moscow: Nauka, 1974), 337–8.

ties with Israel proved to be a real handicap in trying to exert influence both over the course of the conflict and over the negotiations for disengagement agreements that followed. The USSR's inability to exert influence in Israel was a primary factor in Egypt's decision to turn toward an accommodation with the United States.

There were two cases in which the USSR did see fit to keep open some minimal contact with the regime opposing its own client, perhaps recognizing the diplomatic advantage that accrued from such a policy. In Nigeria, the USSR attempted on two occasions to establish minimal contact with Biafra, perhaps as a hedge against the possibility that Ojukwu's secessionist regime would succeed in establishing a new nation, perhaps also in order to gain intelligence about the course and likely duration of the conflict. In Ethiopia, the USSR apparently established contact with a wide spectrum of political groups and individuals during the unstable months after Haile Selassie was deposed, closely following the development of what it saw as a potentially revolutionary situation. Then, even as it gradually switched its support to Ethiopia, military links with Somalia were maintained, enabling Moscow to closely gauge the extent of the Somali offensive in the Ogaden and the amount of assistance Ethiopia would require to counterattack. The USSR was in effect offering to defend Ethiopia against a threat that had been built up and unleashed as a result of its own military assistance to Somalia. In no other instance could Moscow plausibly be accused of having manufactured a threat that it then stepped in to provide assistance against.

On a human level, the performance of Soviet diplomacy has often been mediocre. Soviet diplomats and military advisers have not, for the most part, been popular in the Third World, and genuine trust between them and local leaders seems rarely to have developed. Nor has the Soviet Union's image been helped by some of the transparent and heavy-handed diplomatic manipulation it has attempted from time to time. Examples that come to mind are the open attempt to discourage the YAR from negotiating a settlement with the Royalists, the threat to cut off spare parts to Yemen if it opened diplomatic relations with West Germany, the fiasco of the attempt to achieve a cease-fire in the first days of the October war, the monetary gift given the secretary-general of the OAU in May 1975, the blatant pressure put on Idi Amin to recognize the MPLA, and the pressure brought to bear on Somalia to join in a Red Sea federation under Soviet auspices. Yet, if Soviet diplomacy at the tactical and human level is often crude or heavy-handed, its saving grace has been that a more or less coherent strategic pattern seems to underlie most Soviet efforts and operations. This is not to say that the Soviet leadership operates in foreign affairs on the basis of detailed plans, as is the case in its economic affairs, but it does think strategically, and this gives an overall purpose and cohesion to its foreign policy. American diplomacy, by contrast, has often performed splendidly at the personal level, only to founder for lack of an overarching strategic framework.

Weapons shipments and other military aid

The case studies reveal pronounced, though not steady, increases in the volume and sophistication of weapons transferred to non-Communist Third World clients involved in local conflicts. Table 10.1 illustrates this trend for tanks and combat aircraft only. A roughly similar trend is indicated by the figures for such equipment as rocket launchers, SAM missiles, antitank missiles, and armored personnel carriers, reflecting not only the increasing sophistication of Soviet weaponry per se but also an increasing willingness to transfer technologically advanced armaments in large amounts to the developing nations. The general upward trend is not steady, the October war having marked a peak in the level of Soviet weapons shipments, but the table clearly shows the significant increases from the first two cases to the latter three.

Another trend that can be seen in the case studies is one of increasing sophistication and increasing capability in the logistics of transferring arms to Third World clients. Without the expansion of the Soviet air transport fleet that took place in the 1960s and 1970s, the massive supply operations of the October war, the Angolan civil war, and the Ogaden war would have been unthinkable. The speed and logistical smoothness of the Ogaden operation, in particular, suggest that the USSR has been ascending steadily up a learning or experience curve, with each successive intervention in a Third World conflict enhancing the experience and skill of hundreds of Soviet officials and military officers. The experience derived from each conflict contributed to successful implementation in subsequent conflicts. The cumulative experience of the USSR, together with its growing logistical capabilities, has given it a capacity for rapid intervention and crisis response on a massive scale that was simply lacking before the 1970s.

The timing of Soviet weapons shipments as well as the specific mix of weapons selected for transfer were, for the most part, highly sensitive to the military requirements of each client and each conflict. Particularly good examples of this were the massive provision of Sagger antitank missiles to the Arabs in 1973, the transfer of the BM-21 rocket launchers to the MPLA, and the use of Mi-6 heavy-lift helicopters in the Ogaden war. One exception to this general pattern was the weaponry shipped to Nigeria, which in many instances arrived too late for use in major offensives and was not particularly well suited for furthering the war effort. Low-flying bombers, helicopters, and superior artillery or rockets would have been more effective. However, this appears to be largely the fault of the regime in Lagos itself, which insisted on determining its own purchases.

Not a great deal of significance can be attached to the types of

Table 10.1. *Quantities and levels of sophistication of the large military equipment transferred in the five case studies*

War	Tanks		Combat aircraft		Total tanks and planes
	Quantity	Latest generation	Quantity	Latest generation	
Yemen	Over 50	T-34	24	MiG-17	74
Nigeria	0		50–60	MiG-17	60
Yom Kippur	Over 1,000	T-62	Estimated over 100	MiG-21[a]	Over 1,100
Angola	200–300	T-54/55	10–20	MiG-21	Over 300
Ogaden	350–450	T-62	Over 80	MiG-23	Over 500

[a]There were unconfirmed reports that a number of MiG-25s had been transferred.

weapons withheld from local clients by the USSR, because it was for the most part willing to provide whatever weapons they could both utilize and afford. However, there were two exceptions to this rule. First, the Soviet Union rarely transferred its most sophisticated weapons of any given type to the Third World, probably because few clients really needed them or had the skilled manpower necessary to operate them. Every such transfer is also a security risk, as the USSR has painfully learned from a few instances in which it has made such transfers, mainly to the Middle East.

The second exception is that the USSR generally withheld from its clients bombers and missiles of a range sufficient to make deep strikes against an enemy's homeland, including its population centers. The Kremlin seems to be sensitive to the high risks of escalation associated with conflict at that level and to the adverse publicity that such transfers might receive. This sensitivity was particularly evident in the case of the two interstate wars. In the Ogaden conflict, the USSR did not provide Ethiopia with any bombers really capable of making strikes against Somali cities. In the case of the October war, the USSR did, under great pressure from the Arabs, transfer Frog-7 and SCUD missiles to both Syria and Egypt that were used on a limited scale, but the SCUD missiles at least were deployed where they could not strike at population centers, and both types of missiles saw only restricted use in the conflict.

In the case of the civil wars, on the other hand, the USSR has been somewhat bolder about providing its clients with the capability to make strikes of a strategic nature. The use of Il-28 bombers in the Yemen and in Nigeria is an example. In both cases, the weapons were used to strike against military enclaves of the opposing side, occasionally inflicting substantial casualties on civilian populations. Such incidents received less publicity and had less far-reaching ramifications than would have been the case in an interstate conflict. The apparent use of poison gas in the Yemeni civil war, in Cambodia, and in Afghanistan may also be a case in point. The use of such a weapon by Soviet allies in an interstate conflict has never been alleged.

Military considerations were not the only factors considered by the USSR in choosing weapons for transfer to client states at war. The Kremlin was also sensitive to the symbolic and political significance of military assistance, sometimes making transfers that seemed intended solely to reassure a local ally or to enhance Soviet prestige. The Tu-22 bombers deployed in Iraq during the October war and the MiG fighters transferred to Angola during its civil war seem to fall into this category. Neither type of weapon saw any action in combat.

The naval diplomacy occasionally conducted by the USSR during some of the conflicts, as well as the economic aid granted to certain client states, was also more important for its symbolic value than for its military contribution. One exception was the massive Soviet naval buildup in the Mediterranean during the October war. This does not seem to have been undertaken merely as a show of diplomatic support for the Arabs. The Soviet fleet included *Alligator* troop carriers that conceivably could have landed Soviet troops in Egypt or Syria in order to make good Brezhnev's intervention threat. The buildup in the Mediterranean also served as a precautionary hedge against the small but deadly serious possibility of a Soviet-American clash of some sort arising from the crisis. But most examples of Soviet naval deployments during local conflicts seem to have been motivated by political and diplomatic considerations, rather than by military calculation.

As for nonmilitary forms of assistance, such as economic aid, these played no real role in the relatively short-lived October war, Angolan civil war, and Ogaden war. But Soviet economic assistance to the YAR did enable it to complete the Al-Rawda airfield and the road between Hodeida and Taiz, both projects of notable military and political importance to the regime. The large number of Soviet economic assistance projects initiated in Nigeria during its civil war may have been of marginal military value, but they brought much favorable publicity to Moscow and were an important aspect of its continuing influence in Lagos after the war.

The role of Soviet and East European advisers and Cuban troops

The USSR has been much more conservative than the United States with regard to deploying its own armed forces abroad. From 1945 to 1979, regular tactical formations of Soviet ground troops never once participated in combat outside the boundaries of the Warsaw Pact. On a very limited basis, some Soviet troops were involved in direct combat as fighter pilots or as members of crews manning SAM installations, but their contribution to the actual military outcome in Third World conflicts was marginal. The self-restriction of the Soviet leadership in this respect arose perhaps from its native caution, but it may also have stemmed partly from experience derived in the early years after the Russian revolution. In Chiang Kai-shek's memoirs, he tells about a visit he made to Moscow in the early 1920s to seek Lenin's backing for the Kuomintang struggle for power in China. Lenin readily agreed to supply the Nationalists with ammunition, arms, provisions, instructors, and advisers, but he laid down a firm caveat: Absolutely no Soviet soldiers would participate in combat. Lenin explained that following the Red Army's disastrous losses in the Polish campaign of 1920, he had issued a new directive regarding the future policy for promoting world revolution. He had ruled that Soviet Russia should render the utmost material and moral support to wars of national liberation, but "should never again employ Soviet troops in direct participation."[2]

The historical record suggests that the Soviet leadership felt increasingly cramped by its own restrictions in this regard as the postwar period progressed. The noncombat assignments given to Soviet advisers became increasingly varied and bold over time, going well beyond the routine roles of providing technical assistance to the client and politico-military intelligence to Moscow. In the Yemen, Soviet advisers supervised ammunition depots, assisted with the air transport of troops and equipment from Egypt, and helped plan the relief column that broke the cordon around Sana. In Nigeria, the role of Soviet advisers was limited to technical assistance, probably as the result of a deliberate decision by the FMG itself. But in the Yom Kippur war, thousands of Soviet advisers in Egypt and Syria carried out an impressive and diverse assortment of tasks from extensive tactical planning to troop and weapons transport. In the Angolan civil war, the involvement of Soviet advisers was also extensive, particularly in the area of transport, though it paled before the vastly more extensive contributions of Cuban advisers and troops. In the Ogaden conflict, Soviet advisers made very significant contributions despite the presence of Cuban troops and advisers. Two Soviet generals and other high-level Soviet commanders virtually directed Ethiopia's winter counteroffensive, and Soviet advisers played a dominant role in logistics and communications. The Soviet presence reached well over 1,000 men, who performed a wide variety of combat-support functions. It is probably fair to say that between 1945 and 1979, Soviet advisers participated in virtually every wartime role except ground and naval combat. A number of Soviet advisers are believed to have been killed in local wars.[3]

The sudden introduction of Cuban troops into Third World conflicts beginning with the Angolan civil war was a boon to the USSR's foreign policy. The Soviet-Cuban combat tandem seems to have begun almost as an experiment in Angola, but by the end of the war its fighting potential had been decisively demonstrated. Being highly trained and already familiar with Soviet weaponry, the troops from Cuba provided the key the USSR needed for translating weapons shipments into a military force in which confidence could be placed. Moreover, although Cuban troops in Africa set off alarm bells in Washington, the response from the United States was not nearly as forceful as it no doubt would have been had an equal number of Soviet troops been deployed that far from Soviet borders. The Cuban troops thus enabled operations to take place that otherwise would have been either impossible or too risky.

[2] Chiang Kai-shek, *Soviet Russia in China: A Summing-up at Seventy* (New York: Farrar, Strauss & Cuhady, 1957), 22.
[3] *New York Times*, August 25, 1979.

One impressive feature of the two cases of joint Soviet-Cuban intervention was the close coordination between Soviet weapons shipments and Cuban troop deployments. This was particularly evident in the Ogaden conflict, where some arriving Cuban troops were immediately outfitted with the recently obtained Soviet equipment and dispatched directly to the front. The case studies provide evidence of Soviet-Cuban coordination at the highest levels even before the two respective operations were under way. There is little evidence to provide a basis for the notion that Cuba's African policy has been significantly independent of that of the USSR. However, the case studies do suggest that the Soviet-Cuban relationship, as far as it pertains to Third World conflicts, has not been so much that of commander and subordinate as that of a highly dependent Soviet ally obliging its mentor with enthusiasm. Castro has seemed quite content to play the role of an international revolutionary. Nevertheless, Soviet aims and interests were served much more directly in the two African wars than were Cuba's interests. This was particularly true in Ethiopia, where Cuba had had no traditional ties whatsoever with the military leadership in Addis Ababa and had even rendered support to the rebels in Eritrea only a short while before the conflict with Somalia broke out.

By 1978, over 40,000 Cuban troops were stationed abroad. Cuba's usefulness as a source of proxy forces for the advancement of Soviet foreign policy aims may have been rapidly diminishing simply because Havana was stretching the practical limits of its manpower resources. Cuba could not easily send still additional tens of thousands of soldiers overseas, at least not without affecting its own security in the Caribbean, nor could it transfer large numbers of troops out of Angola or Ethiopia to other countries without seriously weakening those regimes. The USSR again faced the problem of how to make the force of its arms felt in the Third World without trained soldiers to operate those arms. It found one solution in December 1979, when thousands of Soviet airborne and ground troops invaded Afghanistan to intervene in a mounting civil war. That event marked the end of Moscow's long-standing practice of not employing Soviet ground troops in combat outside the perimeter of the Warsaw Pact, and it seems to suggest that the restraining limit once set down by Lenin may be eroding. The Afghanistan war could yet turn out to be the exception that proves the rule, but there is no question that it represented the crossing of a once seemingly sacrosanct threshold.

Soviet-American interactions

In only two of the five cases studied, the October war and the Angolan civil war, did the USSR and the United States clearly stand on opposite sides of a conflict, rendering military assistance to two opponents at war. These were the only two conflicts in which escalation to the level of superpower conflict was a serious possibility and the two conflicts that therefore entailed the greatest risks for the USSR. In the Yemeni civil war, Washington granted early recognition to the YAR and remained almost completely uninvolved in the conflict, except for one short-lived attempt at mediation. In the case of the Nigerian civil war, U.S. public sympathy was strongly pro-Biafran, but Washington remained officially neutral, and there was never any serious contemplation of recognizing Biafra or providing it anything other than humanitarian assistance. In the Ogaden war, the United States opposed Somalia's claims on and invasion of the Ogaden, even after the USSR had become the major ally and arms supplier of Ethiopia. Although the Carter administration gave some consideration to supplying Somalia with defensive weapons after Ethiopia had begun a counteroffensive, no such step was taken.

Despite the relatively minimal involvement of the United States in the majority of these conflicts, the Soviet news media invariably portrayed Washington as the prime instigator in each conflict and the main backer of the side against which the USSR's client was contending. That was the argument even in the case of the Nigerian civil war, where another Western power, Great Britain, was a far more important actor than the United States. Such a portrayal of events is, of course, at least partly for propaganda effect, but it would also seem to reflect the overriding importance that the Soviet leadership attaches to the U.S.-Soviet relationship. The makers of foreign policy in Moscow surely recognize that the United States is the only power in the world that can seriously jeopardize the success of most Soviet operations in the Third World, and they seem to be acutely sensitive to the risks involved in any conflict that might threaten vital U.S. interests.

The timing of arms agreements and arms shipments in a number of the conflicts seems to have reflected this sensitivity. In the case of the Nigerian civil war, the USSR did not sign the arms agreement with the FMG until after Washington had announced its neutrality in the conflict. Even then, Moscow made no public statement of commitment to the Nigerian cause. When the first Soviet arms actually arrived, the U.S. State Department issued a statement expressing regret, but reaffirming U.S. neutrality; only two days later, Lagos publicly admitted for the first time that it had purchased Soviet arms, and this was followed a short time later by a letter from Kosygin to Gowon expressing Moscow's commitment to back the FMG. In the case of the Angolan civil war, the USSR halted its airlift for two weeks in December 1975, evidently because of a U.S. diplomatic initiative. Only following the vote in the U.S. Senate in favor of the Tunney amendment did the arms shipments resume. In the case of the Soviet relationship with Ethiopia, the small arms deal signed secretly in December 1976 seems in retrospect to have been a test both of the U.S. response and of the prospects for a close relationship with the

Ethiopian Dergue. The subsequent massive arms deal of May 1977 did not come about until after it had become clear that Washington would not attempt a diplomatic comeback in Ethiopia and after the pro-American elements in the Dergue had been purged, leaving Washington with little real leverage in the situation. It is also revealing that Soviet arms shipments continued to trickle into Somalia after May 1977, not being terminated until the United States had announced it would not sell arms to Mogadishu. Only then could Moscow abandon its link to Somalia with impunity.

The Yom Kippur war was a special case. In the course of this conflict the Soviet Union took a number of significant escalatory steps involving perhaps the greatest historical risk of superpower collision since the Cuban missile crisis. Yet throughout the war Moscow made efforts to stay in close contact with the White House, and the diplomatic and military signals communicated from Washington essentially established the outer limits of the Soviet involvement in the war. Moscow cooperated closely with the United States to terminate the conflict in short order after Washington had made an implied threat to escalate the level of its own military involvement. It is nevertheless interesting that the Kremlin went as far as it did up the ladder of escalation in October 1973. Soviet leaders had made vague threatening pronouncements in previous Middle Eastern wars, but the threat to unilaterally introduce Soviet troops in 1973 was of a totally different order, if only because the USSR's power projection capabilities were so much greater in 1973 than in previous conflicts in the region. The rapid buildup of Soviet nuclear forces from the early 1960s to the time of the conflict also reduced the risks for Moscow, because the United States could less credibly threaten massive retaliation in conditions of nuclear parity. The worldwide alert of U.S. conventional and nuclear forces did cause the USSR to back down from its threat, but that threat nonetheless served its purpose. It put pressure on the United States to use its influence with Israel to bring about a rapid termination of hostilities lest the Israeli offensive in Egypt lead to direct Soviet intervention. Moscow was, in effect, raising the threshold of risk and engaging in brinkmanship in order to achieve a specific diplomatic end, something it would have been less likely to do in an earlier decade.

The USSR was the only one of the two superpowers to supply arms in the Yemeni civil war, the Nigerian civil war, and the Ogaden war; it was the first to begin transferring arms in the other two conflicts. It would therefore be fallacious to portray the Soviet Union's behavior in Third World conflicts as motivated principally by defensive considerations or by a desire to counter U.S. advances. It is the USSR that has acted as a revolutionary force in Third World affairs in the postwar period, while the United States has acted as a conservative power, generally attempting to uphold the status quo and the established international order. This same conclusion holds true if one considers the two major conflicts of the postwar period in which the United States was the most heavily involved of the two superpowers: the war in Korea and the war in Vietnam. In both cases the United States was acting as an essentially conservative force, attempting to prop up an order that a Soviet-backed force was challenging.

When a limited rapprochement was achieved between Washington and Moscow in the early 1970s, the designers of U.S. foreign policy and a number of Western commentators expressed the hope that the relaxation of tensions would have a moderating effect on Soviet actions in the Third World. This did not prove to be the case. If anything, détente reduced the risks incurred by the USSR for its adventurist behavior abroad. The Soviet leadership had, in fact, never interpreted détente as precluding support for wars of national liberation. Brezhnev, at the twenty-fifth congress of the CPSU, openly stated that détente would not prevent the USSR from supporting national liberation movements, and at least one Soviet commentator identified détente as a principal factor making possible Soviet successes in Third World conflicts.[4]

But the Soviet Union could not forever occupy the untenable position of seeking to enjoy normal and highly cooperative relations with the Western governments while at the same time supporting the maximalist demands of some of their most implacable enemies with military aid and diplomatic succor. Although détente may have indirectly facilitated a Soviet strategic offensive in the Third World in the 1970s, Soviet military involvement in local conflicts in the Middle East, Angola, Ethiopia, and Afghanistan eroded the very conditions that had made a modest East-West rapprochement possible in the first place. By 1980, détente was virtually a dead letter, a victim, in part at least, of the very local wars it had been intended to prevent.

This book is about Soviet policy, but a few observations about U.S. policy may be in order at this point.[5] First, inasmuch as the currency of influence in the Third World is the supplying of arms, the United States suffers from at least one clear disadvantage vis-à-vis the Soviet Union, namely, the cumbersomeness of the U.S. arms transfer process. The USSR can generally transfer greater quantities of arms more rapidly than the United States simply because the entire Soviet arms transfer process operates on command principles, with a single political decision by the Politburo sufficient to initiate action. The White

---

[4] *Pravda*, February 25, 1976; E. Tarabrin, "Natsional'no-osvoboditelnoe dvizheniya: problemy i perspektivy," *Mezhdunarodnaya zhizn'* (January 1978);67. At the twenty-third congress of the CPSU, Brezhnev stated that "there can be no peaceful coexistence when it comes to the internal processes of the national liberation struggle." *Pravda*, March 30, 1966.

[5] For a treatment of U.S. policy with respect to Soviet military involvement in the Third World, see Bruce D. Porter, "Washington, Moscow, and Third World Conflict in the 1980s," in Samuel P. Huntington, ed., *The Strategic Imperative: New Policies for American Security* (Cambridge: Ballinger, 1982), 253–300.

House has no such flexibility, having to contend with congressional committees and a Pentagon bureaucracy not always willing or able to expedite certain decisions. The United States, fortunately, will never act as efficiently in this regard as the Soviet Union – inefficiency being the price of democracy – but some streamlining of the process for the sake of crisis effectiveness might be advisable. One possibility would be to give the president greater authority over arms transfers, including a small contingency fund to be used in critical situations.

A second observation is that the Soviet Union has been keenly aware of the implications of developing conflicts or revolutionary situations well before the United States has awakened to the problem. Top U.S. policymakers generally seem to view the world as fundamentally stable, becoming aware of conflicts only when they reach crisis proportions. This was particularly striking in the Horn of Africa, where U.S. policymakers virtually ignored the development of an anti-Western revolution in Ethiopia until it was too late to exert much influence. By contrast, Soviet leaders seem to view conflict as the fundamental feature of world politics and, as a result, identify incipient conflicts and respond to them at an earlier point in time. This gave the Kremlin an edge in all of the conflicts studied, save perhaps the Yom Kippur war, in which the United States was uncharacteristically on top of the situation.

Finally, the close attention that the Soviet leadership pays to U.S. policy and its understandable concern about U.S. reactions make possible meaningful deterrent actions, short of conflict, for the United States. In recent years, the Vietnam syndrome has sometimes led the United States to view its choices as either inaction or direct intervention, ignoring a whole host of policy options that lie between and that fall into the category of deterrence. More attention and thought probably should be devoted to this middle range of options.

The China factor

Insofar as the Sino-Soviet rivalry has been played out in Third World conflicts, it has tended to take one of two forms. Either Moscow and Peking have competed for influence with the same regime or they have backed opposing regimes or parties at war with one another. In Yemen, the USSR and China competed intensely over many years for influence with the same regime. In Nigeria, China gradually shifted from a position of neutrality to one of backing Biafra, perhaps hoping in this manner to counter what it saw as a Soviet advance. In the October war, Peking sought, through an inflated rhetorical commitment, to outbid Moscow in winning the favor of the Arab states. In Angola, Peking sought to maintain ties with all three liberation movements, thus simultaneously vying with Moscow for influence with the MPLA and backing the latter's sworn enemies. In the Horn of Africa, the USSR and China competed for many years to win influence with Somalia; later, once Mogadishu had expelled the USSR's advisers and Moscow had thrown its support to Ethiopia, the Sino-Soviet rivalry took on the second form mentioned earlier.

Regardless of what form the competition took, China, for the most part, came off second to the Soviet Union. Only in Yemen did Peking achieve for a time a measure of influence with the local regime roughly equal to that achieved by Moscow. But even in that case, Soviet influence increased following the breaking of the siege of Sana, while Chinese influence waned. This was also the only conflict in which Chinese policy seems to have had a substantial impact on Soviet policymaking. In no other instance does China seem to have been a major factor taken into account by the USSR in deciding whether or not to intervene, how extensively to become involved, and what diplomatic course and aims to pursue.

In the case of the Nigerian civil war, for example, Chinese actions had no apparent effect whatsoever on Soviet policy; China took sides in the conflict too late and was too little involved militarily to be a significant actor in the affair. In the end, China's decision to resist the USSR's involvement by backing Biafra only served to set Peking at odds with the OAU. China could do nothing other than watch helplessly as Biafra was finally subdued by the Soviet-backed client. In the October war, the PRC played an equally marginal role because of its inability to provide any significant military aid to the Arab states. In a war of that magnitude, military equipment became the only real currency of political influence, and China had little to offer.

Some Western analysts, Colin Legum in particular, have portrayed Sino-Soviet rivalry as having been a crucial determinant of Soviet policy in the Angolan civil war. But the USSR had been clandestinely involved in Angola long before China, and Soviet arms had been flowing to the MPLA well before a single shipment of Chinese arms arrived in Angola. China, moreover, completely withdrew from the conflict before it assumed the massive scale that followed Portugal's withdrawal. China's policy toward the conflict was impeccably correct from the point of view of the OAU's official stance, but Peking ended up gaining little from its propriety. Instead, the conflict served to enhance Soviet influence in southern Africa, particularly with indigenous liberation movements, at the expense of China. Once Africa had witnessed the potent combination of Soviet arms and Cuban troops, the attractions of Maoist ideology and Chinese economic assistance paled before the prospects of military success. A not dissimilar phenomenon occurred in northern Africa as a result of the Ogaden conflict. Chinese influence increased in Somalia, as might have been expected, but elsewhere the impressive victory of Soviet arms received banner publicity. The events in Angola and the Horn had a considerable effect on African perceptions of Soviet power and of the relative desirabilities of the USSR and the PRC as allies.

It is not difficult to divine the reason for the USSR's relative success vis-à-vis China in the arena of Third World conflict. China has been able to provide some meaningful economic assistance to Third World countries, and its attractions as an ideologically purist, revolutionary, and developing country have been real. But it is simply not able to compete with the Soviet Union in the realm of military assistance, which is the decisive element in local conflicts. Inasmuch as the arena of Sino-Soviet rivalry is that of Third World conflict, Moscow is likely to come away the diplomatic victor in a large majority of instances. China's role will tend to be limited to that of conducting rearguard actions. It is interesting to note that in none of the cases studied did China become militarily involved in the conflict before the Soviet Union, and when it did become involved, the level of its arms supplies was invariably much lower than that of its Communist rival. The one obvious historical exception to this pattern, which was not among the case studies, was the Korean war, in which China intervened with massive numbers of its own troops, playing a role at least as important as that of Moscow. But even in Vietnam, where geographical proximity favored China, it provided far less of the armaments being sent to Hanoi than did Moscow. Outside the Far East, China's capacity to compete as a global power has always been and remains sharply limited.

The outcome

There are at least three levels on which the outcome of Soviet military involvement in Third World conflicts should be evaluated. The first is the tactical military level: How successful was the USSR in contributing to the battlefield performance and overall military success of its clients? The second level is the political and diplomatic: How successful was Moscow in increasing its own influence with client states and establishing long-term relations favorable to its interests? The third level is global and strategic: How did the USSR's involvement in Third World conflicts contribute to its overall foreign policy aims and strategic position vis-à-vis the Western powers?

At the first level, that of tactical and military operations, the record of Soviet involvement in local conflicts has been highly successful. Soviet-backed clients were the military victors in every case examined save the October war, when the outcome was a stalemate, with each side claiming victory. The USSR also achieved a remarkable record of success in other Third World conflicts that were not among the case studies selected for this work. Indeed, throughout the postwar period, the only conflicts in which the USSR became involved in which its client was a clear-cut loser on the battlefield were those in which the Arab states fought against Israel. As noted earlier, Soviet successes at the tactical military level must be attributed, at least in part, to the care with which the USSR chooses which clients it will support and which conflicts it will become involved in. But in at least three of the cases studied – the Yemeni civil war, the Angolan civil war, and the Ogaden war – the USSR's client would have faced a very serious possibility of defeat on the battlefield had it not been for timely and well-structured Soviet assistance. Moscow's contribution to military victory was decisive in each of these cases. In the October war, Soviet arms were not able to achieve a decisive victory for the Arabs, but they did make possible Egypt's recapture of the east bank of the Suez Canal and a modestly credible Arab performance against Israel. Only in the case of the Nigerian civil war would the military outcome of the conflict likely have been about the same if the USSR had not become involved.

The Soviet Union's success at the military level in local conflicts must be attributed largely to its capacity to deliver arms rapidly and in the amounts necessary to fulfill the battlefield requirements of its clients. Adroit use of air transport to transfer arms to local clients who have needed them quickly has also been a particularly noteworthy aspect of Soviet operations. In four of our five conflicts, the civil war in Nigeria being the only exception, the USSR organized airlifts that rapidly reversed a local battle situation that was turning against its ally. This was not merely a technical achievement, but a matter of political will and decisiveness. The decision to resupply the Arabs in the October war seems to have been made and implemented in a matter of a few days (some preparatory steps, however, had been taken before the conflict began). That conflict demonstrated that, in a crunch, the USSR could deliver arms to the Middle East at speeds and volumes roughly equal to those that could be achieved by the United States. The conflicts in the Horn of Africa and in Angola demonstrated that Moscow could also deliver arms quickly and in mass to geographical points considerably more distant than the Middle East.

The role of Soviet advisers in servicing and training was doubtless also a critical factor in each of the conflicts, but their actual influence on tactical planning in most cases is not known. It is believed that some Soviet advisers played a role in operational planning on the Syrian side in the October war, and Soviet commanders and advisers are known to have played a major role in planning and carrying out Ethiopia's counteroffensive against Somalia in the Ogaden conflict. The important contributions that Cuban troops made to the victory of the MPLA and that of Ethiopia also should not be underestimated. Soviet arms shipments alone, regardless of how massive, almost certainly could not have made so decisive a difference in either war, simply because the indigenous armies involved did not have the trained soldiers required to employ those arms.

On the second level, that of political and diplomatic outcomes, the USSR's record has been much more ambiguous. Military victories did not always translate into long-term political influence, nor was there any clear correlation between the amount of Soviet military assistance granted and the resultant diplomatic influence gained. In the case of the Nigerian civil war, Soviet military aid was a marginal factor in the FMG's victory over Biafra, but Soviet influence in Nigeria increased substantially. That influence declined gradually following the war, but not before the USSR's involvement in the conflict had succeeded in prodding Nigeria into the stance of nonalignment that it has assumed ever since. In the Yemeni civil war, by contrast, Soviet arms made a decisive contribution to the survival of the Sana regime, but the YAR began drifting nearer to the West soon after the war had ended; the USSR was left with little enduring influence to show for its long involvement in the conflict. Egypt owed much of its success on the battlefield in October 1973 to Soviet aid, but this did not prevent Sadat from turning away from Moscow and toward the United States once the war had ended. Military and diplomatic outcomes, in short, may be diametrically opposite.

As was noted earlier, the countries of Angola and Ethiopia appear to be examples of the USSR winning enduring political influence as a result of military intervention in a local conflict. It cannot be ruled out that one or the other country may yet reverse its pro-Soviet alignment or at least adopt a position of true nonalignment, but in the several years that have passed since the Angolan civil war and the Ogaden war, respectively, each country has displayed a high degree of loyalty to the USSR and almost total support for Soviet positions in international forums such as the UN. This probably has more to do with ideological compatibility than with Soviet military assistance. Soviet military aid did make possible the survival of each regme, but ideological compatibility with Moscow and the success of each regime in organizing its internal affairs along Leninist lines account more for the present situation. Two cases alone do not prove anything, of course, but all other factors being equal, it does appear that ideologically motivated regimes are more likely to remain long-term allies of the USSR than are those regimes that Soviet commentators would term bourgeois nationalist regimes.

The third level mentioned earlier, that of the strategic outcome of the USSR's participation in local conflicts, is the most complex of all to analyze. It is difficult to distinguish strategic gains that were direct by-products of involvement in Third World conflicts from those that must be attributed to other causes. A number of observations are nonetheless possible.

First, a decisive strategic shift has not taken place in the Third World, despite notable Soviet successes in the 1970s. The entry of such weak and poorly developed countries as Angola, Ethiopia, Cambodia, and Afghanistan into the Soviet camp does not amount to more than a minor shift in the global balance, not even if their collective weight in world affairs is considered. Close alliances with these countries may give the USSR opportunities for constructing military facilities in strategically important locations and opportunities for exerting political influence on neighboring countries, but such benefits are partly offset by the costs entailed in subsidizing or propping up local client regimes.

Second, the Soviet Union's principal gains were neither country-specific nor region-specific. Regardless of what gains or setbacks the USSR has experienced in various countries and regions, the simple fact of its involvement in the Third World has contributed to a weakening of Western influence there. Soviet influence in Egypt waned rapidly after 1973, but this did not mean that the nearly two decades during which Cairo was Moscow's preeminent ally in the Third World were a total loss. On the contrary, the Soviet-Egyptian alliance caused innumerable troubles for the Western powers, reduced their political influence in the Middle East, and strongly affected the evolution of military and political events in the region. The Arabs waged three major wars against Israel with Soviet arms; each war inflicted enduring damage to Western interests. Soviet involvement in the Nigerian civil war did not lead to an alliance between Moscow and Lagos, but it did serve to prod Nigeria into a nonaligned stance, weakening British influence in West Africa. Furthermore, wherever the Soviet Union has been deeply involved in local conflicts and disputes, it has tended to leave behind a legacy of rising militarization, social divisions, and political instability that has weakened the prospects for stable political development and evolution toward more liberal systems. Such a legacy tends to be more detrimental to Western interests than to Soviet interests, for it provides openings for the exercise of influence that Moscow can use to advantage at some future time.

A third observation, closely related to the second, is that Soviet involvement in Third World conflicts has affected the international diplomatic climate in a way that, until recently at least, has been highly favorable to the USSR. Soviet-backed military victories have contributed to a growing perception among Third World leaders that the future lies with the East rather than with the West and that it is, in any event, imprudent not to maintain a good relationship with Moscow. This phenomenon might be termed diplomatic accommodation. Militarily weak powers seek to accommodate the interests of a rising power as insurance for their own future security. A former Ethiopian cabinet minister claimed that after watching what had happened to Somalia in the Ogaden war, not a single black African government dared to denounce the USSR publicly. After that conflict, Somali officials told an American journalist, Kenneth Tomlinson, that "we have learned that there is only one superpower." Colin Legum wrote that numerous Third World leaders and revolutionaries had become convinced that their allies should be chosen on the basis of whether or not they can offer "superior arms" and that many believe the USSR should be that ally. Kenneth Adelman has observed that growing perceptions of Soviet military preeminence have tended to frighten the West but seduce the Third World.[6] Playing on such tendencies, the USSR, in the course of the 1970s, attempted, with the assistance of Cuba, to promote itself as "the natural ally" of the non-aligned movement.

The invasion of Afghanistan somewhat reversed the trend toward diplomatic accommodation on the part of Third World countries by dramatizing the potential of Soviet military power to pose a direct threat to their own security and sovereignty. The overwhelming majority of Third World states condemned the invasion in UN General Assembly resolutions on January 14, 1980, and again on November 21, 1980; this seemed to signal the waning of an era during which an ever-increasing majority of developing regimes had leaned toward the Soviet position in international forums. This trend was further confirmed by the diplomatic setbacks suffered by the USSR over the invasion of Afghanistan at the Third Islamic Summit Conference and the Seventh Non-Aligned Conference in January and February, 1981, respectively. The Soviet Union faced the dilemma that whereas successful military adventures in the Third World often enhanced Soviet prestige, too many such adventures forced other nations to react defensively, and often in alliance, with an eye to their own security. This seemed to be particularly true in cases such as the invasion of Afghanistan, where it was virtually impossible to justify the Soviet Union's intervention on any conceivable moral grounds.

There is a fourth strategic aspect of Soviet military involvement in Third World conflicts, one that is largely overlooked in most analyses of Soviet gains and losses. It concerns the implications of Soviet activities for the evolution of the postwar international order. From 1945 to 1980, the Soviet Union, with increasing capability and confidence, assumed the role of a challenging power within that order. Moscow sought to erode the preeminence of the United States within the global system of nation-states, persistently articulating and pursuing the goal of transforming the structure of international relations in its own favor. The Third World proved to be a promising venue for the pursuit of this aim, and consequently many of the periodic crises that troubled and sometimes rocked the U.S.-Soviet relationship following World War II were centered in Asia, Africa, or the Middle East. The USSR's military activities in those regions, particularly its involvement in local conflicts, constituted one of the more tumultuous aspects of its overall challenge to the West.

The impact of Soviet military involvement in Third World conflicts on the evolution of the postwar order may perhaps best be illustrated by a chronology of firsts, of landmark actions undertaken by the USSR following its rediscovery of the Third World in the mid-1950s. This

---

[6] Interview with confidential Ethiopian source; Kenneth Tomlinson, *Reader's Digest* (September 1978); Colin Legum, *New York Times*, January 11, 1979; Kenneth Adelman, "Fear, Seduction, and Growing Soviet Strength," *Orbis* 22(Winter 1978):734–66.

chronology is drawn both from the case studies and from the historical material presented in Chapter 2:

Egypt, 1955	First overt arms agreement with a Third World client
Yemen vs. South Yemen, 1957–9	First military aid given to a country currently engaged in conflict
Sumatran rebellion, 1958	First military aid to a non-Communist country at war when the United States supported the opposing side with arms
Congo crisis, 1960	First Soviet military involvement in an African dispute
	First Soviet-assisted transport of Third World troops into a war zone.
Laotian civil war, 1960–1	First direct Soviet supply of front-line troops in a Third World conflict
Yemeni civil war, 1962–9	First confirmed participation of Soviet fighter pilots in combat
	First case of Soviet advisers remaining in center of combat
Nigerian civil war, 1967–70	First large-scale Soviet military involvement in a sub-Saharan conflict
War of attrition, 1969–70	First known case of Soviet advisers manning SAM installations
October war, 1973	First massive Soviet resupply effort to a non-Communist belligerent in the course of full hostilities
	First massive Soviet airlift of arms to a Third World country at war
	First deployment of Cuban troops in connection with a Soviet operation in a Third World conflict.
Fall of Saigon, 1975	First major case of a Soviet-backed regime defeating a U.S. ally in war

Angolan civil war, 1975–6	First large-scale use of Cuban troops armed with Soviet arms in a Third World conflict
	First massive Soviet intervention in sub-Saharan Africa
Ogaden war, 1977–8	First instance of high-level Soviet commanders being directly involved in planning a Third World military operation
Civil war in Afghanistan, 1978	First participation by Soviet ground troops in a Third World conflict
	First Soviet invasion of a Third World country

The general trend has been one of increasing flexibility of policy combined with increasing magnitude of scale and latitude of type of military aid rendered. Insofar as the international order is defined by an unwritten set of "rules of the game" – thresholds, precedents, spheres of influence, lines demarcating acceptable and unacceptable behavior, trip-wires, and the like – the USSR's military activities in the Third World have been a series of incremental encroachments on those rules. Furthermore, a precedent, once set, has tended to become the norm in future conflicts, as illustrated in Table 10.2. By advancing incrementally and by carefully choosing the places and times of its involvement in Third World conflicts, the Soviet Union has substantially increased its latitude of action in the world. The cumulative effect has been an evolutionary erosion of the postwar international order, a gradual change in the nature of the game itself. Soviet behavior that was disturbing in 1955 – the arms deal with Egypt – seemed routine within a decade; 20,000 Cuban troops in Africa appeared a profound new threat to the West in 1975, but in 1978 the deployment of an additional 15,000 in the Horn of Africa was downplayed by U.S. policymakers. What the USSR achieved in the Third World between 1973 and 1980 would have been totally unacceptable to the United States only a few years earlier; two decades earlier it might have led to war.

The Soviet leadership seems to have recognized that a certain restructuring of the international order was taking place in the 1970s. As the decade progressed, Soviet leaders and spokesmen stressed that the overall balance of forces in the world was shifting in favor of the Socialist bloc, that a "fundamental restructuring" of international relations was under way. Regarding Soviet advances in the Third World during the decade, A. Iskenderov wrote the following in December 1978:

> But one thing is indisputable: on the whole the national liberation movement is on the ascent . . .

Table 10.2. *The trend of Soviet military involvement in Third World conflicts*[a]

Precedent	Yemen-Aden	Indonesia	Congo	Laos	Yemen	Nigeria	War of attrition	Vietnam	Yom Kippur	Angola	Ogaden war	Afghan civil war
Soviet ground troops												X
Soviet commanders											X	X
Cuban troops										X	X	X
Massive scale								X	X	X	X	X
Soviets in combat roles					X		X		X		X	X
Soviet advisers in war zone					X	?	X	X	X	?	X	X
Direct supply of troops on the front				X	X		X		X	?	X	X
Transport of troops			X	?	X		X		X	X	X	X
Arms shipments	X	X	X	X	X	X	X	X	X	X	X	X

[a]This table illustrates how a precedent, once set, tends to be repeated again and eventually to become the norm in future conflicts.

This is confirmed by the historic victories of the heroic Vietnamese people, the emergence in the course of revolutionary struggle of progressive states like Angola, Mozambique, Guinea-Bissau, and the Cape Verde Islands, the successful course of the revolution in Ethiopia, the revolution in Afghanistan and other revolutionary changes in Asia and Africa.[7]

Boris Ponomarev of the Central Committee Secretariat observed in January 1980 that the past decade had been marked by the continuing unfolding and deepening of the national liberation process and by the erosion of capitalist strength. To the list of successes offered by Iskenderov he added the overthrow of the Pol Pot regime in Cambodia, the Iranian revolution, and the rising revolutionary ferment in Latin America. Echoing Gromyko's words on an earlier occasion, Ponomarev declared that the strength of the Socialist community had reached such proportions that no serious international problem would or could be resolved without its cooperation.[8] In short, he claimed the USSR's full rights as a global power.

In the United States, it has become customary since 1975 to speak of "the lessons of Vietnam," a phrase that usually connotes the declining utility of military power in the modern world and the high risks associated with superpower involvement in local conflicts. It is often overlooked that the Soviet leadership also learned lessons from Vietnam and from other Third World conflicts in the postwar period – lessons not about the limitations of military power but about its manifest political utility. The top leaders of the Kremlin learned that military power, indirectly employed by means of arms shipments, *can* help sustain a client regime at war and that involvement in a local conflict *can* yield significant diplomatic and strategic benefits. Thus, the Soviet leadership has not only been ascending up an experience curve, as was observed earlier, but also ascending up a confidence curve. As for the Soviet armed forces, they have been climbing up a capabilities curve. The combination of rising experience, confidence, and capabilities has been the key to what successes the USSR has seen in Third World conflicts.

Yet it is important not to exaggerate Soviet successes nor view them with unwarranted alarm. The political and diplomatic setbacks discussed earlier were as real as the successes, and they have taken a toll. The United States, from 1945 to 1980, unquestionably lost some ground to the USSR in the Third World, but it remained the most influential of the two powers in most countries and regions; Moscow still had to exercise considerable prudence in its military activities abroad lest it provoke a clash with Washington of potentially great danger. The quagmire in Afghanistan, with all its attendant painful lessons, no doubt has taken some of the edge

[7] A. Iskenderov, "Edinstvo trex revolyutsionykh potokov – vazhneishaya predposylka sokhraneniya i uprocheniya mira," *Mezhdunarodnaya zhizn'* (November 1978):73.

[8] Boris Ponomarev, "Neodolimost osvoboditelnovo dvizheniya," *Kommunist* 1173(January 1980):11; A. A. Gromyko, in *XXIV S'ezd KPSS – Stenograficheskii Otchet*, vol. 1 (Moscow, 1971), 482.

off Soviet confidence and forced the leadership of the Kremlin to reevaluate some of the premises of its foreign policy, even as did the United States in the aftermath of Vietnam. The problem of Soviet military involvement in Third World conflicts is sure to remain a troubling one for U.S. policymakers throughout the 1980s and beyond, but there is no reason to suppose that a skillful and resolute U.S. diplomacy will not be capable of meeting the challenge in a way that will preserve vital national interests, while still maintaining the general peace with Moscow.

INDEX